10/02

12 $\frac{50}{}$

By the same author

Justin Wintle

Romancing Vietnam

Inside the Boat Country

VIKING

for Merlynna Hashim

VIKING

Published by the Penguin Group
Penguin Books Ltd, 27 Wrights Lane, London W8 5TZ, England
Viking Penguin, a division of Penguin Books USA Inc.
375 Hudson Street, New York, New York 10014, USA
Penguin Books Australia Ltd, Ringwood, Victoria, Australia
Penguin Books Canada Ltd, 2801 John Street, Markham, Ontario, Canada L3R 1B4
Penguin Books (NZ) Ltd, 182–190 Wairau Road, Auckland 10, New Zealand

Penguin Books Ltd, Registered Offices: Harmondsworth, Middlesex, England

First published 1991
10 9 8 7 6 5 4 3 2 1

Printed in England by Clays Ltd, St Ives plc
Set in 12/14 pt Lasercomp Sabon

A CIP catalogue record for this book is available from the British Library

ISBN 0–670–83228–6

Contents

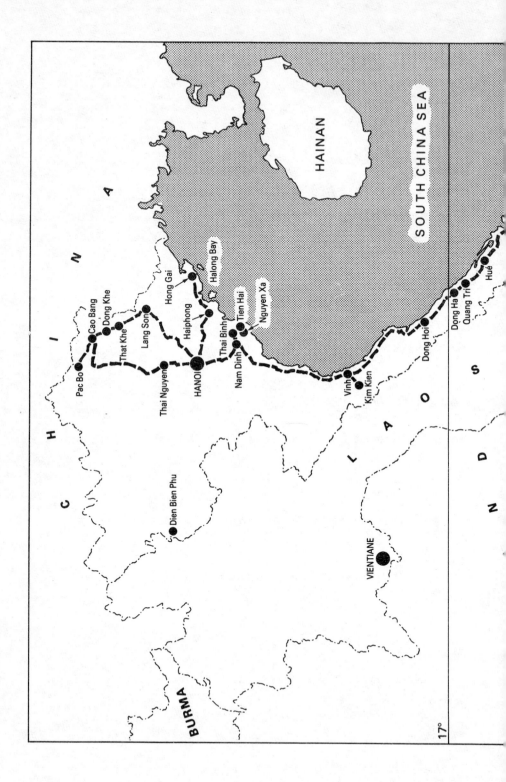

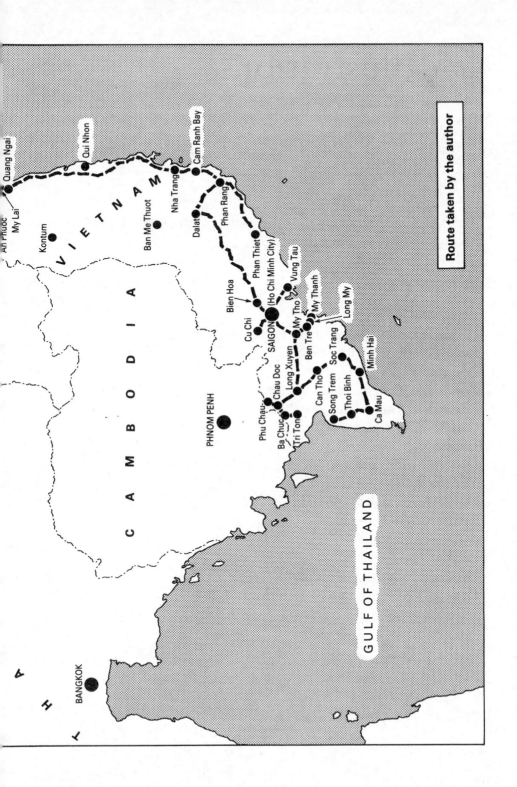

Route taken by the author

Illustrations

Plates

Prologue: Sea of Bones

I was in Vietnam from 4th October 1989 until 3rd January 1990 – that is, a while before relations between Hanoi and Washington began to thaw. I went to that country to research and write this book. Specifically I wanted to furnish an alternative to the received picture, built up over the last forty-five years, of Vietnam as a place of war. Or at least, I wanted to see if this could be done. I felt that at heart Vietnam must first and foremost be part of South-East Asia, that it must have more in common than at variance with Thailand, Malaysia and Indonesia; that in the last analysis geography, climate, agriculture, race and historic culture are more powerful forces than recent events and novel ideologies.

The thought that Vietnam and 'Vietnam' might be separate entities first struck me in a burger bar in Milford Haven, the old Welsh fishing port where I live. The burger bar opened shortly after I moved into an old house down on the water. The quick-food facility brought a dash of the 1970s to an essentially decaying but alas not excessively decadent town. Duly I called in to buy a burger. Whilst I was waiting for my order I noticed a video-game machine. For 20p I could guide two US combat-men out of the Hanoi Hilton – the nickname given to Hoa Lo prison in the capital of North Vietnam where captured pilots were incarcerated and sometimes tortured during the 'American' war. The object was to zap the Vietnamese guards as and when they interposed themselves on the route to freedom. The more guards you zapped the more points you scored. If you didn't zap the guards, then they zapped you and bang went your 20p.

What interested me about this game was that 'freedom' was actually unobtainable. Sooner or later the escapees had to fall. The reason for this was that there was no limit on the number of guards. Kill as many of them as you might, there were always more to kill you, coming ever faster, and in ever greater numbers. 'Winning', therefore, was relative. The best that could be achieved was a high body count, a decent kill ratio. Which of course made it a very nice game for our burger-munching young to cut their teeth on. In a small way it encouraged racism and mindless murderousness.

Imagine it. You are young, and you are playing this game. Whilst you are playing it your taste-buds have been, are being or are about to be wantonly satisfied. Zap zap zap. But the ultimate triumph – evasion of the little yellow bastards – is withheld. They can only be picked off one by one. Collectively they are invincible. The only thing to do therefore, after amassing however many thousands of points, is to have another hamburger. Yumee yumee. We'll get them one day!

Well, I have a joke about Milford Haven. It may be a long way from London, but it's nearer America.

As chance would have it, a couple of days after the burger bar I visited the local video library. The title I took out, the title I had to take out, was *The Hanoi Hilton*.

It was not a movie I wanted to watch twice. The opening credits ran up over airborne shots of a carrier-launched bombing mission to the North. These were backed by a stretch of cavalry-rides-again type orchestral score. The United States, it should be noted, bombed North Vietnam like they had never bombed anywhere before, except the rural areas of South Vietnam.

The storyline, based on the real experience of Patrick Michael Williamson, was simple. An American airman is shot out of the sky. He winds up in the Hanoi jailhouse. There he is tortured in a variety of ways. Rats, strappings, canings, electrics, you name it. Nonetheless Williamson survives. He has character, as do most (but not all) of his fellow inmates – we must remember there are some dud Americans! At first, kept in solitary confinement, he is not aware that he is not alone. But little by little the community of fallen pilots pieces itself together. Communications systems are painfully elaborated, group adhesion created. Finally, after many years of imprisonment, the survivors are released, to fly back home via Hawaii.

Well, it happened. US airmen *were* captured, and they *did* have a lean time of it. What annoyed me about *The Hanoi Hilton* however were its values. It pursued, somewhat relentlessly, a revisionist, we-were-right line. The Vietnamese warders, in marked contrast to the American individualists, were stereotyped, completely lacking in personal detail. Each and every one of them was merely a 'gook', no more, no less. All except the camp commandant that is, a Frenchified psychopath who would never have held down a decent job in a civilized society.

What it was not, this film, in any way, was an attempt to reach an objective understanding of why the Vietnamese may have felt compelled to act as they did: they had, after all, rather better excuses than their Colditz counterparts.

The Hanoi Hilton set me on the trail of other Vietnam movies. I spent many nights watching the likes of *Platoon, Hamburger Hill, Missing in Action, Saigon, The Deerhunter, Gardens of Stone, Full Metal Jacket, Rambo, Apocalypse Now* and *Good Morning, Vietnam* ... the list is almost endless. It was an interesting exercise. While it would be grossly unfair to suggest they were all the same, just as it would be misleading to pretend all Cowboy and Indian films are the same, there were certain constants. One way and another they were all preoccupied with American values, American soldiers, American experience. Some were anti-war, some anti-establishment, some even anti-American, but not one of them was 'about' the Vietnamese. And yet these films, which include some of the mega box-office successes of recent years, provide the resonance of the word, of the term 'Vietnam'.

What Hollywood creates today the rest of the world swallows tomorrow. 'Vietnam' has come to mean an assault course for the American psyche. It was other things as well, for instance it was a real war fought for real causes; but the way it comes across on the screen is just that: not a place, not a country, not a people, but a testing ground where all the hallowed shibboleths of America are blown apart to reveal a rawness, a primitiveness that was not found in the Mekong Delta so much as implanted there.

'God has a hard-on for Marines because we kill everything we see,' says a soldier in *Full Metal Jacket*. 'Welcome to show business,' says another in *Gardens of Stone*. 'Do we get to win this time?' asks Sylvester Stallone in *Rambo*. After a while I began compiling a list of such 'lines'. There was certainly no shortage of them. Yet overwhelmingly I felt that the provenance of each was a matter of accident. Any one line could be transplanted from its mother movie to another. Context and plot might determine its ultimate effect, whether or not for instance a degree of double-take was intended, but as far as basic style went it did seem that the various scriptwriters had access to a common stockpile. The hard-hitting, self-consciously macho quip has come to represent the collective, saleable American linguistic response to whatever it was that went on in Vietnam. And so loud is this response, so brutally insistent, that any other response gets drowned out.

I also discovered that no picture or writing about Vietnam can hope to be authentic unless expletives are present in liberal dosage – although interestingly the film everyone loves to hate, *Rambo*, contains only one f-word, and nobody is called a 'gook'. In a sense, in American cinema and American literature the four-letter word is legitimated by 'Vietnam'. Vietnam is, or was, too real for polite, or at times even meaningful, discourse.

The hallowed shibboleths are blown apart. What the Vietnam veteran lacks in intelligence or education he makes up for in experience. His experience, *the* experience, puts him on a par with, if not above, any Washington congressman or Harvard professor. 'Hell man,' said a real soldier in a television documentary, 'I was *there*, I was the biggest motherfucker in the valley.'

Vietnam, since the withdrawal of American troops in 1972–3, and the fall of Saigon to the communist forces in 1975, has come to mean a peculiarly American dilemma, at least in the West. For all the variety of their intentions, the movies convey remarkably similar impressions of the country and its people. All the young women are prostitutes, hookers. All the young men who are not VC are either pimps or gangsters. Saigon itself is indistinguishable from Bangkok (where, of necessity, a lot of the city scenes are shot). And the villages become mere locations where zealous American soldiers – combat junkies – work out their frustrations by 'wasting' the peasant inhabitants.

Add in Huey helicopters (their blades rotating behind nearly every title sequence), fragging, dope, agents orange, white and blue, napalm, Coke, FACs, Khe Sanh, tunnels, dollars, funky radio stations and a bit more napalm, and you have an instantly recognizable, fully constituted media package.

The result, movie-wise, and also taking into account books like Philip Caputo's *A Rumor of War* and Michael Herr's *Dispatches* ('Vietnam is what we had instead of happy childhoods'), is that the image we have of Vietnam has become static, its ingredients limited. Vietnam is no longer a nation or a people, but a nexus of signs and sounds that describe, simultaneously, American guilt and American prowess. The 'real' Vietnam, elusive and incapable of realization as it may be, is never even given a chance. It has become, culturally, off limits. No longer having anything to do with the United States, it can no longer be used as a sounding-board for American neuroses.

Which is why I went to Vietnam. When I had watched enough Vietnam movies I submitted an application to the Vietnamese Embassy in London. I requested a visa that would last up to four months, and said that I wished to write a book about 'Vietnam now'. People told me I wouldn't get permission, that no western writer who was not a card-carrying communist ever got more than a month; but in fairly rapid time my application was accepted and I was on my way.

Unwittingly my timing had been perfect. In 1986 the Vietnamese government, or Politburo, faced with economic collapse, promulgated a new policy of 'renovation', or *doi moi*. The idea was to get the economy back on its feet by allowing, *inter alia*, private enterprise and other forms of capitalism, notably joint-venture schemes with western governments/companies. It was a while though before anything much happened. By mid-1989 it was still touch and go whether *doi moi* was going to work. The government simply wasn't getting its message through to the outside world. The doors therefore would have to be opened still wider – wide enough at any rate to allow the likes of myself to pass inside.

Naïvely I had hoped to be able to journey around Vietnam under my own steam, in the company perhaps of just one guide/interpreter who would stick with me all the time, in much the same way that I have journeyed around other SE Asian countries. This was not to be. Instead I was given a programme, which usually included a guide, an interpreter and a driver. Regularly I was entouraged. I became used to feeling like a solitary sheep under a heavy escort of many sheepdogs.

On balance I probably saw far more of Vietnam this way than I would otherwise have done. I certainly met many more of the top brass than if I had been left to my own devices. But the arrangement did have its drawbacks. Principally I was confronted with another version of 'Vietnam', the one my hosts from the Ministry of Information wanted me to witness.

Like any western company promoting its merchandise my guardians sought to advertise their country's best features – all the time! Decoding this second Vietnam became an almost daily challenge. If America perpetuates its shame, Vietnam perpetuates its pride. Beneath the land is a sea of bones, the remains of 'fallen heroes' who still cry out for recognition of their achievements. Getting away from the wars was not going to be as easy as I had imagined.

Romancing Vietnam

1989

Wednesday 4th October: Hanoi   Terrific. I'm here. Hanoi. The cockpit of one of the great stories of the century. And my immediate fear has been assuaged. In Bangkok, on my way out, the correspondents and journalists were unanimous. There's no point in going to Vietnam unless you get a good interpreter, they said. Get a bad interpreter and you may as well have stayed at home. At the aerodrome (not big, not grand enough to be called an airport) I am met outside the arrivals hall by a young man from the Ministry of Information called Dung, pronounced Zung. Full name, Le Viet Dung. At once I am impressed by his vitality, his enthusiasm, his engaging laughter. His English is more than passable, it is fun. I'm the one who mispronounces words. Dung dips in the middle, has an oriental inflection. With my ears still buzzing from the scream of the engines of the Thai Inter jet, the best I can manage is Zoom. Zoom laughs. 'Mister Zoom,' he says. 'I like it. I'll zoom about and do everything you want.'

'Then you are my interpreter? You haven't just been sent to meet me?'

'Your interpreter, your guide, your organizer. Mister Zoom can do it all. Don't worry. Zoom knows how to work for you. Cigarette?'

Zoom proffers a packet of 555. '*Nam nam nam*,' he says. 'In Vietnamese, *nam* means five, like our driver, Mister Nam. All the drivers in our company are nicknamed numbers. In the south you'll meet Mister Sau. That's Mister Six. Then there's a Mister Tam, only he's not a driver, he's a guide. *Tam* is eight. It's a custom in our country. For instance, if you're the fourth child, then we call you Mister Five. Mr Nam's a fourth child. He's also got five children. There's no Mister One, Mister Mot, though. Nobody is Number One. Everybody's more than one.'

We both laugh, and I laugh again, because I hadn't expected to laugh so soon in Vietnam. We are sitting in the second row of seats in a Russian minibus. Periodically the driver, Mr Nam, turns round and grins. His face is large, rugged, warm, and confirms my impression that I've struck gold.

'Company?' I ask Zoom. 'What do you mean company? I thought you were from the Ministry.'

'Oh I am. Don't worry. The Services Centre. Only we call it the Company. It's part of the new policy, *doi moi*. Ministries and departments are supposed to earn their own keep, if they can. So we call our department the Company.'

'Sounds a little Thatcherite to me,' I quip, glad for this early opportunity to distance myself from my own 'reactionary' government. The longer I can conceal the fact that I'm not a full-blooded Marxist–Leninist the better I shall prosper. Or so at least I reason to myself. For no sooner have I pronounced the Iron Lady's name than I observe Zoom's thumb upwardly puncture the space between us.

'Maggie Thatcher,' he cries. 'Great woman!'

The joke of course is on me, and doubly so. In Vietnam, or at any rate in north Vietnam, there's no tradition of denigrating national leaders, your own or anyone else's. Rather, the opposite. It would simply be rude, inhospitable, for Zoom to join me in my aspersions. (It would also be un-Confucian, but that's another story.) Secondly, the idea of a Ministry of Information being run on Thatcherite lines means this: if the majority of the Ministry's clients are western journalists and their ilk, then western journalists and/or their sponsoring organizations (newspapers, television outfits, publishers) underwrite the cost of the work of the Ministry. Given that the terms 'information' and 'propaganda' are interchangeable, it bottoms out, or could bottom out, that a communist regime's main instrument for disseminating communist propaganda (and thereby perpetuating itself) is paid for by us.

Cute, huh?

But now is not the moment to embark on politics. My head feels like a waiter in an understaffed and overcrowded café. It is being pulled this way and that. The risk of inefficiency is great. My

4

attention is so fragmented it is hard to achieve coherence in any one direction. Overall I am trying to adjust to the peculiar fact of being in Vietnam in the first place. The sense of personal displacement, inevitable whenever one first sets foot in a new land, is amplified by notions, as much putative as so far actual, of cultural and ideological discontinuity. Then, since it seems likely I shall spend much time in his company, I am striving, with a neurotic western haste, to come to preliminary terms with Zoom himself. His open character, embedded in an open, decent, handsome (if still a little girlish) face, is so very much what I didn't expect. A thin line of hair across the upper lip is one of the very few clues that Zoom is actually the age he says he is (twenty-seven). Also, I am having to resist a trivial fascination with the insides of the Russian minibus: for I have never passengered in a Russian vehicle before. And finally, there is the outside landscape to behold.

The outside landscape began inside the Thai Inter aeroplane. There was cloud cover all the way from Bangkok, or at least all the way from before the Laotian frontier, so that my first glimpse of Indochina was delayed until well after the descent to Hanoi had begun. Even then a pervasive rainy mist meant I saw nothing concrete until the wheels all but touched the runway.

In the next few minutes I observed four phenomena. One, a flatness of land suggesting that I had indeed landed somewhere in the Red River delta basin. Two, in the distance, a handful of designer hills, or mountainettes, mauve creations of an almost Japanese delicacy. (This cannot be Vietnam!) Three, a row of eight or nine mothballed MiG fighter jets. Four, as soon as the plane taxied to a halt, a solitary military uniform: a rather lurid yellow-green cloth, cadmium-red epaulets and a gold star glinting from the band, similarly red, of the peaked cap.

There is of course no docking berth, nor any bus to take one to the terminal. With seventy-odd other passengers, the majority of them from the West, I walk across the tarmac toward a building that time must have forgotten. Without an umbrella I am very slightly drenched. The phrase 'Northolt 1937' crosses my mind, as does, with even greater prejudice, the maverick sentence 'You cannot have access to the documents unless you submit a formal request, and any formal request must be based on a detailed appraisal of the contents of the documents': either a Kafkaesque concoction derived from reading too many reports indicating that Vietnam is still a Stalinist police state, or an ironic comment on the bureaucracy implicit in the absurdly detailed customs declaration form handed to me whilst still airborne.

For those unable to complete the questionnaire before landing several rows of high desks are ready and waiting inside. (This is my first intimation that being in Vietnam is not altogether unlike being back at school, and an English boarding school at that.) The passport control officers are billeted in dark wooden sentry boxes that evidently (like almost everything in Vietnam that has a functional dimension) began life elsewhere.

So much for the sharp end of immigration. Beyond this room is the customs hall, already milling with old boys come to meet new boys, or returning boys, laid out with low tables and more or less official types standing behind them. A woman from the British Embassy, with a Union Jack pinned discreetly to her blouse, pounces on my recognition of the national flag. 'Are you being met?' she asks. 'I hope so,' I reply. Her eyes fill with English disappointment. Receiving unmet Brits at the aerodrome is evidently the high point of her working week. But at least she knows who I am. 'Well, I'll tell the ambassador you've arrived,' she says, and stalks off trawling for other custom.

Baggage inspection is arbitrary. You may or may not be asked to show your chattels. Observing that those who try walking straight through with their cases tend to be the ones who are stopped, I carefully pause to catch the eye of a customs man. This takes some time since none of the customs men seems willing to have his eye caught. However, eventually I land one. To my dismay he beckons me to his table and watches while I heave my excessively heavy suitcase onto his makeshift counter. As soon as I have done this he smiles and tells me to be gone.

And so I am sitting in the Russian minibus, with one eye on Zoom and the innards of the Russian minibus and the other on the outtards of the Red River delta. The flatness is ineluctable, the more so as the vegetation is largely confined to paddy. There are very few trees in sight, even on the dikes that run between the paddies. (A flash of history here: the agronomic subjugation of the delta, the propagation of irrigation, the consolidation of the Viets' mastery over the land, the basics of their civilization, centuries and centuries ago . . .) On the road itself, peasants: ill dressed, on foot or, more rarely, on bicycles; a universal thinness of face, and an even greater thinness of body. The occasional bullock cart, and very occasional car or truck – other than the convoy of engines coming from the aerodrome. Paddy-workers doing everything by hand, or with pre-industrial implements. Very small houses, some of them brick, some of them bamboo. Pigs, dogs, chickens, the pigs not pink but dirty white, like stripped fat. Not idyllic – the sky is still too grey for that – but animated by a species of routine urgency. Like watching 'from behind the lines' war reportage, only that is prejudice again, and of the kind I have come to Vietnam to dispel . . .

Hanoi comes up on the screen with surprising speed, so that its true size is belied. This is because Hanoi is mainly on the south-west bank of the Red River, and is spreading south-west, while the aerodrome is thirty kilometres north-east and nobody wants very much to live across the river. Nevertheless there is a perceptible accretion of buildings from a mile or two out, including a few concrete tenement blocks that no doubt reflect the shape of things to come. And then it is the Red River itself, broad, and really red, or reddish, on account of the clay present in the delta's subsoil, and spanned (at this point) by two bridges: the modern bridge that takes me into the capital, and more famously the Paul Doumey Bridge, which Americans loved to bomb, and stands today in a state of high yet still defiant distress. (Several of its cantilevered sections are no longer there, but enough remain to make it one of the world's premier war monuments.) After which I am suddenly in the middle of Hanoi, for the middle is up near the river, and briefly, before arriving at my hotel, I am dazed by thoroughfares teeming with bicycles and rickshaws (cyclos) and old women carrying baskets of apples and black Soviet-made limousines and Honda motorcycles and peculiar converted sawn-off tractors that are black and make a fearful din, but most of all with the bicycles, because, as Zoom now tells me with another of his fetching, infectious laughs, everyone in Hanoi who's anyone owns a bicycle.

'My dear,' he says, 'the first thing you must do in Hanoi is acquire a set of two wheels.'

7

The bicycles dizzy me more than cars ever could. Probably this has something to do with the intersections. At the intersections there are no traffic lights. The bicycles converge and pass through each other at right angles, like the two halves of a deck of cards being shuffled. In a city where computers are still a novelty, it seems as though the traffic has been elaborately programmed, such is the precision of a hundred near-misses that take place in the blink of an eye.

The effect is phantasmagoric, the more so as it is achieved with relatively little noise. Hanoians it seems swerve on the quiet side. Also phantasmagoric is the architecture. Off the thoroughfare are endless little streets, lined with little houses and little shops, nothing reaching much above the second storey. But every so often something French, a government building or townhouse left over from the colonial period, four-square, classical proportions and classical features, full of imperial purpose, and usually of an ochreish yellow. Slices of Battenburg cake located in a sea of overbaked, broken grissini.

'Weren't they all destroyed?' I ask. 'Weren't they all blitzed by the B52s?'

Zoom shakes his head. 'Not at all. The Americans went for the station, the railway lines, the factories, the bridge. They used laser beams, you see. They left nothing to chance.'

Before I can adjust to downtown Hanoi, before I can comprehend that what I am seeing represents, for three and a half million souls, the state of normality, the minibus draws up at my hotel, the Thong Nhat (Reunification), in French times La Metropole. Around the portico are gathered half a dozen cyclo drivers and a couple of shoeshine boys, only they are not boys, they are men in their late middle age, one of whom I will learn later was a lawyer in French times and would rather the Revolution had never happened. They begin to gather round me, but Zoom sees them off, leaving me and my impossibly large suitcase free access to the revolving door that hurtles me into the vestibule of my first home in Vietnam.

Inside the Thong Nhat all is dim, murky even, for the simple reason that central Hanoi is, at this time, subject to a power cut.

There are, on average, three power cuts a day. The vestibule is long and narrow. At the nearest end a dingy reception desk, at the furthest end an equally dingy bar. The walls are lined by heavy square chairs grouped around low, glass-topped coffee tables. There are one or two beer-drinkers, but mostly guests and their friends (Vietnamese accomplices) are drinking black tea. They talk in hushed voices, as though they too were having problems with energy supply.

Zoom recommends, as though any other course of action were unthinkable, that I take a rest in my room. In one hour, he tells me, Mr Hong will come to the Thong Nhat to welcome me to Vietnam. Meanwhile I should go to my room and take a rest.

I go to my room and take a rest. A porter thinks about taking my suitcase up the stairs, reconsiders, smiles apologetically and picks up my shoulder bag. 'No strong,' he says, by way of explanation. The lift of course is not working. But this has nothing to do with the power cut. The lift hasn't worked for thirty years and, in case any guest should think otherwise, has been sealed up.

To steady myself, now that I am alone, I contemplate my new surroundings. The first thing to be said about Room 137 is that it is big, in keeping with the bygone grandeur of the Thong Nhat itself. The second thing to be said is that it is relatively bare. The eye bounces across an uncovered wooden floor, thin-stripped and dark-stained some aeons ago. Two virtuously narrow beds are separated by a junk-shop bedside cabinet. Each has a white mosquito net folded into a wooden structure curtained with a faded, bluish cloth. One of these I open. A frame of sorts extends above the mattress. The mosquito net balloons out like an expectant wedding dress, which I have some difficulty refolding. Then the windows, fantastically elaborate compared to the modern double-glazed aluminium jobs I am used to in Bangkok. The outer skin consists of louvred shutters, painted green at least once during their history. Then mosquito panels, wire gauze protectors and, on the inside, dilapidated folding casements containing flawed glass. Between the window-sets (there are two of them, shielded by pale blue drapes that definitely do not match the curtains of the beds), a table and tea-set: two minuscule cracked cups and a pot (all made in Czechoslovakia), and a covered plastic dish playing the part of

9

caddy. On the floor by this table a very large Thermos flask that, surprisingly, turns out to contain lately boiled water.

Over in the far corner a desk, replete with elephantine black telephone and a desk-lamp that, once power is resumed, works but only after it is touched with kindness. Two uninviting wooden armchairs, a derelict wardrobe, a useless air-conditioner and a standing electric fan, Sanyo, that, once activated, follows you around, nodding gently like lowing cattle. In Moscow I would immediately have examined this object for a hidden lens, but in Hanoi I have already sensed that the technological resources do not extend to such sophisticated surveillance.

There is, to boot, a bathroom, a place to scrub yourself in, dirty white enamel tiles from floor to ceiling, dirty red tiles underfoot, cockroach stains, but a boiler that amazingly, exhilaratingly, actually dispenses scalding water. A larger Thermos flask, with about as many controls.

I am not displeased. The veneer of austerity in a place that must once have boasted luxury enables me to prepare for my encounter with Mr Hong.

At four o'clock I duly make my way downstairs, noting that in the room immediately opposite mine a Japanese, or maybe several Japanese, have set up a business consultancy, presumably in contravention of their nation's support for the blanket trading embargo imposed by the United States. As I reach the vestibule Zoom zooms in via the revolving door, followed by a grey-haired man in his middle fifties.

We sit at a table, order tea and exchange cards. Duong Duc Hong is the director of the Services Centre of the Ministry of Information. As such he is what Zoom would call a medium big potato. He is not, surprisingly, a member of the Party. Later I am told that if he were a member, then by now he would in all probability be a government minister. The fact that he is not a Party member and still holds down a senior post is an aspect of *doi moi*, the policy of renovation – Hanoi's answer to *glasnost*, *perestroika* and the Deng Xiao Ping reforms. But also the fact that he holds down a senior post and is not a Party member means that, because he has Party members employed under him, he is not altogether in control of his department. Not only is he liable to intervention from above, he is liable to intervention from below. In general, *doi moi* has tended to make office politics more, not less, complicated.

All of this I am as yet unaware of. All I do know is that Mr Hong is Zoom's boss, and that, officially or otherwise, it is his duty to welcome me to Vietnam. Having exchanged cards, we set about exchanging compliments. Since I have spent barely three hours in Vietnam, I am as yet unfamiliar with, and unpractised in, this most essential art. This first assay therefore turns out a somewhat one-sided affair. Mr Hong grasps my hand, tells me Vietnam thinks it wonderful I have come, and several things about myself I have often wished were true but have never quite had the afflatus to believe are. He also makes several inquiries about my family, as if he had known each and every one of them intimately for years. In reply I offer breezy thanks. Then we get down to business.

Mr Hong, whom one might describe as dapper, were it not for a somewhat tousled look and manner, sits on my left. Periodically he leans forward and pumps my knee. He speaks feasible English, but often relies on Zoom to translate. This Zoom does in a low voice seemingly with infallible accuracy.

My major concern is money. To begin with I have $7,000 worth of the stuff about my person, all in US banknotes, having been advised by the Vietnamese Embassy in London that that was the only negotiable form of currency to bring. I am worried about where to keep it, and also how long it will last. Not only did the press gang in Bangkok warn me about the importance of having a good interpreter, but they also alarmed me with accounts about how easy it is to be fleeced by official agencies (never mind about the unofficial ones) in Vietnam. One American had, within the space of three weeks, parted with $5,000, or forty times the local average annual income. Since it is my intention to spend three months in the country, if not four, and still leave with $1,000 or so, I believe it as well to put my chicken-feed straight on the table.

Mr Hong listens to me with the utmost concern, then tells me not to worry. He understands my position perfectly. I am not the employee of a rich corporation that markets newspapers, but a freelance author, and a friend of Vietnam to boot. He will personally see to it that my 'programme' is covered by what I have brought, and that I still have some left to spend in Bangkok on my way out. Incidentally, am I intending to devote a chapter to Ho Chi Minh in my proposed book?

This one I field as best I can. No, I am not intending to include a chapter on Ho Chi Minh. Chapters, I say, are a thing of the past. Very *démodé*. But in any case, that is not the point. How, I ask, could anyone possibly write any kind of book about Vietnam without mentioning Ho's name on nearly every page? In my volume, even though its remit is specifically a study of 'Vietnam now', there will certainly be no shortage of Ho Chi Minh.

Mr Hong nods as Zoom interprets. My imagination perhaps, but it does seem a certain weariness, or wariness, flits across his features. It occurs to me that whichever bigger potato finally authorized my visit may have instructed Mr Hong, directly or down the line, or even up the line, to encourage me at all costs to remember Uncle Ho. To that extent therefore he is doing his duty. When I finish, he reminds me that 1990 is the centenary of the Great Man's birth, so I should bear him constantly in mind. For my part, I feel I have too much to lose by discussing the point further. I return to the topic of my $7,000.

'And my money?' I ask. 'Where can I keep it? Is there a bank nearby?'

Yes there is a bank, and it is relatively nearby. The trouble with the bank however is that if I put my dollars into it, the chances are they will want me to convert them all into *dong* right away. And even Mr Hong cannot bring himself to declare that seven thousand dollars' worth of *dong* is a thing anyone in a reasonably untroubled state of mind should want for himself.

'Then what are the options?'

'Either keep the money on you, or give it to the Ministry to look after.'

And this of course puts me right on the spot. The British Ambassador, I knew, was unwilling to keep it in his safe – I had already asked him back home, and it was against Foreign Office rules – while the idea of stashing it around my corporeal cavities for three months filled me only with terror. The shoulder holster in which I kept my passport had already given me three nightmares. With that amount, one false move and I was so much dogmeat. So there was no option really.

'You mean you'll look after it for me?' I beam. 'You have a safe?'

'Yes, we have a safe.'

Smiles all round. And in retrospect it was absolutely the right thing to do. I wanted them to put their trust in me. It was only correct therefore that I should put my trust in them. The arrangement also had the advantage that, if need be, they could check to see how much I had at any given time. This should ensure that any temptation to overspend on my behalf would be firmly resisted.

This leaves just the matter of my 'programme' to be discussed. I say just the matter. In fact the concept of my programme is new to me. In my visa application I stated that I wanted to spend three to four months wandering around Vietnam either on my own or in the company of a single guide who would double up as driver and interpreter. To save money I indicated that I would be perfectly content to take trains and buses as and when they were available. I had in mind perhaps some novice intelligence officer with a first-class degree in English from Hanoi University who would relish roughing it a bit before settling down to a career.

Such is the stuff that dreams are made of. Although the staff at the Vietnamese Embassy acted toward me with the utmost friendliness, they must have known that my request fell short of both the probable and the possible.

Instead Mr Hong, no doubt after consultations with both his superiors and his inferiors, wants me to have a 'programme', and preferably one that includes ample opportunities to research the life and times of Ho Chi Minh.

'That is what we must do now,' he says, through Zoom. 'We must fix your programme.'

'Will that include the odd train, the odd bus?'

'Maybe. But you must understand, it is essential that no harm at all befalls you. From the bottom of our hearts we want to take good care of you. We are so pleased that you have come. We want to honour your commitment.'

As I will soon discover, and discover again and again, the word 'maybe', when employed by a Vietnamese official or, as they prefer to call themselves, cadre, almost invariably means 'probably not', or even 'quite unlikely'.

I should also mention, at this point, that my original plan was to start off in the south, in Saigon, explore the Mekong Delta, and only then go to the north. My final destination was to have been Pac Bo, a small village close to the Chinese border in the far northeast, or rather a particular cave at Pac Bo.

This cave too needs some explaining. I had no overwhelming interest in visiting it, but it was the place Ho Chi Minh first put up in when he returned to Vietnam after twenty-nine years of self-imposed exile, spent, in the main, globe-trotting. The Ho Chi Minh theme was therefore partly of my own devising. I had put it into my visa application as a kind of bait. By glossing my itinerary as a species of pilgrimage I thought substantially to increase my chances of getting the visa I wanted.

The best justification for such a deception is that it worked. There was however at least one crucial amendment to my itinerary, even before I arrived. I should come to Hanoi first, not Saigon.

Given that anybody who knew anything about Vietnam had told me there was not a hope in hell of my getting a visa for more than three or four weeks, this seemed at the time a relatively minor inconvenience. But now, with Mr Hong warmly patting my knee-cap, I realize that my intended schedule is in tatters, never mind about a programme.

'Let me have a day or two, then I'll give you a list of the places I want to go to, and the people I'd like to interview.'

In the meantime, I suggest, I could begin by seeing what there is to be seen in Hanoi.

Mr Hong, I think with his next appointment already in mind, seems pleased at this. He reiterates his collective pleasure at my safe arrival in Vietnam – I am he says a bosom friend – and assures me that my visit will be a huge success. Then he stands, and I stand, and the next thing I know is I am being hugged.

A word about this hug. It is not a frosty, formal hug, of the televised sort one sees between world leaders assembled to slog it out over some conference table – even though hugging between males is an established convention not just in Vietnam but in most oriental societies. As hugs go, Mr Hong's communicates variously. Partly it fulfils the functions of a handshake: we can work together, we will work together, a deal of some kind or other is clinched. Partly it is a way of saying that the compliments he has paid me are not merely so much pap, but indeed are heartfelt. I am, it seems, to be taken seriously. Partly, in the Confucian mode, it expresses his privilege, the right of the older man to hug the younger if and when he wants. And partly it is ironic. The discussion has taken place, and has been concluded, more or less satisfactorily. Both sides have done their positioning, their play acting. This is to remind us that we are human beings as well, and that should it happen that things foul up, neither of us should regard it as the end of the world.

Perhaps I imagine too much, exaggerate. Perhaps Mr Hong is simply very good at conferring hugs. But the impression of his embrace lingers with me, long after he has disappeared through the revolving door of the Thong Nhat Hotel, and vanished into the darkening street outside. And this impression tells me that Vietnam is feasible, that I am not an utter idiot to have earmarked the next hundred-odd days to a country whose bitter history I know, but only on the page, and whose actuality, today, now, I am wholly alien to.

The epiphany lasts a while yet. Zoom lingers behind a moment, tells me that my meeting with his boss has gone very well, then says that he will join me for breakfast at eight in the morning. Then he too leaves. Shortly afterwards I follow him out, for my first stroll around streets whose names it will take me several days to learn. I turn left out of the hotel, assure the cyclo drivers that I'll require their services soon, point out to the shoeshiners that my sneakers are made predominantly of canvas, and push on. It is almost dark now. Such lighting as there is is dim – an abiding feature of night-time Hanoi, for it is a city of curiously low voltages. I come to the first intersection. I watch the cyclists threading, more slowly now, past and through each other. I notice that many of the women are wearing those conical straw hats one remembers from the movies. I notice that many of the men wear what, in the gloom, resemble pith helmets, a green that is not quite khaki green, the symbol of the cadre. I notice too that the street is lined, more or less, with trees. There is a definite aura of leafiness.

The faces enchant me. There is a dignity about the features one does not always readily associate with South-East Asia. Their eyes look at one with friendly curiosity, but they do not implore, they do not beseech.

I turn into what purports to be a bookstore or stationer's. I take my first look at the local manufactured produce: pens, writing pads, the books themselves. Immediately I feel I have fallen through a time warp. There is nothing here that could not have been produced in Hong Kong in 1955, and even then for the lower end of the mass market.

I come out, and find myself standing at the intersection. The traffic, mostly two and three wheeled, has a contrapuntal flow to it. They drive, or ride, on the right. But on the inside of each lane there are cyclists going against the flow, as they prepare to swing off into another street. Crossing the street, therefore, one has first to look right, not left.

I pass a group of street hawkers, more women wearing conical hats and proffering baskets of apples. (Chinese apples, as it happens, brought in over the mountain passes two hundred kilometres away, usually on foot by the hill tribespeople, and at 4,000 *dong* a kilo not cheap.) I look sideways in each direction. At one end of the new street is – good gracious! – the Paris Opera House. The other way, shops, and one shop with a small crowd gathered outside.

I choose the latter. The crowd is gathered round an ice-cream parlour, the first and as far as I am aware the only one in the north. They sell ice-creams in Hanoi now! The customers are young, and their clothes are not so different from the clothes worn by young people in Kuala Lumpur, Jakarta or Singapore. Designer track-suits, jeans, T-shirts, brightly coloured sweaters. I pass them by. I enter another bookshop, but all the titles are either Vietnamese or Russian, save several piles of English grammars. Then I am pounced upon by a girl who drags me two yards into a narrow alley-way. She is selling books as well, but all her titles are English or French – products of the Foreign Languages Publishing House.

The girl, still holding my hand with hers, which is warm and dry, begins reeling off titles: *Mountain Regions and National Minorities, American Failure, Education in the SRVN, 25 Years of Health Work, Ethnographical Data (Volume One), Linguistic Essays, Ethnographical Data (Volume Three)* ... To stop the flow I seize upon *Dien Bien Phu*, by Vo Nguyen Giap. Since it's my intention to meet and interview the General, I tell the girl I'd like this one, but will have to come back for it as I don't have any money on me.

'Don't come back, sir. Buy it now.'

'But I have no *dong*,' I say. 'Must go hotel, go bank, change some dollars.'

'No problem. Give me dollars.'

And so I am trapped. But who cares? Haggling with a pretty face is always fun, and after ten minutes I walk away with a fat brown parcel under my arm, tied up with yellow string. Inside the parcel, as well as General Giap, are a large English–Vietnamese dictionary, an equally large compendium of Vietnamese literature down the ages, a short guide to Hanoi, a proper map of the same and *Vietnamese Folk Tales*, as well as *Vietnamese Traditional Humour*. Not inside the parcel is *Ho Chi Minh: His Exemplary Life and Achievements*, by Truong Chinh. In all I have parted with twelve dollars, and a promise to come back the moment I have finished reading what I have bought.

The girl's face lights up in ecstasy.

'Come back tomorrow,' she says. 'Have many many more books for you then.'

I walk back past the ice-cream parlour, and the peculiarly fetid stink that emanates from it. At the intersection I turn right. The shops here are smaller: in many cases the entire stock would fit comfortably into my suitcase. More street-vendors, proffering trays of cigarettes – 555, Dunhill, Hero, Ruby Queen – or ancient plugs and even more ancient light sockets.

The pavement, originally laid down by the French, is rough, pockmarked, pitted. On it I observe, for the first time, Vietnamese deep in conversation, squatting not on their haunches, but right back on their heels. Bicycle repairers similarly crouch on the kerb, waiting for customers, with pumps, spanners and jerry-cans of oil-black water.

Something that I can only describe as an intense yet utterly laid-back happiness washes over me, as though I have been given a shot of omnopon. I feel almost as if I have come home. It is silly, but there you have it, that is what I feel. For years and years, when I was young, Hanoi was synonymous with aggression, with what my country's staunchest ally was fighting against. Yet the Hanoi that I see around me is utterly unviolent. Rather it enjoys what trendy sociologists call 'backward advantage'. It is pollution free, it is charming, it is beautifully provincial, it possesses relatively little glass, it is the sort of place most of us would like to live in in the year 2020. All the debris of modernity has been swept away.

I return to the Thong Nhat. A Mrs Moon at reception offers to exchange some dollars for me. The rate is lean, just 3,500 *dong*, but not knowing any better, I comply. (On the street the rate begins at 4,000 *dong* a dollar.) She then invites me to try a restaurant on the other side of town. It is, she says, very good because it has French cuisine. Whatever I do I should avoid eating in the hotel. The hotel cuisine is bad because ... because ... Analysis fails Mrs Moon. 'Tomorrow,' I say, and take my key. After a scalding shower I defy Mrs Moon and try the restaurant. Once more I find Vietnam to be survivable. Chicken soup, fried rice, spring rolls. Nothing for the gourmet, but then, having heard that food in the north is sometimes scarce, I've left that particular set of needs behind.

The dining room is large and square. All the other diners are western. They sit either singly or in pairs. I carefully avoid locking eyes with a scruffy, bearded, lean, bespectacled fellow who looks like a New York intellectual. Something tells me he is a journalist, and for today I prefer to avoid my own kind. I stare, betimes, at the ceiling instead. There are thirty-six outsize fans, arranged in rows. They spin slowly. For a moment it flashes through my head: this is no restaurant, this is a testing station for the propellers of home-made submarines.

Prejudice again!

Dinner over, I pass quickly through the lobby. A bald, red-faced man lurches at me and invites me to join him in a Saigon 33. I resist the non-temptation. I go to my room and open my journal (which in large measure will become this record). Two hours later I unpack my freshly purchased books. I begin my research at the shallow end: folk-tales and traditional humour. The two pamphlets overlap. Seventy per cent, they share the same material, ancestral anecdotes. One way or another, most of the stories concern mandarins. There is one that doesn't, however, which grabs my fancy more than any other. It goes like this:

There was once a miser, the father of two daughters both married to skinflints. On a certain feast day, in accordance with custom, the miser's sons-in-law came to his house to present gifts. Presenting gifts was the correct procedure for displaying filial piety.

The two husbands naturally resented this duty, but both conceded there was no escaping it. Otherwise, when their father-in-law died, they might inherit nothing.

Gifts normally consisted of pigs, chickens, ducks, fruit, rice-wine and so forth. But the young men, although each had more than enough such items, were loath to part with so much as an egg.

The first son-in-law, therefore, went to an artist and, for a modest outlay, commissioned a sketch of all those things that he knew would delight his wife's progenitor: oxen, pigs, geese, wine, you name it . . .

In due course he arrived at the miser's house.

The miser was ready and waiting for him, he was seated in the middle of a divan, the customary position for receiving gifts.

'And what have you brought me this year, my son?' he asked, as soon as they had exchanged traditional compliments.

'This year,' replied the oldest son-in-law, 'I am not so rich. I regret very much that all I can offer is a few oxen, a few pigs, some geese and some wine. Please be so good as to accept these humble offerings from a son who loves you more than life itself.'

The young man then unfurled his painting, and presented it to the miser, pretending to struggle under its weight.

The miser thanked him profusely. 'This is very good,' he said. 'But allow me to remark: perhaps, given your straitened circumstances, you have been a little too extravagant?'

The second son-in-law, meanwhile, had arrived at the house, and witnessed this scene. It was now his turn to present his gifts.

19

He stepped forward and, with a flourish, produced a stick of charcoal from deep within his robe.

'And what is this you have brought your father?' asked the miser.

Rather than make reply, the younger husband bent over and began sketching shapes on the floor: some oxen, some pigs, a few geese, wine and a dozen other things besides.

They were, of course, all much bigger than the beasts and foodstuffs depicted in his brother-in-law's offering.

'I am only sorry,' he proclaimed, ramming the point home, 'that due to lack of space I am unable to present you with even more and even bigger oxen, pigs, geese, chickens, etcetera.'

'Splendid!' cried the father-in-law. 'You have been more thoughtful than your brother. Even so, you have been, perhaps, a little extravagant. But I intend to reward you both. Here, have some wine!'

The miser then went through the motions of opening a bottle and pouring out drinks, all in thin air.

'Cheers!'

The two husbands dutifully went through the motions of raising their glasses. Their father-in-law, they afterwards agreed, was a genius, one of whom they were both unworthy.

I finished reading, unfurled a mosquito net and climbed into bed. It was indeed a bit like trying on a wedding dress. But the effect wore off. Soon I began to doze. But the dozing did not give way to sleep. Suddenly there was a small commotion over by the windows.

I struggled out of my wedding dress, switched on the light and crossed the room to see what the matter was.

The lid of the plastic tea caddy had divorced from the receptacle proper and was lying on its side. Very slightly it rocked.

Damn! I thought. A mouse, or a rat!

I replaced the lid, put the whole ensemble on top of the refrigerator, and climbed back into bed. I honestly thought the creature would simply be unable to scale the machine's enamelled sides.

Ten minutes later the tea-caddy lid ricocheted across the floor.

This time I put the caddy inside the fridge, and a sleeping pill inside my mouth. I was buggered if what had been a good day should be ruined by a pesky rodent.

On my second day in Hanoi I purposefully left three banana skins lying on the table. When I returned a few hours later, two of them had gone. Also missing, half a packet of biscuits I had unintentionally left on the desk.

This confirmed my worst suspicions, that the thing was definitely a rat.

That night, by positioning myself next to the table lamp, I saw him. Not the biggest I'd ever seen, but with a tail that whipped across the floor like a snake.

My third night in Hanoi, at dead on 4.00 a.m., the rat bit me.

Thursday 5th October: Hanoi Zoom is ready and waiting for me downstairs at 8.00 a.m. I invite him to join me for breakfast in the dining room. Again the young man is exceedingly chatty, engaging, candid. We have an hour before Mr Nam is due to arrive at the Thong Nhat with the 'van' (Russian minibus). Zoom tells me a bit about himself. He says he is very fortunate to be alive. When Hanoi was devastated by American bombs he was a kid living in the city. One of them might have landed on his house. Although he was very young at the time he remembers being at an open-air cinema early one evening and seeing a flight of B52s high in the sky above, and sticks falling. More recently, he was with a television crew touring the south when the car he was in, for no apparent reason, exploded. Also, he was almost eaten by sharks when he went underwater filming with some Hungarian naturalists. But worst of all, Cambodia. He did his military service in Cambodia at the beginning of the 1980s, after Vietnam had invaded that country ostensibly to put a stop to Khmer Rouge incursions into Vietnamese territory. One morning he fell off the back of a truck and severely injured his head. He was in hospital for six months.

'I almost died. You should have seen me. I had no weight at all. When I came back home everybody thought I must have been captured and put in a Khmer Rouge labour camp. But really I was lucky. So many Vietnamese died in Cambodia. But I survived.'

Zoom laughs, giving me the uneasy sensation that he regards

living and dying with a detachment that is beyond his years and contrary to his happy, engaged manner.

'One day maybe I won't be so lucky. I've had four escapes. Next time perhaps, no more Mister Zoom!'

After military service he 'hung around' a while, doing nothing in particular. Then he acquired a guitar, learned how to sing and played in a band. His repertoire included several numbers written by the Beatles. But his father, a former army officer turned civil servant, soon put a stop to that. If Zoom didn't pull his socks up then Zoom would be expelled from the family. This threat brought him to his senses. 'You see, in Vietnam, we must respect our parents.' He attended the Foreign Languages College to study English. Then he got his job with the Ministry of Information. Just recently his post was made permanent.

'They want to keep me, you see. Mister Zoom knows how to be a good interpreter, a good organizer.'

'But you can't be an interpreter all your life.'

'No? Maybe not. But it's okay for the present. I meet a lot of foreigners, I travel around. It makes me feel lucky.'

He has, he says, been offered well-paid jobs by the private sector in Saigon, but so far has refused. His salary is 40,000 *dong* a month, or somewhat less than $10. It's not enough to live on, but he is still single and stays with his parents. Sometimes he gets tips from his overseas clients, and that helps. But money is not important. What is important is working hard, job satisfaction. He is, despite his gaiety, an out-and-out Hanoian.

The conversation becomes more general. At one point Zoom proffers a Vietnamese proverb that I'll hear again and again over the coming weeks: 'For a man, the best is a European house, Chinese food and a Japanese wife.' He also tells me about the four symbols of Vietnamese culture: the dragon, symbolizing power; the phoenix, symbolizing beauty; the chimera, symbolizing strength; and the turtle, symbolizing longevity. Then the white-and-blue Russian minibus appears in the street outside and it is time to go.

Nam drives us to Zoom's office, a dozen or so blocks away from the Thong Nhat. By daylight Hanoi appears tinged everywhere with brown. Everything seems in want of repair, and there is a distinct dearth of fresh paint. The streets are full of cyclists. I

22

notice how in many instances passengers are perched on the baggage racks of the rear of the bicycles. In a few cases whole families wobble gamely forward on just one set of wheels. Zoom tells me that the bad bikes are manufactured in Vietnam, the good ones in East Germany or China. Overwhelmingly people prefer a Chinese bicycle, but Chinese bicycles are expensive: about seventy dollars each.

The Services Centre is housed in a substantial brick-and-stone building with various outhouses clustered around a shabby court-yard. The aim of my visit is threefold: to map out my programme, to deposit my money and to meet Mr Le Tien. Le Tien, it is explained, is well connected with the publishing and broadcasting businesses, and will therefore be of singular use to me. He has some connection with the Ministry itself, although quite what will remain a permanent mystery.

'Also,' Zoom adds, 'he is my father.'

'Your father?'

'Well, no. Not my actual father. But like my father. We use such terms to identify each other. Mister Hong, he's my father too. You and I will be brothers, perhaps.'

So I am taken up some rather grand external stairs and led into a square reception chamber. I am introduced to two or three cadres of Zoom's own age and rank before being joined by Mr Hong. Mr Hong shakes my hand if anything with even more fervour than yesterday, then invites me to drink tea. Le Tien, he says, will not be long. Until he comes perhaps we can discuss my programme?

This time, having given the matter some thought, I am prepared. I explain that as nearly as possible I would like to stick to the itinerary proposed in my original application, but since I'm in Hanoi (and not Saigon/Ho Chi Minh City) I'd like to spend a week or two in the capital doing interviews and generally getting a feel of the place. After that I propose flying to Saigon, spending a week or two exploring the Mekong Delta, before journeying, as slowly as possible, all the way back up Highway One to Hanoi, and on to Cao Bang and Pac Bo. In addition, since I've come all this way, I put in a bid to visit Phnom Penh, in order to interview Hun Sen (the effective leader of the much harassed Cambodian government). Also, I would like very much to go to the Spratlys. The Spratlys are a cluster of islands in the South China Sea which, along with the Paracels, are disputed between Vietnam and China. The rumour is that the islands have now been largely overrun by the Chinese, and that there is a little war going on out there.

Mr Hong nods vigorously as Zoom translates my requests. 'Yes, yes, yes,' he says, verging on impatience. 'Everything is good. But as for the Spratlys, I'm not sure. You would need special permission.'

'Then let's ask for it.'

'Maybe.'

At this point Le Tien enters. For the second time I am welcomed to Vietnam from the bottom of the heart, hugged. He is slightly larger than life, disorganized, a touch unkempt. His overriding characteristic is a volubility that denies him the opportunity of listening to whatever it is one might have to say to him. Or it might just be that he is better at speaking English than at deciphering it. Zoom and Hong run through my programme with him and, like Mr Hong, he nods impatiently as though he has heard it all several times before. 'Very good, very good.' And then, the direct question: 'Are you going to have a chapter about Ho Chi Minh in your book?'

I reiterate what I said yesterday.

'Of course, of course, I understand, no chapters. But really, a chapter about Uncle Ho is most important.'

Le Tien is further of the opinion that, whatever happens, I should be in Hanoi on 23rd December, when there will be a big military parade marking some or other revolutionary anniversary that I shouldn't under any circumstance miss.

'Of course,' I say, 'I'd be delighted.'

As for the interviews, no problem. All I have to do is furnish Zoom with a list of those I'd like to meet, and the Ministry will see to everything.

The main business accomplished, Messrs Hong and Le Tien take their leave. Zoom shows me through to an inner room where the safe is kept: another table, more hard wooden seats and a plethora of teacups. Several youngish cadres down newspapers and pretend to look busy as soon as I enter. Zoom laughs.

'They are all having *boc phét*,' he tells me. 'You know, idle gossip. The same as hanging about.'

24

I am invited to join the company and at Zoom's prompting I do so. 'Never refuse tea, it is the Vietnamese way.' The *boc phét* at once focuses on the person of Ms Binh. Binh is the keeper of the safe and general office clerk who also doubles as a French interpreter when one is needed. She is petite and sweet, and blessed with an instant blush that rises to every occasion. Zoom and several of his colleagues strenuously urge me to practise a little French with her. This done, I prepare to give her all, or almost all, my money. Zoom makes me count it first. The others do everything in their power not to look. Then Binh wraps it in a sheet of old newspaper, painstakingly gumming it down on all sides. The office may have a sweetheart, but apparently no manila envelopes.

'Really, you will have to buy Binh some Sellotape,' Zoom mischiefs. 'Then, maybe, she will give you a date.'

'Don't worry,' Zoom reassures me back in Mr Nam's van, 'your programme will soon be under way. But for today you must relax. I have many things to organize on your behalf.' But we do not drive straight back to the Thong Nhat. Nam takes us on a mini-tour of the city. Mainly this means a succession of narrow streets bottled up with bicycles. But it also includes a whip round the southern shore of West Lake, the very large expanse of water to the north of the city where, according to my guide, lovers like to stroll and even boat on warm summer evenings.

Briefly we stop at the Thang Loi (Victory) Hotel, partly built out over the water, an unexpectedly modern, almost stylish construction put up in 1975 after the fall of Saigon. Its reception area is large, cool and studded with fish-pools. A room costs $55 a night.

'But really, you wouldn't want to stay here,' says Zoom. 'It's too far out of town, and designed for diplomats and businessmen.'

'Exactly. And in any case I couldn't afford it.'

This enables me to broach a topic that has been preying on me more or less since I arrived:

'By the way, how much am I paying at the Thong Nhat?'

Zoom thinks somewhere between $25 and $30 a night. A quick calculation tells me that at that rate if everywhere's the same around half my money will go on accommodation – provided I remain in Vietnam for the full period anticipated.

25

'Is there anywhere else I could stay?'

'You're not happy at the Thong Nhat?'

'I'm delirious, but . . .'

'Okay. I understand. I'll see what I can do. But stay there just for a few days, yes?'

It's still only mid-morning when Zoom and Nam drop me back at the Thong Nhat. I take a second, daylight walk and discover Ho Hoan Kiem, or the Lake of the Restored Sword (sometimes called the Little or Round Lake) – the emotional centre of Hanoi. According to legend, the fifteenth-century King Le Thai To was out boating on it one day not long after he had repulsed a Chinese army when a golden turtle pushed up through the waves and reclaimed the sacred sword which the gods of the Fatherland had given Le Thai To to help him ward off yet another assault by Vietnam's traditional enemy. The lake is about the same size as London's Serpentine, and genuinely picturesque. A tiny tower and a not-much-larger pagoda adorn its middle. For me though the real joy is a coffee shop about a third of the way round its perimeter. In a tiny, cluttered room I sit on a tiny, rickety stool only three or four inches off the floor while, with a great deal of commotion and a long monologue, the elderly proprietor, for the equivalent of six or seven cents, serves me with a beverage. I sit for an hour watching the bicycles spin past. Beside me, on an unlit wall, stares a full-size, murky reproduction of the *Mona Lisa*. I have never before considered it a masterpiece of the surreal.

I am less lazy in the afternoon. I apply myself earnestly to the language. Before leaving Britain I purchased a Vietnamese course, the only one available or even known about at Dillon's university bookshop – two cassettes and a booklet. But although I ran the tapes night after night on the player beside my bed, scarcely a word of it sank in. In the darkness of my bedroom I would dutifully repeat the sounds as they were spoken – and wake up next morning with absolutely no Vietnamese in my head whatsoever. The main problem was that Vietnamese offers nothing for an English speaker to get his teeth into. All the words are monosyllabic, irreducible, indigestible. It was like putting a lot of unpolished marbles in the mouth, and then being asked to work out what colour they are. An added complication is the superimposition of a system of accents and tones (which Vietnamese shares with Chinese and Thai); so that even if you land on the right phonemes, the chances are they will mean something totally different from what you want them to mean.

But the course itself was no help either. Published in the United States by a body called Educational Services Teaching Cassettes, and subtitled, for no discernible reason, *Language/30* (unless Vietnamese is in some way or other Language No. 30), it begins encouragingly enough: 'I am Charles Berlitz,' says a soothing voice with a slight Midwest drawl to it. (Whether this is *the* Berlitz is left to speculation.) There are two 'important things' the student is advised to remember when learning a new language, the first of which is 'to be inner-rested in the people, their country and language'. The cassettes then provide 'basic phrases', such as 'Excuse me, can you tell me where the baseball ground is?' and 'I want to book an aeroplane ticket to America now.'

The kit makes no concessions to elucidating Vietnamese grammar, nor are the magic people-and-country-understanding phrases (the longest section is about automobile maintenance) translated word by word, blow by blow. Being in Vietnam I hope will supply the missing key, but after two hours' study in my room I am none the wiser. The phrase I really want to learn – 'Help, I am not an American!' – still eludes me. By a process of double-checked elimination, I am more or less certain that the Vietnamese for 'I' is *toi*, and reasonably confident 'American' is *My*. (*My*, however, pronounced 'me' or 'mi', has an accent that is not tonal so much as hysterical: 'meeeee!' – as though the speaker had just spotted a mouse on the chair-arm. The paranoid inflection? There is no equivalent in Thai, nor, as far as I'm aware, in Chinese.) But how one progresses from 'I am American' to 'Help, I'm not one' is anyone's guess.

Only then, when I have wrenched the tapes out of my machine, does it occur to me to consult the English–Vietnamese dictionary purchased yesterday. In no time at all I come up with 'Cu'u voi! Toi khong phai nguoi My!' I write the words out on a piece of paper and commit the spelling to memory. How they are pronounced is still *terra incognita*, but I feel I am at least halfway to

27

not having my head chopped off by a remnant VC in the jungle, should I ever get to the jungle.

What I don't appreciate yet is that, far from not wanting to see any Americans, the majority of Vietnamese would very much like to see a very great number of them all over their beautiful but impoverished land.

Awarding myself full marks for diligence, and none for aptitude, I cease my studies at the stroke of six. Mrs Moon at reception buttonholes me. Her excuse is a letter for me, her purpose to remind me of my promise to visit the 'French' restaurant. I tell her I'll have a drink first and decide afterwards.

The bar is, or seems to be, one of those good bars one finds in tropical and subtropical capitals, a place of expatriate congregation where no one allows himself reasons for not chatting with anyone else who's around. In the coming evenings it will prove an invaluable source for 'lobby talk': that *ad hoc* mixture of informed expertise and wild guesswork, ideas that the newly arrived needs to give him his first co-ordinates, his first fix. Much of what he hears will later be jettisoned, but at least it provides him with a clue as to what the important issues are. It also makes the honeymoon period (going to a foreign country for any length of time always does have the flavour of an arranged marriage) at least marginally enjoyable.

For now I fall in with a man of my own age, Colin Bullogh, a thin-faced, ginger-haired obstetrician from South Shields. He has been in Vietnam a month, working up country for the World Health Organization on a natal programme. His way of speaking is low key, cautious, eschewing anything flamboyant, which includes anything political. Grist absolute to my mill. We share a beer, swap notes on Mrs Moon, and decide to give her dining tip a whirl. The jungle is one thing, city back streets another. Together, no harm shall befall us.

Mrs Moon writes an address on a scrap of paper. This we show to the cyclo drivers outside. We agree a price with two of them, and set off into the dark. The cyclos clatter, Colin Bullogh and I rattle. I try to keep track of left turns and right turns, but after a while the feat becomes too much. Colin draws alongside and I tap my watch. Colin grimaces back knowingly. But before too very long the cyclos grind to a halt and we are emptied onto the pavement in front of what, our drivers assure us, is the My Vi. We pay them 5,000 *dong* each, and venture inside what seems to be a plain small urban dwelling. To our relief we discover several tables and red-chequered tablecloths. This is *doi moi* in action. The proprietor, who is Chinese, makes the briefest of appearances. Otherwise we are left in the hands of an ageing but capable waitress whose face is not wholly dissimilar to Mrs Moon's.

The food disappoints. That is to say, it is on a par with the cuisine of the Thong Nhat, and a little more expensive. It has the advantage however of not distracting my attention away from my companion. Colin tells me about his work, and the difficulties he faces. There is, he says, no real shortage of hospitals in Vietnam. The Party believes in health care, always did; in the war one of the ways the Viet Cong curried favour with the peasants was by always doing what was in their power to help, but that's not the point. Quantity is no substitute for quality. And the quality alas simply isn't there. The staffs of the small hospitals and clinics he has visited do not want for knowledge; but the knowledge they have is, in the main, gleaned from textbooks thirty or forty years out of date, and has been learned very much by rote. But even up-to-date knowledge wouldn't do them much good, because equipment and drugs are lacking on an unimaginable scale. There is also a question of attitude. In his own field, obstetrics, the prevailing wisdom is to save babies, not mothers. The result is a maternal mortality rate that accounts for more lives even than malaria (still the plague of Indochina). 'It's not . . .' Colin pauses, 'something that would be particularly acceptable in South Shields. One has to say a certain male chauvinism is at work here, for of course there's an even chance the baby may be male, while it's statistically certain the mother isn't.' Thus mature lives, with their accretion of experience and social skills, are lost, for the benefit of infants who as yet have no personality, and who are prone to a number of fatal diseases during childhood anyway. 'But it keeps the great Asian family system going, I suppose. If the mother dies, then the grandmother comes into her own again.'

'Ah, Mrs Moon!'

Our conversation is interrupted by the appearance of the Thong

29

Nhat receptionist. We are not altogether surprised to see her. It is evident she hasn't come simply in order to wish us a belated *bon appétit*. But we are wrong to think she's just here for her cut. The My Vi, as she disarmingly explains, is the family business.

Our cyclo drivers have waited outside. For another 5,000 *dong* they agree to porter us back. The return journey is swift. The restaurant could have been walked in fifteen minutes; or by cyclo should not have cost more than 2,000 *dong*. But how else does one learn?

At the hotel, the bar is crowded. It is less than a week since Vietnam withdrew the last of its troops from Cambodia, and some of the foreign journalists have come up from Saigon and Phnom Penh to nose round Hanoi. (Also, at one of the tables, a group of Vietnamese women, prostitutes, whom the majority avoid since it is assumed that they are run by 'Security'. They actually do have names like Sum Phun and Chew Mee, only they call themselves 'Madame Phun' and 'Madame Mee'.) The troop withdrawal is an integral part of the country's effort to rehabilitate itself on the world scene. The United States long ago made the evacuation of Cambodia a precondition for setting up formal relations between Hanoi and Washington. Vietnam has done its bit, will America now respond? It seems not. The trouble is, America is reluctant to withdraw militarily from Indochina. It supports Prince Sihanouk, and sooner or later a part of the aid that goes to Sihanouk's army finds its way to the Khmer Rouge. As the Pentagon well knows.

Norodon Sihanouk is about the only non-communist Cambodian the West has heard of, and therefore everybody rushes to support him; whereas in reality he is a man devoid of principle. The Khmer Rouge, backed by China and North Korea, slaughtered most of his family after they took power in 1975 (along with two million other Cambodians). Since then Sihanouk has lived mainly in exile – in China and North Korea. Now he is back in Cambodia, the leader of one of three resistance forces hoping to topple the Vietnam-backed socialist government of Hun Sen in Phnom Penh. The three forces have combined in a coalition, so that Sihanouk is, so to speak, in bed with the Khmer Rouge. And America supplies the blankets, as part of its pro-China, anti-Vietnamese policy. Needless to say, the mainspring of this policy is Washington's historic need to counterbalance Soviet power. Washington's objection to Russia is supposedly ideological. So it winds up supporting, directly and indirectly, the Khmer Rouge, who represent the most extreme, and bloody, form of communism. Such are the terms of geopolitical endearment.

The question on everyone's lips is whether the Vietnamese withdrawal from Cambodia is for real. Most of the journalists I quiz are of the opinion that it is. But there are contra-indications. Vietnam has left behind a large number of 'settlers' in Cambodia, supposedly farmers, but who may in fact still be armed. There is also a piece of hot news: five Vietnamese soldiers have reputedly just been captured on the Thai border. This however comes from Hsin Hua, the notoriously unreliable Chinese news agency. Yet it is confirmed by the Thai Foreign Minister.

(Tomorrow the plot will thicken. When the Bangkok press corps rush to the scene of apprehension, the commanding officer of the Thai border army denies all knowledge of the episode. Later, it is said that five uniformed Vietnamese were indeed captured, but they were no part of the Vietnamese Army. Rather they belonged to an insurgent group of expatriate Vietnamese fighting a futile war on the Viet–Laotian border in the hope of one day overthrowing Vietnam's socialist government. The Thais, according to this scenario, since they clandestinely support such groups, in accordance with their Sino–American alignment, had scored an own goal – made possible by a bitter squabble between the Foreign Minister and the Trade Minister, who wants an end to all the fighting in order that the whole of SE Asia may be transformed into a *baht* prosperity region.)

There is also talk of a senior CIA official, a man who carries the rank of a two-star general, having been seen several times on the Thai–Cambodian border. The consensus is that the United States is deliberately stalling over any settlement in Cambodia. A Swiss correspondent who was in Paris during the abortive peace talks earlier in the summer tells me that an American aide said to him: 'Cambodia is a small country, just seven million people, so let them thrash it out in a civil war. Then we'll have a look-see whom we've got to deal with, or not deal with as the case may be.'

Two Australians, not journalists, but aid workers, are particularly glum. The Australian government had agreed that bilateral aid to Vietnam could start immediately after its troops were withdrawn from Cambodia. So last week they packed their bags and flew over. But now the Australian Foreign Minister, Gareth Evans, under strong pressure from America, has backtracked. They tell me that the United States is now imposing a new precondition: there must be an agreed settlement in Cambodia before it will consider lifting its trade and aid embargo on Vietnam. And Canberra must kowtow to brother Washington.

Yet there is dialogue between at least one section of the American political machine and Hanoi. A Norwegian historian, Stein Tønesson, who has come to Vietnam to research the August Revolution of 1945, asks me whether I noticed who else was on board the plane we both flew in on yesterday. No, I say, tell me?

'Senator Edmund Muskie.'

'Are you sure?'

'I am almost certain.' (Stein speaks excellent English with a clipped Germanic accent.) 'I have to say I was a little surprised myself. He was sitting just two rows in front of me. I thought his face was familiar, but that was all. Then I was talking to someone else this evening, a Nepalese diplomat, and he asked me, what do you think Senator Edmund Muskie is doing in Hanoi? He too was on the aeroplane. Having met Muskie once before he was in no doubt.'

'It seems odd,' I say, 'that someone like Muskie should come in on an ordinary commercial flight with no fanfare.'

'That's precisely what I thought. I think we should follow this closely.'

Stein is utterly, therefore comically, serious, and for this I take an immediate liking to him. A tall man in his early thirties, bespectacled, yet strappingly built, he wastes no time in assuring me he is a pukka socialist. As a historian, he abides by Marxist analysis, though his methodology (he hopes) is more idiosyncratic than that. His card reveals that he is a research fellow of the International Peace Research Institute in Oslo. About his whole person there is something charmingly conspiratorial. We are destined, over the next few weeks, to become close friends. Having arrived in Hanoi on the same day, we are travel contemporaries, and we will compare notes about everything as we strive to get to grips with a country that often seems to be teetering on the edge of chaos. At the same time the fronts we present each other will crystallize into opposites: Stein's optimistic, committed, sometimes naïve; mine cynical, disbelieving, querulous. And then, as we become aware of our own personae through each other's eyes, we will each do our best to confound the other's expectations.

Such are the mechanics of an intellectual friendship away from home. I retire to my room happy with the day's progress. I retire to my bed even happier. The letter which Mrs Moon gave me, and which I had forgotten all about once I had slipped it into my back pocket, is an invitation from Emrys Davies, the British Ambassador, for lunch tomorrow.

Friday 6th October: Hanoi Panic! The first thing that happens when I wake up is I discover I have mislaid my zipper briefcase. I remember taking it down with me last night, and I remember clutching something on the way to the restaurant in the cyclo. I don't remember clutching anything in the cyclo on the way back. Therefore I must have left it in the restaurant, if I have left it anywhere at all.

Panic, because the only thing of any value or importance in the case was a notebook containing notes taken during a lunch in London with the Vietnam specialist at Amnesty International. Generously the Amnesty man divulged the contents of a special report on human rights abuses that was not scheduled for release until the middle of November. I was given a good briefing on all the 'sensitive' issues pertaining to Vietnam, and now this, in encapsulated form, might be in anyone's hands.

The sensitive issues included re-education camps, the 'boat people', MIAs, torture and the penal code. By and large my informant was inclined to look favourably on Vietnam. Having visited Hanoi he was convinced that the government was eager to be, as well appear, humanitarian. The re-education camps, set up to deal with non-communists after 1975, were a case in point. They only existed because the bloodbath many had anticipated when Saigon fell did not materialize. True, conditions inside the camps had not been pleasant, and many prisoners had died of various causes, but in part this was a reflection on living conditions in the country at large. There was also strong evidence that in recent years large numbers of prisoners (political detainees) had been and were being released. The problem was in arriving at an accurate assessment of how many inmates were left. The Vietnamese government has a tendency to say one day that only a few hundred obdurates are still behind bars, then the next it proudly announces the release of a further thousand or more.

On the matter of the boat people, or water-borne voluntary exiles, I was told that this matter did not fall properly within Amnesty's Vietnam remit. But the strong impression was Hanoi didn't want these people back, and was only discussing having them back (from Hong Kong) as part of a package which would clear the way for improved relations with the West (principally Britain and the USA). The question as to whether the majority of boat people could rightly be dubbed 'economic migrants', as Mrs Thatcher was currently insisting, was a very large one indeed, and depended upon relativist definitions of 'political', which rather put the issue beyond Amnesty's traditional pale of legitimate concern.

As for MIAs – those listed Missing In Action by the US government as a result of American military intervention in Indochina – Amnesty took the line that the Vietnamese were doing everything that could be reasonably expected of them to locate and return the remains of American soldiers. More to the point, Amnesty had uncovered no solid evidence to support the view that some MIAs are still alive and being held hostage in Vietnam in hidden jungle POW camps. The only contra-indication came from the testimony of a Japanese Buddhist monk, who had been kept in prison (for dissidence) until a year ago. As soon as he got back to his own country he began telling everyone that he had seen Americans in detention, but for several reasons his testimony was suspect.

The areas that did concern Amnesty were law, the judiciary and the prison service. A new penal code has made Vietnam potentially more of, not less of, a police state. There are more restrictions, more rules to break. This makes it wrong to lump *doi moi* together with *glasnost*. *Perestroika* yes, *glasnost* no. The Vietnamese government has generally operated effectively to reduce and contain organized opposition. Two of the old religious sects, the Cao Dai and the Hoa Hao, which played important political roles in the 1950s and 1960s (generally to the advantage of the Viet Minh and Viet Cong) have had their central organizations smashed, although they continue to operate at the village level.

Political 'unity' has been achieved largely through the courts. Trials are not 'fair' in any recognized sense. The state prosecutors enjoy something close to a 100 per cent strike rate. Defendants are normally presumed to be guilty, otherwise they wouldn't be in court in the first place. There are no private or independent law practices, and the best that most state defence counsels can achieve is a reduction of sentence following pleas for mitigating circumstances.

The main charge that Amnesty International would be making in its report was that the law was being used against genuine dissidents who have committed no crime, but who are apprehended under the provision of catch-all 'national security' clauses.

All this was in my little notebook. Clearly if it fell into the wrong hands, and it was not appreciated that I had simply recorded what I had been told, then my 'friend of Vietnam' status would evaporate, and my stay in the country be abruptly curtailed. There was also the small matter of wider consequences. The Vietnamese government could attack Amnesty International before it had published its report, and through my carelessness I could justly be accused of having betrayed that organization's trust.

Unable to find Mrs Moon so early in the day, I sit in the dining room unconsoled by my allegedly continental breakfast. I am also unconsoled by the vision of the bearded New York intellectual a few tables away. He is not alone this time. Rather he is having a heated debate with a French (German? Dutch?) woman. From time to time the phrase 'in a free country', uttered with some vehemence, flies my way. Nothing else. Just that. *In a free country . . .!*

Zoom rescues me. Today, he says, it is his turn to buy me breakfast. Nam drives us to Nam Ngu Street, scarcely bigger than an alley-way but packed full of noodle stalls. Madame Lam, he assures me, serves the best noodles in Asia. Prodding at the contents of my bowl I am ready to agree, though it's Zoom's bounce rather than the vermicelli that stimulates my approval. Zoom explains to me, at some length, about the various kinds of noodles available in Hanoi. I tell him about my little problem, without of course mentioning Amnesty International or its report.

'Don't worry. Really. It'll turn up.'

We drive to a police station to register my name, to the Cambodian Embassy to collect visa application forms, and to a photographic studio to have passport photos taken to put on the forms. For a ludicrously small sum, I think about 20 cents, I get ten copies. Zoom lets me keep eight of them. Then we embark on the first instalment of my 'programme'. This includes visits to the Temple of Literature and the Army Museum.

The Temple of Literature is a nice place originally built in 1070 according to Chinese specifications, and dedicated to the spirit of Confucius. It is rectangular, with outer and inner courtyards. The grounds are studded with stone steles inscribed with the names of those who, in the Middle Ages, won first prize in the imperial examinations – the temple was, in those times, the equivalent of a university. My guidebook tells me that it 'invites quietness and meditation by its harmonious line, the greenery surrounding it, its courtyards and its walls'. It is also one of the very few public places I will visit that does not have the image of Uncle Ho plastered everywhere.

By contrast, the Army Museum is virtually wallpapered with the man and his sayings. It is however a clever, even human place. The exhibits consist largely of photographs, in the main wonderful old black-and-white shots of the French and American wars – rather more of the former than of the latter; of the people who fought them; and of staged revolutionary events. The tone, which is one of some compassion, is spoiled only by the last and newest hall, dedicated to the 'Reunification'. Here, a T34 tank sits defiantly on top of one of the gates from the Presidential Palace in Saigon. I am reminded that I am in Hanoi, not Ho Chi Minh City.

Dropped off at the Thong Nhat, I walk to my ambassador's residence three blocks away. Emrys Davies, whom I have spoken with before but never met, is a modern diplomat: there is not a speck of starch on him, although when I explain about my briefcase and its contents he finds it hard to suppress an involuntary shudder. 'You will keep me posted on that, won't you?' he requests anxiously. There are just two other guests, a medical entomologist seconded from ICI called Graham White, and Murray Hibbert, the *Far East Economic Review*'s Vietnam specialist.

Without Murray lunch would have been a cosy informal affair. Unfortunately Murray is one and the same person as the 'New York intellectual' I have viewed with inner distaste in the restaurant of the Thong Nhat. In fact he is not American, but Canadian. He is also supposed to have a Mormon or Seventh Day Adventist or Christian Scientist background, which both explains and adds to his curiously driven quality. Perhaps something of my discomfort at seeing him communicates itself, for no sooner are we introduced, in the ambassador's drawing room, than he asks, with a sodding sneer, 'I see – and what kind of book are you *trying* to write about this country?' Nor does he find better grace at table. Graham White, in a lengthy and informative digression on the ins and outs of malaria, at one point drops a marvellous comment about the Vietnamese 'eradication mentality'. (The point here is, Vietnam is spending what few resources it has on preventing malaria, rather than on treating it when it occurs. This, in White's view, is the reverse of what should be done.) No sooner is the phrase uttered than Hibbert's notebook flings onto the tablecloth. The ambassador's eyebrow rises. So, for another reason, does mine. When he catches my stare Hibbert I think gets my meaning. If a phrase is that memorable then surely he can remember it later? *Touché*.

Hibbert however, dead-ringer that he should be for a Bateman cartoon, remains unabashed. And this warns me not to scuffle further with him. The man has, after all, a reputation. I have read some of his pieces with admiration. Any animosity should be kept strictly at the private level. The discussion broadens out. None of us can keep off the topic of the boat people for long, even though this discomforts our host, who is obliged, by his position, to stick to the line that Britain considers most of them economic migrants and therefore fit for repatriation. Patently the problem for Mrs Thatcher is that if she agrees to find homes for 55,000 Vietnamese refugees, then she will be under even greater pressure to find homes for three and a half or four million Hong Kong Chinese in 1997. What Emrys Davies does say is that there are approximately 350,000 Vietnamese nationals in China (the result of the anti-Chinese movement in the late 1970s and early 1980s, after China had attacked Vietnam) and Hanoi is worried lest by warranting repatriation from Hong Kong it will tempt China to take the same line. He also concedes that aid is likely to be a significant bargaining counter. Here I venture the argument that if any country deserves a free lunch then that country must be Vietnam. Murray tells me I am ignoring four thousand years of Vietnamese history. I reply that's right, I'm only thinking about the last hundred and fifty. We are at each other's throats again.

I put on a tired, defeated smile and ask Murray sweetly what's new in town, what's happening, what's he doing here? But Murray just shrugs. 'Not a lot.' There's no hair on an iron donkey, as the Chinese proverb goes. Nor, as the Rutland proverb goes, is there much lipstick on a turd.

Mrs Moon is back in harness when I return to base. Is it possible, I ask, that I left a briefcase at her cousin's/sister's/brother's/mother's restaurant last night? Mrs Moon takes immediate offence. Nobody at the restaurant would take anything.

'I'm not saying that, Mrs Moon. Really. But I may have left it under the table, or on the floor beside the chair.'

Reluctantly she agrees to make inquiries. Then Zoom appears. His high spirits are back up where they belong. 'Good news for you, Mister Justin,' he cries. 'I think maybe I've found you a room!'

The room is at the back of the Sofia. In fact I have a choice of three: a tiny cell, a small cell and a medium cell. The walls are concreted, unpainted, the furniture rickety, the vibes oppressive. But each has a cold shower-room, and the biggest, at $10 a night, an air-conditioner that works, as well as a fridge.

The Sofia is a restaurant, originally set up as a Bulgarian friendship venture. Today it is run as a semi-private-enterprise co-operative. It fronts onto Hang Bai Street, a rather impressive boulevard that runs south from the Lake of the Restored Sword. There are dining areas on three floors. Downstairs is a coffee shop backed by a bakery, then a gallery running round the coffee shop and upstairs a spot of faded grandeur: a room of classical proportions opens onto a narrow balcony overhanging the thoroughfare outside. Inside the room, baroque chandeliers, gifts from Bulgaria, and a youngish staff full of curiosity about this oddball westerner who may be coming to stay with them.

Zoom is ecstatic.

'Very good. Really. You can be free here, you can come and go as you please. It's not like the Thong Nhat. And look at the waitresses! Aren't they so pretty? Mister Zoom will come and see you every day!'

But before that we must negotiate with the manageress, one Madame Oanh (pronounced Wine). 'You must understand,' Zoom cautions, 'this is not a usual arrangement. Generally it is better for westerners to stay at the big hotels. But you are our good friend, so maybe it will be all right.' We sit at a table on the narrow balcony and wait for Madame Oanh to join us. After a while she comes, a slightly stout, short woman in her early fifties. Very correctly she shakes my hand. An enchanting younger woman, also called Oanh, Miss Oanh, pours tea. Zoom and Madame Oanh embark on a lengthy discussion. From time to time the older woman looks at me, palpably struggling to reach a decision. About her features is something irrevocably sad. They are childlike, as though she never lost her puppy fat. But the skin is tired, worn out, a little grey.

At length the negotiations are concluded. Madame Oanh rises to her feet (not a lengthy operation) and again, very correctly, shakes my hand. Then she is gone.

'Well?'

Zoom pauses for a double-take, then claps his hands.

'It's okay. You're accepted. Congratulations!'

'Congratulations? It's thanks entirely to you I think.'

'You see? Mister Zoom, he can fix anything!'

It is agreed I will transfer to the Sofia on Monday. For now, Zoom walks with me around the Lake of the Restored Sword, showing me a row of shops on the north side that cater for foreigners. There is nothing in them that I want to buy. Such goods as they have are displayed in ageing glass cases. Because there are so few of them they look forlorn, and that is why they are unwantable. Outside in the streets, because Hanoi is naturally a fussy, intricate *ville*, you don't notice the absence of advertising. In any case red banners with gold lettering – propaganda, messages and exhortations to the people – stretch across many of the roads, and there is usually a portrait of the Great Patriarch somewhere in sight, which is a form of advertisement. But in the shops, the lack of promotional materials makes browsing a dour, almost Calvinist experience.

The art galleries are something else. On the side of the lake nearest Hang Bai Street there are three or four of them. The walls are covered by pastiches of the French Impressionists, with an occasional shot at middle Picasso standing out like a sore, misshapen thumb; also, sculptures of various sizes that owe an obvious debt to Brancusi, and a less obvious debt to Henry Moore. There are, says Zoom, four hundred registered (approved) artists living and working in the greater metropolitan district: Hanoi is the art centre of Vietnam as well as the political capital.

The quality of the paintings, judged from a western viewpoint (in art, the only one available to me), extends from the competent and mediocre to the downright bad. Too many of them have a copybook, art-school texture. In vain I look for something indigenous. In many cases the subject-matter is female, friendly and Vietnamese. Nudes are permitted; but their poses are, in the main, instantly recognizable as deriving from Renoir or Villon or (more exceptionally) early Degas.

Yet it is interesting, this. What the art shops are not full of is social realism. To a very real extent, the Revolution is kept off the canvas. This, in a sly way, makes the art revolutionary. The deliberately slavish emulation of a French school of yesteryear, the eschewing of originality, the pretence of a collapsed modernity, the avoidance of the direct – all add up to a statement of sorts.

In the last gallery (which henceforward I shall call simply the Gallery) Zoom introduces me to Miss Hoa, the manageress. Miss Hoa is exceptionally vivacious, even with Zoom present. She is petite, her teeth protrude a little, but not to the point of caricature, and she is terribly welcoming.

'Oh it's very nice to meet you,' she effervesces, 'very very nice.'

We begin to chat. Miss Hoa's English is good, although whenever

I use a word she doesn't hear or can't understand her small, dollish face threatens to disintegrate entirely. Then, without warning, Zoom takes his leave. 'Forgive me, but I should be getting back to the office. You stay here.' When he is gone, Miss Hoa invites me to the opening of an exhibition tomorrow. An invitation is to hand.

'But how do I get there?'

'No problem, no problem. Be here at two o'clock and we will take you. Miss Dun and Miss Ha are coming too. Only you must bring your camera please. We shall all wear our *ao dai* and we shall want a photograph!'

Mrs Moon greets me, back at the Thong Nhat, with the news that there is definitely no sign of my briefcase at the restaurant, that I can't possibly have left it there, and who would want to do such a thing anyway? Nor has it been handed in by any of the hotel staff. But all's well two hours later when I check in at the bar. The barwoman has been keeping it for me all the while. Before handing it over she unzips it and makes me confirm that nothing is missing. The Amnesty International notebook is safe and sound.

I celebrate by letting Stein buy me dinner at the Dan Chu, the other centre-of-town hotel for westerners. We congratulate ourselves on the excellence of our guides. After that, it's a lot more lobby talk at the Thong Nhat. A United Nations official tells a story that 'sums the whole place up'. His department was approached with a request for emergency aid to the tune of three and a half million tons of rice, following typhoon damage in mid-Vietnam. The official told the vice-minister concerned he was off his face, that three and a half million tons of rice was preposterous given the number of people affected. Two days later the vice-minister returned. He was very apologetic. His department had got its sums wrong. It had applied incorrect statistical analyses. What they actually required was three million four hundred thousand tons of rice.

'Which of course they didn't get. This year, for the first time since Armageddon, the country has actually produced a surplus, of about a million tons. They've begun exporting it to places like Bangladesh and Africa. The main problem is the quality of the grain. They've fallen way behind the rest of Asia. But at least it's edible. We're encouraging them to experiment with new grain-types. We also think the government should build up its own emergency reserves. But the trouble is they've forgotten how to store. They don't have the facilities. On the other hand, they do have an enormous population of rats, and a sizeable national debt. So perhaps they are better off trying to sell the stuff.'

I ask about famine. Before I came out there were rumours of a serious famine in 1988.

'Yes, they've had famine quite recently, though it's impossible to find how many died, if any. They're fond of statistics, they couldn't function without them, but there are some statistics they don't care to release. Mainly it's a problem of supply. Probably there are isolated pockets in the mountains and highlands that do periodically run short of foodstuffs. But in general there's quite enough rice to go round.'

The problem has eased somewhat, he says, since the introduction of *doi moi*. Now there's an incentive for southern, Mekong Delta farmers to sell their produce wherever they can. Before, it was up to the Party machinery to shift grain, and the Party bureaucracy was as bad then as it is now at getting anything done.

'That's right,' says a back-door Australian entrepreneur. 'Thank God for the IMF is what I say, sport.'

The International Monetary Fund, according to this man's testimony, was more or less responsible for imposing *doi moi* on the Vietnamese government. No economic reform then no loans was its message. Inflation had run away, and the gap between official and black-market exchange rates was also out of hand, roughly on a 1:2 proportion.

'Last year I could get seven thousand *dong* for my dollar in the street. Now it's down to four thousand or four thousand two hundred. The official rate is pegged up to three thousand eight hundred. Even so it boggles the mind to contemplate how many man hours must be wasted counting *dong*. It puts two minutes onto the average transaction. Aggregate that nationally, and you've probably got three per cent of your workforce counting money at any one time.'

And that wasn't the only brake on doing business. 'Sure, the government boasts its new investment laws are amongst the most open in the world. A foreign outfit can come here and own up to 100 per cent of its venture. The top tax rate is only 15 per cent. But that's only what it says on paper. In practice it takes about six months to work out who you are dealing with and who you should be dealing with. That's because of the rift between central government and provincial government. Central government doesn't like it if you deal directly with the provinces, and the provinces don't like it if you come to them with central government's blessing. In the end, you go up and down the bureaucratic ladder seven times and still end up having (a) to pay at least two parties a substantial backhander, and (b) to let at least one of them control a substantial share of your business. And that, matey, is what joint venture means. A lot of applicants are turned away, and a lot more turn themselves away.'

Opinion about *doi moi* as a national salvage programme working is sharply divided. Vietnam's future oscillates between the sublime ('another South Korea in ten years' time') and the woeful ('its only hope is to become a dumping ground for the civilized world's nuclear waste'). The only consensus is *doi moi* will only succeed if Saigon is given its head.

In the immediate wake of Tiananmen Square the question that everyone seeks an answer to is: could the same happen here? Again, opinion varies. One speaker thinks a bloody backlash is as certain as night follows day. Another concedes that the People's Army is genuinely of the people, that it knows the meaning of blood too well, and would never move against the civilian populace. Someone else says, never underestimate the Vietnamese army: it's capable of anything, 'as the whole world knows to its cost'.

After a while I rob myself of any illusion that the discussion is informed by anything other than wish fulfilment and prejudice on the part of the individual speakers. I take my Russian brandy, which is better than Spanish brandy but a pale imitation of French cognac, and sit with Stein at one of the tables.

Stein, a little tipsy, becomes peculiarly dogmatic. Vietnam now, he assures me, can only be understood in terms of Vietnam then, 1945.

He lends me a paper he has written about Cambodia, which I take with me to my room. Before turning in I read it. As one would anticipate, it is strong on Marxist reasonings. This however only makes Stein's conclusion the more startling. Endearingly, as though the Khmer Rouge are only waiting to be given membership of the Reform Club, his proposed solution for the Cambodian crisis is the imposition of nationwide elections leading to a Westminster-style parliamentary democracy.

Yet I shouldn't laugh. On the other side of the world half of Europe is poised for one of the big political explosions of the century. The peoples of Poland, Hungary, Czechoslovakia, East Germany, Bulgaria and Romania, raised on a diet of communism, fundamentally think the same thoughts as my Norwegian friend.

I read Stein's paper, and sleep. At 4.00 a.m. I am bitten by the rat. It is short and sharp. In fact, it is very much like an electric shock. It galvanizes the whole body. One moment I am deeply en-slumbered, the next I am sitting bolt upright shaking uncontrol-lably. The only equivalent experience I can think of is when my dentist pulled a wisdom tooth without telling me that's what he was about to do. Only, instead of the vile crunch of bone that engulfs the brain, there is just the vileness of the apprehension: now I am rat-bitten.

I stare at the point of puncture, on the tip of my little finger on the left hand, which I had left hanging over the side of the bed as I slept. There is no mark, no scar, no gash. Yet I know I have just been bitten there. I squeeze the flesh. Immediately blood forms. It diffuses over the top of the finger in a kind of gouache. There! You see! I was right! It wasn't an evil dream. It is an evil fact.

I take my finger to the bathroom, run it under cold water and plunge it into a bottle of disinfectant. I leave it there a good two minutes, take it out, squeeze more blood, then return it to the liquid.

Later I take my little finger to the desk-lamp. Sure enough, barely discernible, is a tiny oblong incision. The impress of the rat's tooth.

It takes me half an hour to get over the sheer nastiness of the *idea*. Then I laugh. Christ! The wounds men endure in battle, the things they survive! The things they don't survive!

I am even, in a while, able to derive some comfort from the

44

event. I prepare to sleep once more. The only precaution I take against a second attack is to leave the desk-lamp switched on. As my head burrows into the pillow, I think to myself, Wait till I tell Stein about this! And anybody else who cares to listen!

For the second time since my arrival in Vietnam I feel as though I am back at school: a schoolboy who wants to show off bruises acquired honourably on the games pitch.

Saturday 7th October: Hanoi In the last dream I have before waking up I am being exterminated by a gang of American journalists. I am harmlessly sniffing the bottom of a drainpipe when the leader spots me: 'There's one! Let's get him!' Large boots begin to rain down on the ground around me. 'Harder! Harder!' shouts the leader (who is bearded, bespectacled, driven . . .). 'Yah,' screams one of his accomplices, 'a dirty little friend of Vietnam! The rat!' More boots rain down. Then the boots turn into clouds of white powder. Warfarin! I look at my fingers. The blood flows freely from them. The ground becomes like a piece of grey blotting-paper spread out over a red puddle . . .

Saturday is a working day in Vietnam. At least, the morning is. Zoom and I have a session in the lobby downstairs, going over my programme. Mr Hong has suggested that rather than fly down to Saigon and then drive back to Hanoi, I should do it the other way round; that is, I should fly back to Hanoi via Phnom Penh. Also, my departure date for the south is set for Monday 6th November. If I want to go to Cao Bang therefore I should do so before then. In fact there are quite a lot of places for me to go before I set off south. Halong Bay and Thai Binh have been added to my list.

'Where?'

'Halong Bay and Thai Binh.'

'Where or what is Halong Bay?'

'It's very beautiful. It's a resort beyond Haiphong.'

'A resort! But I'm not here on holiday, I'm here to work.'

'We'll have a good time there. Really. You'll see.'

'And Thai Binh? What's that?'

'Mr Hong wants you to see a farming collective there.'

'How far is it?'

'Oh not far,' says Zoom. 'About four hours' drive. We'll stay there overnight.'

'Isn't there a model farm any closer?'

'Oh yes. We have plenty of model farms. But the one near Thai Binh is the best.'

'And how, exactly, would you describe the Ministry of Information's work?' I ask.

'Propaganda,' smirks Zoom. 'But don't worry. You must understand. In Vietnam propaganda is not a bad word like it is in your country.'

'Will you be coming with me to these places?'

'Of course, my dear.'

For the first time I am very slightly annoyed with Zoom. Well, not with Zoom, but with the set-up. By way of revenge I press Zoom on the interviews I want. I give him a long list of ministries and institutions. I also give him the names of several individuals: Party Secretary Nguyen Van Linh; Nguyen Co Thach, the Foreign Minister; General Giap, the victor of Dien Bien Phu, and architect of the wars against France and the USA . . .

'And I must meet someone who can talk authoritatively about the economy. Also I'd like to meet some film people.'

Zoom responds that he has already fixed my first interview, for next week. The Department of Tourism has agreed to field a spokesman.

'Great. Tourism!' I say. 'Oh thanks.'

The compliments are over now. The battle has begun.

At noon I am in my room. On the stroke of twelve two sounds outside mingle to produce the distinctive signature tune of Hanoi: the air-raid sirens on the replica of the Paris Opera House, and the cathedral-like chimes of the clock of the main Post Office. The latter merely mark the time; the former is an instruction to cadres to down tools/pens and take a lunchtime noodle break. Together, they make an eerie counterpoint: authority, fear, joy, structure, trust, nutrition – all are there, ringing across the city at noon.

I take lunch at a restaurant in the same street as the Thong Nhat – the Bac Nam, a place where the sweet-and-sour pork is sometimes authentic and where the waitresses are always gay, the more so if you need to change some dollars . . . On the stroke of two I present myself at the Gallery. Miss Hoa, whom I shall soon call Miss Honeymouth, and then Queen Honeymouth, greets me ecstatically. 'How nice! How nice! You remembered my invitation!' She introduces me to Misses Dun and Ha. All three are wearing *ao dai* of various hues and cuts. The excitement at my burgundy camera case is enormous.

The 'opening' is at the Museum of Modern Art. To get there we ride bicycles. I take Miss Hoa's, Miss Hoa goes on the back of Miss Dun's, Miss Ha rides alone. Miss Hoa's machine is antiquated in the extreme. The front wheel is bent, one brake sort of works, and the upward-pointing, immovable seat pinches where pinching hurts most. The unevenness of the roads plays havoc with my testicles. The crossroads are an added nightmare. I simply do not have the nerve to aim straight ahead and accelerate. Instead I slow down and politely give the cross-traffic right of way. The cross-traffic powers past and usually I am stranded for up to a minute. On the straights I wobble gamely forward. And yet there is something joyous about this escapade. Except when I am left behind at the intersections, the girls ride abreast of me and insist on keeping up a conversation, as though we were all seated in the comfort of a limousine. I also experience a curious, fleeting intimacy with hundreds of other cyclists. Westerners on two wheels in Hanoi are not unknown, but they are still novelty enough to make the Vietnamese want to slow down, take a closer look and, depending on their gender, issue one with smiles betokening either complicity or bashfulness. I am also aware (a) of how healthy this is, compared to cycling in the carbon-monoxided cities I know, and (b) of several teenage cyclists who are obviously cruising: boys float up to girls as though they had not a care in the world, introduce themselves and try their lines. It makes me want to be very young again.

The museum, another old French building, is jam-packed. There is a sort of loggia where a good proportion of Hanoi's four hundred registered artists (the opening is a state-sponsored do) are grouped around pillars sporting blue berets and lavish batik shirts. My three companions, who seem to know everyone, are spirited away – they have been enrolled as official hostesses. For a while I am left to fend for myself. Several artists speak good English, but insist on restricting themselves to rotten French. One in particular buttonholes me. I shouldn't waste any of my time here, he says; rather I should come with him, *immédiatement!*, to an alternative, rival exhibition of 'minority art'. Something about the way he holds my hand makes me resist the invitation. Also, misunderstanding the meaning of 'minority', I feel it is perhaps too soon to be mixing with cultural subversives. (In fact, minority, in this context, means of or pertaining to the hill tribes, of which there are about sixty in Vietnam.)

I enter the salon. The exhibition seethes with people: mainly artists and their attendants. The exhibits are poorly lit, and when a power cut strikes, not lit at all. When the power comes on again a video crew is seen to be at work. Sub-Picasso and sub-Matisse have the edge over sub-Impressionist. Apart from a few Hanoi street scenes, charming in their nunkykrunkyness, I look in vain for much that can be called authentic Vietnamese. A brooding self-portrait by one artist, his face a study in dejection, wittily parades under the title 'The Future'. A large red canvas which depicts a dragon preying on a frail human being of indeterminate sex in the jungle – presumably a reference to China – holds the eye for a minute. But apart from these, and the profusion of oriental faces, there is little that would look out of place at the annual exhibition of the works of the students of Putney Art College.

Hoa, Dun and Ha are by now wandering around with their arms intertwined effecting such introductions as they can. I am introduced to a wispy older *peintre* who insists on giving me his address several times over, who extracts from me the promise of a visit and whose French makes me shudder. Ten minutes later he is at my side once more, and the process begins again. The whole thing is very Bohemian, and even the casual friendliness of the gathering is studied, and desperately sincere. *He who would a modern be . . .* One feels that, at any moment, someone will stand up and make a startling announcement, such as man has just crossed the Atlantic for the first time *in an aeroplane*.

I take photographs of the girls in the forecourt afterwards. With the sun hiding behind the building, there is only one place the light is good enough for my kind of photography: on a mound of earth beneath what I take to be an Asian mulberry. Lifting their *ao dai*, they group themselves. But before I can click the shutter Miss Hoa, convinced that her ankles are about to be devoured by ants, loses her nerve. The girls regroup in the shade, are joined by various passers-by, and in no time I have used half a roll.

'Very very good,' Miss Hoa beams, then leads her companions away to change out of their formal costumes. A group of artists sitting on the steps, one of them with a guitar, invite me over to share a glass of 'vodka'. Determined not to sniff, I open my gullet and drop the stuff into my stomach. It tastes like a duodenal ulcer. It's not vodka at all, but a very crude rice-wine. The artists laugh, offer more. To my relief I see *les trois demoiselles* waiting for me by the bicycle racks.

We head back toward the Gallery. Miss Hoa insists I come in for tea. She has bought some apples, and these Miss Dun begins judiciously slicing. I see Stein stalk by and invite him to join us. He tells me the Thong Nhat has a dance on in the evening, so why don't we invite the girls? With a little coaxing Miss Hoa and Miss Dun agree. But when, a few hours later, it comes to it, they absolutely refuse to dance. Their excuse is, they've never had dancing lessons. (Young Vietnamese take dancing incredibly seriously, and one of the by-products of *doi moi* is several dancing schools that throb away unexpectedly in the dark streets of Hanoi between six and nine in the evening.) They promise, however, that if we invite them again then they will take lessons beforehand.

Nothing will deter Stein, however. With two or three litre bottles of Saigon 33 inside him he rapidly ceases to be the Marxizing history professor. The dining room of the Thong Nhat has been turned into a party room, a desultory band plays sambas and foxtrots. Young Vietnamese move with grace and erudition. Stein goes it alone. The word 'antics' springs immediately to mind. He is like a Prussian officer high on sukebind. When he returns to the table he assures me, triumphantly, that he 'has a lighter side'.

'I never doubted it,' I say.

'Then you should have, my friend. We should doubt everything until we see it before us with our own eyes.'

The girls leave at nine. They are still living with their families, and it doesn't do to be late. Stein and I join the bar crowd. Stein tells me at some length about the beauty and the love of his wife. Two new faces interest me – young fellows with straight backs and half-smiles. To my surprise they are English, and belong to the Royal United Services Institute for Defence Studies. In some mysterious, semi-official capacity they have been monitoring the troop withdrawal from Cambodia. As regards what's happening in Cambodia, they have the honesty not to speculate. Pailin may have fallen to the Khmer Rouge, but then it may also have been retaken by government forces. Whether fighting has begun around Battambang depends on which news agency you follow. It is impossible to confirm whether or not there have been 'terrorist' incidents in Phnom Penh.

I ask the more forthcoming of the two, Christopher MacKenzie Geidt, if Vietnam really has pulled all its army men out. Again he is non-committal. It would appear that the uniformed battalions have all been withdrawn. It would not surprise him though if some advisers have been left in place. These would now be wearing Cambodian uniforms, so you would have to get close to them before you could decide one way or the other.

He tells me what he has been able to find out about the Vietnamese Army itself, which is not a lot. The main thing, he thinks, is that it is not updating its equipment. It is also the case that most of the soldiers returning from Cambodia are being demobbed, so that in a while Vietnam's army may no longer be the fourth largest in the world, but the fifth or sixth. This would seem to be in line with the stance Vietnam is pursuing through its diplomacy: that of a beleaguered, impoverished nation that wants nothing so much as to be friends with everyone. I comment that certainly from what I've seen it doesn't appear either a very militaristic nation, nor for that matter the police state I'd been led to expect.

Christopher says it's difficult to get a true picture from just looking at the capital, although the people he's spoken to say that within the last nine months there has certainly been a move away from 'visible security'. But then he describes an incident he and his colleague have just witnessed in the streets outside. The police had sealed one street off, for whatever reason. An unlucky cyclist, either because he didn't see the tape, or because he realized his mistake too late and his brakes weren't working, turned at speed into the street. Within a trice he was set upon by three or four heavies, who proceeded to give him a severe beating with the butts of their guns. When the man's friend tried to intervene, he too was pulverized. The police then made it obvious that they would use the other ends of their weapons unless both men lay quietly on the road.

'And all because of a minor traffic offence. You spend hour after hour listening to the humanitarian whingeing of officials, and then you see something like that, and . . .' Christopher gestures with his hands.

Sunday 8th October: Hanoi The daytime is spent working on my journal. At some point in the morning fire crackers explode at the back of the Thong Nhat, somewhere just outside my room. For a moment I think it's a machine-gun, but fail to dive under the desk. On my way out for another lunch at the Bac Nam I collide with Stein in the revolving door. He tells me, in a dropped voice, that Senator Edward Muskie is definitely in town, though he still can't discover why. In the evening we go to the Dan Chu to dine with Graham White, who makes even better company than he did at the ambassador's. A university professor as well as a senior employee of ICI, he has a subtle, open mind that looks for the humorous yet is prepared to laugh at the coarse. 'Eradication mentality' is just one of many happy phrases at his disposal. He tells me a great deal about health care and the health service in Vietnam, in which my interest is not entirely impersonal. The main killer diseases are malaria, tuberculosis, rabies, Japanese encephalitis and dengue haemorrhagic fever. Cases of cholera, typhoid and bubonic plague occur in some districts. AIDS is officially unknown – yet! Malarial infection rates reach 15–20% in the worst areas: the foothills and forests – due to the specially dangerous species of *Anopheles* mosquito breeding there. Half the cases are of a relatively mild, relapsing type (*Plasmodium vivax*), half non-relapsing, more serious (*Plasmodium falciparum*). The malaria mortality rate is difficult to ascertain since, despite Vietnamese love of lists and statistics, those who die suddenly from malaria fever may have been debilitated by other ailments, making it unclear which to record as the cause of death. Japanese encephalitis is on the increase. Infection rates however mean nothing as 99% of those who acquire the causative virus remain healthy. The disease is transmitted mainly by *Culex* mosquitoes which pick up the virus from infected pigs and cattle ('amplification hosts') to which other mosquitoes transmit it from migratory birds ('reservoir hosts'). Man is the 'dead end' of the circulation.

The health service is run on a shoe-string 'with much community participation'. Funds are both raised and administered through the hierarchy of local People's Committees. Unfortunately, the poorest areas tend also to have the poorest authorities and the most disease. (Later I will learn that there is not always sufficient lateral communication: neighbouring villages separated by a provincial boundary but faced by a common epidemic will tend not to pool either their experiences or their resources.) On the other hand, health care is taken seriously. Again and again, Graham tells me, he has seen Ho Chi Minh's dictum, to the effect that a doctor should treat his patient as a mother would her child, inscribed on hospital walls. 'And the words really do mean something to practitioners.'

'The manpower is there, the spirit is willing,' Graham continues. 'The overwhelming disadvantage is the shortage of pharmaceutical supplies. Production of medical drugs is one of the six priority programmes of the Ministry of Health, with much emphasis on the modern development of traditional medicines such as anti-cancer and anti-malaria pharmaceuticals extracted from certain plants. The only mass-scale answer to malaria the Vietnamese can get their hands on however is DDT for spraying houses, so as to kill the *Ampheles* mosquito vectors whenever they come indoors. The DDT comes from Russia, which gets it from India, in a complicated tripartite barter network in which the real winner seems to be the Soviet Union. Hanoi needs far more DDT than Moscow provides from its "quota" of counter-trade.'

Graham's job involves demonstrating that a new pyrethroid insecticide manufactured by his own company would in the long run be more cost-effective in controlling malaria vectors. But the immediate funds simply aren't there.

'You see,' he says tersely, 'problems don't generate resources. Resources generate solutions. The thing that constantly amazes me is the continuance of traditional medicine in Vietnam, though this varies north and south. In the north traditional medicine means ancient Chinese medicine, while in the south it takes on a more Indian complexion. But every little hospital has its herbarium.'

The seminar ends when a waitress with the face of an enchanting fourteen-year-old, at least seven months pregnant, comes to our table to clear the dishes.

'Will you come to bed with me?' Graham asks her.

The waitress looks at him, and giggles. Then she shakes her head in disbelief.

'You see,' says Graham, 'that's my trouble. Always flirting with the impossible. Like trying to control malaria in Vietnam. Call it a control mentality. That's what I've got, a control mentality.'

'Talking about controls,' says Stein, 'has anyone said anything to you about Senator Edmund Muskie being here?'

'Not a thing. Should they have?'

To amuse ourselves we manufacture all the possible reasons why Muskie might have come incognito to Hanoi at this time, viz.: 1) the Democratic Party of America has surplus funds and wants him out of its hair for a spell; 2) Muskie has a relative who went MIA and whose body has just been found in the jungle; 3) Muskie's relative is in a re-education camp and Muskie has brought him some early Xmas rations; 4) Muskie has come to return Ho Chi Minh's pecker, which his former boss Lyndon B. Johnson said he cut off back in 1964; 5) . . .

'But it is a most interesting problem,' says Stein. 'The cloak of secrecy, the unannounced arrival and the fact that Edmund Muskie is no longer a big man in his party. Perhaps it has something to do with the Orderly Departure Program.'

'Have you asked your guide?'

'Of course. But Lam does not know anything more about it than I do. Even Murray Hibbert, who I was talking to only yesterday, didn't mention Muskie once.'

'Ah well, perhaps we know at least one thing he doesn't.'

The mention of Hibbert gets Graham White going again. Graham was not unaware of the ill feeling between us at lunch on Friday, but he thinks I should apply the angles to Hibbert's opening gambit: 1) It was a gambit, not a stiff, boring, conventional courtesy; 2) he was defending his own patch; 3) he wanted to test the psychology of a potential rival; 4) . . . And so the night continues, a series of multi-faceted excavations until there is only one possible reason for retiring: exhaustion.

Monday 9th October: Hanoi   The new working week is a little late to begin, but Zoom arrives full of vim.

'Congratulations, my dear. You were on television last night!'

'Who? Me?'

'Yes, Mister Justin. You. At the Museum of Modern Art. Now you are famous. Everybody will know who you are.'

Zoom, alas, exaggerates. The state-run television channel is not something anybody except ageing cadres watches from choice, particularly since the advent of the video and video-cafés. Most programmes seem to be about building bridges in the provinces. Shot of the bridge, shot of the chief engineer, shot of his Russian/ East German/Polish/Cuban adviser, seven shots of the local People's Committee congratulating themselves. Plus, of course, most households in Vietnam do not own a TV set; and it's not invariably because they can't afford one.

Today my guide has his father's motorcycle. We zoom off to the Cambodian Embassy to submit my application. Then we return to the Thong Nhat to await Mr Nam and the van before carting my belongings across to the Sofia. The rest of the morning is spent at the Museum of the Revolution – in many respects the same as the Army Museum. (Museums in Vietnam are like cinemas: very often they're running the same film.) Again I am halfway around the exhibits when the building starts closing for lunch. 'Never mind,' says Zoom, 'we'll come back another day.' (We never do.) In the afternoon he takes me to the History Museum. Several of the exhibits – sculptures, porcelain, vast bronze drums (very ancient) – are world class. But what holds my attention is the arrangement at the far end of the main hall: six or seven stakes, nine or ten feet high, and up to nine inches in diameter, eroded by time and water. These, an elderly guide explains, are a thousand years old, and were used by the Vietnamese to impale a Chinese navy as it sailed up a river with an army of invasion on board. The Vietnamese army stood on the shore as though to defend themselves, then began to retreat. The ships came forward and smashed into the stakes concealed below the water-line. The tide ebbed, and the Vietnamese came forward to pick off the remains of their enemy. General Westmoreland, I thought, had he come to this place with half an imagination, could have saved his country vast amounts of men and money.

Once again, the museum closes before I have seen everything. Zoom and I sit *boc-phét*ing on stools at a coffee stall not far from the Opera. He tells me for the first time about his girlfriend and their plans to get married next year. She is, he says, a tailor, and the main reason why he is usually so smartly dressed. She wants to open her own business, a shop with perhaps two or three girls working under her. The fact that she is already earning more money than Zoom doesn't bother him. 'In Vietnam,' he says, 'a husband and wife are very close. We can share everything, don't worry. That's because so often in the past husbands and wives had nothing to share, but still they shared it.'

I stroll back to my room, calling in at the Gallery on the way. Stein and I have decided to have a dinner party at the Sofia tonight, to celebrate my move, and invitations have been extended to Misses Hoa, Dun and Ha. Now I meet a slightly older woman, Mai Trang, an artist, long-haired, more than a trifle voluptuous. The shop is full of customers, including a preen of Italian diplomats. Mai Trang tells me two of her own paintings are being exhibited in another gallery across the street, whither she leads me. Her work is somewhat conventional – Hanoi street scenes – but the woman herself intrigues. She has, she says, a Swedish boyfriend whom she hopes to marry, but there has been trouble with the 'authorities'. She also has a brother who is an unregistered sculptor. I shouldn't bother about her own efforts, she implies, but her brother is something else. He is, to boot, the friend of Nguyen Huy Thiep, one of the 'best writers' in Vietnam. If I like I can meet him. Eager to extend my acquaintance beyond official, authorized circles, I add Mai Trang's name to the dinner list.

At the dinner, however, Mai Trang is more shy, more easily

overwhelmed. She is not especially close to the other three women, who maintain a front of giggling inseparability. Miss Dun shines the brightest. Her English is fluent, a little archaic, and she is full of questions, though not always willing to listen to the answers if they are not what she expects. She is also prepared to discuss politics, though in this respect she is hard to read. She seems to have no special feelings about the government, which of course makes one suspect 'reactionary' tendencies. But then nor does she particularly relish *doi moi*: Hanoi, she says, was so much nicer to live in a year or two ago, before the temperature started rising.

The food is incomparably the best so far. Bulgarian kebabs (or *brochettes de boeufs*, as the freshly printed menu calls them) and breaded prawns at once create and satisfy the appetite. The waiters and waitresses crowd eagerly around the table. I try the very few Vietnamese phrases I have managed to half-acquire. Already I begin to feel part of a family that sees in my foreignness a virtue, not a liability, and when our four guests, mindful of a different kind of virtue, leave soon after nine, Stein and I continue drinking for a while, before taking a slow and very philosophical walk around the Lake of the Restored Sword.

Tuesday 10th October: Hanoi My programme temporarily stops. Zoom tells me at breakfast it takes time to organize interviews and visits. It is better if he spends the day at his desk making telephone calls on my behalf. But one thing: he has asked his friend Thang to come and see me. Thang will help me with my Vietnamese. Also he should be useful to me in other ways. He works for the national radio network, the Voice of Vietnam. His job is sensitive. He is one of several cadres assigned to 'sift' news as it comes off the international wires. He should therefore be able to keep me abreast of what's happening in the world at large. He will come to my room at six.

'Should I pay him?' I ask.

'You don't have to,' says Zoom. 'But give him some small money wrapped up in some paper one day. Tell him it's for his family and then he won't be able to refuse.'

So I spend the morning sitting with my notebooks on the balcony of the Sofia overhanging Hang Bai Street. In a while the new staff-shift get used to me, and learn that I like a cup of milk coffee (*caphé sua*) every three-quarters of an hour or so. I take great delight in watching the 'traffic' from the elevated point of view. Every so often a tram trundles by, like a dusty duchess. The bicycles and cyclos also move forward enveloped in their own space, so that, against the plain background of the road, they are like so many portraits on the go. I am particularly struck by one tricycle that carries a dead pig in the wide passenger seat, wedged in beside a bookcase filled with hats. The pig, despite its condition, looks incredibly comfortable, at ease. It wears the same smile as a group of older matrons, who, dressed in fineries that date back decades, seem the only well-fed people in the city.

Lunchtime, and I again bump into Stein in the revolving doors of the Thong Nhat.

'I'm afraid I have to tell you,' he conspires, 'that I have discovered nothing new whatsoever. I saw our friend Murray Hibbert this morning and asked him directly whether he knew of Senator Muskie's being in Vietnam. Hibbert replied that he did know because he had lunch with him last week. I asked him if he had been able to find out why he was here, but he only told me no, it had been the most boring lunch of his professional career.'

'Ah,' I say. 'That I'm sure it wasn't. Do you want to have lunch with me at the Bac Nam?'

When Stein says sorry, he can't, he has to be somewhere, I continue into the hotel, only to be waylaid by Mrs Moon.

Mrs Moon makes a great point of telling me how happy she is that my briefcase has been recovered. She knew all along that it couldn't have gone astray at the restaurant because nobody at the restaurant would do a thing like that. Then she sighs deeply. If only she were so lucky! Because Mrs Moon has been overtaken by a terrible calamity. She has made a mistake at reception. She is twenty dollars down, and the missing money will have to come from her own pocket. Mrs Moon is in despair. Perhaps she should kill herself. Where, she asks, imploring me with a steady eye, is she to find $20? Oh, if only she was as lucky as I am . . .

I give her five, which I reckon more than enough to rectify any aspersions I may have cast on the honour of her family's bistro. Mrs Moon takes the note and with the speed of a lizard's tongue vanishes it somewhere about her person. Then she says woe is me, where on earth am I to find the other $15? I tell her that with a bit of luck there'll be some new arrivals who will want to change some money.

'So Mrs Moon, all you have to do is give them the official rate, or even something below the official rate, as you did with me when I first came, nip out round the corner, change the money for the commercial rate and keep the difference. I can even tell you where, if you don't already know. Alternatively, pack them off to the My Vi and get there in time to collect the tips.'

Mrs Moon affects to miss my drift. 'But no one else like you,' she pleads, 'no one else such a good man English.'

Thang comes on time. He is very different to Zoom. More than usually lean, deadly serious about everything, sallow, he has about him the air of a puritan who has stumbled into a party at La Jolla. Things were never terribly good in the past, and they're diving for rock bottom now. At first I take him to be a disaffected Marxist, but become less confident of this the more I see of him. Zoom, always inclined toward a romantic view, will tell me that his accidie is the result of a disappointment in love. But accidie is too much a part of his character for this to be the whole truth. In Thang's case disappointment in love will only have enhanced tendencies already present in his character. One senses that the real inner conflict – and Thang is a young man who has Inner Conflict written all over his face – has much more to do with disentangling the relations between morality and ideology. His is one of those minds that fiercely craves order and decency. Vietnamese socialism putatively provides the order, but he is not convinced it also provides the decency. Yet, because he is a cadre, he must to a degree turn away from his own thoughts. The potential separation of morality and ideology threatens a collision – between nurture and perception – of enormous magnitude, which is only held at bay by an equally intense negativity. A third (or fourth) force, ambition, is also present. But it is unresolved as to which of the other forces his ambition should attach itself. This makes him interesting. That it also makes him likeable takes more time to register.

We do not, today, make any effort to study Vietnamese. We indulge instead in 'free talk'. Thang tells me that many 'current problems' stem from the government's inability to pay its cadres a living wage. Largely this is because of overstaffing in every department. Nobody, not even top officials, is paid more than 60,000 or 70,000 *dong* a month. The average is 30,000 to 40,000 – enough to pay for a medium-heavy smoker's cigarettes and nothing more. For the very top officials this is no very great hardship since, one way or another, the state pays for its senior nomenklatura's lifestyle in kind. (Later I will hear it rumoured that Nguyen Van Linh, the Party Secretary, has a personal medical team that includes no less than nine qualified doctors. Whether this is true or not is almost immaterial. The fact that the rumour exists reflects on the cynicism with which the higher echelons of the Party are popularly regarded.) There are houses that go with ministries, as well as cars that come with chauffeurs. At the provincial level, local People's Committees also see to it that their members live well. But for the middle- and junior-ranking cadres the only solution is, and has been for a long time now, to moonlight. Since this is widely deemed a necessity, a blind eye is turned when most cadres only show up at their offices two or three days a week. The rest of their time is devoted to marginally more profitable pursuits in the private sector, for example selling apples in one of the city's many markets. Before *doi moi*, this translated as the black market. The black market, as a necessary prop to the official structure, came into existence more or less immediately after Reunification in 1975.

The most interesting feature of this arrangement, which Thang can only intimate obliquely, is that in order to derive personal benefit from either the black market or *doi moi*, it helps to be a cadre (*can bo*, or government worker). Indeed it is almost essential to be a cadre, because being a cadre affords protection, licenses the other activities. Viewed this way, Vietnam (like most other formal socialist states) looks like one large protection racket, in which the state plays the role of the Mob or the Mafia or the Triads or the Yakuza or whatever else you like to call it. A disease which is commonly regarded as affecting parts of the capitalist body politic in fact affects the whole of the communist body politic.

Being a cadre however is not the same as being a Party member. It is merely a stepping stone in that direction. To become a Party member, unless you are an army officer, is in fact quite difficult. For the bureaucrat it depends on innate ability, and a certain willingness to fit in with the plans of those who are already members. Blackballing is rife. The elite knows how to look after itself, and its ranks are not open to just anyone. Conversely, to become a member is to arrive. Once a member always a member, unless for some obscure and perverse reason the individual decides to turn in his card.

Family connections can be and usually are important. For the surprising aspect of the Party elite (away from the army) is how it largely incorporates the families of the older, pre-revolutionary elite. (Many of the revolutionary leaders, including Ho Chi Minh, Pham Van Dong, Le Duc Tho, Von Nguyen Giap, Truong Chinh and others, traced their descent from mandarin forebears, or at the least from richer, landowning farmers. And inevitably so. Their background enabled their education, and their education selected them as leaders.) But there is a further subtlety. Most cadres have relations in the south who are not cadres, and certainly not Party members. Indeed, both before and during the period of the war between North and South, many 'families' deliberately opted to split themselves up between the two national factions, ensuring that whichever side 'won' the family itself would still have someone on the winning side. Who went where was often decided by the family head, according to a time-honoured Confucian convention. The important thing was that individual fortunes were subordinated to the family's survival and ultimate prosperity.

The individual's two-timing therefore (office work and moon-lighting, replicated by what Thang calls a system of 'office think-ing and 'home thinking') is but a microcosm of a larger strategy. This will explain perhaps what Vietnamese mean when, as they very frequently will, they tell me that 'in Vietnam, the family is most important, as important as the Party'.

All this is pieced together from what Thang tells me. Our talk is 'free' only in the sense that he provides sufficient clues for a picture to be drawn, but does not give the picture itself – which therefore is prone to double falsification: the bias of his comments, and the bias of the construction I put upon those comments. Much has to be extrapolated from what he tells me, under gentle cross-examination, about himself, his own life.

There is much that Thang resents. Thus he explains how in his 'spare' time he gives English lessons to private classes, indicating that in the best of all possible worlds this wouldn't be necessary. Again, he describes how he is saving up to buy a property in Hanoi. Ideally he would prefer to depend on the state for reasonable accommodation, but because the private sector is now encouraged, he recognizes it would be foolish to get left behind. He is involved therefore in what he sees as a series of obligatory compromises. His greatest scorn however is reserved for what he rather quaintly calls 'ladies of the night'. A by-product of *doi moi* is increasing prostitution on the back streets of Hanoi after dark. This he will have nothing to do with. And yet one cannot help suspecting that the puritan in him is more than usually fascinated by the phenomenon. He recounts how he's heard (but it's only a rumour) that the International Club is about to be refurbished. The new fittings include a hundred 'uneducated' peasant girls who are being trained, by an Indonesian expert, in the art of full-blown massage, to satisfy the 'needs' of an expected inrush of western tourists. In addition, they are being given 'basic English' lessons. He has heard about AIDS, indeed the state-controlled press has recently run a series of 'educational' articles about the disease. He agrees that it is almost as though the virus were being granted a special entry visa. 'Ladies of the night' takes on new tones of doom and gloom. His voice, pitched flatly, nonetheless masks the unmistakable throb of original horror.

Otherwise . . . otherwise the most interesting thing Thang has to tell me is about a growing rift between the government and the Pathet Laos, always regarded as the good disciples of the Vietnamese Communist Party. It has been discovered that a delegation of high-ranking Laotian politicians recently visited Beijing for secret talks. Hanoi is very upset, just as it is upset by the growing number of Thai–Laotian joint ventures. Vietnam is threatened with even greater isolation within the international arena.

I draw Thang's attention to the growing number of joint ventures between Vietnam and western countries. He nods his head, then adds: 'But you already know perhaps, there is never any news of these in our papers. Most people are not aware of any joint ventures at all.'

Wednesday 11th October: Hanoi In the morning Zoom takes me for my first interview, at the Vietnam National Administration of Tourism, a non-ministerial body answerable directly to the Council of Ministers. All does not go well. We sit in a room with an older man, Nguyen Cuong Hien, who introduces himself as the head of the International Relations Bureau (and therefore, in Zoom's parlance, a 'big potato'), and a younger man, Nguyen Hu'u Thuan, a 'specialist' from the same department. It is Mr Hien who does most of the talking. Alas, Zoom does rather less than half the translating. The moiety is given to one of the administration's own interpreters, a slow-witted girl, probably a novice, whose principal concern seems to be not to relay any question that might give her superiors offence.

To begin with though there are no questions. As I am destined to discover again and again, an interview in Vietnam does not mean the same as an interview anywhere else in the world. Rather it is seen as an opportunity for an official body to express its views and its statistics. Particularly its statistics. Preferably the interviewer should be seen (scribbling furiously in his notepad) and not heard. Ideally he should be muzzled.

I am treated to a seminar on the history and future of tourism in Vietnam. The VNAT was founded in 1960. The war however effectively put a halt to its programme. After 1975 it catered in the main for Comecon citizens whose governments wanted to reward their long service with holidays in the communist tropics. Since 1986 and the promulgation of *doi moi*, a determined effort has been made to widen the net. With one eye on the transformation of neighbouring Thailand, tourism has been given high priority as the likeliest means to lead Vietnam out of grim recession toward the sunlit uplands of the Pacific Basin Century. Now it is all systems go – as far as the systems allow.

These mighty strides forward will not just be accomplished by the Party apparatus, although the Party will guide progress every step of the way. Everyone must row together, including private enterprise. There is also maximum scope for participation by outside interests, in the shape of joint ventures. Sixty overseas companies have already held talks with the VNAT, and so far two deals have been clinched. The Vina Group from Hong Kong is building the new 'Friendship Hotel' in Haiphong, and the Pulman Company of France is going to convert the Thong Nhat into a 300-bed deluxe palace.

I ask about 'green tourism'. Mr Hien nods enthusiastically. To be sure, he says, 'we want to avoid violating local custom'. Then I ask about the International Club rumour. Has the VNAT given AIDS a thought? The girl translates. The reply is given as 'Yes indeed, a new airport is being planned for Haiphong.' I look to Zoom for help. Zoom is busy drinking tea. I try a second shot. What about improvements in the infrastructure? From everything I've heard the main national trunk road (Highway One, connecting Hanoi with Saigon) is a shambles. Again, the answer bears no relation to the question.

This time I catch Zoom's eye, and force home my inquiry about the International Club. Mr Hien and Thuan hold a discussion between themselves. Mr Hien then pronounces that his government is well aware of the AIDS epidemic and has the situation under review. He does not want to comment specifically about the International Club, but does concede that 'the economic imperative is strong'. Mr Thuan puts it more bluntly. 'Vietnam needs hard currency,' he says. Another confab follows. Abruptly both men stand up to shake my hand. The interview is over.

A visit to the Hanoi Literary Publishing House in the afternoon confirms my feeling that getting anything useful out of official sources is going to be an uphill struggle, though this has nothing to do with the quality of the hospitality offered. I am introduced to several editors, translators and 'specialists'. My visit, they say, is a great honour. Because Britain has tended to follow the United States' policy of non-co-operation with Vietnam, of non-involvement, it has become increasingly hard to keep up to date with literary developments in London. I am therefore to be congratulated on making my visit.

Other compliments are pushed in my direction while tea is served and the first cups drunk. Then the history lesson begins. The company was founded in 1948 specifically to promote Vietnamese literature and provide translations of world literature. Up until five or six years ago it was 'the only literary publishing house in Vietnam', with the exception of the Women's Literature Publishing House. The editor of the English language section reels off English authors and titles: Dickens, George Bernard Shaw, the Brontës, Henry Fielding, Walter Scott . . . Lewis Carroll (for adults). Shakespeare is the enduring stock-in-trade. Forthcoming titles include Swift's *Gulliver's Travels*, Somerset Maugham's *Of Human Bondage* and *The French Lieutenant's Woman* by John Fowles. Equal attention is given the work of new Vietnamese writers, who, the editor-in-chief tells me, 'must shoulder the task of preparing a new literature'. The all-time bestseller however remains Ho Chi Minh's *Prison Diary* (not a diary at all, but a collection of poems that rather closely follow the form of the classical Chinese quatrain – further evidence of the great patriot's mandarin turn of mind). To date, seven hundred thousand copies of this have been sold.

The HLPH is however having a lean time of it. Average print-runs, which used to be 20,000 to 30,000, are now closer to 6,000. In some cases – new works by new authors – only 1,000 copies are printed. The reason is competition, not from publishing houses in the private sector (there aren't any), but from 'companies' run in and by the provinces. In future it sees its role as the self-appointed guardian of the 'classics' in Vietnam. It will reprint the 'best works' issued by its new competitors, thus conferring 'status' that ultimately can only come from central government: for of course the house itself falls under the direct supervision of the Ministry of Culture (soon to be amalgamated with the Ministry of Information).

This leads into a somewhat wooden discussion of censorship. I mustn't think, I am told, that the house is directly censored in its work. Oh no. Rather it has editorial freedom. The director is allowed to exercise his own judgement. Only, when his judgement falters, he may find himself sacked. In theory he could be taken to court, although (I am assured) this has never happened yet. Also, once a book has been issued, it can always be recalled.

'And this is a very good system for delegating responsibility.'

'But doesn't it encourage too much caution?' I ask.

The heads confer. The consensus is that caution is generally preferable to mayhem. The moral and political effect of a work is always rigorously considered in advance. That, after all, is what editors are for.

'Then what about *Lady Chatterley's Lover*?' One of the last newspaper articles I read before leaving Britain, in *The Guardian*, reported that *doi moi* had advanced so far that translations of D. H. Lawrence's book were on every stall.

'A good example,' comes the reply. 'That had to be carefully edited. Our translation has been very correctly expurgated.'

So much for the Prague Spring reaching Hanoi. The meeting ends with an equally sterile discussion about *doi moi* and the 'way ahead'. Mainly, the way ahead means 'applying the brakes' – otherwise chaos will reign, and anarchy abound. I am intrigued by one twist however. When I ask for an example of a controversial author, the name I am given, the only name, is Nguyen Huy Thiep. His crime, it seems, is to have written a story in which the private life of an ancient national hero was shown to be at odds with his public image. If Nguyen Huy Thiep were to start writing stories about contemporary heroes, then the shit would really hit the fan. Which is why his work is no longer published.

Mentally I make a note to press Mai Trang for the promised introduction.

Later, Le Tien comes to see me at the Sofia. He has heard about this afternoon's visit to the Hanoi Literary Publishing House. Indeed, he probably set it up. He brings with him a list of titles that another house, in Saigon, wants to publish. The books, he says, have just been 'approved' by the Ministry of Information. He invites me to run through them. I do so. One name among the hybrid foreign authors stands out. Barbara Cartland. No risk there, I say, of *doi moi* running amok. Le Tien smiles, and is still smiling when he leaves.

Thursday 12th October: Hanoi   Again the working day is divided up into two parts, two visits: the National Youth Theatre in the morning, the Temple of Literature again in the afternoon. I am taken aback though when Zoom begins with a caution about Mai Trang. I should be careful, he says, not to get involved with her. When I ask why, he becomes evasive.

'Come on,' I say, 'you can't just throw that at me.'

'There was some trouble she had about a motorbike.'

'What kind of trouble?'

'Really I don't know.' Zoom shrugs. 'Also, she knows too many western men.'

'Yes I know. She wants to marry one.'

'It's not that.'

'Then what is it? Is it because her brother is an unregistered artist?'

'Maybe.'

'And in any case, how did you know we'd met? Did Miss Hoa tell you?'

'No. I haven't seen Miss Hoa since I introduced you.' Zoom shifts uneasily. Deception ill becomes him. 'As a matter of fact she was seen coming here the other night.'

'By whom? Someone working in this restaurant? In which case they must also have seen her leave. Early.'

'No. Nobody who works in here. By someone who sells noodles in the street.'

At this I laugh.

'Security?'

Zoom makes a face and looks away.

'It's too much,' I say. 'Really. Whenever we have *boc phét* you tell me I should find myself a Vietnamese girlfriend. But as soon as a poor defenceless woman upon whom I have no designs joins in a dinner party, whoomf!'

'It's not like that. I am just asking you. Be careful. We want you to be happy here, that's all.'

For the moment, to avoid causing him further embarrassment, I take him at his word. We set off on his father's motorbike for the tall narrow building not far away that houses the National Youth Theatre, where I am introduced to Madame Thanh, the director.

Madame Thanh is small, robust, powerful. We sit in a tiny, cluttered, windowless downstairs office. No sooner has tea been poured than there's a blackout. At once an oil lamp of low potency is found and lit. I take notes as best I can. Madame Thanh's chiaroscuroed face leans toward mine. Her voice takes on a rainbow of tones. Before she became a director, she tells me, she was an actress. Eighteen years ago she enrolled at the Theatrical Institute in Moscow. She spent six years there. Then she came back to Hanoi and helped found the Youth Theatre. She and its activities are answerable to the Ministry of Culture, which provides half her funding. The other half must come from the box office. The trick therefore is to put on shows that have audience appeal, but which are not ideologically offensive. A recent production was *Love Story* (she had seen the film in Russia). This was done as a mimed operetta. Using mime, she hints, it is possible to stage almost anything.

'*Doi moi?*'

Yes, since *doi moi* things have changed a bit. In the old days she tended to stick to 'revolutionary theatre': 'character then was like advertising'. Now, the theatre can be used as an agent of social criticism, although since many of her productions are of foreign classics (the Russians, Shakespeare, Molière) no distinction between then and now is absolute. But theatre she thinks shouldn't simply be about education, or simply entertaining: it should occupy a non-dogmatic position in moral debates of the day.

'For example, right now I have a play called *Evil Living Together with People*. This shows the hard times still endured by peasants. I hope very much we can put it on, but I am still waiting for official approval.'

The script has been written by Nguyen Huy Thiep.

She frowns, puzzled by her own analysis.

'But we're not the same as Moscow. We have less talk, less ideology, less philosophy. More action.'

The students are all aged under thirty, and competition for the three-year courses (in both drama and music) is intense. Only one in eighty applicants is successful. Also, living is difficult. She can only afford to give her students a grant of 10,000 *dong* a month.

They need some support from their parents, although in their second and third years they can earn additional 'performance money'. They badly need new premises too. The building we are in was constructed as a house. One day, she hopes, 'we'll get something purpose-built'.

To illustrate this last point I am taken to the top floor, the rehearsal room – smaller, I realize guiltily, than my own study back in Milford Haven. The class is breaking up for lunch, but for my benefit it agrees to enact a 'scene'. There are no props beyond what would be readily to hand in any classroom: a table, two chairs, a crate. The place is a prison. There are five parts: a warder, a thief, a fool, a prostitute and another woman who decides now is as good a time as any to give birth. But is she really having a baby, or is it just a ploy to persuade the jailer to allow a compassionate visit by the husband? The thief dresses up as a doctor and tells the warder that the woman might die at any moment. The woman starts screaming. The fool starts pawing the prostitute. End of scene. Despite a tendency for the cast to stand in a line while delivering their lines, at the audience, and not to each other, I am impressed by an underlying vitality. I'm not sure all the laughs are scripted, but those that are are as natural as those that aren't.

(Curiously, I have witnessed one other student rehearsal in the Far East, at the drama department of Chulalongkorn University in Bangkok: the action also took place inside a prison, and involved a prostitute, a thief and a childbirth . . .)

I am taken to another room, full of singers and mimics. They too are breaking for lunch, but treat me to a sample of their skills. An exceedingly pretty girl squirms in front of a shaken blue cloth as an exceedingly handsome young man cajoles her into doing something or other which is forbidden. This is followed by pop songs (Vietnamese as well as western) sung by five more enchanting adolescents who pass their guitar along the bench they sit upon. Finally the teacher of mime, an epicene fellow probably a year or two older than myself, and trained under Etienne Ducroix in Paris, stuns me with a Marcel Marceau routine.

'I like to mimic people's bad behaviour,' he tells me afterwards, widening his eyes in an otherwise pancake face, 'so that people can know what good behaviour is.' Wink. Only he was too much the artist, had too much of the divine spark about him, actually to have to make the gesture.

For lunch, Zoom and I eat fried noodles at the Sofia. This man Nguyen Huy Thiep, I can't help commenting, seems to be on everyone's lips. Zoom prevaricates. I know that he knows that I want to meet him.

'It is difficult. You must understand he is not a member of the Writers' Association.'

'Perhaps that's why I'd like to see him.'

'It's difficult.'

'Not at all. He's a friend of Mai Trang's brother.'

'Has she invited you?'

'Yes. As a matter of fact, she has. Though we haven't fixed a date yet.'

I feel a cur. I am making Zoom's life, Zoom's job, difficult for him. But I have my work to do as well.

We revisit the Temple of Literature in the afternoon, to attend a celebration for the fiftieth anniversary of the death of the author Vu Trong Phung. The celebration consists for the most part of a seminar held in one of the long thin chambers that line the walls of the innermost courtyard. Various professors give short talks with readings. One professor gives a longer address, full of a withering passion. (His voice is not a big voice: the effect is achieved precisely by the physical strain expended in attaining so much feeling.) The room, hopelessly crowded, pressing from all sides on the long table around which the professors are seated in committee, is all rapt attention. For a while, I can believe in the Prague Spring analogy after all.

Vu Trong Phung is presented as a naturalist/realist enamoured of certain French authors (Maupassant, Flaubert) who produced his best work in the 1920s before turning to alcohol and dying relatively young. Currently he is being rehabilitated. But, the professors slyly caution, his rehabilitation should not deflect attention from the rich quality of his writings. His chosen themes were picaresque: his characters are drunks, prostitutes, gamblers and

69

other destitutes (which Zoom translates as 'nasty people'). At the present time the government sees a virtue in this, which it didn't see before. Under *doi moi* it is no longer held as 'incorrect' to draw attention to the fact of such types' existence. This is because *doi moi* sets out to cleanse (renovate), and so of course there must be something to cleanse in the first place. But it would be wrong to credit Vu Trong Phung simply because he fits in with present propaganda requirements: rather his merit should be acknowledged at all times, as a feature of Vietnamese literature . . .

The ensuing debate is noisy, vigorous, but also cultivated, restrained. Nobody loses his or her cool and stomps out. The issues are real, urgent, however *réchauffée* to our ears. And because they are real, everybody stays to hear them thrashed out.

Listening, I am reminded of the assurances I had yesterday at the Hanoi Literary Publishing House: the Vietnamese take their writers seriously. In this place, that point is made.

Zoom takes me to a photographic shop where I deposit a roll of undeveloped film. The shop has a new Fuji developer. As the girl is writing out my receipt there is yet another power cut. From the back of the shop, a loud oath. What's the point in importing the latest technology if you can't use it? Or if you can use it only part of the time?

In the evening Thang comes to give me my first Vietnamese lesson. His expression is grim. According to the Chinese newswire 700 of Hun Sen's Cambodian government troops have been captured by the Khmer Rouge in Pailin province. The lesson however goes well. I begin to distinguish between one monosyllabic nugget and another. Thang is a patient, diligent teacher. I try to be a patient, diligent student. We are still a little way off banging our heads on my appallingly low language ceiling.

Later, we talk about the Soviet Union. Thang tells me why the Russians are not especially popular in Vietnam. One, their language is unpleasant, not beautiful at all. Two, despite all their help, nothing much has improved. Three, they are the big brother of the communist world, and they never let you forget it. Four, very few Russians have condescended to marry Vietnamese women . . .

*   *   *

Friday 13th October: Hanoi   Just one programme item today: a visit, in the morning, to the Viet Duc Secondary School, in central Hanoi. I am received by Do Thanh Toan, the deputy head. There are 1,359 pupils, who attend the school in two shifts. This is normal practice: there are simply not enough schools, not enough teachers in the country, so existing facilities have to be worked overtime. The Viet Duc is a little special however. It is twinned with a school in East Berlin, even though German is no longer taught.

I am taken over the mandatory national syllabus. Every school must offer at least two of three foreign languages: Russian, French and English. At the Viet Duc, French and English are the choices. Every pupil must learn one of these. Other subjects include maths, literature, physics, chemistry, history, geography, biology and politics. Politics means the basics of Marxism-Leninism, and the thoughts of Uncle Ho. Every three years pupils must sit a national examination. After twelve years there is the final exam, in four subjects: maths, literature, one foreign language and physics. Soon this will be changed to an examination in five subjects. The results decide who goes on to higher education and who does not. At the Viet Duc some 25% 'pass', which is rather better than the national average (10%).

Discipline is good. If a pupil persistently misbehaves, then the teacher will talk to his or her parents. If he still misbehaves, he will be publicly warned in front of the whole school. If he still doesn't fall into line, then he will be suspended for one year – the ultimate sanction. During this period he will probably be sent to a reform camp, run by the state security forces.

'The secret of our educational system,' Do Thanh Toan tells me, 'is in the words of a nursery song. A mother and a teacher are two teachers. Two teachers are two mothers.'

I am taken on a tour of the school buildings (they used to be a French monastery), and asked to sit in on an English lesson. The classroom is large and dark. It is lit by just a single overhead bulb of dim wattage. An ancient blackboard comprises the only teaching aid. The teacher stands rigid at the front of the class and does her best to impart the secrets of my tongue in not very ringing tones. Those immediately in front of her can probably tune in if they want. For those at the back of the class, it is a pretty pointless exercise. On the teacher's own admission, when I ask her afterwards, probably only thirty per cent of the fifty or sixty pupils present are in a position to derive any benefit. Nonetheless, when the class ends and I make my exit, they all rise to their feet simultaneously and offer polite applause.

I look in on other lessons. The chemistry and physics classes are identical to the language and literature classes. One blackboard, one teacher, one dim lightbulb and nothing else. A new science lab is being built (I am told), but otherwise the scarcity of resources rules supreme.

And this presumably is a showcase school. Otherwise, would I have been brought here?

Zoom comes with me to the photo shop, but it will be half an hour before my pictures are ready. We sit in an adjoining video-café, a product of the new private enterprise. I observe to the owner that he has splendid taste in equipment and furniture. Everything is new, expensive. Does he have relatives in France or California? No, he doesn't. Simply his family is/was rich. After the Revolution, it literally buried its gold under the floorboards. Socialism couldn't last forever. 'The Viet Minh and then the Viet Cong were patient. But we were even more patient.'

There are two photos of Zoom, and these I give to him. Then we go our separate ways, Zoom promising he will call for me at the Sofia early tomorrow morning. I spend the afternoon writing notes in my room. Before that, I drop in at the Gallery, where Miss Hoa practically explodes with pleasure on being given snaps of her and her friends in their *ao dai*. 'How very very beautiful,' she enthuses. I tell her to give some to Dun and Ha. Then Mai Trang appears, and we firm up a date for my meeting with her brother and Nguyen Huy Thiep. Next Tuesday at six. At six today Thang comes to my room. After another Vietnamese lesson I take him to the Bac Nam for some sweet-and-sour. Unusually he agrees to a beer. Generally he doesn't drink, because of his 'high blood pressure', but today, why not? A couple of Saigon 33s and his defences lower. He tells me about his routine. Working at the Voice of Vietnam or teaching. In his spare time he reads. Most nights he stays awake until two or three with a book. There is a little lamp beside his bed. He has a thirst for knowledge, a fear of wasting his time. I ask whether he intends getting married. Thang says yes, one day, but so far he has never fallen in love. He is quite insistent about this. 'As you may know, one cannot afford to make a wrong choice. Many of my friends have made a wrong choice, and there is not much I can do to help them.' By preference, his choice would be plump and intelligent. Beauty, he says, is not so important.

As it happens, one of the waitresses is plump, intelligent and beautiful. She has a motorcycle and on my previous visits I have sometimes joshed her about taking me for a spin round Hanoi. She is also the daughter of the assistant manageress at the Sofia, so in a sense we are family. Since the other tables are emptying fast, I propose, for the sake of teasing Thang, that she sits at ours. She complies with blushes and good humour. To balance numbers, another girl, younger, Englishless, sporting a loud canary-yellow T-shirt, also joins us. For half an hour we make *boc phét*. Then we are joined, at his own invitation, by a man claiming to be an ex-Gurkha.

He seems to know something about me. He has, he says, in almost impeccable Hong Kong English, seen me visiting the British Embassy to collect my mail. Sometimes, he says, he works at the embassy. Foolishly, I take him at his word. I am so astonished at meeting a Gurkha in Hanoi that I regale Thang with spicy Gurkha tales, aware that in so doing I must sound like an old imperial fruitcake. The man, who is in his fifties and actually looks Nepalese, sits and smiles. But when I put questions to him I begin to have doubts. For one thing he says he has spent two years at college in Beijing. For another, the words 'booze' and 'tiffin' are foreign to him. I am just wondering whether in fact he is an impostor, and if so an impostor in what cause, when he turns to the pretty plump girl. He tells her she is late going home, that his old friend her father has sent him to collect her with an umbrella. It is raining outside, and she should certainly come with him now before it really pours.

The girl does not comply. For one thing she is talking with her 'friends', for another she has never in her life seen him before and he is certainly not a friend of her father's. To my astonishment she

73

reaches for her bag and pulls out a letter from a London polytechnic. This is an offer for a place in the coming academic year. She wants to go, she says, but so far she has been unable to find the fees. And that is why she is talking to me.

The 'Gurkha' will have none of this. He insists that she accompany him at once. Thang taps my foot with his under the table. I tell the girl that really she should go, that we can discuss the polytechnic some other time. Sulkily she collects her coat and is escorted out.

'Security?' I ask Thang on the street afterwards. 'Or a possessive boyfriend?'

Thang thinks security. You can always spot the secret police, he says. Invariably they have close-cropped hair, and invariably they are stupid.

'Not so stupid,' I say. 'He certainly had me fooled for a few minutes.'

'Oh yes,' replies Thang. 'You must know, they are also trained to be very clever at times. I just hope for your sake there won't be any trouble.'

'Trouble?'

'He'll probably make a report. You gave him your card.'

'Sure. And why not? I'd always give a Gurkha my card.'

I repair to the Thong Nhat. Stein and others are at the bar. I tell Stein about the Bac Nam, also about my projected meeting with Nguyen Huy Thiep. Stein says he would like to come along too, but should talk to his guide – Lam – about it first. We are both mildly excited by the prospect of tasting that which is forbidden.

Saturday 14th October: Hanoi So, within ten days of my being in Vietnam, there are three black marks against me. One, I have spoken to a woman whose brother knows a dissident writer. Two, I have expressed a desire to meet that writer. Three, I have detained another woman in her place of work during her working hours for the purposes of conversation. I am up early, awoken by a cock in a nearby courtyard that gargles as it crows. The rain comes down in heavy vertical lines, inducing an incredible display of antique umbrellas. I wait for Zoom on the balcony overlooking Hang Bai Street. He is supposed to come at eight. By nine there is no sign of him. By ten there is still no sign of him. By eleven there is absolutely no sign of him. I decide to walk the short distance to his office. I have the uneasy intuition that today I am not a friend of Vietnam.

Zoom is sitting with his feet up on his desk, reading a newspaper. Mr Hong is also at his desk, typing furiously, but leaves after giving me a rather sporadic hello.

'So what's up?' I ask my guide.

Zoom tells me nothing's up. I remind him that he had said he would show at eight. Zoom lamely tells me he tried to phone, but 'the phone was down'. There was nothing for us to do this morning, he explains, and the rain . . .

'I wish I had known,' I say. 'At least I could have done some work, instead of hanging about waiting for you.'

'Sorry. Really.'

Oh Christ. A straight, open-faced bat's the only answer. I tell Zoom two things. I tell him first of all that I've now made an appointment to meet Nguyen Huy Thiep. I say that I appreciate the Ministry of Information may not want me to meet Nguyen Huy Thiep, but that if the book I'm going to write is to have any credibility for the western reader then I simply cannot be restricted to seeing just the things that a government agency wants me to see. That will do Vietnam no credit whatsoever. And in any case what about *doi moi*, what about 'openness'? Secondly, I give him an account of last night's proceedings at the Bac Nam.

'I don't know if the man was security, but if he was, and he makes a report, I'd quite like it if my version of what happened is registered.'

Zoom nods, murmurs understandingly. Then he tells me that I may have to leave the Sofia, may even have to go back to the Thong Nhat.

'I'm sorry. But there are some Bulgarians coming. It's un-expected, but they have priority. I'm sorry.'

Zoom also tells me that I may be assigned a new guide.

'Of course, Mister Zoom wants to work with you, but Mister Zoom also has to do what the Company tells him to.'

Shall I book a plane out now? I almost ask, but don't.

'Oh well, let me know. I'll be at the Sofia.'

And without more ado I leave. Within a short time of my returning to the Sofia however Zoom is on the line. The phone is up again. I must be ready at two, he says, still wanting cheeriness. He's taking me to meet a proper 'big potato'. My programme is back on the road, temporarily at least.

At lunch I discuss matters with Stein. Stein however is also evasive, even a touch tight-lipped. Finally he comes out with it. 'I don't want to know anything I'm not supposed to know,' he says baldly. In response to my expletives, he tells me that nothing must stand in the way of his primary objective, which is to research the August Revolution. Clearly, either as a result of whatever conversation he may have had with Lam, or through the medium of his own deductions, he has arrived at the conclusion that I should, for the immediate present, be kept at arm's length.

Stein, I remind myself, through his years of study, knows the system better than I do. It is hard though, in my heart, not to chastise him a little.

There is a horrible, horrible moment, just after two o'clock, when I am confronted by the prospect of humiliation. The 'big potato' Zoom takes me to interview is Lu'u Van Dat, the Director General of the External Economic Research Institute. The institute is supposed to have played a lead role in shaping the government's strategy for economic renovation.

At five to two I don't know this. All I do know is that I am going to meet an economist. The only time I have to prepare my questions is a few seconds on the back of Zoom's motorcycle. Before I can properly collect myself I am being introduced to a large, well-built yet lean individual whose face is a mixture of the austere and the implacable. With his grey hair swept back he looks Chinese.

The exchange of compliments is perfunctory. I have hardly sat down when I am invited, by the institute's own interpreter, to put my questions. Glancing quickly at Lu'u Van Dat's card, I ask whether the institute is a think-tank. Yes, comes the monosyllabic reply. Which deals with the trading relations between Vietnam and the world at large? Yes. Any more questions?

Quickly I improvise. It must be something that can't be monosyllabicized. What I would really like to know about, I suggest, is Vietnam's future import policy and future export policy. The interpreter interprets. Lu'u Van Dat gives me a quick sharp stare, and then looks down to the table at his own empty notepad. A dreadful pause ensues. Even Zoom seems uneasy. I am thinking to myself is this it, am I on my way out, is this how they display their disappreciation of errant writers in Hanoi? But then Lu'u Van Dat, as undemonstratively as possible, writes a couple of notes to himself and begins his lecture. The panic recedes. The man has a highly organized brain, and for the next two hours he gives me the full benefit of it. A lot, if not most, of what he tells me is propaganda, but at least it is propaganda worth listening to. It is as fair and square, horse's mouth a summary of the official Vietnamese position as I am likely to get.

The prosperity of Vietnam's economy, the big potato begins, will depend on the development of four economic conditions: its rich natural resources; its abundant labour force; the quality of that labour force; and the presence of 'remarkable' skills. Combined, these give Vietnam an advantage in the international manufacturing market. He wastes no time however in telling me that the advantage has not been sufficiently exploited in the past. The reasons he gives for this are the endless interruptions caused by the struggle for 'national salvation' (the wars against France, the United States, the Khmer Rouge and China), and the 'absolute policy' directed against Vietnam by America since 1975.

'In my view,' he says, 'the policy of the United States has not changed at all up until this point. Previously they gave as their reason for not withdrawing their embargo on our presence in Cambodia. Now we have withdrawn from Cambodia, but still the embargo remains. Nor will they talk to us in any meaningful manner. Their latest excuse is there hasn't been a comprehensive solution to the Cambodian problem. But sometimes I doubt whether there will ever be a change, even if a satisfactory solution to the Cambodian problem, which is no longer our problem, can be found. Countries ought not to impede other countries' economic development. Our struggle against the United States in the war was one of reluctance. It was America who came to our land, not vice versa. Again, our reasons for invading Cambodia in 1978 have never been willingly appreciated by the outside world. The invasion took place because it was necessitated by reasons of national security. We couldn't look forward to stable development so long as the Khmer Rouge were in power. Everybody knows about the atrocities perpetrated by the Khmer Rouge, but only we were prepared to act, even though the economic cost was great.'

Wryly, Lu'u Van Dat compares Vietnam with other Asian economies. Japan and South Korea, in the not too distant past, were both 'broken countries'. Even Thailand, compared to Vietnam fifteen years ago, lagged behind in development terms. But the reason why the Vietnamese economy has remained static is not primarily one of political systems: it is simply that 'Vietnam has had to pay for the world's sufferings'.

'Japan, South Korea and Thailand have had different kinds of regime: the unifying factor is that they haven't had to labour under the deadweight of American animosity.'

But the picture is not uniformly bleak. Even if Vietnam must largely go it alone, Lu'u Van Dat says, Vietnam will get there in the end. In 1988 exports amounted only to one billion dollars. For 1989 the projection is one and a half billion. Most significantly Vietnam has ceased being a net importer of rice, and has become a net exporter (to Bangladesh, India and Africa). With a million-ton surplus, this puts Vietnam third in the world table, behind Thailand and the USA. The main resources for the future are agriculture, forestries and fisheries. But there is still 'much to be done' before Vietnam can switch from being essentially a storage ('control') economy to being a market economy.

Most significantly, the state has abandoned its rice monopoly. Thus, whereas the state used to supply 100% of the rice consumed in Hanoi, it now supplies 25%, and that only as a means of stabilizing prices. The other 75% comes from Vietnam's new free, internal market. And that, it is urged, is the measure of the economic transformation, the economic renovation that is taking place.

After agriculture, Vietnam looks toward low-tech light industry and mineral extraction along with mineral products to boost her exports in the mid- to long term. Among 'invisible' exports, Lu'u Van Dat confirms that tourism is the 'key industry' of the future, though he adds hurriedly, before I can quiz him, 'We will not pursue tourism Thailand's way. Rather we will develop it while maintaining the traditional moral values of our country.'

Pausing slightly, Lu'u Van Dat turns his attention to the question of imports. In a controlled economy it is not only vital, but it is also possible, to gear an import policy to basic macro-economic needs. The first priority is to bring in modern technical means to rapidly improve an infrastructure that at best is an anachronism. Unless the infrastructure is updated, nothing else can happen. If it is updated, then the scope for foreign investment will be considerably widened, and 'take-off' can occur. Then secondary priorities can be considered and hopefully financed. For instance the equipment for a planned oil refinery in the south can be purchased, so that, as more oil fields come on line, it will no longer be necessary to export crude oil only to import it as petroleum later.

The current inflow of consumer goods (from Japan, Taiwan and Korea via Singapore) is 'not our policy', and Lu'u Van Dat envisages future restrictions. The country's trading deficit is still considerable. But progress is being made. Since new, liberal laws on foreign investment were promulgated in 1987, eighty-five licences for joint ventures have been granted to companies from both western Europe and the Far East, representing a total overseas investment value of $700 millions. Indeed, the only negative pressure comes from the United States, which, as well as discouraging its political allies from sanctioning investment in Vietnam, also works indirectly by applying back-door pressure within such international bodies as the IMF and World Bank.

Even so, the government has done everything in its power to meet demands and criticisms levelled at Vietnam by those bodies. Key indicators – exchange rates and the gold price – have been brought under control and stabilized.

'And we are confident of success. At some point the American policy must collapse. There is a growing moral obligation to change. Even one of America's leaders, Senator Muskie, who was here last week, has now made a statement in Washington calling for the restitution of official diplomatic relations. If Washington does not respond, then the United States will begin to lose its friends.'

And what about China? I ask. Is all the blame to be laid at America's door?

For once Lu'u Van Dat's impassive features break into a somewhat toothy smile.

'Yes,' he acknowledges, 'China is a big power in our head. As you know, relations between China and Vietnam have not been good, because of Cambodia. China is now pressing us to allow the Khmer Rouge a role in Cambodia's future. We must wait to see what happens. A big brother will always put pressure on a smaller brother. But we wish to normalize relations with Beijing just as we wish to be friends with every other government in the world. That I think is our national aim.'

Lu'u Van Dat finishes by expressing an earnest personal wish for improved relations between his country and Britain. He adds that he hopes I have enjoyed our 'open, free talk' and that I will speak well of *doi moi* when I leave Vietnam.

So much kidology? It is not until I read through my notes later that I discover causes to suspect the relatively liberal façade Lu'u Van Dat has presented me. Mainly I have been taken in by a conspicuous absence of Marxist terminology. Yet the real measure of his flair for public relations is my inability firmly to conclude that he may after all be a hard-liner in sheep's clothing.

There is however one immediate dividend. As soon as we are outside Zoom asks whether I am pleased with the afternoon's work.

'Yes,' I reply. 'Very. It's quite flattering to be given so much time by a big potato.'

Zoom smiles, is his charming, youthful self again.

More Bulgarian brochettes at the Sofia for dinner, then Thang arrives to accompany me to the cinema. We were to have escorted the pretty waitress from the Bac Nam, but this, both us 'working boys' agree, portends more trouble than it's worth. As we walk half a mile up (or down) Hang Bai Street, Thang periodically crosses the road. When I ask him why, he tells me it is to avoid the doorways of 'rotten places' where 'ladies of the night' are known to hang out.

'As you may know,' he comments when I laugh, 'ladies of the night carry several sicknesses. And no matter how much money you have in your pocket, one way or another they will have it all.'

The film is called *Unfinished Spring*, a love story set during the French period, although there are no French parts. An almost preposterously smart young man from Hanoi falls for a village beauty, whom he meets on a train. The girl is facing hard times. Her father has died, and she has set her heart on providing her younger brother with an education. The local mandarin, an evil, lecherous plutocrat, blocks the sale of the family house. If she wants to sell the house, he tells her, she must become his fourth wife. The preposterously smart young man comes to her rescue. They marry, and have a child. This however does not meet with the approval of the hero's mother, who wants her son to marry a society girl. The parental pressure is relentless, filial piety triumphs. The village beauty is abandoned. Many years pass. The preposterously smart young man has remarried, but his new wife cannot bear him children. His thoughts keep returning to his true love. The mother also experiences a change of heart. A country grandson is better than no grandson at all. But the girl, and particularly the girl's brother, now a schoolmaster, will have none of this. Her pure heart refuses the father of her child a second chance.

In the last scene, the hero's mother visits the country in a final attempt to claim her grandchild. The girl rounds on her, despite the difference in their social status. 'This is my house,' she says, 'and in it I can say what I want.'

This earns a round of applause from the audience. It is difficult though to tell whether this is because the tyrannical old woman (the enemy of love) has got her come-uppance, or because the younger woman has made a principled stand in defence of home ownership.

The overriding (and unexpected) virtue of *Unfinished Spring* is its oblique approach to moral issues. Cinematically, its values are distinctly Swedish: at several points I am reminded of *Elvira Madigan*, although some of the joints need oiling. Both the acting and the camerawork tend toward the static. Surprisingly too, the film makes no attempt to depict the degradation suffered by the Vietnamese at the hands of the French in the period when *Unfinished Spring* is set. Rather, there is a constant evocation of beauty: the beauty of the people, the beauty of the nature, the beauty of the past . . .

This contrasts starkly with the squalid machinations of the secondary characters (the mandarin, the mother, even the brother). It also contrasts with the squalor of the cinema itself. The heat-oppressed auditorium is contaminated by a world-class stench emanating from rat-infested toilets on either side of the screen. Throughout the show urchins scuttle busily underneath rickety old seats. Nor are there any decorous usherettes selling ice-creams from shoulder-trays in the interval. Instead the audience regroups in the foyer, where moonlighting office workers proffer fruit and sticky sweets through the bars of the iron gates that have been drawn across the exits to the street and are now locked.

Afterwards, Thang and I walk the dim Hanoi streets until we find a deserted coffee shop where Thang can be reasonably confident we will not be assailed by any lurking ladies of the night. I ask him about his army service, and am surprised to learn that he avoided it. He was not conscripted, he says, because he was able to show that his family was in trouble and needed him. At the time the Chinese war was on, and Thang tells me that he was frankly afraid to fight. He did not however pay over any cash, as he knows some others did. Nonetheless, his conscience continues to be troubled.

'As you may know,' he says, 'the Vietnamese have many skins.'

'You mean they have more than one face?'

'No. The expression means that when a Vietnamese wants something, he is prepared to wear out many skins getting it.'

I am not sure what relevance this has to our conversation, but thank him for the explanation. I also tell him about my meeting earlier in the day with Lu'u Van Dat. Thang offers two insights into the economy of his country. In the first place, *doi moi* has made it harder, not easier, for the speculator. Beforehand, when prices lacked stability, a lot of money could be made by illegally moving rice from one area to another and reselling it. In the second place, Vietnam is now confronted by the 'rice trap'. Once there is a surplus of rice it becomes relatively hard for the government to seek international aid. Instead of appreciating Vietnam's ability 'to get things right', outsiders will simply say, 'Oh, there's a nation that doesn't need aid any more.' Outsiders, Thang's insinuation is, will always find a reason not to share their plenty.

'So you see,' Thang continues, 'there are so many problems. Everything results in the opposite of its intentions. Take for example the cinemas, since we've just been to one. Vietnamese film-making is supposed to be going through a revival, but I doubt whether in three or four years' time there will be any more new films. The cinemas are owned by the state. Under the new *doi moi* system, cinema managers are given quotas they have to meet. If they exceed their quotas, then the cinema co-operative can benefit. Because now there are so many video-cafés, managers can only get audiences into the cinemas by showing foreign films, especially, if they can get them, American films. And why, if they can make double the money running something like *Platoon*, are they going to bother with what we can produce ourselves?'

Sunday 15th October: Hanoi I get up early to pack my bags ready to leave the Sofia – and who knows, perhaps Vietnam as well. I have just fastened the clasps of my suitcase when Zoom crashes joyfully into my room.

'Good news, Mister Justin. The Bulgarians are not coming after all. We have just had a telex. You can stay on at the Sofia. Also, Mr Hong has said I can continue working with you. Really. And another thing, we are definitely going to Halong Bay on Wednesday.'

Were the Bulgarians ever coming? Have I been reading too much into trivial events? At any rate, I am *persona grata* again, and that is all that matters. I take Zoom downstairs and order fresh pastries. On the video set this Sunday morning the staff are watching a tape (*Paris by Night*) made by *émigré* singers in France. Elvis Phuong croons his heart out over a floating montage of the Champs-Elysées. Later, working at my customary table on the upstairs balcony, a midday banquet erupts at my back like an inexhaustible firecracker. Army types rub elbows with men in blue berets proposing toasts. Among Vietnamese males it is a tradition to drink your companions under their seats. One by one, clockwise around the table, each banqueter stands and raises his glass. The last one able to stand wins. For my own lunch, I order plain rice, prawns and a bottle of Russian mineral water. Then I remember: I have promised to call on an elderly artist introduced to me by Miss Hoa.

'How very very nice to see you!' ejaculates Queen Honeymouth as soon as I have set foot inside the Gallery. She has not forgotten my appointment either, but regrets she cannot take me to the artist's house. There is no one else to look after the shop, and the shop must stay open all afternoon. Instead, Miss N. will go with me. Within the minute Miss N., herself an artist, taller than the average Hanoi female, appears in the doorway. Her hair is in the Japanese mode: straight, fringed, shiny. But what strikes me, what strikes everyone about Miss N., is the width and sleekness of her eyes.

We set off on bicycles for the West Lake, calling first at the 'National Exhibition Centre', a large concrete hall sparsely packed with small stalls selling mostly manufactured goods either imported or from the provinces, and impregnated with the unhappy air of a true bargain basement. Victorian electrics charm but do not shine. An antiques corner displays gaudily painted wooden puppets that grin at one like Haitian *primitifs*. A liquor stall proffers several varieties of snake-wine: one-snake wine, three-snake wine and five-snake wine. Inside the bottles the reptiles hang like the sprigs of tarragon in the vinegar I use at home.

We hang around a good hour. Miss N. runs into some doctor friends outside, and much *boc phét* is discharged. I take photographs of them, they take photographs of me. When finally we reach the artist's house, down the end of a back lane that leads off another back lane which itself can only be approached by a series of back lanes, the light is already beginning to fade. For the second weekend running I find myself contemplating art in near-darkness.

The artist, Ngoc Tho, accosts me with a shower of greetings twittered in French. There is about him an insistent fragility that has the power to wear one down fast: the sweat of one's own vacillations, between a perceived duty to take an interest in everything he says, an irritation at how he says it and a kind of useless

84

pity. For his is a poor house. A bed, a small table and some stools are the only furniture. But it is not an empty house: canvases, stacked three or four deep, line the walls of all three rooms, making the abode cramped.

We sit at the back, overlooking a patch of wasteland that backs onto other houses. Ngoc Tho's wife, also an artist, creates a repast of sliced apples and peanuts, washed down with a strangely thick green tea in which several weedlike herbs have been deposited. Ngoc Tho meanwhile, leaning a diminished bulbous face into mine, so close that I can taste his breath, twitters on. He shows me, and presents me with a copy of, an art journal that has an article about himself in it. In the claustrophobic world of Hanoi art he is, like so many of his peers, an academician. His small income is derived chiefly from teaching. But for how long he can continue he doesn't know. He is old, his limbs are very thin, perhaps soon he will die. But he does not intend to die before he has made a decisive contribution to his craft. He turns a canvas around from the wall beside where he is sitting to reveal the face of what, in the gloom, I take to be a tiger. But a part of the beast glitters by the light of the oil lamp his wife has hurried to fetch. Embedded into the paint are several strips of gold leaf. Yes, he promises, his work is already valuable. Economic realism?

He shows me more. There are some reasonably striking portraits of young women with clothes on, and some less reasonably striking nudes. As I look at them my imagination perhaps plays games with his French. He is talking about Picasso and Braque. Does he really say 'pubism' for 'cubism', or is it just my ear? Miss N., at an opportune moment, suggests I should offer to buy something. I express an interest in seeing any drawings or etchings he may have done.

We go through into the front parlour. I am aware of more tigers beckoning at me, now with gleaming horses' hooves. Ngoc Tho apologizes. He has done very few drawings. But perhaps I would examine his wife's? Large folders are produced. Inside, better than average Hanoi street scenes. This work I like, but there is too little light for me to want to commit myself to a purchase. I tell them I have no money on me – 'pas beaucoup d'argent sur ma personne' – but promise I will come back.

Miss N. and I push our bicycles through muddy stones back toward the surfaced street. Returning to the Gallery is a species of murderous hell. The streets are all but blacked out, another power cut, and bicycle lamps are few and far between. Shapes whiz past me in every direction. The crossroads are lethal. But somehow we make it without being toppled.

Dinner with Stein, who apologizes for his comment yesterday. 'Now that I have thought about it,' he clips, 'it was not very thoughtful.' We toast each other with Heineken and Russian cognac. Stein asks if it's still possible for him to come with me to meet Nguyen Huy Thiep on Tuesday.

'You tell me,' I say.

'I have spoken with Lam about it, and Lam says that if you can go then I can go.'

We exchange thoughts on Vietnam Now. We agree that Vietnam is an exceedingly pretty dame who knows how to play hard to get too well. I suggest there are three great mountains in the landscape: the Party, the Provinces and the Army. Stein nods, then comes back at me. The Party, he suggests, is more like a high ridge that connects the other two. Have it your own way, I say, as long as the mountain on the right doesn't erupt like a volcano. We are both still at sea in this land, and relishing every moment.

Monday 16th October: Hanoi On Tuesdays, Thursdays and Sundays an English class is held in one of the back rooms of the Sofia, for the benefit of the staff. About ten of them, including Madame Oanh, attend. There is in Hanoi at this time a craze for learning English that amounts almost to a phenomenon. This is confirmed in the morning when Zoom takes me to his *alma mater*, the Foreign Languages College.

The size of the place, founded in 1959 on the outskirts of the city, impresses. There are three long, large buildings, each of three or four storeys, around 3,000 students and 200-plus teachers. Up to fifteen languages can be taught, and the staff includes Russians, Australians, Bulgarians, East Germans, Czechs, Frenchmen, Poles, Cubans and one American 'volunteer' (a Mennonite). There is also an enrolment for overseas students. Additional courses include

86

gymnastics and philosophy, as well as part-time technical language training for scientists, medics and technicians. Courses vary from between three and five years. The college is both the country's powerhouse for turning out cadres with the essential communications skills for forging relationships with the outside world, and the chief source of domestic foreign language teachers. Its graduates are scattered throughout the land. Some of these work in other language centres, which the college services.

There are forty classes in all, twelve of them in English, only three in Russian and one in Chinese. Half the student's fees are paid for by the government. The balance must be found elsewhere. In the case of 'advanced' students, however, the state pays all. Eighty per cent of the students are girls.

I am escorted round by Mr Van, a vice-director and one of Zoom's old teachers. (Zoom puts on a little show of cringeing, but in fact he is having something of a field day: he did well here, and has done well since.) Having given me the figures, Mr Van tells me about the shortcomings. Shortage of materials is the greatest handicap. In the print-room I watch the pages of a second-level English language course written three decades ago roll off a squeaking Roneo machine. A Czech-manufactured language laboratory has broken down beyond repair. There is also, Mr Van says, increasingly a problem with the commitment shown by the Vietnamese teaching staff. Most of them of necessity moonlight. Their minimal salaries have not kept pace with inflation, and the pickings in the city for those with advanced language skills are relatively rich. They can teach privately, or translate, earning more in a day outside the college than in a month at the college. Those teaching English are particularly advantaged. Those teaching Chinese are close to suicide. Would I like to take a class?

Before I can refuse I am dumped among fifteen second-year students. Yours for the next hour, chum. Zoom is delighted, the students' official teacher, an Australian called Andrew Burnett, even more so. All the world likes to see an Englishman make a fool of himself, and in my case the chances of that are high. I have never taught a class for anything in my life. There are two things going for me however: 1) the relatively small, therefore potentially manageable, size of the group; and 2) the fact that way back I once worked as a trainee director with a London street theatre outfit called the Dogg's Troupe. By getting everyone to shift their desks back to the wall and sit in front of them in a circle I seize the initiative. From then on it is plain sailing. We play basic language games in which everyone has no option but to participate. Nobody can escape telling me his or her name, or what kind of mood they're in right now. This enables me to drive home the elementary pedagogical point that there's no point in learning a language unless you're prepared to be up front with it. There are only two bad moments. The first is when a peculiarly quiet young man finally summons up the courage to explain that the way he's feeling right now is very very hungry: he hasn't had a proper meal for two days. The second is when I ask what kind of animal everyone would like to be if the human option wasn't available. Andrew, who has shown all the signs of being the happy-go-lucky type Australia produces by the shipload, decides he would like to be a dog, barks, bounces across the floor on all fours and gives my ankle a well-aimed nip.

By a curious coincidence I meet Andrew again in the afternoon, when Zoom escorts me to the overseas broadcasting division of the Voice of Vietnam. To my immeasurable glee I discover that the name he is known by is Mister My Wife. His spouse works in the Australian Embassy, and Andrew is in Vietnam for the ride. To fill in time, he has become a sort of alternative Peace Corps worker, taking on a number of odd little jobs like teaching English twice a week at the Foreign Languages College and checking the grammar of the news items that the Voice of Vietnam broadcasts in English to anyone who might be listening out there. Nobody can quite understand his volunteer status, so he constantly has to explain himself, beginning with the words 'My wife . . .'.

The big news at Voice of Vietnam is that limited advertising has recently been introduced. The government, sick of having to pay for everything, has told its media to try and earn some of their own keep.

Rather than put me through the ignominy of taking down lecture notes in front of a fellow Caucasian, Nguyen Thi Hue, my hostess for the hour, presents me with a Voice of Vietnam pocket notebook. A brief introduction gives me all the facts I need. The Voice of Vietnam dates back to September 1945, one week after Ho Chi Minh first proclaimed the Socialist Republic.

> In more than 30 years of struggle against French colonialism and US imperialism, the VOV has sometimes evacuated to the jungles and even [been] subjected to heavy raids by American aircraft of different types including B52s. However, the VOV continued its signal tune (music to the song *Smash Fascism*) and its proud introduction: 'This is the voice of Vietnam, broadcasting from Hanoi . . .'

Today, as well as supplying domestic programmes, the VOV, imitating the Voice of America and the BBC World Service, broadcasts in twelve languages.

The pocketbook also provides a translation of the Vietnamese National Anthem. Verse One goes:

> Soldiers of Vietnam, we go forward
> With the one will to save our Fatherland.
> Our hurried steps are sounding on the long and arduous road.
> Our flag, red with the blood of victory, bears the spirit of our country
> The distant rumbling of the guns mingles with our marching song.
> The path to glory passes over the bodies of our foes.
> Overcoming all hardships, together we build our resistance bases.
> Ceaselessly for the people's cause we struggle,
> Hastening to the battlefield!
> Forward! All together advancing!
> Our Vietnam is strong eternal.

The second verse is no improvement.

Work finished, I repair to the Gallery. Hoa, Dun, Ha and Miss N. have invited me to walk with them in Lenin Park. There is a lake, and an island to be gained by a picturesque footbridge. The only upset is the path around the perimeter of the lake which has become muddy after the recent rains. Miss Hoa decides she can't go any further, and stays behind with Miss N. while the other three of us press on. I buy Dun and Ha orange juices at a hut on the island, and listen as Dun delivers an articulate dose of social criticism. On the way back Miss Ha holds my hand, which is unexpected. Miss Hoa and Miss N. are nowhere to be found. We cycle back to the Gallery. Miss Hoa, for some reason, seethes when she sees us. Her dudgeon is as high as normally her greetings are ecstatic. It occurs to me that that she may have misinterpreted what she might have seen across the lake. If so, it's a pity, because from the outset it's been my policy not to show any one of these girls more favour than the others.

I dine alone, and then drop in at the Thong Nhat, to swap notes with a team of British film-makers who have come to make a documentary about Vietnamese film-making. We are interrupted by a Dutch UN Development Programme (UNDP) man called Hermann who crashes into the only empty wooden chair remaining. For half an hour he treats everyone to a non-stop tirade that dispenses with any kind of subtlety. The Vietnamese, he says, are ignorant, the lot of them. 'And when they're not ignorant they're stupid. For example, they know, they've learnt, that wiring systems need to be earthed. But will they earth their bloddy systems? Never! Aid programmes are simply a waste of everybody's time and money. The government keeps half the money and gives the rest to local People's Committees which use it to build themselves nice new homes. And that wouldn't be so bad if they really built themselves nice new homes. But they don't. Rather they build themselves nasty new homes which in a few years' time will fall down, and then they'll have to waste more aid money building themselves more nasty new homes. Give them any equipment and the chances are it'll be sold off as scrap. They keep their old equipment going, but even so they don't *look after* it. So they waste all their bloddy time on repairs which should never have been necessary in the first place. But then it's a filthy country, so bloddy squalor is the only thing they recognize. Except a racket. When it comes to a racket the Vietnamese are geniuses to a man.

Show me a racket that doesn't exist in this country and I'll show you how to turn cement into gold.'

Etcetera.

Later I learn that Hermann does this once every three months. For the rest of the time he is as decent, hard-working and pro-Vietnamese a sort as you could wish to find. He has been in Vietnam for two years engaged in a hydraulics project that involves no fewer than thirteen different departments. What has driven him to exasperation is that no one department is willing to accept a cent less in aid than any other department. Their costings have nothing to do with the job in hand, only with inter-departmental pride and competition. The project therefore is no nearer getting off the ground than when he first arrived.

'And look at their bloddy bicycles. Doesn't anybody here know what a bicycle is? Has nobody heard of brake-pads?'

This raises a storm of protest. Everybody loves the Vietnamese and their bicycles, Hermann should never have mentioned the bloddy things, and so now he is attacked from all sides. This however only confirms him in his views.

'No I will not be bloddy reasonable,' he shouts. 'Listen to you all. I don't believe my bloddy ears. But that's what happens when people come to this bloddy country. They become warped the moment they step off the aeroplane, totally bloddy warped, each and every one of them. Goodnight!'

Tuesday 17th October: Hanoi I'm beginning to think a short snappy break in Halong Bay is not such a bad idea after all. In the morning I play guest at the Writers' Association. The writer as a conceptual entity poses an insoluble problem for the Party/government. In essence writers are, or should be, perceived as the salt of the earth. In the war, the best Americans were writers to a man. By telling their country the truth about Vietnam they greatly contributed to Nixon's decision to pull US forces out of Indochina. Because of the stance taken by the more liberal elements of the press he had little other option. Similarly, North Vietnamese writers and journalists played an integral part in sustaining public morale during the conflict. They also contributed manfully to the unrelenting propaganda effort to undermine the 'puppet' regime in Saigon. However once reunification of the country had been achieved, and the Revolution spread throughout the land, the attractions of free speech became less obvious. The Party now had a position to defend, rather than a regime to attack. The tragedy of Vietnam (and perhaps of Communism generally) is that the Party, having achieved the improbable on at least three occasions – by defeating the French, the Americans and the Chinese – has simply been unable to deliver the goods as regards the promised benefits of socialism. The will was there, but the system and the resources weren't. Yet precisely because of its past successes, the Party has been psychologically unwilling to contemplate its own short-comings. And writers are expected to toe the line.

Individually I find nothing objectionable about the half-dozen males I meet at the Association. The poets, novelists, translators and editors Zoom introduces me to are all cadres. Most of them fought in at least one of Vietnam's wars. They are therefore to be admired, in the same way that, whatever one's race or creed, one admires David as opposed to Goliath. The Revolution after all was a heroic enterprise brought off heroically. I am aware as I talk to them that little in my own experience matches theirs. As an institution however, the Association does nothing but rankle as far as I am concerned. The thought of all writers belonging or striving to belong to one body is anathema; rather it is part of the writer's job to 'stand apart'. In good times he sides with the devil; in bad times he sides with the angels.

This visit promises therefore to be little more than an exercise in (at best) high-minded fatuousness. It is not for me to begin wielding the cudgel of western liberalism amongst those who, having wielded cudgels in the heroic phase of their country's emergence as a nation, have now largely laid cudgels aside. Similarly, on their side, I sense a certain unwillingness to tangle with substantive issues. If I play the guest, they play the hosts.

Vu Tam Nam, the Association's publishing director, middle-aged and stiff, inducts me into the facts and figures. The organiza-tion is a national body that has 450 members. As well as this office in Hanoi there are branches in Hue and Saigon. Funding is tripar-tite: a direct government grant, and earnings from its book and

92

magazine publishing divisions. Membership confers official status on a writer. In most cases before joining this, the national association, a writer will have been a member of a provincial writers' association. Quality control is the name of the game. Under new regulations, a writer will be considered for membership when he has written some 'good books', and when he has two sponsors among existing members. When he becomes a member he may, from time to time, be offered a 'scholarship': enough money to live on for three or four months while he writes his next 'good' book.

From this Vu Tam Nam passes to a synoptic account of modern Vietnamese literature. The wars, he tells me, provide the main 'focus' for the majority of writers. Overcoming difficulties and hardship is the theme of themes. Many generations of writers grew up and matured during those hard times. It is only right therefore that their experience should be celebrated. Since 1975 however, writing about the wars has become more 'vivid'. Now it is not just the heroics that are written about, but the tragedies as well, and the effects (long-term as well as immediate) on daily life.

The conch passes to a poet, Bang Viet, marginally younger than Mr Vu, who tells me that the battlefield is one of the hardest places for testing a human being. In battle, all a man's qualities are revealed. Wartime therefore is a good field for a writer, the more so if he is a participant as well as a witness. It enables him to 'follow reality'. But since those times writers have struggled to become more critical of their experiences. Under fire, the quality of men's prose was not always that hot, and certain 'distortions' were permitted. Today, 'We are striving for a deeper, more far-reaching understanding. We must look at the losses of the people, which, for a long time, we couldn't write about. For the sake of morale, that kind of reality had to be hidden.'

Does that mean, I ask, that an anti-war literature is now in the offing? Bang Viet shakes his head. He talks about the example of western 'anti-war' writers, including Mary McCarthy and Graham Greene. Their preoccupation was with the 'non-humanitarian attitude' of the US government. The Vietnamese view was necessarily different. Since the Vietnamese were not the aggressors, since their cause was primarily defensive, Vietnamese felt 'reluctance' at the 'necessity to fight' while never disputing the necessity itself. With victory behind them, the task rather is to 'show respect for our losses'. At the same time there is now, particularly since *doi moi*, a tendency away from war as a subject-matter. Many new books hardly mention the war at all. There is a 'new focus' on 'love and domestic issues'.

'But perhaps that is what you mean by an anti-war literature?'

Addressing 'domestic issues' extends to acknowledging that poverty and hardship are still at work in Vietnam. 'There is a new dialogue between writers and the public, reflecting the greater democracy within the government system.' Bang Viet reminds me that local People's Committees have been granted the right to criticize the National Assembly, just as the National Assembly can criticize the Council of Ministers. In the same way readers are encouraged to make comment on the books they read. Writers are becoming more conscious of a need to satisfy their audiences . . .

Quickly Vu Tam Nam intervenes, lest I should think Vietnamese literature is on the brink of running amok. It is the Association's duty to nurse Vietnamese literature through the difficult period of transition, from the old pre-*doi moi* 'rationalism' to a more open era when outside influences will inevitably enter on the scene.

'Recently we have had to fight against black videos and black books. One of our tasks is to maintain and improve literary standards. To this end we have been encouraging the translation of good books from abroad. For example, the stories of Somerset Maugham, *The Black Prince* by Iris Murdoch . . .'

How safe can you get? I almost ask. The Writers' Association is exactly what I had anticipated it would be: an organ of indirect censorship, offering guidance to a profession that should not require any guidance at all. Of course its operations are not censored. It is the censor.

Briefly, the conversation opens up around the table, becomes nothing more than lists of 'favourite authors'. An intrinsic feebleness is compounded by this diffusion. Beyond compliments, nothing important is exchanged. Zoom asks whether there are any other questions I would like to put. There aren't. Egoistically I wonder to myself whether there is any chance that the book I am writing (this book) will find its way into Vietnamese translation. Under the existing set-up I realize the answer has to be, will be, one hundred per cent and categorically negative.

But the proof of the pudding is in the eating. There is still my interview with Nguyen Huy Thiep to come, in the evening. Nguyen Huy Thiep is not a member of the Writers' Association, nor is he likely to become one. If asked to join, he would refuse. He does stand apart, and thereby embodies at least some of the values the others like to venerate: hardship, dedication, sacrifice . . .

Our meeting is bizarre in the extreme. Zoom expresses his regret that he cannot come in person to interpret for me. Instead he arranges for Stein and me to be accompanied by Thang. The three of us rendezvous at the Thong Nhat at six. To get to the address which Mai Trang has scribbled on a piece of paper, Thang takes us on an unnecessarily long route, via the curving Tran Quang Khai, a broad, dismal thoroughfare that follows the bend of the Red River. One side is lined with grubby houses and grubbier shops, the other with a continuous steep bank, presumably a defence against flooding. We follow this almost to the slip-road that leads up to the Doumer Bridge, before cutting in down a passageway that takes us to Mai Trang's brother's door. The way back is considerably shorter, and will prompt Stein to wonder whether Thang deliberately took us the long way round to ascertain whether I already knew the way, i.e. whether I had been there before.

The house is tiny, poky, an unlined concrete wastepaper bin, square, with an upper platform inside that makes for an extra floor. Downstairs is partitioned in two: an antechamber stacked full of canvases, half-sculptured stones, bicycle wheels; and the main living area, almost entirely taken up by a wooden double bed. On the bed is a square jute mat. Here, having removed our shoes, we are invited to sit crossed-legged.

This is where Mai Trang's brother, Nguyen Hong Hung, his wife and their two children live. Of Mai Trang herself there is no sign. We are, however, expected. Tea is served. And because we are the first foreigners to have come here, a packet of biscuits is rapidly purchased from a stall outside. I feel guilty at not having brought any gift with us. If we hadn't shown, I know the biscuits would not have been purchased. The sense of poverty is considerable.

There are three men there: Nguyen Hong Hung; an elderly, shaky, thickly bespectacled poet called Duong Tuong, who has translated *Twelfth Night* and *Wuthering Heights*, possibly the poems of Keats as well; and a small figure who crouches in one corner. This is Nguyen Huy Thiep. His handshake is perfunctory. He does not indulge in compliments. He seems inclined not to open his mouth. But his eyes turn you over on all sides, inspect you top to bottom, make of you a relentless study; even, they accuse.

There is a definite tension. When Nguyen Huy Thiep can be prevailed upon to speak, the first thing he says is that five years ago, if we had met him like this, he would certainly have been arrested and put in prison. Thus Thang translates. It is a warning, and a forward apology. Nguyen Huy Thiep does not know Thang, therefore cannot decide whether he is to be trusted. Through Thang I tell him that Thang has assured us he is off duty, that he has come along solely to help. Nguyen Huy Thiep digests this without visible emotion, save a slight flick of those penetrative eyes, asking: And what if you are wrong? On whose head will it fall? Through his fear, his caution, he is the master of us all. In the ordinary sense, the interview is a non-starter from the moment go. It is Catch-22: without an interpreter we cannot have a conversation, nor can we with one.

Nguyen Hong Hung meanwhile has set brush to paper. Quickly he sketches me. The result becomes the talking point. He has projected something of his friend into my features. The eyes are more intense than mine, there is something fugitive about the lines, I look older than I am. Stein clucks his approval, but is less satisfied when Nguyen Hong Hung fails his portrait. 'He is sorry,' translates Thang, 'but he cannot find your character.' As though to prove he has a character. Stein launches into a diatribe about the August Revolution. Though I have heard much of this before, I am nonetheless impressed by the speaker, by Stein's determination to pursue his subject no matter what the circumstances. Nguyen Huy Thiep stares coldly at his feet. 'What about the future?' I ask through Thang. 'What about Vietnam in the next five years, in the coming decade?' Thiep's reply, given without a moment's reflection, is as pithy as it is incisive: 'Ask the politicians.' Could anything be more bald, more provocative?

Tặng :
JUSTIN WINTLE

Nguyễn hồng Hưng
46 trần nhật Duật .

H.Y. H.

17.10
1989

I begin to see why he is disliked by his non-colleagues at the Writers' Association. They would happily discuss the future for an hour, and all you'd get would be the diluted thoughts of General Secretary Linh. I press my inquiries. Thiep refuses to be drawn about his work. In particular I ask about the story that has brought him notoriety, the unkempt other life of the national hero. Did he mean this to pack a topical punch? But no: the story is only a story, he cannot be responsible for what the reader thinks or feels. About his life he says: 'Chance is everything,' and 'Nothing happens except by chance. So what is the point in my telling you about my life?' Then he looks at the picture his friend Hung has done of me. 'Anger,' he says, 'there is anger in your face!'

Stein and I exchange rapid glances. It is as though everything that is said is in code, as though by putting or discovering the quality of anger in my face they wished to convey that that is what they feel: anger. Anger generated by the fact that under a regime whose roots are sunk deep within an ideology evolved from a determinist view of history nothing of any consequence is left to chance. But we cannot be sure, even though our glances confirm we are thinking along parallel lines. There is a sort of ghastly, drained *Alice in Wonderland* atmosphere in the room. The games, the paradoxes, the concealed meanings, if there are any, are strangely monochrome. Or it could just be we are having a highly awkward exchange in which neither side knows how to make proper contact with the other.

'Where do you get your inspiration?' Stein asks Thiep: a clever question, one which I, as a writer, would never ask of another.

'From my feelings,' Thiep responds, without any. 'Whatever feelings chance inspires.'

In a while Hung shows us one of his works, a powerful sculpture called 'Faces in the Revolution'. It is a slab measuring about one foot by two. On it, in full relief, are a dozen or so heads, arranged in rows. These represent Vietnamese types: I recognize many if not all of them from faces I have seen in the street. It is a sort of portable demotic portrait gallery, and the only piece of modern sculpture I will see in Vietnam – save perhaps the figures at My Lai – that I can warm to.

Stein too is impressed, although he immediately seeks to stifle his admiration with a piece of pedantry that makes me reconsider whether in fact we are on the same wavelength tonight. 'But surely,' he says when Hung explains that all the faces belong to his friends, 'they can't have looked like that at the time of the Revolution! They can only have been children then!' For Stein there is only one Revolution, one period of the Revolution, and that was in August 1945. In Hanoi Stein is like a schoolboy who, having stumbled into what he thinks is the sweetshop of his dreams, discovers that some of the sweets on sale don't taste at all like candy.

Hung, Thiep and Duong Tuong announce that they are bored of talking about the Revolution. Again, there is an ambiguity. Do they mean they are bored of talking about it now, tonight, or that they are bored with the topic in general? Thang catches my eye and surreptitiously taps his watch. It takes twenty minutes at least to say goodbye. Then everyone files out into the alley-way, Thiep and I bringing up the rear. I turn to shake his hand. Our hands however do not shake, rather they grip each other tightly. It is almost a species of Indian wrestling, for Thiep stares at me, unblinking, some demonic purpose in him, as though he were determined I should never forget this quietly eerie moment (which I never shall). I believe too that for some reason he is suspicious of me, and that he is measuring his suspicion against his own stare as it is returned by me in full.

We take the short way back, through a brightly lit night-market selling mainly new clothing from Thailand. Stein and I invite Thang to have dinner with us at the Dang Chu. Although we are anxious to discuss meeting Nguyen Huy Thiep between ourselves, we are also curious about Thang's reactions. Poor Thang! Stein has conceived the notion that Thang is 'security', that he would not have come with us otherwise. It is possible that Stein is right, but for my money it's doubtful. Thang, whom I have known a little while now, seems to me unusually agitated this evening. More likely he is worried that going to a house full of dissidents may rub back on him, even though, equally as likely, he will have had official clearance of some kind to make the visit. He tells us that, as we were leaving, Nguyen Hong Hung quizzed him about where he lived and where he worked, in short about just who he was.

Thang's explanation of this is cynical in the extreme, and cuts no ice with Stein: namely that these unofficial artists were anxious to develop a relationship with him in order that he might bring any other foreigners he has contact with to the house in order to purchase some of their art. 'Artists,' he says, 'are like that, whether or not they are recognized by the state. All they're really interested in is dollars.'

'Why don't you?' asks Stein. 'It would help them, and perhaps it would help you.'

'I have too much to lose,' answers Thang.

For Stein, this is proof conclusive of Thang's complicity in his country's security arrangements. For me it is strongly suggestive of the opposite.

'But you see,' says Stein, 'the reason why our friends asked Thang about his job is because they suspected him of being an undercover person. Don't you think that was so very obvious? So why then did Thang make a red herring about them wanting him to take other foreigners to buy their art?'

'Indeed. But then why did Thang bring it up in the first place? Perhaps he really does have his prejudices, just like everybody else.'

In truth, this business about who may and may not be 'security' I find a little academic, a little wearisome. Whether formally or informally, I consider it unlikely that the essentials of one's activities go unreported. Also, there seems to me a crude fairness in whatever arrangements may have been made. I have come here to make my report on them, so why shouldn't they keep a file on me?

'Obviously, Thang may be asked by someone how the evening went, and Thang will make his reply. I don't think we need worry ourselves unduly though. Both our guides knew about it in advance.'

Stein nods his agreement, but I can tell there is still some angle that bothers him. Is his own guide, Lam, in on the act as well? Yet whatever it is there is no time to find out. Our debate is displaced by a matter that gives far greater cause for concern. We are joined at our table at the Thong Nhat by the small band of English film-makers. They have heard, they tell me, about my rat-bite. The story, it seems, has been merrily going the rounds. But have I considered, the producer asks, the possible consequences?

100

'Consequences? What consequences?'

'Well, for instance, rabies, love. Shouldn't you see a doctor at once?'

Wednesday 18th October: Hanoi–Halong Bay (Quang Ninh Province) 'I think,' I tell Zoom when, at the crack of dawn, he arrives with Nam and the van to spirit me away to Halong Bay, 'I should see a doctor at once.' Zoom pulls a face, he really wants us to make a quick getaway before the Haiphong road clogs up, but agrees to stop off at the 'Swedish Camp' first. The best doctor in town is Georg Dalén, staff physician to the Vietnam–Sweden Health Co-operation Programme. The camp is a cluster of Scandinavian chalets close by the Swedish Embassy some distance away from the Sofia. As Dr Dalén doesn't arrive at his consulting room until 8.30 we must 'hang about' in the lane outside. At 8.30 however I am seen to promptly. Dr Dalén is tall, bearded, methodical, unflappable. I explain about the rat-bite, twelve days ago now. Dr Dalén says he is not aware of anyone contracting rabies that way. He pulls down a medical reference book and checks it out. 'Dogs, cats, bats, yes, but not rats.'

'There's always a first time,' I suggest. 'Do you have the facilities to run a test?'

Dr Dalén shakes his head. 'There is no test.'

'Then why not give me some vaccine? I had a couple of shots in England, human diploid cell or whatever, so all I need is a booster.'

'But that would cost you eighty dollars!'

'That's not a frightful amount.'

'You see, people always say life is cheap out here in the East, but in fact the truth is the opposite. When the average per capita income is less than a hundred dollars, life can be very expensive.'

'I think my life is worth eighty dollars, and as it happens I have eighty dollars on me.'

'No, really, I have never heard of anyone getting rabies from a rat.'

'Then at least tell me what the symptoms are, so I can have the injections if the need arises.'

101

Dr Dalén looks at his book again.

'Hydrophobia. Initially, muscle ache, uncontrollable twitching, spasms. But once the symptoms start, there is nothing that can be done. There are only five or six cases where someone has survived the onset of symptoms. You are as good as dead.'

'Then give me the vaccine.'

'I think not. I think you should save your money.'

There is no way through the Swede's defences. I leave rather less reassured than he intends I should. Zoom on the other hand is very happy. Now there is nothing left to delay the trip further. As we put Hanoi behind us he becomes distinctly chirpy. I try telling him about last night, about Nguyen Huy Thiep, but Zoom has no ears for that sort of thing. 'Don't worry,' he says, 'we are going to Quang Ninh Province now. We're going to have a good time at Halong Bay. Really. Lots of pretty girls there maybe. Today we are gangsters.'

He starts crooning verses from some of the songs he sang in his pop group. Nam, at the wheel of the Russian minibus, also looks happy. He is wearing shades and a white hat with the words 'Saigon Tourist' stitched on it. Zoom and I designate him Chief Gangster, and at this he breaks into a broad grin. 'Gangster,' he repeats after us, and keeps repeating periodically, all the way to our destination. 'Gangster, gangster' – and each time Zoom claps his hands with glee.

The day is overcast, humid. It is a hundred kilometres to Haiphong, the halfway point, and all the way the landscape is unrelievedly flat, colourless. The only sizeable town is Hai Duong, where, after an hour, we stop for coffee, fruit and peculiarly powdery confections – little cakes the size of Oxo cubes – made from beans that must be taken with tea. Otherwise there are only villages, spotted about the delta plain at more or less regular intervals. Trees, stagnant mosquito-breeding ponds, duck-houses, huts, gateways, war memorials, sometimes a small pagoda, all huddled together as though intimidated by the monotony of endless paddies. The occasional river, straight as a canal, edged with houseboats. Peasants wading in the rivers, bending down for shrimp, mostly women, all wearing the traditional shallow conical hat. Water buffalo, with small boys straddling their necks. And a railway line, running along the top of a two-metre dike. The national flag (gold star on a cadmium background) is unbelievably dramatic as it flutters, above a station that is no more than a pale concrete shed, in a light wind that crosses the plain unopposed, therefore undetected, except by this singularly livid splash of colour.

The road itself is halfway decent. Nam drives *à la mode d'Indochine*, that is, right at the oncoming traffic until the last moment, when he swerves to the left. The oncoming traffic does exactly the same, so that everybody keeps to the centre of the highway for as long as he dares. Horns and hooters are used unsparingly. If a slower vehicle is in front – and most vehicles are slower, lorries, feeble pick-ups, clapped-out buses – you start hooting him from about a hundred metres behind. When at last he moves in to let you overtake, there is another slowcoach in front, and you start hooting *him*.

One reason that drivers stick to the centre is that long stretches of the road are lined, on either side, with grain, levelled out to dry. This is against the law, but since there is nowhere else to dry your crop (every last square centimetre of the land is used, the soil isn't good, adequate harvests are never guaranteed) you spread it on the road. Vehicles drive over your grain, which must therefore constantly be relevelled, at whatever personal risk from the oncoming traffic. Hay for the animals is dried in the same way, so that the road becomes the conveyor belt of Vietnam's agricultural industry.

After the animals have been fed, if there is any hay left over you cook a pot of rice over it. Zoom tells me that this is a delicacy of the northern delta. 'It's very wonderful. Really!'

I look more closely at a passing village, the passing houses or bungalows. Mainly they are very small indeed, sometimes two or three rooms, sometimes only one. The only buildings that have more than a single storey belong to People's Committees. They are either constructed from wood, or made with concrete. They all have gardens however, with a great variety of animals: pigs, chickens, geese, ducks, dogs, buffalo. It is difficult to imagine that the word 'privacy' exists in such places.

After two hours we reach the outskirts of Haiphong. The ponds here are jammed with long logs that, once the sap has been soaked out of them, will be used for building houses. The skyline in front of us is dominated by an unmoving, towering belch of smoke that comes from a cement works situated near the docks. Along the road now are heaps of scrap iron. It is not at all a pretty place, a sprawling area of urban wreckage in fact. Some of the central streets – narrow, noisy and rotting – remind me of Hanoi, but from this cursory glance it would seem that the chief attraction of Haiphong is the ferry that takes you beyond, across the estuary into southern Quang Ninh.

There is a long queue of lorries and buses waiting for the ferry – a barge that is powered by a tug-like vessel to one side. Zoom offers the ferry-keeper a handful of my cigarettes and we are waved ahead to pole position. A second ferry, another handful of cigarettes, and the scenery is suddenly very different. Pointed limestone mountainettes stud the landscape. The delta is behind us. The road begins to wind. Increasingly the land is uncultivated. Various kinds of quarry – sand, limestone, coal – abound. The air is sometimes full of dust. We drive through a small town that is almost entirely colonial French in character: a place that was never bombed by the Americans, or shelled by the Chinese. Yen Hung, I think. The road begins to coil as well as wind. Its surface deteriorates, causing the van to creak and stutter. And then suddenly there it is, the sweep of Halong Bay, a lengthy shoreline that has the same mild curvature as the Côte d'Azure at Nice, and a sea littered with hundreds upon hundreds of tiny, jutting, craggy islands.

These too are limestone. Once they were mountains. Now they are a numerous, miniature archipelago; mindless shapes that a child might have sculpted in dark Plasticine (mauve, grey, black, purple, streaks of green) and put on a silver tray.

'That's nice,' I say.

'Very beautiful. Really!' replies Zoom, who has been here several times before, but appears not to mind returning.

Halfway round the bay Nam stops at a larger house that purports to be the Foreign Relations Bureau of the provincial People's Committee. Zoom goes inside and after a few minutes I am invited to follow him. I meet the deputy director, one Tran Xuan Nguyen, a fifty-plus-year-old with large hands and a large, serious face that emanates courtesy. What is supposed to be a five-minute formality extends past the hour. I tell Mr Nguyen (as Zoom suggests I call him) a little about myself, and he reciprocates. He is a cadre, he was once a soldier. Then he offers a summary of the wartime history of Quang Ninh Province. The important coal-mines to the north of Halong Bay escaped American attention, although a power-station was destroyed. In the 1979 war with China, 60,000 out of 63,000 ethnic Chinese fled across the border. For several months before their invasion the Chinese had waged an intensive propaganda campaign, warning the Vietnamese Chinese that if they did not return to China they would be regarded as traitors and punished accordingly. So the majority of Chinese packed their bags and left. Yet, when the war came, only a few Chinese squadrons penetrated Quang Ninh. Those Chinese who had stayed behind, Mr Nguyen assures me, have prospered since, far more than those who resettled in Kwangsi or the Yunnan.

He also assures me of the relative prosperity of Quang Ninh, definitely one of the most go-ahead provinces of the country. Then he makes inquiries about my family. Zoom, on my behalf, asks about his. Mr Nguyen beams. As well as a family, he says, he has a garden. I ask to be allowed to visit his garden. Mr Nguyen beams even more. Even though no westerner has set foot on his property before, I will certainly be invited before I leave Halong.

Zoom is highly pleased with my interest, my attention, my performance, the impression these things have created. 'Travelling outside Hanoi should be easy for us,' he ventures. 'I think already you understand the Vietnamese way.' As a result he has been told that there is no need for us to stay in an expensive hotel. Instead we can put up at a 'working people's guesthouse'. Until I see the guesthouse I am in two minds about the benefits of this privilege. I have a vision of a stifling, airless barracks. Various papers are exchanged with minor functionaries, and then we are on our way again, a short ride back the way we came. We are accompanied by a small man with simian features called Vinh, assigned to be our guide for the duration of our visit. I see now several very large edifices on the medium-steep hill-line that fringes the bay. Most of these are hotels. The place really is the resort of the north. At least, I think to myself, I know what I am missing. But suddenly the van swings into a rising drive. Through a checkpoint we come to the portals of a building that is just as big as any other. Four storeys, and a capacity for at least three hundred guests. The small-scale world of Hanoi is a thousand thousand miles way. The workers' guesthouse is in fact the Trades Union Hotel. My own group apart, the only other people staying there are either Russian or Czech, along with their interpreters and drivers.

My room is large, has two double beds, hot water, a refrigerator, an air-conditioner that works, a good table for me to write at, oodles of space to pace up and down in, a balcony overlooking the sea and a ten dollar tariff. For Zoom and Nam, sharing an identical room next door, the tariff is seven.

'You like it?'

'Mnnn! I'm even flabbergasted. It could be the Black Sea.'

'So you see, Mister Zoom really knows how to make you happy. Now, take a rest, you must be tired after such a long drive. Have a bath, take a shower, lie down a while, anything. Then later we will go downtown Halong and have a special dinner.'

Downtown Halong turns out to be a short, unmade street with a few stalls, a few shops and a couple of restaurants. In Vietnam, I have yet to see a single strip of neon. The restaurant we choose though is well lit, with an upstairs as well as a downstairs. The four of us compress ourselves into low seats around a low table. Zoom is at his uninhibited, irrepressible best. Tonight, he announces, we are having king prawns and Chinese beer. Chinese beer is more expensive than Vietnamese beer, and in its export incarnation is supposed to suppress sexuality, but that is propaganda bunkum, and in any case I'm paying, so Chinese beer it is. Zoom reminds everybody that it is the year of the snake, the year of the cobra, and therefore it behoves everyone to go out and kill a cobra. 'But my dear, there are many ways to kill a cobra, and many different kinds of cobra too!' Other dishes are served, but beside the king prawns, which are as succulent as the waitress who serves them, they pale into insignificance. The *boc phét* surges. I take time out however to notice that Vinh finishes his food quickly. Thereafter he goes to work with a toothpick – not the discreet legerdemain practised in European or Japanese eateries, but a full-blooded oral surgery. Nam and then Zoom follow suit. Also, there is scant respect shown for either the table or the floor. The debris of prawns and chicken-wings is dropped anywhere. I contribute by inadvertently smashing my beaker. 'Just push the pieces over the edge,' counsels Zoom. 'They'll clear it up afterwards.' The proprietor, a slightly nervous, bespectacled type, grins approvingly. This, apparently, is the way to make an evening of it.

Afterwards we drop Vinh off, and Nam takes the minibus to visit a 'brother' who lives in the area. 'It's a good chance for him. Really!' Zoom admonishes. 'In any case, that means you and I can take a massage.'

Oh yes? We stroll along the front. We look over two of the hotels, which again, after the confines of Hanoi, surprise me with their amplitude. Between them I observe a squashed scorpion lying in our path, but Zoom assures me it is an illusion. 'I promise you, no scorpions in Vietnam Mister Justin!' Then what exactly is that? 'A member of the scorpion family. But not a real scorpion. Believe me!' And so we come to the massage house, a largish, well-appointed bungalow. To my slight relief, and perhaps disappointment, I learn that it is a state-run establishment. The masseuses, neither very young nor very old, sit circumspectly at a table on the veranda. Also the massage rooms, or cubicles, have large windows which are only half-curtained. It looks and feels safe. For half an hour I am hit by a pleasant creature I think is called Tui, or Thuy, sometimes with her fists clenched, sometimes with her palms open, slapping, sometimes with both hands interlocked. She pulls my fingers and twiddles my toes. She also butts my head with hers. As I lie on my belly she grabs a hold of my ear, pulls it, then jabs her forehead into my temple, hard. For all this I pay the equivalent of three dollars. When it is over I am neither happy nor unhappy.

Zoom, finished before I am, is waiting at a table on the veranda. We drink more Chinese beer and talk about Hanoi. It is now that Zoom tells me, feelingly, about Thang's broken heart. He asks me about Nguyen Huy Thiep – away from Hanoi these things can be discussed openly, honestly. I forget what I tell him. The issue of 'security' comes up. Zoom is at pains to tell me he is not security. I test him with my latest thoughts on the subject. Western journalists, I say, can be intolerably arrogant. They arrive in a foreign country and expect to be able to see whom they please when they please. If a big potato is too busy running the country to be seen, then they start kicking and screaming, reading all sorts of bad things into the refusal. Somebody must be hiding something, there's a cover-up going on. Really (I tell Zoom) we're a two-faced bunch and shouldn't be trusted an inch. One law for ourselves, and another for the rest of the universe. 'Isn't that too much, don't you think?'

Zoom agrees, but I think he is just being polite. I'm not sure, but perhaps I'm not liberal enough for his tastes. In any case, he's not the sort to relish the theoretical end of things. In his job, a surfeit of theorizing can spell trouble. His interest is in doing the job to the best of his abilities, in keeping everybody happy. Everybody includes his clients, like me, and his superiors, like Mr Hong. Serendipity is the only universal safeguard.

We make our way back to the Trades Union Hotel. With so much beer inside me, sleep should be no problem. In fact, it becomes a huge problem. My lovely, beautiful seaside room is riddled with woodlice, and tonight I learn just what a racket they can make. Even the thin struts that support the mosquito net above my bed are heavily inhabited by the things. The noise is extraordinarily exasperating, and curiously electric in its textures. There is a steady background hiss to the erratic, shrill picking of the insects. Perhaps Miss Thuy's ear-trick has tuned up my ears too fine. In the event the only solution is to turn on the air-conditioning full blast, to provide a counter-sound. The body chills, a superfluous coma sets in.

Thursday 19th October: Halong Bay   The thing to do in Halong Bay is take a boat. The Quang Ninh Province Tourist Authority, a department of the People's Committee, owns several vessels of various types and sizes. You take either a three-hour trip, a four-hour trip, a six-hour trip or an eight-hour trip. The last will take you to the centre of the archipelago, and includes a visit to Monkey Island, and the old man from the south who has lived there forty-seven years. To do Halong Bay properly however takes at least three days. There are supposedly 1,600 islands, dotted around fifteen hundred square kilometres of sea. Not surprisingly, the area, once infested with pirates, has become one of the favoured exit points for the boat people. Because the islands lie close together, you could spend a lifetime chasing your prey. Many of the island passes also afford perfect sites for the counter-ambush.

We do not spend three days out in a boat. We do not even spend eight hours. Instead we cadge a three-hour ride on a clapped-out pleasure-steamer that has been hired by a group of East Germans. Before that, we must take a ferry across to Hong Gai, the provincial, coal-mining capital at the northern end of the bay which shelters under a mountain – in effect another limestone island that has moored up alongside the mainland. The ferry casts off at Bai Chai, which means Burned Out, or something similar. A young woman whom we have collected from the *bureau d'étrangers*, our special guide for the day and whose name eludes me, explains: during the Mongolian invasion of 1228 a Vietnamese general, pretending to be a fisherman, approached the Mongolian fleet with a tether of dinghies filled with dry wood and oil. At the appropriate moment his men hurled torches, and the bomb-boats did their trick. Unfortunately, the wind blew the flames ashore and burnt all the trees. Hence the name: Burned Out.

As the steamer sets sail, the woman continues to feed me scraps of information through Zoom. The big island that shelters Hong Gai is called Poem Island, because in 1464 King Le Thanh Tong, finding the spot to his liking, ordered his secretary ('chauffeur') to inscribe some verses he had just composed on the face of the rock. Only two of the sixteen hundred islands are inhabited, although there are plenty of caves where fishermen sometimes rest for several days. One of the islands we won't be visiting today is called Maiden Island, because a rich man once imprisoned an unwilling virgin he had taken a fancy to in one of its caves, as a punishment for her reluctance. Her legs have turned to stalactites, her head is a boulder on the floor. About a third of the islands have names, the rest don't. Mostly the names derive from the islands' shapes. Dog Island is so called because it resembles a dog. Is there a Teapot Island? I ask. The guide is unsure. She will have to ask. If I succeed in finding an appropriate name for an unnamed island then that's what it will be called ever after. That one over there, I say, should be called Island Without A Shape. The guide shakes her head. I will have to do better than that. Halong itself means Dragon

109

Landing. One legend goes that the dragon who is the mother of all dragons descended from heaven one day to assist the Viets in their fight against another host of seaborne invaders. From her mouth she spat pearls like cannonballs. These later became the islands. According to a second legend, the islands are themselves dragons, the children of Mother Dragon. According to a third, the islands were always there, but one day a monster was seen prowling among them. Because the monster *looked* like a dragon, the place became known as Halong. In any case, it's where Ho Chi Minh had his summer residence.

The steamer nudges past an especially steep pinnacle of an island. This is called Titov Island, because it's where Ho Chi Minh once bathed with Titov the astronaut. Over there, Turtle Island, Parrot Island and I Can't Remember But That One Also Has A Name Island. And that one is called Head Of Man Island. Then there's Saddle Of Horse Island, and Mother And Son Waving To The Father Island. And those, those are coal barges. This is Gates Of Heaven Pass. You see the two gates? And the pass between them? On the other side is Surprising Cave, so named because it is 'surprisingly' beautiful.

The steamer puts in at another cavern on Pelican Island. There used to be a great number of pelicans here, but the tourists have frightened them away. The East Germans and I scramble ashore and explore the darker recesses. In one corner are three stone shapes that look like men huddled over a chess-board, so perhaps one day it will be called Chess Island. The East Germans decide they want a swim, dive into the sea from the back of the steamer, then decide the water here's no good for swimming, and clamber out again gashing themselves badly. A junk with a black sail glides silently, menacingly by, the steamer's master rings a bell on the bridge and the boat turns round. A middle-aged Vietnamese whom I hadn't noticed before starts smiling inanely at me. When we reach Hong Gai he sneaks up behind me as I am waiting to disembark and covers my crotch with his hand. The fact that I am not remotely amused by this does nothing to discourage him. I am aware, as my party walks towards Nam's waiting van, that he is standing still and following me with his eyes, and that his inane smile has now become an inane grin.

110

We take lunch in the same restaurant where we had dinner last night. Fried rice is accompanied by portions of grilled chicken. In no time at all Zoom has cleaned all the meat off the bones. Then he puts the bones in his mouth, crunches and swallows. 'It's wonderful,' he says. The food is washed down with rum and coke. The rum is Cuban and has been purchased across the street for two dollars a bottle. In Hanoi it goes for four dollars a bottle. We plot to load up the back of the minibus when we return. For now, we proceed to get drunk. Three sheets to the wind and all of that. Afterwards I treat Zoom to a haircut in a newly opened salon two doors away. He bubbles as the young lady hairdresser pays him excessive attention. While this is going on I examine a small market behind the shops. There is nothing there I would want to buy in a million years. When I get back to the salon, Zoom is under a drier recovering from ecstasy. As well as a cut he has had a shampoo, a shave and a neck massage. 'Oh, her touch is so good,' he enthuses. 'Miss Lien has very special hands. Why don't you try?'

I decline. It is enough for me that Zoom himself is happy on his holiday. We take an interior path back to the Trades Union Hotel, what Zoom calls the Ho Chi Minh Trail. On the way we pass a splendid French building that used to be the summer residence of the Governor-General of Indochina, and a deserted naval hostel. In the afternoon I take a swim with a group of Russians while Zoom and Nam have a siesta. The water is warm but polluted. A Canadian frolics with his female guide in the dirty waves. As I dry off a Frenchman, ill dressed, his hair done in a bow at the back of his head, asks me whether my name is Alexander Hamilton. When I tell him it's not, he says it's a pity because Alexander Hamilton owes him a lot of money. Do I have any money I can give him? Does it look like it? I ask, shaking my empty towel in the breeze. The unkempt Frenchman wanders off.

Late afternoon Zoom greets me with two invitations. Mr Nguyen has kept his promise, and the vice-chairman of the Quang Ninh Province People's Committee, Vu Dat, will see me tomorrow. More, we are all invited to an 'official banquet'. This, Zoom assures me, should please me very much: Vu Dat is a genuine big potato, the second most important personage in Quang Ninh.

At 5.30 we make our way to Mr Nguyen's house, a short

111

distance up the hill. I inspect his garden. Amazing marigolds, azalea, exotic daisies, banana, cassava, cambola, oranges, many medicinal herbs and a steamy, sweltering pig. Clearly Mr Nguyen, off duty and therefore ultra-relaxed, has worked hard at his plants. It is the house itself however that interests me more. By Hanoi standards it is decidedly large. There are three good-sized rooms. The absence of a ceiling renders them pleasantly cool. There is something admirable about the simplicity of the furnishings. Only a glass cabinet, stuffed full of ornaments, scrolls, photographs, books, a camera, suggests clutter. The place is the loyal Party member's just reward: God's, or Lenin's, Plenty. I have heard too often of corrupt cadres out in the sticks not to believe they don't exist by the drone, but I know instinctively Mr Nguyen is not one of these. I like the man.

I am given tea, cambola, apples, nuts, bananas, Russian vodka, all except the last served by Mr Nguyen's prospective daughter-in-law (already being trained to make herself useful about the house). Unusually, his wife sits in on my visit: an upright, slightly wizened woman whom I also like. When I leave, she gives me flowers.

The talk ranges freely, propped up or undermined by constant toasts. Coal-mines, tourism and the army are the topics, though I forget the details: vodka before dinner destroys the memory. Yet for once the details are not the point. What is important is that I am here, that the encounter happens. Mr Nguyen I think really is satisfied that, in the autumn of his life, he finds himself entertaining a westerner in his own home. In convincing me that the wars are a thing of the past he also, perhaps, convinces himself.

At any rate, the vodka is drunk. At the restaurant I endeavour to wash it out with Chinese beer, and so become paralytic. Whatever it is that Miss Thuy does to me tonight I am too far gone to notice. Tomorrow I will vaguely remember a steam bath – I believe unaccompanied – and the figure of her mother, waiting proprietorially for her daughter on the veranda. And so to bed, and the deranged march of the woodlice, noisy Russians carousing somewhere outside, and lightly coloured, diaphanous dragons playing hide-and-seek among three thousand voluminous lavender rocks suspended in all directions around my bed, which floats in or on the air.

112

Friday 20th October: Halong Bay Halong Bay is such a tease. I thought that having got away from Hanoi I had also got away from writers in their collective form, but no: Quang Ninh has its own word-farm. My body, when I wake up, is still sodden with alcohol. Therefore I don a pair of white Japanese tennis shorts and a blue Japanese tennis shirt with macho stripes across the chest. I haven't set foot on a tennis court since I was fifteen, but the gear is ideal for drying out. When Zoom tells me that we must spend the morning at the Quang Ninh Arts and Cultural Association I offer to change into something more uncomfortable, but he assures me I'm fine as I am. Nam drives us across to Hong Gai, where anthracite is being loaded onto a filthy freighter that flies the Maltese flag. Hong Gai itself is a bit of a sprawl and cruising through it does nothing for my hangover. Beyond, Nam parks the minibus at the side of the road beneath a cliff and we climb a steep path to a series of single-storey buildings that command an astonishing view across a thousand islets.

I am greeted by the Association's director, Hoang Thuan, and by a floppy photographer dressed in a floppy tweed suit and equally floppy tie. Smiles all round. This is a friendship visit. I am taken inside, where compliments are exchanged over tea. At 9.00 a.m. sharp the tea is replaced by bananas, nuts and beer. The nuts and bananas I can take, the beer I can't. Looks of disappointment when, on my behalf, Zoom requests mineral water instead; but smiles again when I tell them to carry on regardless. Now that the Saigon 33 is flowing, we are joined by two more figures, including the vice-president, Le Vien Cuong. He tells me that the Quang Ninh Arts and Cultural Association has seven branches: one apiece for writers, sculptors, photographers, architects, musicians, theatricals and fine artists. Since I am a writer he explains about the Quang Ninh Writers' Association. It has seven members, one of whom is also a member of the National Writers' Association. Quang Ninh writers, I am assured, take pride in being free to tackle their 'inside problems'. They are fluent in 'many styles', and the province itself is relatively literate. The annual consumption of books is between three and five per head of the population. This compares to the national average, which is only two books per capita per annum. One reason for this is that the provincial

113

People's Committee is friendly and supportive toward the arts. In other provinces writers are not always so lucky. And of course, where there is no official patronage, the arts can't flourish at all.

I am presented with two copies of the latest edition of the *Quang Ninh Cultural Newspaper*, a broadsheet that is soft in every sense (but which has, I am promised, a circulation of at least 3,000). The sit-down meeting finishes and I am taken to an adjoining room to inspect a photographic exhibition. The Quang Ninh Photographers' Association has been very busy. Two large tables pushed together are covered with photographs. Mostly they are black-and-white, and mounted on thin sheets of office paper. The slightest draught, and the exhibition would take to the floor. Mostly too they are shots of Halong Bay. They have a certain charm, in that there is little to suggest they couldn't have been taken in the 1920s. Halong Bay, one would have to say, represents the ultimate in safe subject-matter, and I can't help thinking that is why the Quang Ninh school of photography is located here. Six or seven photographers are in the room, watching my every move, my every expression. One of them does so with a camera. I smile. Then I am presented with a colour shot of a typical Halong Bay sunset. Each of the photographers inscribes his signature on the back. Did they all take it? Perhaps Mother Moscow or Papa Beijing has sent them a collective camera: the shutter won't click unless everyone presses the button.

Having met the photographers I am walked to the 'writers' camp', next level down the hillside. Do I laugh or do I cry? The writers' camp consists of a row of large cells: unlit rooms each of which has a writing table and a couple of chairs. I imagine that when the writers are at work (tackling their 'inside problems') the director or the president or the vice-president of the Quang Ninh Arts and Culture Association periodically walks up and down the building's veranda, keeping 'an eye on things'. 'Comrade Nguyen, your punctuation is looking distinctly revisionist today.' At present however none of the writers is writing. Rather all the writers are gathered together in one of the cells for a 'discussion'. Or perhaps it's just their tea-break. At any rate I am asked to join them. In my tennis shorts and sports shirt I feel an absolute interloper. (A poet, sizing me up, asks whether I am a follower of Ernest Hemingway.

Truthfully I answer no, I am not at all a fan of the man.) Beer is proffered, and again declined. Formalities and compliments are exchanged at unusual length. I endeavour to get a conversation going, but conversation is never more than sticky. Feeling uncomfortable, I apologize to them for interrupting their *boc phét*. Momentarily the temperature rises. A perturbation ripples through the group like a Mexican wave. Their spokesman responds on behalf of the company. They are not having *boc phét*, they are engaged in serious and earnest discussion. What about? I ask. About the upcoming National Writers' Congress of course! Talks about talks. The congress takes place once every five years, and follows hard on the heels of the cinquennial Congress of Journalists. This year's congress will be the first since the promulgation of *doi moi*. It promises therefore to be particularly lively.

But when does it actually take place? I ask. Very very soon. At the end of the month. In fact, the Journalists' Congress has just finished. And what was the outcome? A statement has been issued. Henceforth journalists are to enjoy 'more democracy' and they are to exercise greater 'self-restraint' in their political reporting.

'Aren't those two things contradictory?' I ask.

The reply is mind-boggling:

'Oh yes,' says the Quang Ninh Writers' Association, 'we have heard how Mrs Thatcher visited the victims of the Clapham train disaster in hospital.'

Either Zoom has elected not to put my question, or the Association has elected not to hear it. Instead, the oldest member of the group starts up. The tragedy is, he says, that the old practice of hanging poets' verses inscribed on large pieces of wood outside your house has been allowed to die. In times gone by when you built a house you adorned it with choice adages by choice poets. But then the wars came and the inscription boards were taken away to fuel the trains or for other purposes, and since the wars have finished no one has seen fit to revive the custom. Today people would rather use good wood for building boats, etcetera. In modern Vietnam, literature is losing its customary respect.

Nods all round. Nobody can disagree with such sentiments. Faces animate. The old man has put his finger on it. A national scandal.

115

Zoom gives me a nudge. It is time to go. Any more of this and his holiday will be spoiled. Clambering down the path to Nam's van though he starts laughing. '*Boc phét!*' he exclaims. 'You really pulled their eggs in there. That's what they do all day. Make *boc phét*. Really!'

'Don't you mean pulled their legs?'

'Pulling their eggs or pulling their legs – it's the same thing, isn't it?'

'Yes,' I say to Zoom, 'exactly the same.'

There is still plenty of morning left. We stop at an office in Hong Gai to collect a cadre and authorization for my group to visit whatever there is to be visited. I am shown around an astonishingly modern theatre/convention hall. This it transpires was built (in 1976) by the Vietnamese but funded by the Japanese. But which Japanese remains a mystery. The story I am given *in situ* is that the theatre was a gift from Japanese trades unions, who wanted to express solidarity with the socialist regime after Reunification in 1975. Elsewhere though I hear two different explanations: that the building represents belated war reparations following the Japanese occupation of Indochina in 1941; and that the building was a way of saying thank you to Vietnam for setting up trading relations prohibited by the American embargo. Conceivably it was both, or even all three. To the Japanese certainly there would be no contradictions involved. What is not disputed is that the money for the theatre originally went to Hanoi, which then decided Halong Bay was as good a place as any for Party and other conventions.

Next I am taken across to Poem Island. Even though the island is attached to the mainland, the trip requires a boat ride. We drive through some particularly squalid back streets until we arrive at a small landing-stage. The air is bright, clean, the blues of the water and the cobalt of the ring of surrounding rock starkly beautiful. There is some problem in finding a boat, until two women in a sampan agree, for a modest quantity of *dong*, to ferry us across. Both in their late twenties or early thirties, they pull up their neck-scarves over their faces, so that all that can be seen under their conical hats is their laughing, beguiling eyes. Working hard, they never quite look away from one. Unexpectedly, it is one of those moments when the East of one's boyhood fantasies becomes a reality.

Alas though, it's not a long journey, just a couple of hundred metres or so around the base of the mountainous promontory. At another landing-stage we disembark and thread our way through a closely packed village of huts and shacks. It is a tidy place, and reminds me of the Greek side of the Adriatic. Immediately I am tailed by a crowd of children who all want a tug at the hair on my arm. At the end of an unmarked alley between two sheds, I am brought to the poem inscribed by King Le Thanh Tong's secretary. It is set into the rockface about four metres up from the ground. Most of the lettering (in the old-style *mon* alphabet based on Chinese hieroglyphs) has been weathered away. In fact, only a dozen characters are strictly discernible. Looking at them reminds me of a sonnet from Spenser's *Amoretti and Epithalamion*, perhaps the only whole poem I learned by heart at school which still sticks:

> *One day I wrote her name upon the strand,*
> *But came the waves and washed it away:*
> *Again I wrote it with a second hand,*
> *But came the tide and made my pains his prey.*
> *'Vain man,' said she, 'that dost in vain assay*
> *A mortal thing so to immortalize;*
> *For I myself shall like to this decay,*
> *And eke my name be wipëd out likewise.'*
> *'Not so,' quoth I, 'let baser things devise*
> *To die in dust, but you shall live by fame;*
> *My verse your virtues rare shall eternize,*
> *And in the heavens write your glorious name:*
> > *Where, whenas Death shall all the world subdue,*
> > *Our love shall live, and later life renew.*

Substitute limestone for strand, and there you have it. The Hong Gai cadre, who has something to do with the People's Committee's Department of Culture (quite distinct from the Association), opens a notebook and offers a rough précis of the royal stanzas: *Let the people of Vietnam stop fighting among themselves and begin*

117

reading poetry forever. Then, after looking at several other inscriptions made at a later date, and which I am assured are not worth translating, we march back to the sampan. As the women punt us back, the cadre opens his notebook at a blank page and invites me to write something, anything, preferably in verse. For a few seconds I consider writing out Spenser's sonnet. I also consider writing that Hong Gai culturologists should do something to preserve their heritage instead of drinking beer at breakfast, but refrain from that as well. In the end I can do no better than: 'How wonderful to come to Halong Bay, and how even more wonderful to see the King's hand on Poem Island.' Decidedly I have been caught out, though later the right answer comes: 'Is it the poet that makes the poem, or the poem that makes the poet?' *Esprit d'escalier*, with apologies to Li Po. It occurs to me that, collectively or otherwise, the writers and poets I met earlier would have bested me, at least in this; and so I am punished for my sneers.

The gods don't love me either. The last stop before lunch is the Long Tien or Dragon Fairy pagoda. According to the best loved of all Vietnamese legends soon after the Dawn of Time the lord of the Lac Viet (the original Vietnamese people), Lac Long Quan, married a beautiful princess called Au Co. In due course she bore him a hundred sons. After this he lost interest in her. 'I am a Dragon,' he announced one morning, 'and you are a Fairy. So really, my dear, we'd better split up.' Lac Long Quan then took fifty of his sons off to the coastal plains, while Au Co was left to take the rest of her brood up into the mountains. One of Lac Long Quan's fifty, the strongest, disliked the arrangement however, and set about reuniting his family. He was after all both a Dragon and a Fairy. Eventually he succeeded in founding the Hung dynasty, which provided Lac Viet with eighteen rulers. Ever since, the Dragon Fairy has been an important deity.

The Long Tien pagoda was built in 1941, after the French, in order to gain access to coal which they badly wanted to give their Japanese masters, had destroyed another, much older place of worship. Inside is spacious. There are three altars, dedicated to the Buddha, the Tran Dynasty and, on the right, the Heavenly Princess Lien Hanh. Lien Hanh, so the story goes, once came down to earth to share her heavenliness with mortal men. There were offerings (joss-sticks, fruit, rice, money) on all three altars, but rather more on the altar of the Tran Dynasty.

Zoom suggests I offer a bunch of joss-sticks myself. The pagoda could do with the few hundred *dong* they cost. Not wishing to be mistaken for a royalist, I plump for the Heavenly Princess. At first they don't light, then suddenly they flare up, showering my hand with burning cinders. This hurts.

Lunch at the same place. Today, grilled 'greenbird', a sparrow-sized flyer that tastes like frog. Zoom tells me another local legend. A miserly merchant from Annam fell off his boat among the islands and started drowning. Soon a fisherman noticed his distress and rowed toward him. When he was near enough he stretched out his hand for the merchant to grasp, but the merchant thought the man was asking him for money and refused. So he drowned anyway.

We chat about the law, the legal system. There is, from what Zoom tells me, no civil code in Vietnam. Civil matters, such as small claims and matrimonial disputes, are dealt with by local People's Committees, which have the power to impose moderate fines. Women tend to do particularly badly in divorce proceedings for a variety of reasons: the committees are male-dominated, and there is no tradition of property division. Unless she is confident that she will remarry, a woman will tend not to sue for divorce. If a man refuses to abide by the decisions of the local People's Committee, then he will begin to find that things go badly for him. He may lose his job, or not get promotion. In the worst case, he may become a non-person, an outcast. People's Committees also have the choice of handing offenders and defendants over to the courts, in which case it becomes automatically a criminal matter. The courts only deal with crimes. This is likely to change soon though. *Doi moi* and the growth of the private-sector economy mean that more and more people are immunized against many sanctions at the disposal of the People's Committees. Also there is as yet no machinery for resolving disputes between Vietnamese companies (whether state owned or private) and foreign or 'international' companies. Indeed, the British Bar Association has been invited to frame an appropriate code.

Zoom complains that he is beginning to feel ill, dull. I tell him to take a rest, never mind about me. I spend the afternoon swimming, walking, relaxing. The evening promises big things. We convene at the External Relations Bureau at six: Zoom, myself, Vinh, Mr Nguyen and, arriving punctually five minutes after everyone else, the big potato himself, Vu Dat. The compliments and formalities are particularly elaborate, particularly cloying. The vice-chairman/ deputy surprises me somewhat. He is tall, lean, curly-haired and self-evidently a ladies' man. He reminds me of the sort who used to get the starring roles in B-movies thirty years ago. He reminds me in particular of Canadian actors, who had the looks but were a little wooden, a little predictable in their movements. He has recently returned from a trip to the UK, he tells me. The English girls were very very lovely.

After half an hour we repair to a private function room at what I can only describe as the People's Committee clubhouse. Zoom and I are presented with statuettes, cast in glazed china, of prancing lions with the letters *UBND Tinh Quang Ninh* inscribed on the bases. The food is lavish – crab, duck, broiled fish, salads, rice. The compliments continue, except now each compliment is accompanied by a standing toast. Vietnamese vodka, beer, ginseng wine. Just about I hold my own. Vu Dat apologizes that he cannot drink too much because he has had to spend the afternoon entertaining some businessmen from Hong Kong, but keeps raising his glass anyhow. The English girls were very very lovely, and now he comes to think about it so were the videos. The videos were full of lovely lovely English girls exposing themselves, it's a pity he didn't bring any back with him. But if there's anything I want then he can organize it for me. I have only to tell him and he will give the word. Mr Nguyen, concentrating on his food, avoids my face. Zoom nudges my foot and, pretending to translate, says: 'Pay no attention, he doesn't mean it. He's only being hospitable.' Ominously, loud music begins to seep through the double doors leading to the next room. What, Vu Dat suddenly inquires, do I think of Vietnamese women? After the banquet there will be, there must be dancing. He will choose a Vietnamese girl for me to dance with, we will all dance together. Zoom tells me that perhaps we should be getting back to our rooms. I say no, we can't do that, it would be impolite. Not yet, anyway.

120

Suddenly, without warning, the ensemble is joined by two fellow Brits, almost as though they were a part of the entertainment. A sharp-faced fellow called Brian, and his colleague John. John is a plant manager, Brian has a more senior title. They are working for a mineral extraction company that has a joint venture going with Quang Ninh Province to sort out the coal industry. But of more interest right now is Brian's guide/interpreter. He knows Zoom, and, apparently, he knows about me. As soon as we are introduced he floors me by saying: 'Oh yes, Mister Justin. Mister Justin is writing a biography of Ho Chi Minh.'

I give Zoom an especially filthy look, which Zoom ducks. Vu Dat meanwhile is staggering to his feet. He begs our forgiveness, but there is another banquet he must attend. He will return later, but until then why doesn't everyone join the dance next door? Zoom prods me until it hurts, but I tell him I'm staying, I want to talk to Brian and John. The doors are opened, we are led through. Madonna screams from new Japanese speakers. On the floor, two Hong Kong Chinese businessmen are romping with each other. A waitress leans against the wall, almost rigid with fear. And that is the party.

'So, shall we go now?' asks Zoom.

'You go if you like, but I'm staying. I told you, I want to chat with my compatriots.'

Vu Dat briefly reappears, dances with the Hong Kongites, generally cavorts, embraces me, pressing wet lips against my cheeks, and is gone forever. The evening ends around a table on the terrace outside. Zoom stands off, or rather sits off, either still ill with having eaten too many greenbird bones, or in some kind of dudgeon. But this suits me well. Brian, John and I are free to talk among ourselves. Brian tells me about his business, about how his counterparts in Quang Ninh actually are forward thinking, and outlines the advantageous deal secured by his company. As a matter of course I inquire whether any backhanders were involved. Brian absolutely refuses to answer, but in the interests of bonhomie feeds me with an even more intriguing titbit. I may have noticed, he begins, how the Russians are not altogether flavour of the month in Vietnam. The reason for this, he has it on reliable authority, concerns an oil rig. A while ago Moscow told Hanoi that it would sell Vietnam a brand-new oil rig at the knock-down price of 25 million US dollars. On the open market it would cost at least 35 million. All Hanoi had to do was pay over the cash, and the oil rig would be dispatched forthwith. Hanoi responded with alacrity. A very large proportion of state reserves was immediately made available for the transaction. The dollars went post-haste to Moscow. But Vietnam did not get her new rig. What she actually got was a clapped-out, third-hand rig the Russians had scrounged off Indonesia for the modest sum of 5 million dollars. The anti-imperialist, anti-capitalist Soviets therefore had realized a 400% profit on a piece of brokerage that anywhere else in the world would have led to the suspension of diplomatic relations.

Saturday 21st October: Halong Bay – Hanoi Up early for the journey back to Hanoi. The owners of the downtown Halong Bay restaurant have become like family and it's sad to say goodbye. We call in at the bureau. Mr Nguyen has made a point of being there to see us off. The diminutive Vinh alone seems happy. Zoom explains afterwards: he has given him twenty thousand *dong* out of the kitty. 'Don't worry, it's just small money.' As the minibus picks up speed I hear the chink of bottles in the back. There's a crate of Cuban rum under a blanket. Zoom and Nam were up even earlier.

I give Zoom a pair of sunglasses purchased yesterday. I thought I had lost mine, but it wasn't so. So now all three of us wear shades. 'Gangsters,' exuberates Zoom, 'real gangsters.' With a van-load of hooch. I teach them the gangster song:

> *I'm an easy sort of guy*
> *But I like to have my way . . .*

Zoom picks it up immediately, and pretty soon Nam is honking his horn even when there aren't any rival vehicles to be cleared off the road ahead.

The weather justifies the shades. The sun burns, the water flashes in the paddies once we're past Haiphong (which, Zoom the true Hanoian now tells me, should really be called City of Thieves).

122

There's nothing new though, nothing that I didn't notice on the way out. Except that, in the heat, a lot more peasants are out in the fields, or fishing prawn and crab in the canals. They seem content to spend their days half-submerged. Seem content . . .

It feels good to be back in Hanoi, back at the Sofia. The staff are genuinely pleased to welcome me back. Madame Oanh pumps my hand a full half-minute. Miss Oanh gives me a quick hug and giggles. The only bad thing is the man who has moved into the room next to mine. He's different from all the other Vietnamese I've met. Short, swarthy, over-confident, dressed in a baseball hat, he hails from Saigon. He presses his friendship on me like a parking ticket. 'Madame,' he says, pushing his way uninvited into my own room, and pointing at my bed. 'Madame!' To get rid of him I pack off for a walk around the Lake of the Restored Sword. Then I creep back and write some notes. In the evening I drift down to the Thong Nhat, to catch up on lobby talk.

There's no sign of Stein, and nothing much has happened in the four days I've been away. An Australian entrepreneur though tells me a good story about a UNDP project leader whose speciality was fisheries. After a fortnight's formalities, compliments and preliminary discussions however he discovered that what his Vietnamese counterpart from the Ministry of Agriculture was really after was a submarine. One of the waitresses I'm fairly confident I've never seen before grabs my hand and won't let go until she suddenly decides my hat is dirty and needs a wash. She returns after fifteen minutes with a clean hat and resumes holding my hand. Cross-examined, she concedes that she has two children and that her husband is a policeman. But she goes on holding my hand. It actually does mean nothing at all.

Cognac. I am joined by two British hydraulics experts. They begin having a passionate argument about the future of Vietnam. One believes economic take-off is on the cards, the other believes it's a permanent impossibility. I suggest that take-off may be the wrong concept, that progress will be more piecemeal, partial, as it is in Indonesia. This somewhat spoils the party.

I return early to my room and work. For no good reason I experience a slow dejection. There are moments when the lack of facilities, of comforts, gets through to one. I take a shower, but

123

realize this is a mistake. The water is cold, and the air is cold too. The clear sky has let the daytime heat escape into the stratosphere. My room I notice has become a cold fug. Too much tobacco. I open my door and stand outside, where it is marginally warmer. For a few minutes I observe the courtship ritual of two rats on the ground two storeys below. I return to my work. Then there is a tap on my door, then another. My neighbour, the Saigon type. He whistles between his teeth and beckons me to his room. I shake my head and point at my typewriter. He comes in, picks up a bottle that has four inches of whisky left in it, and whistle-beckons again. Okay, I'll have a whisky with you, but that's as far as I go. A little to my surprise there are two women nestling on his bed. 'Madame,' he says, 'madame, madame.' The Saigon type makes gestures with his fingers. The women are not unattractive, and for a moment I am tempted. In a trice the Saigon type starts scribbling figures down on a piece of paper. The gist of these is that I can have a madame for $25 not $50. I begin to feel decidedly untempted, the more so as it dawns on me that my neighbour has probably had his way with both of them already. I laugh, shake my head, and rise to go. I am halfway out of the door when one of the women cries plaintively: 'What's wrong with me? Is it because I'm Vietnamese?' It's the first indication that either has a word of English, but it doesn't stay my feet. I bolt my door and sleep, ten hours of it.

Sunday 22nd October: Hanoi Think think think, write write write, smoke smoke smoke, until the early evening when after much haggling I take a cyclo to the Thang Loi. Brian, whom I met in Halong Bay, has offered me dinner. The Victory Hotel, I now learn, was financed by the Russians and built by Cuban engineers. Probably the only piece of real luxury in the north. While I am waiting in the lobby I fall in with some Afghanis. Diplomats, presumably. 'And how is the situation in Afghanistan?' I ask. 'Oh very good,' the man replies in perfect, Eton English. 'The rebel rockets are only falling on civilians.' Steak and real French red wine. Brian talks technicalities, the problems of grading coal so the right quality can be sent to Europe. His company is also trying to get in on the prawn industry. Tells me about a colleague who took

124

pity on a Vietnamese girl and married her, only to discover her family was incredibly rich. Bits and pieces of property all over the country. Gave him a French villa as a wedding present. Rolls-Royces are not unknown, only no one dares take them out on the roads. The roads would chew them up in no time at all. Not because of what the neighbours would say.

Outside the Thang Loi my cyclo driver, who promised to wait, has scarpered. Being a snob place where diplomats stay the hotel doesn't have a cyclo bay, so I am obliged to take a taxi. Having negotiated an astronomical price, the car fills up with Viets who want a free ride into town. I find Stein dining alone at the Dang Chu, writing up his journal. His handwriting is military medium, and I see he has already reached page 100. Most of my stuff is still in note form only. Little pangs of guilt.

Stein too has just been to Halong Bay, and is full of it. But in a while his conversation returns to the August Revolution. Gently I suggest that Vietnam hasn't always been and may not always be a socialist state. Stein sticks to his guns, and wonders whether the Vietnamese aren't over-educating too many of their younger cadres. 'I can see no benefit to the state in sending so many students to college,' he says, knitting his brows, but immediately retracts his thoughts when I unleash a spray of expletives and offers to buy me cognac.

'It's good to see you again,' I say.

'And it's very good to see you,' says Stein.

We talk late. To my dismay I spot Saigon Man hanging around the entrance of the Sofia. He whistles through his teeth at me, a singularly unpleasant tone. I wave at him and walk by. The pavements are deserted, the streets dead dark. Mooning cyclists waft by, heads turning to see who I am. Even at this hour (after eleven) I occasionally pass an old woman trudging along with her pole and baskets. A few cafés are still open. I slip into one where an American video is showing, order a Saigon 33. I watch the film for twenty minutes or so. The violence, pegged out with guns and planes and rocket-launchers, is endless. Slowly it dawns on me that the joint is not only or even primarily a video-café. From another room at the back I hear the cries of a woman or a girl being strapped by someone or something. At first I had thought it was another film, but when the fellow behind the bar starts making signs at me I realize my mistake. Sick, man. I leave my beer and go. Outside it has begun raining. I take shelter under an awning outside another café with a group of Viet workers. As conversation is impossible they offer me vodka instead, the crudest brand money can buy. Ordinarily I would refuse, but tonight I say yes, why not, what the hell. The fact that a westerner is prepared to sit and drink with them makes them immensely happy. It lifts some of the gloom for me as well. So I drink vodka, glass after glass of it, and once again Hanoi by night becomes quite beautiful. But no amount of vodka can ward off Saigon Man. He is waiting for me outside my room, grinning his fucking head off. The girl with him I can have for $18. The tariff is virtually pinned on her bodice. There is no end to his persistence.

Monday 23rd October: Hanoi Not an early start, but considering the impurities of what I drank last night, a surprisingly clear one. Mindful of Stein's progress I begin journalizing at nine. Zoom rolls up at noon. He fills me in on the trip to Cao Bang, which is supposed to start tomorrow. We can't take the minibus because the minibus won't stand up to the roads. Also, Nam has other business to attend. But no worry. Zoom has arranged to hire a jeep and driver from the Foreign Ministry's Transport Company. It shouldn't cost too much. All we have to do is go there this afternoon and sign a contract. For now, why don't I let him treat me to lunch? There's a place in the Chinese quarter . . . And he's asked Thang to join us.

I'm not sure it's a place I would go to again, except to look at. The restaurant has rooms upstairs and down. The walls are plain and peeling, but the windows, overlooking the narrow bustling street below, are magic. There is not the slightest pretence at elegance, and the service is minimal. There's only one dish on offer, the house speciality: fish that has been marinated in a thick yellow sauce for a day at least and is grilled on a charcoal burner at your table. When it's cooked, you tear it to pieces and dip the bits in another sauce. This second sauce is shocking pink in colour, being made, in the main, from puréed shrimps. The fish tastes of nothing special, but the shrimp juice lingers in the mouth so long you wonder why someone doesn't arrest it for loitering. Mercilessly, I join Zoom in teasing Thang about his celibacy. Under fire however, Thang refuses to change his dour expression. For some reason this fills Zoom with joy absolute. His face shines in the bleak surroundings like a lightbulb. Perhaps because he knows he's paying, because, on his way to becoming a bigger potato, he likes to be the host.

Then the contract-signing ceremony at the Foreign Ministry's transport depot, which is nowhere near the Foreign Ministry. Only the contract isn't signed. First off I am introduced to another man called Dung or Zoom, who assures me he really does know how to drive a jeep, and is something of a mechanic as well. It'll cost me $320, though my Zoom quickly beats him down to $300. Then we go inside, to meet the deputy manageress in her office. An appealing woman in her early forties, she is less keen on the scheme. In fact she is completely unwilling to risk one of her vehicles in the mountains. There are too many rocks, she says, which have a habit of not falling off their high perches until they sense an approaching vehicle. Then we discuss my proposed trip to Dien Bien Phu and the picture changes. If I agree to sign a contract for both trips, then she'll give way. Rocks are things that can be chanced after all. But then she quotes a figure, and we both realize the whole thing's a charade anyway. Probably the Foreign Ministry doesn't have a jeep. Zoom rattles away in Vietnamese for a while, then explains that the real problem is $300 doesn't leave anything for the driver. Then how much does the driver want? I ask. $20! That's okay, I say. But by now neither side is willing to compromise, to lose face, so we leave empty-handed.

We zoom off on the motorbike to another 'company', owned by the Ministry of Transport. Zoom leaves me on the street for fifteen minutes and returns triumphant. $200 only! Including the driver! You see! Mister Zoom never let you down. Mister Zoom always know how. Only problem is, they can't supply anything until Wednesday.

'Is that all right for you, Mister Justin?'

'Yes, Zoom. It'll have to be. Thanks.'

'Don't worry. Mister Zoom will organize a programme for tomorrow.'

127

Which means, rather as I suspected, there's no programme for me today, or what's left of it. The afternoon and evening follow a by now predictable course. A little work, dinner with Stein, expat *boc phét* at the Thong Nhat, rounded off by avoidance of Saigon Man. But Saigon Man is not so easily evaded. In the twenty-four hours since I saw him last Saigon Man has reached the conclusion that I must be in need of a wife. Tonight Saigon Man is waiting outside my room with no less than three potential brides. God knows where and when he has found them, but they have all been briefed. Collectively they present an impression that there's nothing more they would like than to become Mrs Justin. The best I can do is look at the fellow, shake my head, close my door. For an hour or so there is a series of furtive knocks on my window, but these I ignore, burying myself instead in General Vo Nguyen Giap's account of the battle of *Dien Bien Phu*.

Dien Bien Phu, fought in 1954, was the shock victory that effectively marked the end of French dominion in Indochina. It was not achieved without considerable *matériel* and advice from Red China. In the edition of Giap's work I have in front of me however, the fourth, published in 1984, Mao Tse Tung's assistance goes unacknowledged. But by then, 1984, China was Vietnam's enemy.

Nineteen Eighty-Four . . .!

Tuesday 24th October: Hanoi   Zoom at 10.30 a.m.: no, we're not going to the Transport Ministry to sign a contract. He's found another place, a semi-private concern, that's got a brand-new Russian jeep and will only charge us $120. He can pay the advance out of what's left of the money I've already given him (for the Halong Bay trip). And another thing. Dien Bien Phu. I can fly there for only $40. Zoom's seat on the same plane will cost $15. And then we can take a bus back, since there's only one flight a week, and nobody stays in Dien Bien Phu for more than two or three days. How's that?

'Fabulous. But are we going to Cao Bang tomorrow or aren't we?'

'Definitely. I promise. And I've arranged for you to meet Professor Tran this afternoon. He'll come here at two. So be ready.'

'A big potato?'

'Yes,' concurs Zoom, 'a big potato.'

Tran Quoc Vuong is not a minute early, not a minute late. He is head of the archaeology department at the History Faculty of Hanoi University. He speaks 80% English, so Zoom's services – for once – are not required. We sit on the balcony of the Sofia, drinking coffee, tea and later beer. He has the erratic appearance of a professor, and some of the eccentricities. He exudes charm. From time to time during our talk he blows his nose into pieces of newspaper he keeps in a shoulder-bag. Newspaper has been invented, handkerchiefs have not. It cannot be poverty, because he has about him a supply of Dunhill cigarettes, the most expensive in Vietnam. He appears completely at ease, is unusually corrigible. But this is only his manner. When he sits down he unstraps his watch and periodically looks at it. By pre-arrangement, Le Tien will join us at four. It is no coincidence that our 'informal chat' reaches a climax at precisely one minute to. He starts off and ends on a French note. It is only afterwards that I realize he must have had what he wanted to say to me mapped out beforehand. Our meander has never lost sight of its destination, despite my frequent interruptions.

'I spoke French in my mother's belly,' he begins. He was born in Hanoi in 1934, the son of a 'French' functionary, that is, a Vietnamese of the mandarin class who worked for the colonial administration. All his family were bilingual, and French was the language spoken at table and in front of guests. At secondary school however he refused French classes, and took English instead, as 'a symbol of patriotism'. In this he had his parents' blessing. After December 1946, when the French hit back at Ho Chi Minh's August Revolution, his family evacuated from the capital, to become soldiers and communists. Tran, the youngest child, remained in education. His mother wanted at least one son who was not going to be killed. By 1952 he was still a student. The Resistance had opened a university, but even by 1954 there were only three faculties running: Medicine, in the mountains of Viet Bac, Mathematics and Physics, exiled in China (Kwangsi), and Literature and History, in the fourth 'Inter-zone' (northern Annam). And when the war ended, the grand tally of professors amounted to only twelve, half of whom were doctors.

Tran joined the faculty of Literature and History at its inception, in 1952. But he never became a Marxist in the formal sense. 'With respect, I should like to become a Marxist, but it is very difficult to apply Marxism to "traditional" Vietnam.' For a moment Tran digresses. He recalls how the first Secretary of the Southern Party, Tran Van Giau, before resigning his post in 1951, wrote that the fate of Vietnam would be decided by an elite of forty individuals. War is a great social leveller, but it is also a social elevator.

In Vietnam however the greatest social effects of war were on the family. This was particularly so of the US war. It not only divided the country north and south, but it divided every Vietnamese family, 'especially the downtown families'.

I ask Professor Tran if he agrees that 'reverse reunification' is appropriate as a description of what is happening now. He sees my point without my having to elaborate further, and after a pause nods. 'In some ways,' he says, and quotes Heraclitus. Every great victory leads in the end to a great defeat. Saigon is rich again now, Hanoi is not. Hanoi is still very poor.

'There are so many ironies. After 1945, my father became a communist, a cadre, a *can bo*. Under the French he had been a smoker and a drinker. It had not been such a bad fate, from the personal point of view. But now the communists showed him that in fact he had been a slave – even though he was paid ten times, fifty times what his son earns today. My mother never had to work before 1946. She had servants to teach her children. I had my own nurse. I think I had more difficulty raising three children than my own parents had in raising thirteen! The system that permitted those things was wrong, of course! . . . But from the personal point of view . . .' Professor Tran throws up his arms and smiles wistfully. In the French war his family lost everything. Later he inherited a small house from his father, but that too was bombed by American B52s. He remembers the date: 26th December 1972. Afterwards the ruins were photographed by *Le Monde*, under the headline 'Is it the United States' Military Aim to Destroy the Homes of Famous Vietnam Historians?'

In 1954 Tran enrolled as a founder member of Hanoi University. It took him twenty-five years to become a professor however. At the beginning he taught at a secondary school, and thought of himself as a generalist rather than a specialist. In 1960 he founded the department of archaeology. 'By that time, India already had two thousand archaeologists. We had none, except perhaps myself. The French were to blame.'

I interrupt. 'What took you into archaeology if there were no archaeologists, Professor Tran?' Again the wistful smile, the wave of the hands. 'There was no decision, at least by me. It was fate, just as it was fate that took my father's property from him. One cannot complain, and one should not rejoice. It was fate.' But at least fate worked in the interests of a good cause. Professor Tran and Hanoi University matured together, and the university, he says, leaning forward to touch my arm, has much to recommend it. It is 'a very rare democratic institution': 'We elect our president and the deans, who choose their own deputies. Each department has its head, and unlike in America, he must stand for re-election every three years.' The picture though becomes a little less clear as Professor Tran adds detail. Most of the faculty deans are Party members. Thus it is not unusual for a professor (like himself) who is head of his department within a faculty to have to serve under a dean who was formerly his student, but who joined the Party. 'But that is changing now. Party membership is not as important as it was.' Academic qualifications have begun to count for more. 'And in any case, the system is not so bad. We need younger, more dynamic leaders.'

Leaders? I put the stock question, about rumoured divisions in the 'Red House'. 'One hears reports, factions in the Politburo, and so forth.' Tran smiles, 'I am an archaeologist. I live only in the past. But yes, I would like to see more liberals. For the sake of variety perhaps.' And then: 'At the university, most of the leaders are in the centre, waiting ... What will happen? A university, particularly the capital city's university, is a symbol of the nation's life. At Hanoi University, we try to maintain a relativist point of view about most things. About Great Britain, for example: Madame Thatcher is not our ideal girlfriend.'

The Professor looks at his watch, scans the agenda inside his head. Enough of this idling, he thinks, and slips into a higher gear. What is my subject? I want to know about Vietnam now? Then the Professor will tell me about Vietnam now. Hold tight! But first, to understand Vietnam now I must learn a little more about Vietnam as it was. 'You have observed, you were about to ask about, the role of women. Today there are fewer women in politics than there were during the wars. When Ho Chi Minh was alive, there were always a few women at least at the top. But that has changed since he has gone. You should believe what is said about Ho Chi Minh. He was indeed the binding force, the father. This is proved by the way he developed the Viet Minh as the envelope of the Communist Party. He managed to persuade people of all political convictions to join against the French, even those who were opposed to communism. That I think was genius. But after the August Revolution in 1945 he was sanctified. He ceased to be a person in the ordinary sense. And his closest colleagues became his disciples. Yet one has to look at those men, great though they were. There were three of them. Giap, Pham Van Dong and Truong Chinh. Giap came from a peasant family, a rich peasant family, but the other two were of mandarin birth. Indeed nearly all our leaders have been the sons of mandarins. Perhaps this was unavoidable – since who except mandarin children had the education to lead? But the mandarin element was a fact, and has served to perpetuate aspects of traditional, historic Vietnamese social structure. In the old days there were four classes: mandarin, peasant, worker or artisan and merchant. And perhaps today you can still find them. For example, if a professor indulges in a little trade on the side, then that is frowned upon. In the order of things, a professor should be a professor, a merchant should be a merchant. The two should not be confused. And traditionalism perhaps is at the root of the antipathy felt toward the Russians. Have you noticed how they are alien, unpopular among us? Orthodox communism runs counter to our culture.'

What is forty-five years in a history that stretches back four thousand years? And things are already moving, changing. Both classical socialism (Stalinism) and classical capitalism are already dead. There is a universal tendency toward the middle ground. In hindsight, the origins of Marxism-Leninism are specifically European: the German philosophers, the French Utopian socialists, the British economists. Again, Marxism has even older roots in Christianity. As an archaeologist, those are the layers that Professor Tran uncovers, and is bound to uncover. Small wonder then if Marxism turns out not to be too well tailored to the needs and conditions of the Vietnamese.

'Marxist determinism, Buddhist fatalism, Confucian order, you might think: the same! But there are subtle differences that can become enormous!'

The Professor reaches into his bag and fishes out a newspaper cutting. I think he is about to hand this over, but no, he blows his nose on it, then lights up his umpteenth Dunhill.

'But then I think back to what I once read in André Malraux, that capitalism and communism are one day bound to meet. It must be so. Not in Washington, though, and not in Moscow. But perhaps – who knows? – I am Vietnamese – they will meet in Hanoi! Though not in my lifetime, nor in my children's lifetime, nor in a way that either you or I would recognize.'

Down in the street the familiar figure of Le Tien, stepping off a bicycle. Professor Tran just has time to deliver his summation:

'One last idea I wish to put to you, at the end of our open, free talk. The human way is and always must be between heaven and earth. We are animals, we are angels, we are both, we are neither. But when capitalism and socialism do meet, there will be a new society, a synthesis of all the perfumes of humankind, from primitive times until the present. Perfumes which include liberty, fraternity and equality!'

What on earth is one to make of Professor Tran? The man exhibits an independence of thought I have not encountered before in Vietnam, and will not encounter again. At home, I would regard him as garrulous, entertaining, mildly crackpot and completely harmless. But here? In Hanoi? The question I have to ask myself is: why have I been introduced to him? I had asked for contacts at Hanoi University, but my request was hardly more specific than that. Several possibilities must be considered: 1) Professor Tran is a state-approved stooge, wheeled out to impress western visitors that liberal thought is alive and kicking in the Socialist Republic; 2) Professor Tran has spoken out of turn, has indeed been using me to convey his opinions to the outside world; 3) his international connections and good humour give him a certain immunity; 4) I have misheard or misunderstood much if not most of what he has said; 5) liberal thought in fact is alive and kicking in the Socialist Republic, Vietnam is more pluralistic than I have so far been led to believe, and I should put a stop to my cynicism, my disbelief.

Le Tien comes up the stairs and greets us both as bosom friends. More beer is ordered. Did I know that Professor Tran is a close acquaintance of General Giap? He can help arrange my interview. Professor Tran is a highly popular fellow – something Professor Tran confirms immediately: 'Yes, I am very popular. Everybody in Hanoi knows my face.' By way of confirmation Madame Oanh appears and greets him. They fall into a long, animated and flirtatious conversation. Le Tien explains: Professor Tran has recently lost his wife. He would like another. He is hoping that Madame Oanh will find him one. Since he is growing old now, a young wife would suit. Saigon Man appears briefly in the doorway. I contemplate the advantages and disadvantages of introducing him to Professor Tran, but before I have time to decide Saigon Man has vanished. He has sized up the company at my table, and it is not at all to his liking . . .

Wednesday 25th October: Hanoi – Cao Bang   Up at 5.30 a.m. for a 6.30 start. The idea is to get to Cao Bang before dark. The Russian jeep is almost new. Four of us set out in it: myself, Zoom, the driver Chinh (or Ching or Chin) and Tam. Tam is Zoom's age, and a T'ai ethnic. Supposedly once we're up in the mountains he will provide invaluable additional support, especially if we have to have any dealings with the T'ai *montagnards*. As it will turn out, local People's Committees will provide all the shepherding we need and more, and I can't actually believe the Company doesn't know this already. However, Tam provides excellent companionship for Zoom, and an occasional back massage for me whilst the jeep is bouncing over rock and shingle. The vehicle has a tidy little engine, but next to no suspension. Tam speaks scarcely two words of English, but makes up for this by bearing, at times, an uncanny resemblance to Mick Jagger.

I had wanted to take the old (French) colonial Route 4, via Lang Son, Thatkhe and Dongkhe, close to the Chinese border – to see the several places where the French Expeditionary Force suffered its first humiliating defeats against the emergent Viet Minh – but Route 4 is apparently closed. Instead, heading almost due north, we must take Route 3, effectively a continuation of Highway One, which therefore connects Vietnam top to toe. The flatness of the delta lasts an hour or so, although, unlike the road to Haiphong, the lower stretches of Route 3 are often tree-lined, which breaks up the monotony somewhat. Our first stop is at Thai Nguyen, on the very edge of the great basin fed by the Red, Black and Clear rivers, an industrial city specializing in steel, iron and coal, well laid out, but with a profusion of Sovietski architecture that causes aversion in the eye. Just beyond Thai Nguyen we take breakfast in a roadside shack belonging to an elderly crone who, it just so happens, owns one teapot, four teacups and as many teeth.

From Thai Nguyen the road deteriorates as it climbs, and the traffic steadily thins out until soon there is rarely another vehicle in sight, lolloping bullock-carts and bouncing motorcycles apart. Picturesque wooded village succeeds picturesque wooded village. In Thailand, each of these would have at least one gleaming white temple, decorated with gold, red and green. Here, it is the war memorials that express spirituality, shrines to the fallen heroes.

We lunch on noodles, yam, fatty pork and beer at noon in Bac Can, as the crow flies two-thirds of the way to our eventual destination. Zoom has said that in the far north I must expect to eat only to survive, yet I do not see that his voracious appetite is rebuffed. The electricityless restaurant is a family business, the eating area mostly swallowed up by a vast bed that is a thing in itself. Carved and assembled from a sturdy, teak-like wood, it is a composite of several pieces of furniture. At its head there is a large panelled mirror and an artificial fish tank. At its foot, a bank of cupboards, one of which is glassed and houses ornaments. All the external surfaces are lined with beer bottles, empty Saigon 33s. Just the sort of apparatus, in other words, that would make sense of an average New York bed-sit.

Above us, a wall shrine, crowded with jars of spent joss-sticks. Zoom explains: if a joss-stick disintegrates into ash and powder after burning, then that is bad luck. If it retains its shape and bends a little, then that is good luck.

135

'But surely,' I say, 'it's got nothing to do with luck. All you have to do is buy good-quality joss-sticks in the first place.'

'Of course! Why not?' Zoom laughs. 'Have money, buy better joss-sticks. It's luckier to be rich.'

The bridge across the river in Bac Can is broken, unusable. This says Zoom is our 'first obstacle'. Instead we ford across, the jeep crashing through the water as it slips and scrapes on the stony river-bed. From now on it's mountain country. 'Where there are many mountains it must be very very beautiful,' Miss Hoa decreed in Hanoi, when I called at the Gallery to say hello, goodbye. She is right. It is. Very very. *C'est vraiment magnifique.* A sort of warmed-up Snowdonia, the undulating hills carpeted with luxurious greens of many shades. Glinting streams, accreting mists. Chinh though has his job cut out. The road gets worse and worse. Our speed drops to thirty, twenty-five, twenty, fifteen kilometres per hour. The pot-holes are treacherous. Soon we are all banging our heads against the jeep's steel frame. Tam gives me my first *in situ* back massage. As he does so, 'minority' people appear on the roadside. Mon. Villages are fewer and fewer. None of the houses, or huts, have tiles anymore. Tiles have been routed by thatch. Thick, coarse, grey thatch, like the stuffing of a horsehair mattress.

But all the time we are inching toward Cao Bang. The rolling hills become steep-backed mountains, the landscape phantasmagoric. I begin to understand why the Bac Viet region was the French administration's undoing. It is untameable, can only be lived in by the truly hardy. And anybody forced to live in Bac Viet, by a rampant French army for example, will become truly hardy, invincible. On the top of one mountain I spot – the first sign of the military I have observed – a radar station, pointing north-east. That means we must be close to the Chinese border. Zoom concurs. Now we are probably less than twenty kilometres from Cao Bang. But these twenty kilometres contain the worst stretch of the entire drive: nine kilometres of road that is being remade from scratch. The jeep must negotiate a tract of cut, white, lunar rocks. 'Our second obstacle,' says Zoom. I grip the bars of the jeep's frame, but still I am knocked to pieces. There is no question of getting off the rubble and trying the fields because there are no

136

fields. The road hugs the edge of a mountain. How Chinh manages to drive at the same time defeats me, but for his skill Zoom and I confer upon him the title of honorary gangster.

Suddenly the torture stops, the jeep glides over concrete slabs. A few more minutes and we begin passing the meagre outskirts of Cao Bang. Trails of smoke rise from clumps of trees in the pale gold of the mid-afternoon air. The sense of arriving is curiously strong, curiously satisfying. Already the pale gold is enriching: the surrounding ring of peaks darkens stupendously in the developer's tray.

The jeep stops outside the offices of the Cao Bang Province People's Committee. Zoom returns shortly with the news that while the committee is too busy to receive us tonight, they certainly will tomorrow, and meanwhile would we like to stay at the People's Committee guesthouse? My first-floor room, while not quite on the scale of the accommodation at Halong Bay, is better than expected. The water may not be hot, but it runs freely. There is an air-conditioner that works when the electricity supply comes on (about half the time) and a mosquito net that unfolds. The view too, over the bend in the river where Cao Bang is situated, with leaning mountains in the distance, is excellent. What more could a fellow want? Zoom however seems less than pleased. 'Are you sure it's okay?' he keeps asking. From this and other things he says I gain the impression Zoom is not altogether thrilled to be where he is. I notice too that he treats various minor functionaries with some disdain, and very slightly he pulls rank on a cadre who in due course comes across from the committee to inquire after our comfort.

'We stay here just one day, okay?'

'So long as we get to see Pac Bo I don't care how long we stay, Zoom.'

Before dinner, I look round the town's market, a medium-sized densely packed affair offering farm products and both Thai and Chinese imported goods. Most of the stallholders are minority people, but only the older ones are dressed in the traditional rags of their tribes. The youngsters wear what all young Vietnamese people wear, and it is hard to distinguish them. What is different though is the number of fires that have been lit. No sooner has the sun disappeared than the cold strikes.

Incredibly fresh duck, egg-rolled pork, boiled chicken, bread, rice, bamboo-shoot soup and Chinese beer await our return. Sight of the spread brings cheer to the faces of my entourage. Up country is not so bad perhaps. But afterwards, with nothing else to do, we turn in early. For a long time I lie awake in the semi-dark, pondering Vietnam, the extraordinary friendliness of her people, listening to Zoom and Tam *boc phét* in the room next door. One of them, it seems, begins scratching on the wall. Then I realize the scratching is on my side. A rat, godammit. Also, some strange nightbird enjoying a lonely party on my balcony. But I allow neither to bother me. The bird is outside, and the statistical chances of being bitten twice by a rat in the space of one month are slim.

Thursday 26th October: Pac Bo   I am already up, showered and shaved when Zoom knocks on my door at 6.30 a.m. Today is a big day, the day I visit Pac Bo. The start however is delayed. After a lacklustre breakfast we all have to hang about. A junior cadre, Huy, comes across from the committee to apologize. In the meantime he is anxious to practise his English, which he has been teaching himself. Painfully I learn that in 1979 the Chinese occupied Cao Bang for seventeen days, killing four thousand of its population. Zoom grows impatient, goes off to find out what's happening. He learns that there has been some kind of 'incident' on the border, and that our trip may have to be delayed further, even cancelled. But when I ask what kind of incident, he becomes non-committal, mentions the word 'tobacco', but beyond that just doesn't know. But then another messenger arrives to tell us not to worry, the trip can go ahead. Mr Vuong will be with us shortly.

Mr Vuong, a member of the People's Committee secretariat, arrives accompanied by a second jeep and another driver. Since Huy is coming too, my little convoy, as it sets out from the guesthouse, contains seven persons in all. I sit in the first jeep beside Chinh, with Zoom and Mr Vuong behind. Mr Vuong half-smiles. He is clean shaven, smooth skinned, well fed, and has

138

about him the imperturbability of an angler. Later I learn that he is also a minority person, a Nung.

We drive north-westwards, out through the hills, and presently find ourselves snaking through a valley full of limestone crags the shape and size of those in Halong Bay. The cultivation is various: maize, soyabean, tobacco and fruit orchards as well as rice. Every once in a while we pass a burnt-out building: the remains of a school or a hospital destroyed ten years ago by the Chinese. Hoc An district gives way to Ha Quang district. The scenery once again becomes more expansive, more sweeping. The valleys widen, and lengthen. We stop at a village People's Committee. The form seems to be: to visit anywhere, permission must be 'sought' from the local dignitaries, even though one may be travelling with their superiors. That is socialist democracy. We are invited into the committee's hall, a long hut of a place bedecked inside with red banners embossed with gold letters, for tea and compliments. When the convoy sets off again, it has two more attachments: the local deputy, and his assistant. Mr Vuong proudly points out a minuscule hydraulic plant. Traditionally the minority people of these parts, the H'mong, had to walk all day to fetch and carry water. Now it is being piped straight to them up the mountainsides. Thus we come to the last valley before the Chinese frontier. At the top of this is Pac Bo.

Pac Bo is the place where, when Ho Chi Minh returned to Vietnam in February 1941, after almost three decades of voluntary exile, he first settled on his native soil. He found a vacant cave and moved straight in. From this, for a few weeks, he directed the operations of an incipient movement that would, thirty-four years later, win national independence, smashing the French and humiliating America along the way. Whatever one's political sympathies, it is hard not to see in all this one of the few real epics in modern history.

The jeeps get to within a mile or so of the cave. From then on my entourage of nine must proceed on foot. With Zoom and Mr Vuong at my side, I advance along a path between two paddies. At the end of this are a stream and some relatively smart looking houses. These belong to a community of T'ais, whose parents helped Ho and his colleagues in those early days. The stream is called Lenin Stream, renamed by Ho himself. We walk along its

139

western bank. On the other side is an arching, tea-cosy-shaped hill called Karl Marx Mountain. Then we cross over, to stumble through an overgrown garden. The path leads up, into a tangle of shrubs and boulders. Below us, a slightly milky pool, the head of Lenin Stream, fed by three or four concealed springs in the rocks. Immediately ahead, a gash in the rockface: the entrance to the hallowed hollow.

The cave itself, one has to say, is nothing special. A deep pocket in the side of a mountain (not Karl Marx Mountain) and nothing more. Twenty feet down, a floor of sorts, and the squarish, flat-topped rock Ho Chi Minh used as a writing table. Other, smaller rocks that served as his 'kitchen'. I climb down into it, helped by Tam. The others stand in the mouth looking down. There is, I can't help noticing, a lot of rubble about. A great slab of rock lies right across the mouth, cutting out much light. I call up to Zoom, suggesting that the place could be better cared for. Zoom consults with Mr Vuong, then explains. It *was* well cared for. But when the Chinese Army passed by the Chinese officers, knowing all about the cave, mortared and shelled it, purely out of spite. The lump I am standing next to was deliberately destroyed by them. It used to be a statue of Karl Marx, which Ho Chi Minh himself carved when he lived inside the cave.

I look at the lump beside me. Nothing about it resembles the eponymous father of Marxism. Either the Chinese made a very good job of their wreckage, or Ho Chi Minh was an inferior sculptor. One thing though: its very existence answers, for me, one of history's conundrums. Some commentators have insisted that Ho Chi Minh was first and foremost a nationalist, that he only espoused Marxism-Leninism as the necessary means to the desired ends. This surely must be wrong. Anyone, returning to his country after an absence of twenty-nine years, who carves, out of solid rock, the image of a man must love that man and everything he stands for.

Alone in the cave, I compose a poem:

> *It was the habit*
> *Of Uncle Ho,*
> *When he was old,*

To dress in white.
But when he was young
His habit was red.

Then I climb back out, up into the air. My party has now been
joined by another, a detachment of the military. The two merge.
Having had one inspiration, I am about to have another. Rather
than go back the way we came, I suggest making our way around
the pool at the head of Lenin Stream. My motive is simple. I have
seen a place where clear water gushes out of the rock and I want a
drink. Drinking fresh mountain water is one of the joys of life, and
Uncle Ho or no Uncle Ho I am damned if I am going to be robbed
of that pleasure.

I reach the spot, crouch on the moss, bend right forward, get my
lips around the flow and swallow. Just as I had imagined, the
water is brilliant, particularly on a sticky day in the tropics. I
drink, wash my face, and drink again. Indeed, so good is the liquid
that I empty my water flask of whatever was in it and fill it up
with the gods' own number one. Then, and only then, do I stand.
Everyone, my own entourage and the visiting soldiers, is standing
still and staring at me. Come on, I say, have some, it certainly
won't hurt. And then, for once remembering the right Vietnamese
word, I cry: 'Nuoc Lenin, nuoc Lenin!' (Lenin water, Lenin water!)
Suddenly, everybody wants a drink. My flask (an 'army surplus'
flask, manufactured in Taiwan) is passed round, drained, refilled,
drained and refilled again. And everybody cries, 'Nuoc Lenin!
Nuoc Lenin!'

Zoom particularly is ecstatic. I have, quite unwittingly, done
something the retelling of which can do my standing nothing but
good. Later, as I make my way to the southernmost tip of the
country, to the town of Ca Mau in Minh Hai Province, the story
will accompany me. Often, when I am introduced, I will hear the
magic formula 'Nuoc Lenin!' tucked in among the formalities. And
among cadres, among former VC, among potatoes big and small
alike, among real heroes even, it will always raise a smile, or at the
least a nod of approval. It reflects, not untruly, that a part of me is
willing to be bonded to the people I have come to study.

*   *   *

We walk back towards the jeeps. One of the soldiers points to a high ridge behind us. 'China,' he says. In 1979 the Chinese winched tanks right up over the ridge, thus bringing them into an area where no one had expected tanks. To get into the valley, the Red Army tanks drove straight along the shallow bed of Lenin Stream. Zoom picks up the empty case of a landmine and gives it to me as a souvenir. The building ahead, he tells me, is to be a Ho Chi Minh Museum. Cao Bang Province is doing everything in its power to get the site ready for the centenary of Ho Chi Minh's birth. The trouble is there's no money. That's why so many of the schools and hospitals shelled by the Chinese remain in ruins.

We bid farewell to the army detachment, and stop at a place in the fields where Ho returned in 1961 and met the assembled locals. Then we clamber into the jeeps. Lunch however is taken al fresco, at a memorial halfway back up the valley. The second jeep is crated up with beer, eggs, bread, roast pork and bananas. The memorial, well set to one side of the valley beneath craggy limestone heights, is dedicated to the memory of an early revolutionary 'martyr', a Nung minority man called Noang Van Dem, but better known as Kim Dong. The leader of a group of 'pioneer scouts', in 1940 and 1941 he co-ordinated some 'secret' operations against the French. He met his death – a 'big contribution to his country', according to the memorial tablet – at 5.00 a.m. one day in 1943, while guarding a meeting of cadres. The centrepiece of his monument is a statue of the man, in fighting pose: a somewhat uninspiring, even vulgar bas-relief in the social-realist manner, but which, Mr Vuong tells me, is most lifelike, 'except Kim Dong was even more handsome'. To the left, his mother's grave.

We burn joss-sticks and scatter flowers in a large white dish set, altar-wise, in front of the statue, then, still within the memorial precincts, spread a newspaper on the ground and begin the picnic. Sixteen bottles of Saigon 33 are given short shrift by nine thirsty blokes. The conversation, all of it *boc phét*, rises, then dissipates. When there is no longer any beer with which to toast each other, my comrades for the day raise and chink bananas and eggs. The hilarity, at this place of death, is seemingly unquenchable, until – as though an unseen signal were given – all fall silent for a ten-minute nap. Zoom, usually slow to reminisce, lies on the grass beside me talking almost in a whisper about his own experiences in the military. There was no pay, just food and clothing. A bottle of beer then was a dream.

The convoy sets off again, but instead of turning left for Cao Bang at the head of the valley, my jeep turns right. I am being taken to another site, to get a better look at China. A second valley, even grander than the one we lunched in, is traversed, and we arrive at an undermanned border post. A lieutenant is found, his permission to proceed further sought and granted. He packs into the back seat between Zoom and Mr Vuong, so that once again my entourage is swelled. The jeep rattles on for another kilometre, then stops before an impassable bomb- or mine-crater. We have entered a third valley, broader and flatter than its predecessors. Somewhere on its paddied floor is the frontier. Vietnam here, China there. Until recently, all this was one great minefield. Now, a group of Nung hill-farmers have been encouraged to bring their skills downstairs. The minority people have become a buffer people.

We walk on, along the road/path that hugs the side of the valley. The object is to reach a distant house and say hello to some Chinese. We pass a belt of land that remains uncultivated, uncleared. Nonetheless the tiny figures of two T'ai women can be seen advancing across it. 'Traders,' says Zoom. 'They know there may be mines there, but they are taking the risk. They stick to the paths made by others. So long as there are no heavy rains they should be safe.' Heavy rains are the nightmare of Vietnam, not just here, but anywhere mines have been laid in the last thirty years. During the monsoons the land becomes like a soup. Mines drift, from uncleared fields into cleared paddies. Even today, a mine explodes at the touch of a peasant's hoe every week, every day. Thus, in a time of peace, casualties continue to mount.

'Then why don't they use this path?' I query. 'The monsoon floods can't reach up here.'

Zoom shrugs, but the answer comes a dozen paces on, around a rocky corner. In front of us three sappers with metal detectors. The path we are on is still being cleared, and it is difficult to tell in which direction they are working. Little white sticks have been planted in the ground before and behind them. One of these is only a few inches from my feet.

143

'Maybe mines, maybe not,' says Zoom. I ask to take pictures, and surprisingly permission is given. As I look at the three men through my viewfinder I recall that, in Cambodia, along the Thai border, there was a forty per cent casualty rate among Vietnamese sappers. Prod prod prod. The man with the earphones holds up his hand. Another white marker goes in the earth. Then we turn back. I'll make it to China some other time.

Back in the big valley we climb a hill, a moraine shaped 'like a sleeping dragon'. It commands an altogether worthwhile view. Forty years ago, it housed a French garrison. The sleeping dragon had been turned into a 'hedgehog'. Hedgehogs, bristling with the latest in European arms, were supposed to keep Indochina firmly within the French pale, but it didn't work out like that. On the flat top of the hill signs of a former encampment are hard to detect. The place is overgrown. Tam grabs my arm as I almost fall into the remains of a concrete bunker. There are no mines up here, but still one must walk warily.

Back in '79, an artillery battery, sweeping the valley below, could have caused the Chinese problems. But because the hill had once been French, it was abandoned. A few more years, and the dense undergrowth will have regained the status of jungle.

In Cao Bang I am driven around the perimeter of the old French citadel. Its blackened concrete walls impress me with their size. There was a certain scale to the French occupation, even at this outpost, which one seldom finds in latter-day Vietnamese projects. Then a confusion at the guesthouse. Huy, whom we thought had gone home for the night, hot-foots it from the committee. My party is invited to dinner there. Zoom, who clearly wants some quiet time to himself after working hard all day, is angry. He tells me that Huy has made a mistake, that he is a provincial who doesn't know his own business. At length we reach a compromise. We'll dine at the guesthouse, then join the committee for a film show.

The film turns out to be a video, a piece of propaganda designed to showcase Cao Bang Province and its contribution to the Revolution. I don't know it yet, but it follows faithfully a tried-and-tested formula. It begins with an extended agricultural montage: rice, tobacco, cereals, soyabean production. Then the industrial sector: tin, textiles, a small paper-mill. There are intermittent reminders of the Chinese invasion. The revolutionary history proper is introduced. Footage of Ho Chi Minh's 1961 visit to Pac Bo, stills of other, local revolutionary heroes. Another look at the agricultural prospect, and a flip round the minority peoples: ninety per cent of the provincial population is 'ethnic'. Then the big parade through Cao Bang town. Old T34s, a celebration of forty years' independence. Red flags flying, Party supremos smiling. Cao Bang: the socialist republic within the Socialist Republic. *Fin.* Technically, all the quality of a 1950s Pathé Movietone.

This has been watched by an audience of a hundred *can bo* seated on hard wooden chairs in a long room hung with maps and red banners. Behind the video screen, a much larger than life bust of Uncle Ho, who, from his expression, appears to contemplate the back of the video set with bemused indifference. Zoom and I have been given privileged seats in the front row. The man sitting on my right is Vu Ngoc Bo, the chairman of the People's Committee and also a deputy of the local Party committee. This combination of appointments makes him an extra-special big potato. Yet, when the lights go on, I am almost startled by the open-faced simplicity of the fellow. He is very much a salt-of-the-earth type, and almost casually he invites me to call on him after breakfast.

My acceptance however is not entirely to Zoom's liking. Zoom had been hoping to make an early start to get back to Hanoi.

'We'll just say hello and then we'll be away,' I console.

'Maybe,' says Zoom. 'Or maybe we'll have to stay the night in Lang Son.'

'Lang Son?'

'Didn't I tell you? Route 4 is open after all.'

Friday 27th October: Cao Bang – Lang Son   Sitting across from us at a long table in the People's Committee at half past eight in the morning, Vu Ngoc Bo continues where the film left off. He is anxious that when I leave I take with me as good an impression of Cao Bang as it is possible to take. He also sees to it that I am

145

acquainted with the early history of the Revolution. I am encouraged to make notes.

Vu Ngoc Bo volunteers little about himself except that he is a T'ai, and has worked thirty years for the Party. The rest has to be dug out. He joined the Revolution in 1941 when he was a lad of 14 or 15. In 1943 he left his family to follow Vo Nguyen Giap and Pham Van Dong. In 1947 he became chief of the youth union in Cao Bang; in 1956, a deputy chief of the administrative zone of Viet Bac, the mountainous north-east of the country. Three years later he returned to Cao Bang, where he has remained ever since. He is regarded as a trouble-shooter among cadres. 'Everybody knows me, and respects my early connections,' he grudgingly admits.

Many of these connections are dead. For a while Vu Ngoc Bo tells me about the first communist leaders of Cao Bang Province, the men who joined forces with Ho Chi Minh to defeat the French. But the man he really wants to talk about is Ho Chi Minh himself. 'You see,' he says, 'the great thing is that Ho Chi Minh only became known as Ho Chi Minh when he crossed over from China in 1941 and started living in the cave at Pac Bo. Before then he was known as Ai Quoc, and various other aliases. So in a sense you can say that the Revolution began here, in this province.'

And this was always bound to be. As early as 1930 Ho had decided that the north-east, with Cao Bang at its heart, collared by Ha Tuyen, Bac Thai and Lang Son, should be the springboard of the movement for national independence. 'The mountains were good to attack from, and a safe retreat if operations went badly.' There was the added advantage of the long border with China behind. Ten years later Ho's thinking remained unaltered. With real pride Vu Ngoc Bo opens a book and quotes a letter written by Ho Chi Minh in November 1940: 'Cao Bang resistance base should pave the way for the revolutionary movement in the whole country, because Cao Bang has a revolutionary tradition and because of its geographical location. But the movement should be extended southwards, to take the whole country, so that when we launch our military movement we can attack or defend according to conditions.'

When Ho took up residence in his cave the Viet Minh front, a coalition of anti-colonial forces, was already being cemented. But although the Viet Minh was not an explicitly communist organization, the Party saw to it that it retained control of all the key positions. Many members kept their membership secret. The priority, for all Vietnamese, was national liberation.

Vu Ngoc Bo tells me this with pride. 'The French were ruthless, and at the end of the day only the communists could stand up to them. Only we had the purpose, only we had the ability to organize the whole people.'

The Japanese occupation of Vietnam both complicated matters for the Viet Minh, and gave them their chance. Because the French were allowed to retain nominal control of Indochina, *à la Vichy*, the Viet Minh still had the French Sûreté to contend with, as well as the dreaded Kempeitei. But before being defeated by the Allies, the Japanese, determined to free Asia from European domination, turned on the colonial power. The French were seized, their arms confiscated. Momentarily, in August 1945, there was a political and military vacuum. The Viet Minh, under Ho's leadership, marched on Hanoi and proclaimed a republic.

The Japanese had maintained control by positioning their own troops at key strategic points. One of these had been at Cao Bang. Toward the end of the war the garrison was regularly attacked by Allied air forces operating out of Kuomintang China. One American plane was shot down directly above the town. The pilot (Lieutenant Shaw) baled out and landed in the nearby village of Ngan. There he was picked up by the Viet Minh, and brought before Vu Ngoc Bo.

'I realized at once he was a foreigner and decided to shoot him. But he also looked extremely poorly. I thought at first he must be an enemy, but it soon became apparent he wasn't a Frenchman. At length we found someone who could translate English, and we discovered who he was. He asked for safe conduct, and stayed for two days to recuperate. Then he returned to China. One thing though. He wouldn't eat in the Vietnamese way. We prepared sticky rice for him, but he wouldn't touch it. The next day I saw to it that he had enough food – meat and so forth – to feed ten people. At that time we all thought very highly of the United States, and even though we didn't have enough food for ourselves we didn't want this man to leave us feeling he had had insufficient hospitality.'

147

In fact at this point in time the Viet Minh were being supplied by the Allies. The Viet Minh base at Lang Son received regular air-drops of food, clothing and light armaments.

The August Revolution did not last. With considerable help from the British and the Kuomintang, the French returned in force to Indochina, to reoccupy what they regarded as their inalienable possession. Cao Bang, however, remained what it had been during the critical world war years: a defensive–offensive fastness.

'The Revolution, you see, was always rooted in Cao Bang, just as the Cao Bang revolutionary movement was always rooted in its ethnic peoples. That is why we are building a museum for Uncle Ho at Pac Bo. We think we still bear a debt for the whole country, and we must show ourselves still equal and willing to pay that debt. Otherwise . . . otherwise the younger generations will forget!'

But Cao Bang has other problems to contend with as well. Although economically it is approaching self-sufficiency, there is still some way to go. The potential – tin, tobacco, soyabean – is there, but the technology to exploit it is lacking. Ruefully Vu Ngoc Bo tells me that central government even took away a soyabean processing plant in 1976.

'Probably though this was just as well, for we would have lost it in any case. In 1979 the Chinese came and destroyed everything.'

Ah, China. The chairman's face darkens. China continues to represent a threat. There are still pressure points along the border. Parts of Cao Bang remain 'not so safe for our friends'.

Vu Ngoc Bo describes how, in 1977, prior to Vietnam's invasion of Cambodia, he headed a provincial delegation on a visit across the border. 'I talked to the Chinese. We said we don't want to quarrel with you. The Chinese gave us so much help against the French, against America. But after the war, after Reunification, we also took help from our other socialist friends, and this angered them. I told them we could never forget their help, that we must always be brothers. Then they invaded us. I just couldn't under-stand their position. After all, we are all socialists, we share the same ideology. But when I addressed them, the Chinese just smiled, and said nothing.'

The Chinese however were ill advised. In Cao Bang Province alone their Red Army lost thirty thousand troops. It was the old story, the same as Korea. The Chinese advanced too far too fast. Their supply lines stretched and snapped.

Vu Ngoc Bo himself took the surrender of one Chinese battalion. 'They were so hungry I had personally to supply them with rice. I locked them up in a military barracks. The next day I told them I wanted their photograph taken, to send to Hanoi. Their senior officer refused. I asked him, Where is your discipline? Then he consented. His soldiers stood in a line and we took their picture. Then the officer asked to speak to me again. He requested, nay begged, that we tell China that his men had been captured, and not that they had surrendered. I agreed. Otherwise, when they returned home, they would have faced certain death.'

It is eleven-thirty already and we break for lunch. Before I go, Vu Ngoc Bo tells me, he wants to toast me at a banquet. The banquet is laid on back at the guesthouse. Another long table, myself and a dozen cadres of various levels, including the cautious Mr Vuong. The food is simple and excellent, the vodka and beer continuous, the compliments extravagant. It is hard to get away from China however. Although the 'Chinese war', according to the history books, began and ended in 1979, incursions – 'artillery practice', as it was euphemistically called – continued up until 1987. Vu Ngoc Bo lets slip that there are still eight or nine spots where detachments of the Red Army are still lodged on Vietnamese territory. He recalls with bitterness the 'well atrocity' – 42 old men, women and children dropped into a hole in the ground by the Chinese, who then grenaded them. What makes it particularly painful for the local chairman is that, before the war, many of the local Chinese leaders across the border were his personal friends. In the '60s and early '70s the Red Army had helped the Vietnamese build many of the roads and bridges in the north. Then they came and blew them up. And most probably, Vu Ngoc Bo tells me in between one small beaker of rice-alcohol and another, the Chinese still have spies all over Cao Bang. Who knows which peasant selling apples in the market is working for them and which isn't?

Yet Vu Ngoc Bo remains a happy, fulfilled person. I have simply touched a raw nerve, nothing more. The China problem will resolve itself, he tells me, as, when the midday banquet is over, we stand outside the guesthouse to allow Zoom to take photographs of us with my camera.

The ring of mountains suggests confined horizons. I feel faintly patronizing toward the man. Cao Bang, Ho Chi Minh and the Revolution, with not much else. Yet this feeling is defensive. I am actually envious of the chairman. He is someone for whom life has meant something. His long hug goodbye is not long enough.

Route 4! We make our getaway. It is 140 kilometres to Lang Son, and it takes five hours. The road is not as bad as I had feared, and every bit as dramatic as I had hoped. About 25% of the original French surface remains, but the rest has not been excessively eroded: built to serve a military purpose, its commercial use has been limited. In the back of the jeep Zoom and Tam slap each other's thighs continuously as they chatter away about all the things that add tonic to young men's lives. *Anh yew em*, they insist on teaching me: *I love you*. Or if a girl wants to say it to a fellow, *em yew anh*. Beside me, Chinh confirms his recent promotion to the status of honourable gangster. The needle on the speedometer rarely flicks past the thirty mark, but, except round dangerous bends, it rarely drops below fifteen.

Yet there are plenty of bends, corners, climbs, switchbacks. From Cao Bang the road climbs swiftly and steeply into the mountains. The limestone crags make for a succession of miniature valleys. Where these are flat-bottomed they are farmed, sometimes just a single, pocket-sized paddy-field. More often than not they are no more than inverted cones, extended crevices offering nothing at all for the farmer. Creeper country, tiger country. The road itself is like a ribbon tied halfway up the sharp slopes, often overhung by crags, sometimes smashed by fallen boulders. For mile after mile no sign of human habitation whatsoever, and then a bigger valley, huts, bended backs, the flash of a hoe, or of a long, deadly sickle.

One admires, and pities, the French. To have ever built such a road in terrain that was doubly inhospitable was a feat of guts and determination. Yet to have built it at all was the mark of a supreme stupidity, of a misplaced confidence. At any point between Cao Bang and That Khe (roughly the halfway stage) one could stop and point to half a dozen places where a well-laid ambush

150

would give an enemy an incalculable advantage. And this is exactly what happened, from 1949 onwards. The French had a chain of garrisons, from Lang Son up to Cao Bang. Yet to supply and reinforce these, convoys had constantly to run a murderous gauntlet. In the end the road they had built proved their grave. To the Viet Minh on the other hand, it was nothing but good news. They fattened up on the captured rations, weapons and ammunition that the French so thoughtfully sent in regular supply. And at the end of the day they possessed the abandoned arsenals at That Khe and Dong Khe.

An hour goes by, and suddenly I realize: we haven't passed a single vehicle, nor have we met any in our path, travelling in the same direction.

'I don't suppose,' I inquire of Zoom, 'there are any bandits up in these parts?'

Zoom confers with Tam and laughs.

'Maybe,' he says, 'but I think maybe not. From Lang Son to Hanoi, between ten at night and five in the morning, plenty of bandits. That's why we must stay at Lang Son tonight. But up here – I don't think even bandits would take the risk!'

I'm not convinced, and I begin to relive some of the horrid fear experienced forty years ago by the French Expeditionary Force. In four decades, not a lot has changed, except the road has deteriorated. A puncture I'm sure would do for us. Stop for five minutes, and it wouldn't just be mountain leopards rustling in the undergrowth.

And yet there are delights as well. Once in a while the road goes over instead of round a mountain, and there is a short-lived vista, a thousand-peak ecstasy. And slim green canyons filled with butterflies like water in a lake.

Five kilometres out of Dong Khe an especially treacherous pass, where I don't have to be told that the French suffered a particularly thorough drubbing. Then a descent of sorts into a proper valley, though still none too large, and the clustered dwellings of a shabby town ridden by the granite of another French fort. Gap-toothed ethnic peasants, women mainly, their tight breeches revealing a basic, scrawny sexiness. From behind, impossible to tell how old they are. If they are young, and beautiful, Zoom or Tam calls out,

'Anh yew em', I suspect principally for my own amusement/educa-
tion. They are determined I shall learn the phrase. The women
turn and stare at us. Sometimes they smile, more often they don't,
but one thing is they never frown.

Out of Dong Khe, the previous scenery reasserts itself. I observe
many more places ideal for staging ambushes. In the space of ten
minutes we pass three motorcycles and two trucks, and something
within me relaxes. When the jeep slows however, as slow it must,
every sixty or seventy metres, to negotiate another bend, I notice
the crushing heat. How the hell did a marching infantryman
endure it? I asked myself. *Why* the hell? But of course it was fear
that kept him on his feet, slogging onward, from overhang to overhang.

Little by little the valleys lengthen, broaden, as the road locks
into a now continuous descent. The sensation is not unlike being in
an ancient cargo plane at the end of a journey between continents.
There is population here, scattered, and unexpectedly a river to
our right. That Khe has outskirts. A hydroelectric dam, a beautiful
lake. We have entered the biggest valley yet, eighteen kilometres or
so long, the same size more or less as Dien Bien Phu. After the
mountainous privations, there is a sense, almost, of prosperity.
That Khe itself, another small town, but more dissipated, is charming but asleep. Everywhere is closed. Even the dogs yawn on the
cracked sidewalks. In vain we look for a place to have coffee, a
place to have tea. More French bunkers, more French fortifications,
all overgrown. One or two new buildings that somehow succeed in
looking nice. But nowhere anywhere that can sell us coffee.

Out of That Khe. Empty road, a bend, the river again, a huge
bridge, built by the Chinese and destroyed by the Chinese, jutting
out from a cliff, sawn off, wasted. We stop at a group of houses
and more or less insist that the four of us are served with tea. It
takes a while to brew, but when it comes it refreshes like an ice-
cream sundae. The young of this outcrop of That Khe (which of
course, even today, is an outpost) gather round, and in no time at
all a packet of Ruby Queen vanishes. They're welcome to it. Let's
push on. We push on. Another crawl up into the mountains,
another murderous pass or two, followed by a long lyrical passage
high above the river. The river, says Zoom, turns into China,

152

comes back again, goes back to China, swapping its nationality several times on its way to the sea. More traffic. And then down, down, down, into valleyland, a plain, histrionic summits in the far-off distance, drenching in the gold of an early tropical evening.

We swing close to the border (always the border!), and there suddenly appears a shanty town, a newly sprung line of shacks along the highway, a flashpoint of the new trade with China, which is behind a wall of mountain to our left. Tribeswomen descending the cliff face with baskets on their shoulders, baskets on their heads, goods to bargain over with the drivers of lopsided trucks lined up in front of the shacks. Only the tribeswomen don't reach the shacks. They are met by the drivers, relieved of their burdens for small money, so that they are free to climb back up over the peaks, to collect further merchandise from their Chinese counterparts. Ahead of us now, lorries groaning under the weight of Chinese beer and Thermos flasks and woollen coats and apples and all the other things that Hanoi will require in the morning.

This place is too new to have a name. The jeep is brought to a standstill in the throng of traders. I jump out to take photographs. Zoom follows hard on my heels. Be quick, he says, there are real gangsters here, gangster gangsters. I find it hard to believe, but perhaps he's right. Further on a checkpoint. Excise. The police want to search the jeep, but Zoom persuades them there's no point. My white, western face provides the password.

To the west, more high canyons are turning gold. Dust rising from the road, dust that lasts all the way and into Lang Son. Lang Son a boom town now. Into it, over the bridge that has twice had to be rebuilt. First the Chinese came, then a massive flood. But the long, long market street, steamy, milling, is oblivious to such calamities, man-made or natural. *Dong* and dollars are the only authorities here. An aspect of Asia, hectic and mundane, I haven't seen in Vietnam until this moment, but which I recognize at once.

We thread our way through to a guesthouse that belongs to one or other of the local Lang Son committees, the People's or the Party's, I'm not sure which. Our plan is to get in and out of Lang Son without attracting official attention. Neither Zoom nor I can face another history lesson just yet, and also our papers are not strictly in order. Because we'd thought Route 4 was closed we don't have the documents for Lang Son Province. We could stay at a commercial hotel, in Lang Son there are some, but that would be expensive. Zoom has an animated conversation with the manageress, explains our situation. Eventually we are told we can have two rooms, for $20.

A swarthy type shows me to my quarters. He sprays my sheets with the cheapest of cheap perfumes. There is no running water, only a pitcher full of a tepid liquid that cannot have been changed for days. The Thermos flask is all but empty. I add a healthy measure of disinfectant to a plastic scoop and endeavour to wash off at least some of the grime of the day's long drive. A little dislodges, but mostly it remains in place. We take a filthy meal in a filthy bistro. Having already conceived a robust loathing for Lang Son, I quiz Zoom about crime in his country. What about the death penalty for instance? Zoom replies that the death penalty exists for treason, rape and 'serious murder'. What do you mean, 'serious murder'? Serious murder means any murder that would not be regarded as justifiable homicide or accidental manslaughter in the West. Because there is no civil code, the concept of homicide does not exist. All homicide is murder. Somehow the conversation passes on to Tiananmen Square, the savage slaughter of Chinese civilians by the Red Army in the centre of Beijing earlier in the year.

'Now come on, Zoom, tell me, could it happen here, in Vietnam, in Hanoi or in Saigon? I need your thoughts on the subject. Off the record if you like.'

The routine question unexpectedly pays a dividend. Zoom tells me the story which, in a sense, I've been looking for all along. In a way Vietnam has already had its Tiananmen Square, a student protest at the Transport College, *before* Beijing.

'What happened? Was the army involved?'

Zoom shakes his head, almost as though he thinks he is about to disappoint me.

'Not at all. There was a sit-in for a few days, then the two sides talked. That is the Vietnamese way. Some concessions were made to the students, the strike ended.'

'Just like that?'

'Just like that.'

154

'What was the problem?'

'I think it was money. The students didn't have enough to live on. But I'm not sure.'

'Can we find out? Can you fix some interviews for me? The college authorities, the student leaders, everybody concerned. Someone from the Ministry of Education perhaps.'

'I'll try,' says Zoom. 'Is it so very important?'

'Yes, very.'

Zoom promises he'll try his best. We return to the guesthouse. By half past nine I'm in bed. At twelve I take a sleeping pill. The usual rat problem. But it's been a good two days, a brilliant two days, and Lang Son I can take for one night.

'His bust adorns the country everywhere, but it's not the bust of Mars.' My last thought before the pharmaceutical blackout. God knows why, but I will remember it tomorrow, when I wake up at six.

Saturday 28th October: Lang Son – Hanoi   When I get up there is no sign of Zoom, Tam, Chinh or the jeep. In fact I am kept waiting two hours before there is any sign of them. The staff of the guesthouse are also curiously unhelpful. It takes half an hour to rustle up a cup of weak, lukewarm coffee. I am just beginning to think that my little entourage has packed off to Hanoi without me when the jeep slides into the forecourt. Zoom is sincerely apologetic. He tells me they simply went off to have breakfast with some of Chinh's relatives, nothing more. Probably they have been scouring the market street for bargains – a hypothesis that is confirmed by the presence of new cardboard boxes in the back of the jeep. I don't recriminate, but I keep to myself on the drive back. Being unwashed doesn't help, and the landscape is monotonous paddy-scape nearly all the way. Once again it's good to get back to the Sofia, even though my room has been changed for a smaller one. Nonetheless, after the squalor of Lang Son, its cold shower has all the comfort of a luxury.

I say hello to the girls at the Gallery, walk, work, dine at the Dang Chu, call in at the Thong Nhat. No sign of Stein, but some French relief workers from Médecins sans Frontières provide some company. They have come to help mop up in the wake of a typhoon that has supposedly devasted mid-Vietnam, to the south of Vinh. It's the ninth typhoon this year, and so is called Number Nine. Bernard, a former journalist with one eye for the ladies, tells me that the official death toll has been put at 56, but the true figure is probably half that. 'It's always the same. Any natural disaster, and every death from whatever cause during either a week before or a week after in a fifty mile radius is added to the list of casualties. But it's a poor area, they need medicines at the best of times, so we play along with – how do you say in English? – conniving officialdom.' He also tells me the story of a little Cambodian boy who was smuggled from his country into Thailand. In order that his identity be preserved, his family arranged for a letter to be rolled up in a plastic tube that was then surgically implanted into his chest. The idea was that when the child grew up he would be shown the letter, and could return to Cambodia to find and save his parents and siblings. Unfortunately he developed an infection from the implant and died.

I quit the bar early and stroll the streets. To my surprise, and slight dismay, one of them has transformed, in the space of just five or six days, into a busy night market, offering the now familiar array of imports from China and Thailand. Another bit of old Hanoi bites the dust!

Meanwhile, back at the Sofia, Saigon Man too has disappeared – though not, it seems, without first having left instructions with the night porter. I have to bang on the doors to be let in, but then I am more or less pulled into the unlit downstairs restaurant. There is a female shape sitting in a chair. The night porter points at her. 'Madame,' he says, 'madame you.'

Sunday 29th October: Hanoi　It's a rough night. After three days in the jeep I ache all over. Worse, I begin to twitch. A muscle in the leg throbs like a pump. Convincing myself that this is not the onset of rabies is harder than convincing myself that it is. Am I doomed?

To take my mind off thoughts of an imminent demise I explore a part of Hanoi that is new to me, up above the Lake of the Restored Sword, behind the cathedral. In no time at all I am lost in a maze of streets, many of which specialize: furniture street, metal workshop street, trouser street, the street that makes and sells flags for every occasion. More by accident than by design I thread my way through to the Red River, emerging near the end of Doumer Bridge, emerging also therefore near Mai Trang's brother's house. My instinct is to walk on, but I decide that would be to kowtow unnecessarily to the prevailing wind. The brother is at home, only despondently so. He takes me round the corner to Mai Trang's apartment, a single-roomed dwelling which Mai Trang has transformed into an ersatz bower of earthly bliss. Mai Trang is with her Swedish boyfriend, about whom I remember little except that he smiles a lot and wears a bermuda shirt. Mai Trang seems slightly wary of me (has she been 'spoken to'? I wonder), but gives me a name-card: not hers, but a French–Canadian journalist's, Carole someone or other.

Soon I leave. Hoping to find a short cut back to the Sofia I once more plunge into the Hanoian labyrinth, only to find myself more thoroughly lost than ever. It is only now that I realize I have wanted to get lost in Hanoi ever since I arrived. This peculiar obsession we have of wanting to know where we are all the time, and what direction we're headed in. For a while it's pleasant, it acts as a kind of therapy, an emptying out. But hours before I need start worrying about where I am I begin asking directions. It's stupid, I could have drifted around until seven or eight in the evening, but in the end I don't, and that says something about me I can find little cause to admire.

Soon I am back at the Little Lake (as it is also called). Miss Hoa yanks me into the Gallery, to meet a Yugoslav who haggles endlessly about the price of a stone statuette that would be cheap at five times the price Miss Hoa wants for it. I ask him what he's doing in Hanoi. He says he's chairing a three-week seminar at the university. A seminar in what? In economics, he replies sheepishly. 'Oh don't laugh. I know we're bankrupt too, but the difference is Yugoslavia is not as bankrupt as Vietnam. If Vietnam could raise itself to the level of Yugoslavian bankruptcy it would be doing very well! You have my word for it.'

To my joy, Stein knocks on my door almost the moment I return to the Sofia. We dine at the Bac Nam, droolingly comparing notes on what we've seen and been doing. Stein as it happens has also been to Lang Son, where he was taken to be shown the burgeoning Vietnam–China trade. He went to a 'free zone' which charged an entry fee of 2,000 *dong*, or slightly less than 50 cents. On one point though I have to reprove him. I tell him about my visit to Mai Trang's boudoir and show him the Canadian journalist's card. 'Oh yes, Carole,' he says. 'She's staying at the Thong Nhat. She wanted to interview Nguyen Huy Thiep, but couldn't get approval. So I gave her the address.'

'Thanks!'

Stein peers at me quizzically through his thin spectacles. I explain. In the first place, giving her the address will probably rebound on me, in the second I'd gone to some trouble to set up my own interview with Nguyen Huy Thiep. Now I'd be scooped.

Stein apologizes, which only makes me feel guilty. I don't *own* Nguyen Huy Thiep after all, why shouldn't others see him? One of the bad habits of journalism which is why I'm not a full-time journalist. I offer to buy Stein a plate of papaya at the Dang Chu. Then we go to the Palace.

My curiosity has been exercised by the Palace ever since I first heard about it (from Zoom). Situated almost next door to the cathedral, it is the new night-spot for the young of Hanoi. It is unlike any other building in the centre of the city, being modern, white and dome shaped. In Bangkok or Manila you'd pass it without looking twice. But in Hanoi? . . . Stein and I buy 70 cent tickets at the door and make our way inside. A circular dais for dancing, a circular gallery for eating, a band lined up at the back of the stage and a young man shouting western pop songs. Did I say Bangkok? All that's missing is a plethora of tarts.

For now, perhaps because it's Sunday, the dance floor mainly writhes with dancing families, parents being taught to twist and rock by their six-year-old children. Once in a while, when the singer wants a rest, the band plays a samba, a tango or a foxtrot, and the adults come into their own. They rehearse their steps meticulously, expertly, as though judges were present.

Soon Stein can no longer resist the temptation to test his legs. Willingly he responds to the invitation from a gaggle of Vietnamese youths to join them on the floor. Stein prances, energetic, angular,

158

resplendent. I use his absence from the barstools we have occupied to case the joint. Who owns this place? Where's the finance from? But my questions fall on deafened ears until a Palestinian diplomat, slight and perfumed, fills me in. The money came from Saigon, the permission and the site from the Hanoi People's Committee. A consortium of three businessmen have combined forces with the city fathers – a typical intra-society joint venture.

The singer stops by and, still panting, introduces himself. Joseph. 'I sing only American,' he says. Stein returns, assures me that I'm mistaken in my opinion of him if I think he doesn't know how to enjoy himself, and continues dancing on his stool. Over his shoulder I observe one of the Thong Nhat madames; also, one of the girls Saigon Man tried to get me into bed with. The girl behind the bar asks me why I haven't danced. The reason is because, Stein excepted, I'm probably twice as old as anyone else, but I tell her it's because she's the only one I'd care to dance with. To my surprise, she vacates her post and leads me to the floor. We dance. The girl has a slightly long, well-formed face, beautiful eyes. She moves well. Her hips see-saw gently under my hands. She is young, unspoiled and adorable. At the end of two dances she says thank you and returns to her position behind the counter. More beer, and then we say goodbye. A philosophical spin around the Little Lake. Stein, having demonstrated his serendipity, reverts to serious. He is developing the thesis, he confides, that the Communist Party actually did dissolve itself at the end of 1945, when Ho Chi Minh did everything in his power to broaden the social basis of the Viet Minh resistance. I am not convinced. I remember the statue of Karl Marx in Pac Bo. Another reason presents itself when I return to my room and dip into a volume of essays on *Uncle Ho*. There is a particularly fine piece by General Giap, who recalls Ho Chi Minh saying to him: 'The Party is like a family to us.' Just as the Vietnamese family could split up or bury its wealth for however long events necessitated, so too the Party could go into hiding. Communism was like the family gold. It could be concealed, but it was never abandoned.

Monday 30th October: Hanoi   No sign of Zoom until noon. I

159

begin to fret lest my admonitions to Stein about handing round Mai Trang's address were not as paranoid as I thought. Zoom's excuse this time is that the Ministry of Information has been moving office, and it's been all hands to the deck. This being Monday, he of course tells me that the trip to Thai Binh, scheduled to begin tomorrow, won't happen until Wednesday. He also requests that I prepare written questions for my short list of really big potatoes: General Giap, Party Secretary Nguyen Van Linh and Foreign Minister Nguyen Co Thach. I mildly protest. How can I know what are the best questions until I have seen the whole country? Zoom's response is – never mind, the questions are only for the secretariats, to get my foot in the door. Once I meet these people I can ask them anything I like. We also decide to axe my visit to Cambodia on the way back from the south. Primarily this is for financial reasons, though a couple of reports about terrorist attacks on western journalists in Phnom Penh by the Khmer Rouge help decide me. This trip after all is about Vietnam. Zoom further suggests there might not be any need for me to come back to Hanoi from Saigon, that I might consider flying straight on to Bangkok, but this I resist. What about Linh, Giap and Thach? I tell him that how much value I get from my six or seven thousand dollars will be a part of my story. Zoom sees the point, and apologizes.

'Forgive me, but I must get back to the office. No programme today, Mr Justin. Sorry. Perhaps we'll do something tomorrow. For today why not . . .'

'. . . have a good relax?'

Zoom laughs, is gone. I spend the afternoon preparing big potato questions. Dinner alone at the Sofia. Afterwards I contemplate another pile of books purchased from the charming, hand-grabbing girl in Trang Tien Street, but decide I can't face any more propaganda tonight. I look in my suitcase for whatever else I may have brought with me. Ernest Gellner on *Nations and Nationalism*. Either that, or Stanley Karnow's fat history of *Vietnam* at war. Nothing else. For the first time in my life I suffer a strong craving for P. G. Wodehouse. Properly regarded, books are like medicines. You reach for the bookshelf to right some wrong within you. If you take a lot of books, then you have to take even more, to maintain metabolic balance. There are books that are uppers, and books that are downers. The *Selected Writings of Truong Chinh* are definitely a downer. I need a lightning pick-me-up, like Wodehouse, or a draught of Evelyn Waugh. Or a dose of Dorothy Parker perhaps. Not Tom Wolfe, and certainly not Tom Sharpe. Nor García Márquez. Too narcotic, too addictive. Gore Vidal, at a pinch. I *need* to feel facetious. None of your broad-spectrum stuff – Shakespeare, the Bible, Tolstoy. They should be withheld for emergencies, otherwise a resistance develops. I could do with Doctor Johnson, his traditional cure. But Gellner will suffice. He always does. Once you get into him. Like oil of cloves applied to the cerebellum.

Tuesday 31st October: Hanoi Another no-happen day. Zoom is still shifting boxes for the Ministry – though curiously the offices of his department, the Services Centre, are to remain put. I have a working lunch with Ben Fawcett of Oxfam though. Thus do I partially meet my daily learning quota. Oxfam has been in Vietnam since 1980, when a typhoon that devastated the Red River delta led the charity to donate £250,000 of foodstuffs and materials. In the intervening decade it has set up 85 projects, covering a third of Vietnam's forty-five provinces. The majority of these are seeding projects. Oxfam provides expertise, some equipment and some finance, but only on condition that its funding is at least matched by the provincial or central government. Generally the organization prefers its contribution to be around the 35 to 40 per cent mark.

If you want to know about a place, ask an overseas aid worker. Ben is both well informed and sanguine about Vietnam's prospects. Vietnam, he says, is well conditioned for the kind of programme Oxfam offers. 'Money doesn't go missing very often, and we've enjoyed a good strike rate here. Only three or four projects have failed to bear fruit. Out of eighty-five, that's a real success. In some countries where Oxfam has a presence, the success rate is nearer 50 per cent.' For a few minutes he talks about 'push' factors and 'pull' factors. The one-party state, the struggling economy, frequent agricultural failures in the past. The boat people, arriving in Hong Kong and transmitting a 'very negative' picture of the country they have come from. (Most arrivals are nowadays from the north, but this distorts the reality: those setting off from the south are less likely to reach a 'safe' haven, are more likely to die or be killed by pirates on the way.) Set against the boat people, two million Vietnamese living abroad, by and large in reasonably comfortable circumstances.

Ben finds little to object to in the 'system': 'There is a structure here, which can get to everybody, and therefore includes everybody.' Bureaucracy hath its advantages. I ask about famine and famines. Ben nods. Yes, there have certainly been serious food shortages, although the situation has eased somewhat since the market economy has begun to bite. As recently as last year though some areas of the country were chronically short. Since then, co-operatives have been instructed to retain a portion of each harvest for 'welfare' purposes. One of the problems in the past has been that the government hasn't always been eager to publicize, or even admit, difficulties. The old propaganda trap. A socialist economy is inherently superior, therefore food shortages can't happen, therefore they don't. The view of Vietnam, or of Vietnam's government, holding out its begging bowl at the slightest provocation is wrong. Generally Vietnam could have asked for a lot more aid than it has. There has also been a reluctance to have too many 'helpers' swarming over the countryside, though that too has changed for the better. When Ben first arrived, he discovered that provincial and district cadres had been 'trained' in what they could and couldn't say to foreigners. Now it is much easier to come by essential information. Cadres have been instructed to open up to foreigners, at least those who have come to help. Ben finds he is free to come and go as he pleases, within reasonable limits. Also, he has now been granted permission to open his own office in Hanoi.

I tell Ben that a fair proportion of the UNDP officials I've met have a somewhat less positive attitude about working in Vietnam. Ben says yes, but that's because UNDP operates at central government level, and is indirectly involved in formulating national policies. Therefore UNDP people are more likely to be caught in the crossfire of ministerial rivalries. Oxfam works at the local level, in a particular village or district. There it becomes a question

162

of knowing a need – usually something like a new bridge or a new pumping station – and then devising a plan to meet that need.

Having once worked in the voluntary sector myself, I am curious about what took Ben into Oxfam. Ben, a slight, efficiently built individual, grins. By training he's a public health engineer. His last private-sector job was on a multi-storey car-park in Aldershot. When it was finished he realized that sooner or later it would be blown up by the IRA. That perception made him rethink his values.

One thing though. At the end of our lunch, he requests that I clear anything I write about Oxfam in Vietnam with Oxfam's headquarters in England.

'Censorship?'

'Accuracy.'

'And what if the Ministry of Information makes the same request?' (As indeed, before I leave, it will . . .)

'Censorship!'

As it happens I have dinner with a UNDP man, Barnard with an 'a', a new friend of Stein's. Four of us eat at the Dan Chu, where it's music night. There are three musicians, all male, all slim, all dressed in shabby-genteel white shirts and ties. Their faces are sad, and eminently suited to the schmaltz they play on their piano, violin and flute. The more schmaltzy the music, the more gusto they play it with. Barnard, an expansive, cultured Corsican in his middle fifties, comments that this must be the last place in the East possessed of the spirit of Somerset Maugham. The fact that he is himself palpably a Somerset Maugham character no doubt contributes to this perception. Probably anywhere that Barnard goes takes on a little of the spirit of Somerset Maugham, just as anywhere that Stein goes takes on a little of the spirit of Thomas Mann. Barnard is expecting to spend two years in Vietnam. His background is biology, though neither his English nor my French is able to reveal much more about his project other than that it has something to do with water. Stein speaks perfect clipped French in the same way that he speaks perfect clipped English, but it would be too laborious to get him to translate. In any case Barnard is more interested in telling me about his wife, who sits beside him, the fourth of the above-mentioned four. She is twenty-seven and comes from Cameroon. Barnard married her three years ago. Then she was slim and beautiful. Now she is plump and beautiful. Can one, in this age, speak of extravagant black upholstery without being racist? Or sexist? Barnard's wife's extravagant black upholstery is divine. Even so, Barnard is hoping she will once again become slim and beautiful. That is one reason he has brought her to Vietnam. 'Ooo knows, maybe she catches *la dysenterie* or the dengue, and then, oo la la, she is slim and beautiful again.' Mostly when he speaks about her though he speaks in French, so that she can understand what's being said. Far from resenting his comments, the Cameroonienne, who is called Camille or Ipolyte or Iphigénie, one of those, appears pleased. For a moment she stops eating, smiles her African smile and . . . spoils it by giggling. 'Son problème,' dit Barnard, 'est tout psychologique.'

Wednesday 1st November: Hanoi–Thai Binh–Tien Hai Zoom's on time, as he always is when he has to be, 6.30 a.m. We're off to Thai Binh, in a white Russian limousine, a Lada that has curtains fixed across the back window. The driver is another Dung/Zung/Zoom. Also in the car Tam, and Tam's brother. Tam's brother, who doesn't look at all like Tam, wants a lift as far as Nam Dinh.

'Remind me why we're going to Thai Binh,' I ask Zoom as the Lada sheds pace in the busy early-morning throng of Hanoi bicycles. If I sound bitchy then that's because I mean to. Since Thai Binh is a flat, seaboard province without mountains it's unlikely there'll be any minority people around. As much as I like Tam, at this hour in the morning it's hard not to see him as a supernumerary mouth to feed.

'To visit a model co-operative,' Zoom answers, slightly aggravated by my apparent forgetfulness.

'Is it really necessary?'

'Mr Hong wants you to go there. But don't worry. We'll have a good time. Really.'

'I hope so.'

We take Highway One as far as Nam Dinh, deposit Tam's

164

'brother', and then take the secondary road for Thai Binh city, the capital of Thai Binh Province. It's neither a very long nor a very exhilarating journey. About three and a half hours through flat delta-lands. By mid-morning we are arrived. The secondary road, I observe, is somewhat superior to the national trunk. At several places the national trunk is reduced, for long stretches at a time, to single-lane traffic. Since there are no flow-control lights the only thing to do is position yourself behind a larger truck and let it bulldoze a path through for you. But the way from Nam Dinh to Thai Binh is straight and generous. Thai Binh too is well laid out, with broad, relatively undusty streets. The city was levelled by US bombers, so the slum clearance has been done already. There are many solid edifices.

We are early, but the People's Committee's lunch-break is even earlier. The committee buildings are deserted. After twenty minutes however Zoom manages to buttonhole a youngish female cadre on her way through the gates and discovers that someone has gone over to the People's Guesthouse to welcome us. The guesthouse, when we find it, turns out to be a five-storey tourist hotel. The room, or rather rooms, I am given are quite the best I've had so far. A suite, no less: a drawing room, bedroom, bathroom with hot water, separate lavatory and no rat, and all for $20. Or rather $10, once Zoom has negotiated a special tariff for this 'friend of Vietnam'.

I begin to feel less negative about Thai Binh. I had rather feared having to sleep in an ideal bullock shed in the ideal co-operative, where I would certainly contract malaria or Japanese encephalitis or the plague or all three. Downstairs in the lobby I am introduced to a Mr Thanh, from the Bureau of External Relations. We all repair to a private dining room. Mr Thanh rattles off provincial statistics. I listen with half-ears. There's a limit to the amount the non-agriculturist wants to hear about the rice crop whilst he's eating. I gather that production has increased by 50% since 1986. Mr Thanh, hollow-faced and probably a time-server, makes no bones about the fact that Thai Binh is one of the richer Red River delta provinces. Jute, he tells me, is of the essence, and other crops to boot. But there are also hardships. Once every two to three years a typhoon rips across the paddies. They have just experienced the whip-end of Number Nine. And then of course, the US bombers. Thai Binh city was directly on the flight path to Hanoi, so American pilots made it a habit to unload any unused cargo 'on our heads'.

Post meridiem, the first part of my Thai Binh programme, which has been thoughtfully arranged for me in advance. I am driven, in the Lada, to Tien Hai, an outlying coastal district forty minutes away. Mr Thanh accompanies us. Tien Hai, I am told, is, or was, an important centre in the war of resistance against the French. It is not the promised model co-operative. At the local (district) People's Committee they are waiting for me, three of them: Pham Quang Tiep, the deputy chairman of the local Party cell; Nguyen Anh Doai, the deputy chairman of the People's Committee; and Phan Nhoc Yen, introduced to me as 'a historian'. I am ushered into by now familiar surroundings: a long room with a long table, a portrait of Ho Chi Minh, one or two red banners, a map of the district and a wall chart of production-output figures. I sit opposite the officials as tea and compliments are served. The young historian is twitchy, smiles apologetically whenever he is obliged to speak (which is hardly at all). Zoom whispers in my ear that I should take out my notebook. Nguyen Anh Doai has taken out his, a thick wad of papers. Clearly it is his intention to run through them all for my benefit. The Party man sits silently, terrifically solid, but also wreathed in smiles. Another provincial seminar is about to commence.

Mr Doai kicks off with the economic facts and figures. Tien Hai District contains 2,300 arable hectares and supports a population of 85,000. The main produce is rice, plus a little maize and enough natural gas to power two West German turbine generators. Tien Hai also has 23 kilometres of coast, so of course there are shrimperies too, and an annual production of between four and five thousand tons of salt. The biggest problem is the weather. Up to a hundred people a year die as a result of typhoons and storms, and thousands of homes are shattered. Much manpower must be expended on maintaining and strengthening the dikes. Even so, little by little living standards are improving. Though it is hard to drag small boys from the backs of their fathers' buffalo, 30% of Tien Hai children now attend primary school. Cultural projects that will

166

remind people of their history, and therefore encourage their resolve to build tomorrow's world, are in hand. Tien Hai has a good revolutionary record. Seven of its citizens have received the official designation of 'hero' from Hanoi since 1972. Five thousand families also share the honour of being 'fallen hero families'. There are over two thousand invalided soldiers living in the district.

The three Tien Hai men smile. Beer appears, mineral water, fruit, nuts. The main course is on its way. The farmers' uprising of 1930.

Tien Hai District, Mr Doai continues, was created in 1828, by a Nguyen dynasty mandarin called Nguyen Cong Tru. Under his regime life was tough. Ninety per cent of the land belonged to landlords. The French regime that followed however was even tougher. The French imposed a crippling salt tax (rising from 200 francs a ton to 2,000), and they cared nothing about education. Their only interest was profit. There was also a series of severe natural disasters; 1926 and 1929 especially were years of terrible famine.

But conditions in Tien Hai were no worse than in the rest of the country. It had taken the French thirty years to bring Vietnam under their control, and there continued to be 'problems', sporadic local uprisings. But so long as these remained sporadic, uncoordinated, local affairs, they presented no real threat to colonial rule. The difference in 1930 was that the uprisings were co-ordinated and, if not nationwide, then at least widespread. They did not, finally, succeed, but they pointed a way forward for the Vietnamese people. There was a new force in the land: the Communist Party of Indochina, created by Ho Chi Minh at the beginning of the year. The Revolution had begun.

The point that Mr Doai is anxious to make is that Tien Hai played a forward part in these events, that Thai Binh didn't wait until the bandwagon was already rolling.

The trouble started in Nghe Tinh, a larger province occupying much of southern Tonkin. On 1st May 1930 the whole province erupted. The French were temporarily banished and a system of soviets put in their place. Nghe Tinh in itself was worth nothing, but the French knew that if they didn't act swiftly and brutally they risked a general conflagration. Therefore they acted swiftly and brutally, although it was many months before the last of the local soviets was disbanded.

The incipient Party, which had only been partially responsible for the Nghe Tinh insurgency, looked on approvingly. At the same time it sought to spread the unrest. Tien Hai was selected as being as good a place as any. It was resolved that local Party cells should support the Nghe Tinh Soviet with a peaceable strike. Five demands were to be put to the French authorities: 1) there should be no interference with the Nghe Tinh Soviet; 2) construction workers on the Coc Giang canal (running through the heart of Tien Hai District) should be paid for their labour; 3) an end to the land-owners' monopoly, transferring all land to public ownership; 4) an immediate reduction on salt and other taxes; and 5) no interference in the salt and wine trade.

October 14th was chosen as the date for simultaneous uprisings in three of Tien Hai's villages. Early that morning the people of Nho Lam, Thanh Giam and Dong Cao converged upon and massed at the central market of Tien Hai. They came along the dikes shouting slogans and demands, seemingly from all directions. The local mandarin, Phe Huy Thiep, a French puppet, took one look at the crowd and retreated into his fortified residence with his sixteen armed guards and his assistant, Be Van Thanh. Be Van Thanh however thought that such evasive measures would not be enough to save their skins, and ordered the guards to fire on the people. The guards lined up and raised their rifles. A heroine, Lung The Nguyet, then nineteen or twenty years old, stood forward and dared the soldiers not to fire. She reminded them of the people's poverty, that they were all members of the 'same family', and finally appealed to the mandarin 'not to attack the Nghe Tinh Soviet'. The soldiers listened; then they pulled their triggers, killing eight, including a pregnant woman, and injuring another thirteen. One old man, Lung Van Sang, standing at the front of the crowd, was hit in the belly. Flinging his intestines at the heads of the soldiers, he cried out 'Long live the Communist Party!' before falling to the ground.

Such guts in the face of the enemy however did not deter the inevitable outcome. The 'puppet troops' moved forward and arrested ten of the crowd, including six Party members. The unarmed gathering dispersed, and by 10.00 a.m. the uprising was over. By 12.00 noon reinforcements were on their way to the three villages, on the orders of the Sûreté. The houses were looted, then burned. Seventy-eight more arrests were made, including 33 Party members and 8 women. Finally, the 'colonial army' moved out into the countryside and laid waste the paddies.

The eight who had been killed were buried and their graves put under guard. A band of activists however secretly entered the cemetery and posted a poem commemorating the lives of those who had fallen:

> *These women, these men –*
> *All worked for their country,*
> *Their perfume lingers forever.*

That, at least, was the gist of it. After three days, the coffins were exhumed, by the French, and the corpses photographed. The hope of the Tien Hai's People's Committee is that one day these pictures will be found, whereupon they can be hung in the local museum, a 'story for all succeeding generations'.

As Mr Doai finishes, a junior cadre tiptoes into the room and places a cardboard box beside Pham Quang Tiep's elbow. The local Party deputy rises to his feet and, with a considerable verbal fanfare, presents the box to me. Inside are three Chinese-style figurines, representing wealth, happiness and longevity. They are not the finest porcelain you'll ever see, but, coming immediately after the tale of the uprising, delivered with a combination of emotion and apparent care for the facts, I cannot help being a little overwhelmed. Apart from anything else, the gift is unexpected, and unexpected gifts always do tend to choke me.

'Are these really for me?' I ask Zoom.

'Yes. Of course. Why not? You see, this is the first time a western writer has visited Tien Hai since French times and the People's Committee wants to express its gratitude.'

'I wish I could express mine. Really.'

I am taken to the local museum, a short walk away. Most of the exhibits concern the events of 1930 – photographs, models, farming implements the crowd took with them to shake at the puppet mandarin. Nothing very special. Then we drive to a pagoda four or five miles away, one of the early-morning gathering places of Mr Doai's tale. With the sun beginning to set, the place today has a bucolic magic about it. Some farmworkers are raking rice at the back of the building, on a sort of patio that overlooks a small complex of paddies and irrigation channels. Then we return to Tien Hai and say farewell beneath a tall public statue outside the museum. I have that warm feeling that comes of making new and unexpected friends. The statue, set on a plinth fifty or sixty feet above our heads, depicts a small group of those early revolutionists. One of them has a buffalo horn raised to his lips, summoning the people to the confrontation. Another beats a drum. It's the usual piece of social-realist iconography, but at least I can understand what it's doing there. At least the non-artistic elements of my sympathy are aroused.

We drive back to Thai Binh and dine in a large room more often used for wedding receptions. One entire wall is covered with a crude painting of an idyllic couple waltzing through an idyllic, fairytale landscape. Above this, banner-wise, an exhortation to happiness, *hanh phuc*. The couple however are not Vietnamese. They are Caucasian – Russian, or East German perhaps. We are joined by Mr Thanh, who tells excruciatingly inconsequential stories about Bulgarian and Hungarian foodstuffs. He is an old-fashioned didact of low wattage, but because of the national respect for seniority Zoom and Tam are obliged to hear him out in silence. Afterwards we go *jalan jalan* around the front streets and back streets of Thai Binh. Finding nothing doing, we retire to our rooms. For half an hour I wallow under my hot shower, then I sleep extraordinarily well.

Thursday 2nd November: Thai Binh–Nguyen Xa–Hanoi And so to the model collective. After a breakfast of black coffee and bananas, again with Mr Thanh in attendance, we drive forty kilometres or so to Nguyen Xa village. Today's indoctrination is undertaken by the chairman of the village People's Committee, a

Mr Tuan. I learn about peasant life – the life and soul of Vietnam – sitting across another table in another long-tabled reception room. Mr Tuan is flanked by several of his fellow committee members, one of whom, for a change, is a woman. The first thing to be said about Mr Tuan is that he is young, not at all your traditional village headman type. He is thirty-two if a day. The second thing is that he is so ardently in favour of *doi moi* that I am tempted to call him a militant renovationist. The third thing is that he has a set of full metal teeth. It is difficult to resist the hypothesis that his position has much to do with his biting-power.

There are, he says, getting down immediately to life-giving statistics, 1,530 families in Nguyen Xa. Out of a population of 6,266, 4,200 may be classed as labourers. These are parcelled out among three co-operatives: agricultural, 'trading credit' and crafts (artisans). The village has 300 hectares under cultivation, with an average product of 12 tons per hectare. There are two harvests a year. The whole shooting match is run by the People's Committee, which consists of three executive members (chairman, vice-chairman and secretary) and four 'ordinary' members (the chief of the agricultural co-operative, the head of the militia, a treasurer and a 'land manager'). Prior to 1986, all the land in the village belonged to the co-operatives, hence in effect to the People's Committee. Since 1986, the land has been leased to individual farmers, in the first instance for a term not exceeding ten years. These new short-term owner-occupiers are expected to pay 'agricultural' taxes, irrigation fees, a contribution to the upkeep of the militia and a Labour Day tax. In addition they must make a contribution to the co-operative's own funds. In all, these tithes amount to approximately 30% of a farmer's annual yield. The remaining 70% the farmer is free to market as he pleases. He is not free, however, to build on his land. The house he lives in is separately owned, the area it occupies designated as housing land. On any spare land surrounding its house, a family is at liberty to raise ducks or chickens or any other small livestock.

This package is the reality, the substance of *doi moi*. And so attractive is it, Mr Tuan tells me, that in Nguyen Xa there has been a 100% take-up. This may have something to do with the fact that

171

between the People's Committee and the village Party cell there exist 'exceptionally good relations'.

Membership of the committee is decided by elections in which, initially, all adults vote. The Party cell provides lists of candidates seeking election to the People's Council, and the People's Council then selects committee members. Currently, elections are held every five years. They used to be held every two years, but, says Mr Tuan, that was 'too bureaucratic'. In all there are thirty-two people's councillors, so that every 200 head of the adult population has a representative. In addition, there are 290 Party members in Nguyen Xa, so that all in all the label 'participatory democracy' is not a bad one to apply to the system.

'But can anyone stand for election?' I ask.

'Yes of course, provided his name appears on the list of candidates prepared by the Party.'

(In the old days, at the local level, Vietnam was ruled by mandarins, the educated, landowning elite who had the power of magistrates. Below the mandarins came village heads and village councils. But because the mandarins were not in any sense beholden to the villages, rather the reverse, power was simply and purely authoritarian. In this context, the socialist system is indeed a great leap forward in terms of participatory democracy. Only at the very top of the system – the Politburo and Council of Ministers, which to all intents and purposes are self-electing – is democracy found completely wanting. For the ordinary Vietnamese, mandarinism has somewhat 'retreated' into the clouds. However, thanks to the Party network, lightning can always be transmitted swiftly and ineluctably back down the line, to its furthest hamlet terminals.)

To conclude, Mr Tuan dwells on the 'problems' of Nguyen Xa. These he sorts into four catgories: investment, lack of new grain varieties, management structure and weather. Money for new projects is available from the district bank, but the interest rate varies according to the nature of the loan. If a project is agricultural, interest can be as low as $3\frac{1}{2}\%$; if it is commercial, the rate may rise to 9%. However, the great beauty of *doi moi* is that well-run collectives like Nguyen Xa can become progressively self-capitalizing. This year three hundred tons of rice will be converted into a hundred million *dong* which will be used for improving roads and 'upgrading cultural life'. Other expenses include the maintenance of schools and health clinics. These are not however a very great drain on the village purse: teachers' salaries are paid for by central government, as are medicines and health-care training.

'And how much does Nguyen Xa have to give to the district and provincial coffers?'

Mr Tuan flashes his ironmongery in what I take to be a smile.

'Oh very little,' he says, 'except for specific projects such as irrigation, which of course are of benefit to us.'

'And management structure?'

'We have a very good management structure.'

'You said it was one of the four problems.'

'Oh yes. Sometimes there is a lack of harmony between the managers of the different co-operatives. But the harmony is always restored by the People's Committee. That is our job, so really, we have a very good management structure.'

I am not taken out into the fields to see the agricultural co-operative at work. Instead I am taken over the road to look round Nguyen Xa's village museum. This concrete example of the upgrading of cultural life is similar to most other museums I have seen or will see, except it is on a much smaller scale: photographs of war heroes, pictures of Ho Chi Minh, archaic weapons, a map of the area with a résumé of paddy product. Also, one or two pictures of distinguished visitors. From these I learn that I am Nguyen Xa's forty-first foreign caller.

Finally a look-in at a fifty-loom jute workshop, also close by, a walk round the village war cemetery and an inspection of Nguyen Xa's collection of water-puppets.

'It's a great pity,' says Zoom, 'that you can't see a performance, but all the puppeteers are in the fields.'

Now I know all about rural Vietnam. I thank Mr Tuan for his trouble, and the white Lada turns round.

As soon as we pass the village boundary Mr Thanh addresses me from the back seat. It is not true, he wants me to know, that the village makes only a token contribution to district and provincial funds. On the contrary, 30% of its income must be passed on to central government!

Which is the thing about the deep country. You never quite

know where to expect a hornets' nest. Under a bush, down by the stream or in the back of a Russian limousine.

Back to Hanoi after lunch. In the early evening drinks with Peter Whitehead in his flat above the British Embassy. Peter, a tall man who rarely speaks above a whisper, was on the plane from Bangkok with me, and holds the rank of first secretary. Since the embassy in Hanoi does not normally have a first secretary, and his posting is not permanent, I assume he is a special envoy of some kind, possibly something to do with the boat people. Peter keeps tight-lipped on this subject however: negotiations about what to do with the 55,000 refugees in Hong Kong are at a 'sensitive' stage. He does though fill me in on what's been happening in Eastern Europe, in Poland and Hungary. How, I ask, is the Vietnamese government taking it? Not well, says Peter. General Secretary Linh has issued a statement in which he deplores moves toward liberalization in Budapest. Is that window-dressing, to help Hanoi keep in with Beijing? I ask. Peter shrugs, shakes his head. The embassy is paying credence to Linh's remarks.

'What does that forebode for the future?'

'It's so hard to say. Our view, our observation at the present, is: the government here is anxious that new political formations do not appear inside Vietnam. Partly this is a matter of continuing jobs for the boys, but partly, among older cadres, it is also a matter of ideological commitment being a very real factor. If you're asking whether there'll be a political backlash, then everything depends on the success of Linh's reforms. As you know there is great emphasis on developing state industry, or rather, on developing industry through the state, even at the cost of going into more joint ventures than ideally they want. Either that works, or it doesn't.'

'Aren't they trying to have it both ways? Moving closer to China now that the Soviet Union looks like going the way of all flesh, while priming themselves up as a trading partner for the West?'

Peter's hand pats the arm of his chair. 'One can always look at it like that,' he says. 'More whisky?'

My glass replenished, I try to steer the conversation nearer home. In Vietnam I am dismayed by how little Britain seems to be doing in what is a situation ripe with opportunities.

'The British Council should be here, but isn't. Aren't we being a little too American? Shouldn't we be giving them all the books they ask for? Wouldn't that be a good way of building up a friendship, while disseminating our own liberal culture? If we're not in favour of sanctions against South Africa, why are we in favour of what amount to sanctions against Vietnam?'

Peter listens, but of course there's nothing he can say. Government policy is government policy.

'It's an almost criminal neglect of a golden advantage,' I say in a last attempt to break the mask.

The mask quivers, but does not break.

'Any response that any of us here can make, one way or the other, to a remark like that,' Peter replies in measured words, 'would have to be off the record. More whisky?'

Friday 3rd November: Hanoi   No big potatoes, no small potatoes, no programme, and Zoom at his briefest. A day of reflection, cogitation, 'relaxation', followed by high jinks at the Sofia in the evening. Tonight's the night that Stein, Barnard, his wife and I have a party. To celebrate, a bottle of Johnny Walker Black Label, which until now I have managed not to open since bringing it out of Bangkok. Stein is the star. I persuade one of the waiters, Doan, to clear the floor for a stupendous demonstration of dancing technique, and Stein gives it to them. In a trice the classically proportioned room is full of Stein's legs, and the shadows of Stein's legs. Barnard's wife smiles her African smile. Tonight she does not giggle. Doan turns the volume of the restaurant's cassette player up and up and up, and Barnard keeps saying, 'How colonial, how colonial.' The Harry Lime theme from *The Third Man* fills our ears. Stein reaches out for madness. His movements are cunning visual dithyrambs. Beneath his spectacles his grin profanely elongates. In the midst of his flailing limbs his head is often still, stiller than those dire Bulgarian chandeliers above, which perform a rumba of their own. In a while a waitress, one Miss Hanh I think, consents to take the floor. Having prepared her steps, she is elegant, and an incomparable inspiration to my Norwegian friend. In his hands, she bends back, curving like a length of Plasticine.

175

Stein bends forward. Both avert their heads, toward the table. Barnard rejoices. An attempt is made to lift his wife, but the girl from the Cameroons will not be moved. I offer Doan whisky. Modesty retires Miss Hanh. Stein continues, solo virtuoso. Madame Oanh materializes. Stein dances with her, I dance with her, Barnard dances with her. Madame Oanh dematerializes. Stein takes to his chair, pants, and tells us what he's learnt about lotus tea. Lotus tea, he says, is made from the dew that collects ovenight on lotus leaves. Before it can be imbibed however the liquid must pass another night 'between the breasts of a beautiful virgin'. Barnard nods as he listens. 'Bien sûr,' he says, 'bien sûr.' The whisky is consumed. 'May I?' asks Doan, helping himself to glass after glass. It is his first time to drink neat Scotch. He takes it like rice-alcohol, *chuk xu khoe* and straight down the hatch, one hundred per cent. Gimme another. Doan is very drunk. Who are these crazy foreigners? Where are they from? What are they doing here? In Vietnam? In Hanoi? In *my* city?

He straightens up, blows his cheeks, rubs a face that has turned tomato red. The crazy foreigners are about to leave. Automatically, Doan begins rearranging chairs and tables in their proper order.

Saturday 4th November: Hanoi   Major-General Tran Cong Man is sixty-three. He was born in Nghe Tinh Province, the same as Ho Chi Minh. Many years ago he joined the army. He has fought against the Japanese, the French, the Americans and the Saigon Army. For twenty years he has been a commander, at various levels, including the divisional. Infantry and engineering. He teaches at the Military Academy. He has also, for the last twenty-five years, been a journalist. In 1964 he was appointed deputy chief editor of the the *Quan Doi Nhan Dan*, or *People's Army Daily Newspaper*. In 1976 he became chief editor. He is also vice-president of the Vietnam Journalists' Association. Early in the morning I am taken by Zoom to interview him at the offices of the *Quan Doi Nhan Dan*. We are met at the gates by a smartly uniformed aide. I am about as far from 'Fleet Street' as it is possible to be.

General Man is polite, cordial, but not especially forthcoming. His responses to my questions tend toward the minimalist. He is not a willing lecturer. His paper has a circulation of 150,000, making it the second largest in the country, after the *People's Daily*. It was first launched on 5th August 1945, as a quarterly. It became a daily in 1965. Most of the articles it carries are about army activities, but it also provides commentary on economic and political affairs. Since 1975, it has become more 'vivid'. On occasion it has even offered criticism of political errors, and criticized selected leaders. In 20% of cases such criticisms have led to an 'improvement'. In 25% of cases they have been disapproved of. Man reminds me that General Secretary Linh has spoken out against the 'silent majority' in Vietnam. However, 'between the *Army Daily* and the Politburo there exists no real conflict. Rather, there is a feeling of fellowship between the two bodies.'

Man supports *doi moi*, but prides himself on having been among the first to attack 'black videos' two years ago. *Perestroika* without *glasnost* should indeed be the nation's goal. Discussions at last month's sixth congress of the Journalists' Association reflected some of the problems associated with an 'open door' policy. At the conclusion of the congress it was agreed that literature (*sic*) must 'continue to serve the interests of the country'. Journalists agreed to promote 'social love' and 'non-violence'. They also agreed that it was important to curb the excesses of some of their own 'emotionalism'.

'We must be responsible for our society, and for our work,' says Man, wearing both his hats.

I ask about the army. Man tells me the army is shrinking, now that troops have been pulled out of Cambodia. This is in line with the new humanitarianism of government policy. (He does not mention the unwillingness of Moscow to go on subsidizing the Vietnamese military, according to some analysts the major reason for Hanoi's decision to withdraw from Phnom Penh.) Very soon Vietnam's army will no longer be the world's fourth largest. Already it has fallen below a million men. In 1975 the figure stood at 1,700,000. Now, half a million have been demobilized. In the short term this means a dramatic rise in unemployment, but General Man hopes provincial authorities will find a use for such manpower. The demobilized should be regarded as 'economic troops', fit to reconstruct the country's ailing infrastructure. Some are being sent to Eastern Europe to learn new skills. Care is being taken to ensure that ex-officers are placed in 'suitable positions'.

We discuss China. The General becomes almost brittle. In reply to my question, could Tiananmen Square happen in Vietnam, he answers no, most certainly it could not. There is a historic bond between the people and the army, the people trust the army, there is strong mutual involvement, the army would never turn upon those it is its duty to protect. Also, the people would never create an atmosphere in which the army might feel obliged to act. He recalls an incident in 1954, after the French withdrawal. There was hostility against the Catholic population in the North. The army moved promptly to protect the Catholics, but they did so without weapons. 'That was one of our victories.' The General reminds me of the many elements that go to make up Vietnam. Catholics, Cao Dai-ists, the minorities . . . Vietnam is a pluralist society. He agrees that the process of reunification has yet to be completed, and that there remain some groups that are 'very right wing'. But he sees no need for military interference at the moment. And if there were to be interference, then it would be 'non-violent'. All of which makes Vietnam a very different proposition to its mighty neighbour. In the past, China and Vietnam were good friends. 'Our two armies had good connections, and we learned how much the Chinese Army contributed to Chinese development. But now all that has changed. The friendship finished in 1979, and the Chinese leadership have put the interests of China's military above the interests of the Chinese people. That is the opposite of how matters stand in Vietnam.'

Chinese belligerence remains a threat. The policies of the superpowers and the economic situation have seen to that. But fortunately, at the present time, 'China is not strong enough to attack Vietnam, which perhaps is why her army attacks her own people.' Yes, there is tension in the Spratly Islands (in the South China Sea), but no fighting between the two nations at the moment. The archipelago is divided. Half the islands are under Chinese control, half under Vietnamese. The Spratlys however remain a potential flashpoint. 'The Chinese are used to setting traps. They know very well how to provoke an incident, so it is important we exercise vigilance and restraint.'

We try other topics. We talk about joint ventures, Thailand, the orderly departure programme for Vietnamese wishing to leave for America, the unlikeliness of an early normalization of US–Vietnamese relations. The General relapses into platitudes. He offers nothing new, nothing that provokes thought. By pre-arrangement Zoom lingers behind when I leave. He slips General Man 20,000 *dong* wrapped up in a piece of newspaper. About $4.30 c. That it seems is the going rate for an hour's worth of a major-general in Hanoi. It's the only interview I knowingly pay for. A whore for the same period of time costs 40,000 *dong*, or so I'm told.

But one must have some sympathy for the editor of the country's number-two newspaper. Younger cadres can take time off to sell apples in the market. The more senior you get, the harder it is to earn money on the side. Everyone must improvise the best he can. I've heard of at least one senior Vietnamese diplomat who necessarily works as a carpenter in his spare time.

Lunchtime. In search of Stein, I run into a curiously unsettling individual, name of Nigel Cawthorne, at the Thong Nhat. Since Stein is not to be found, I sit at his table. He is writing a book about MIAs (American soldiers listed 'missing in action'). He is determined to demonstrate what has never been adequately demonstrated before, namely that some of those MIAs are still alive and being held either by the Vietnamese themselves, or by the Russians. The crux of the matter he asserts is a letter written by President Nixon in 1973 promising Hanoi $3.25 billions in war reparations, subject to congressional approval. (Congress did not approve.) The living MIAs are being held hostage, against payment. Washington prefers to keep this under wraps because it doesn't want any further attention to be drawn to Nixon's pledge.

Cawthorne tells me he has a copy of this letter, but backtracks when I ask to see it. (In fact Nixon's pledge is already well documented.) Then he expatiates on his theme, spinning a web of intrigue that is at once fantastically complex and egregiously naïve, so that after a while I begin to wonder what it is he wants to convince me of: the survival of some MIAs (including, it would seem, some nuclear physicists) or the existence of UFOs? The only plausible moment comes when he puts the question, why is it that all the American prisoners of war who were returned to America in

1973 were in full possession of all their limbs? 'Surely you would expect some of them to have lost an arm or a leg in battle before being captured?'

'But then surely too,' I quiz, 'if the United States thought there were still POW camps in the jungle it could detect them with its satellite surveillance systems.'

'Of course it could. Which is why it doesn't. If Washington could prove the existence of such places, then it would come under pressure from the MIAs' relatives to make good Nixon's promise. And the last thing Americans want to do is pay Vietnam a single cent.'

'But I thought a lot of Americans are outspoken in their insistence that such camps exist?'

'Yes. But they are *different* Americans.'

Little by little Cawthorne backs himself into an incredible maze of supposition and evasive counter-argument.

'How on earth did you get a visa?' I ask at length.

'Easy,' says Cawthorne. 'I applied for one. I sent the Ministry of Information a copy of my first draft, and they invited me to come . . .'

'So you could see for yourself there's nothing doing.'

'Exactly!'

'But you of course will prove them wrong.'

Cawthorne doesn't answer, he just grins. His face is very modern. The back of his head is straight, his cheekbones are wide, and he sports a pencil moustache. He is clean-shaven and wears the sort of shirt that might not look out of place on Waikiki Beach. My instinctive inclination is to dismiss each and every one of his theories as so much tripe. So at any rate I tell him, though the effect of my reproof is so much water off a duck's back. But this also says something about myself. After a month in Hanoi I am quite prepared, it seems, to take the line the Vietnamese would wish me to take over what is a sensitive issue.

Sunday 5th November: Hanoi What Cawthorne hasn't told me is that he has entered Vietnam in the slipstream of Tim Page. So at any rate Tim Page tells me. Page is a revenant, a part of the

180

'Vietnam' I'm here to deconstruct. Most people think he's a madman who nourishes a hyperactive death-wish. He came to Vietnam at the height of the war as a teenage photographer in search of adventure. He found so much he's never been the same since. He took his cameras so close to the action that several times he was almost wasted. Many professional soldiers would be proud to show the number of wounds Page can.

The details are recorded in his autobiography, *Page after Page*. I haven't read *Page after Page*, but if I ever see a copy then I will. It is highly recommended by its author. When I discover Page holding court in the lobby of the Thong Nhat soon after six he is doing just that: highly recommending his autobiography. 'As usual you see I'm broke,' he says as soon as Cawthorne, playing the part of Page's social secretary, has introduced us, 'so why not get yourself a copy?' There is a group of Scandinavian photo-journalists hanging on his every word. Like me, they first encountered Page in Michael Herr's *Dispatches*, where he comes across as the lone Brit trying, and generally succeeding, in outflanking the Yankee combat junkies. 'Take the glamour out of war!' Herr quotes him as saying:

> I mean, how the bloody hell can you do *that*? Go and
> take the glamour out of a Huey, go take the glamour out
> of a Sheridan . . . Can *you* take the glamour out of a
> Sheridan . . . Can *you* take the glamour out of a Cobra or
> getting stoned at China beach? It's like taking the glamour
> out of an M-79 . . . Ohhhh, war is *good* for you, you
> can't take the glamour out of that. It's like trying to take
> the glamour out of sex, trying to take the glamour out of
> the Rolling Stones.

'No,' says Page to one of the Scandinavians, 'I don't do many royal weddings.' Not only does he talk the way Herr has him talk but he also talks the way he writes. Page doesn't have a copy of his autobiography with him, but he does have a copy of *Tim Page's Nam*, a deluxe paperback selection of some of his better war pix, accompanied by a dancing dervish of a text. This he hands round, just in case there's anybody who doesn't know who he is. When you've been made to rub bellies with death three or four times you're entitled to your fame. Having bought my own copy a year ago I restrict myself to just a few lines of Page's prose before passing it on: 'I am not sure if most, even in the depths of the soul-searching hawk and dove debates, really weren't out there mainly for the hell of it, for the kicks, the fun, the brush with all that was most evil, most dear, most profane; maybe we were there because we had to be, because it was there.'

'Sometimes,' says Page, to no one in particular, 'I feel my fate is bigger than this country.' Cawthorne smiles. His protégé, who must be getting on for twice his age, is performing well. Then Page, to substantiate the point he has just made, or to gloss the joint he has just rolled, tells everyone about a meeting he had with General Giap, down in Ho Chi Minh-ville (Saigon) in 1985. Giap agreed to have his photo taken by Page one hour before Page was due to fly out to Thailand. Because he'd given up on meeting Giap, Page immediately rolled himself two joints. The best Thai-stick money could buy, or somesuch. The second of these he was still smoking when he entered the room where Giap was waiting for him. 'In my excitement I omitted to put a stub on the roach. I also began tripping over my own wires. I started rolling across the floor, but I still had my camera in my hand so I started flash-zapping like a machine-gun because I didn't know when the General would kick me out.' But Giap didn't kick him out. Giap was rather tickled by this fellow who arrived puffing marijuana and took photos of him from under a table. There and then he dubbed him 'Professor Can Sa'. *Can sa = gan cha* = grass = weed. Page tells everyone to look at his lapel, where he's got the words sewn into his blue denim waistcoat. 'There's the proof,' he says. He also hands round his joint. What he doesn't say is that he has a doctor's prescription for the stuff. It's the only thing that can keep a man who has been shot five times on the rails.

Meanwhile Stein has appeared. He looks at Page's book while listening to the tail-end of Page on Giap. Stein solemnly asks if Giap has seen *Nam*. Page nods.

'And did he indicate which photographs he liked best?'

Page nods. 'The one with the soldier grinning as he sniffs the bone of a dead VC.'

182

'How interesting,' says Stein. 'How very very interesting.'

'Yeah. He said it was the picture that most showed the callousness of the Yanks toward his people.'

'But surely he couldn't have said he *liked* it . . .?'

There is a sort of pause while Stein and Page look at each other and wonder whether what they see is in any sense real. Quickly, and unfairly, I introduce Stein as the only Marxist I've met so far in Vietnam, hoping Page will laugh and forget Stein's pedantic query. Instead Page gears into one of his set-pieces. From Marx to Marxism is a short step, and from Marxism to every other kind of -ism is even shorter. Page preaches the death of all -isms, that's what's happening in the world now, Marxism, liberalism, capitalism, shamanism, every four-lettered -ism in the book is swilling its death juice, haven't you read your television lately, haven't you read your radio? Stein parries, but Page is adamant, Page is dogmatic. Isms are out. That is his dogmatism. His speech is vigorous and vivid, but lacks subtlety. Suddenly he swerves off into a diatribe against his fellow photographers. They come to Vietnam in choppers and their feet never touch the ground. A good photojournalist gets out among the people. Otherwise – Page abruptly swerves back again – he's just another ism-monger.

'I think I can understand what you want to say,' says Stein. 'But is there not a risk that if you get out amongst the people too much you will over-reflect a popularist-romantic notion of what the country is?'

'Uh?' says Page, having to think for a moment. Then, with magnificent lateral-mindedness, he pronounces: 'It's like this MIA thing. Sure there are a few hundred Americans unaccounted for. But think of the millions of Vietnamese who wound up shrouded. People will always care more for the very few than they will for the very many.'

Stein and I slope off to the Dan Chu for a somewhat downbeat dinner, but not before I have cadged a photo-call off the hero of the moment.

'Sure,' says Page. 'I'll portrait you. But not until six-thirty tomorrow morning. Sometime between then and nine the light'll be fine. There's no other time.'

*   *   *

183

Monday 6th November: Hanoi   The thing about Tim Page is that at heart he's a great big softie. Corny, but true. At around two in the morning there's a power cut that lasts until four. During this time it's impossible to sleep. I rotate in my narrow bed in a lather of my own sweat, serenaded by invading mosquitoes. Then my fan starts up again – there's no conditioner in the smaller rooms at the Sofia – and I sleep until 5.30 when a dog that crows like a cock or a cock that barks like a dog wakens me. At least it's not raining. I ask myself if having one's photograph taken by Tim Page is really worth getting up so early for, but before I can decide I fall asleep again. I dream I am on board a submarine that is making a geological survey underneath a football stadium where some great leader is addressing an enormous crowd of chickens. At 6.12 I wake up a third time. The answer is yes, I want Tim Page to take my pic. At 6.30 I stumble anticlockwise through the revolving door of the Thong Nhat fully expecting Page to be nowhere in sight. In fact he is there, sitting heavily in one of the wooden chairs. He looks up and smiles. At this time of the day his voice is flat, his remarks mundane, stripped of any argot. 'We had a power cut here last night,' he begins. 'You're lucky I decided to get up.' We order *caphé den*, black coffee, as opposed to *caphé xua*, white. Remarkably, it is served within the minute. Then we set off for the Opera. Tim has decided to make a session of it. He wants a bag of Hanoi shots for his library. Perhaps he'll flog them to *Elle* magazine.

On his feet he limps. He also can't hear out of one ear, and only one of his eyes is good for taking photos with. The old head wound. To have any conversation I have to walk on his right. On average he stops every ten paces to photograph someone or something. He is a tall figure and there is something comic about the way his long lenses home in from what must seem like the sky to the early bicycle-tyre mender he wants to capture. You can tell if Tim really wants to photograph what he is taking, because only then does he reduce his elevation. Lowering himself is painful, crouching hell. Mostly he keeps upright. He struts forward. There is something splendid about his well-groomed raffishness. He is forty-five, and has a mop of well-brushed silver-grey hair. His spectacles are a touch too optical to be entirely elegant. There is a

184

Union Jack as well as 'Professor Can Sa' sewn onto his waistcoat. He has gone to some trouble to make his non-conformity apparent. He also likes to talk. Mostly he talks about himself, but then I lead him anyway. The 'insanity', he tells me, started in Laos, where he spent a part of his childhood. It was in Laos that, aged sixteen, he 'died' for the first time. The second time he died was when he was pronounced brain-dead on his arrival at the Saigon Military Hospital, having been strafed by a USAF pilot who'd gone berserk. That was the most serious of his deaths. When he was well enough he began writing up what had happened to him. Then the authorities sent him his hospital bill. He sent the bill back with a copy of his report attached and never heard another word.

Having been shot-up three times already in Vietnam, he returned in 1968 after the beginning of the Tet Offensive. 'I couldn't bear seeing all my friends' pictures appearing in the magazines and not being there myself. Also there was a question of money. In my first week back here I earned $5,000.'

We pass the Opera House and cross the big road, Tran Quang Khai, that runs parallel with the Red River. We climb over a steep bank, and down into the belt of slums beyond. At once we are made a big fuss of by countless children. Page continues to photograph everyone and everything. Whenever he can he leaves them with a smile. 'Otherwise,' he says, 'it's like killing them, like zapping them.' He is particularly pleased with an old woman who sits on a tiny stool beside a brown cow that stands side-on under the thatch of a more than averagely grimy hovel. We thread our way through to what used to be the landing-point for a cross-river ferry, and is now a human toilet area. 'This will do.' Page asks me to squat Vietnamese-style on the slippery slope, so that he can get both bridges behind my head. But it's easier said than done. On a flat surface I can just about manage the heel-squat, but not on a one-in-two gradient. 'It's your jeans,' says Page. 'You should stop wearing jeans.' 'It's not my jeans, it's my hamstrings.' Page takes his time, clicks his camera twice, then gives up. It's impossible for me to relax my face. 'We'll try again later.' We hit the main thoroughfare of the Red River village. A considerable crowd has gathered twenty or thirty paces in front of us. Many brightly coloured vertical banners, reds and blues with gold lettering. A lot

185

of people dressed in white, with white bands around their fore-heads, and a musician who produces a caterwauling wail from a curious, shawm-like instrument.

'How terribly fortunate,' says Page, 'a funeral!'

He dives into the mêlée. Inside the house, the funeral parlour, which is on a corner of the street, a local photographer is taking shots for the family album. I watch Page's head bob up and down just above the milling crowd. Nobody seems to mind his intrusion. Death in Vietnam is not a particularly private affair. The more people who pay their respects to the dead person, the more honour accrues to the family. In this case the dead person is a fifty-seven-year-old male. As the wailing music rises, the relatives and well-wishers jabber more and more excitedly. Some of them, one would have to say, are even merry. Page pushes his way right inside the building, disappears. Outside a traffic of trucks and motorcycles hoots and toots its way through the congestion. I keep to the periphery of the crowd, guarding Page's spare camera and lenses. Some girls begin making friendly eyes at me. A gaudy wreath drops in the dust, but is quickly snatched up again and shaken down. In a while Page reappears at my side. Do I remember the picture of the grief-struck women in the book he was passing round last night? 'Well, I've just improved on it, I've just gone one better. How fucking fortunate this funeral is!'

We head back over the dike and find a place that sells coffee. As I sit on a nine-inch-high stool Page takes my portrait. 'Say Turkish delight and think of something sensual.' But it's not until a Viet-namese in a cadre helmet lights up a cigarette behind me that Page gets what he's after. 'You'll like that one,' he promises, putting a match to his own kind of cigarette. 'That funeral. It's drained me. It fucking has. You've no idea. I mean the effort it takes to control something like that. You really have to get your Zen-set right.'

Zen-set? Or do I mishear? Is it something technical, to do with his lenses perhaps? I hesitate to ask. Page has already made one comment about my never having worked with a photographer before, after I pass him the wrong camera for one of his street shots. But then I've never been a golf caddy either.

We set off again. The light is already losing its depth as the day-volume rises. The streets are now alive with Chinese goods and all

186

the people who buy and sell Chinese goods. It's close on 8.30 a.m. Page takes fewer and fewer photographs. A basket of ducks, an outdoor barber's chair, once the ejector-seat of a US Starfighter. People no longer interest him. Except perhaps myself. 'I hear you're writing a book about Ho Chi Minh?' he asks. 'Where'd you hear that?' I reply. 'In Oxford,' says Page. In Oxford! But Page pushes on with an explanation of what he was doing in Oxford in the first place. He was a guest of the Oxford Indochina Committee. One of its members was once French Ambassador to Cambodia, so probably it was she who'd heard about me. Page is not just in Hanoi to take photographs, Page says. There's a new scheme afoot to solve the boat people problem and help the Vietnamese economy in one stroke. The idea is: create half a dozen special economic enterprise zones, like free ports, and give the boat people special economic status inside those zones. This will surely encourage the refugees to return to their country. Somewhere along the line, Page intimates, Oxfam is involved, to give the scheme cachet. Page is acting as an intermediary. Freelancers often are used as intermediaries, Page comments: it makes the Vietnamese feel more comfortable.

'You don't really believe the government would give the boat people any status, let alone special economic status, do you?'

Page pauses to snap a goat tethered to a barrow full of cabbages.

'Probably not,' he says, 'but you must agree, it's a brilliant, brilliant idea.'

'The only brilliant idea is the idea that works,' I can't help remarking.

'This works,' says Page, patting his camera and putting it back in its case. We have reached the Lake of the Restored Sword and are about to go our separate ways. 'Though maybe you're right. The boat people are like the new Vietnamese. It seems reasonable to suppose that maybe twenty or thirty of all those Americans who came to Vietnam stayed behind of their own volition. Of course, that's a totally insignificant number compared to the gross numbers involved. But America wouldn't want them back any more than Hanoi wants 55,000 of their own back from Hong Kong.'

I have about half an hour to myself at the Sofia before Zoom arrives to take me off for the morning's work. This is my last day in Hanoi. Tomorrow we set off for the long journey down Highway One to the south. Zoom confirms that everything is ready, that all the necessary plans have been made.

'But I must tell you, I can only come with you as far as Hué. After that Truc will be your interpreter. I'm sorry, but Mister Hong insists. There's so much work for me here. In fact he didn't want me to go at all, but I told him, I must be the one to show Hué to Mister Justin.'

'Who's Truc?'

'Haven't you met him? He works for the Company. He was in my class at the Foreign Languages College. He's very good, don't worry. And from Hué there'll also be Mister Sau to look after you. Mister Sau is Number One in the whole of Nam Bo. You'll understand when you meet him. He's a driver too. Mister Nam will drive us down to Hué, then Mister Sau will take over.'

The prospect of Vietnam without Zoom doesn't hearten me, nor does a sudden change in the weather. By the time Mr Nam drives the minibus into the compound of the Vietnam Documentary Film Studio, in the west of the city, a cold rain is bucketing down. Today's potato is Lu'u Xuan Thu, the studio's director and, according to Zoom, a 'high honour artist'. Thu is a big bustling man in his early to mid-fifties who wears thick-framed media spectacles and laughs a lot. Indeed he laughs so much that it becomes hard to reconcile what he says, or what Zoom tells me he is saying, with its source. We are joined in his office by a man called Sy Trung, an assistant scriptwriter and director. Sy Trung also laughs, but cautiously. He listens to what his boss has to say, waits for the laugh and then joins in.

The rub of it is that, since *doi moi*, documentary film-making in Vietnam has not done well. The government thinks the studio should earn most if not all its keep, even though its principal role is to produce propaganda for the government. However, revenue is hard to come by. This is largely because as more and more people have a choice of watching imported videos, 'black' or otherwise, more and more people are not watching state propaganda. Nor do the cinemas have any appetite left for documentaries. The argument is that if people want to watch documentaries then they can sit at

188

home and watch the television, if they're unlucky enough to have one. But alas, the state-run television service, which used to be the studio's keenest customer, has less and less money with which to buy its product. It too has been told to rationalize its finances.

Lu'u Xuan Thu heaves and shrugs his shoulders mightily. But then from the look of him, he has spent most of his life heaving and shrugging. He is a born heaver and shrugger.

The revolutionary film industry began in 1945, as soon as Ho Chi Minh's forces had entered and taken Hanoi. The Viet Minh leadership had a keen appreciation of the power of celluloid. In 1946, with a handful of films, a special mobile projection unit commandeered a railway carriage and piggy-backed rides at the rear ends of trains using the Tonkin rail network. The carriage would be uncoupled at each town, and a film show mounted in the station yard. The audiences, sometimes running into four figures, would come in from the surrounding countryside, often walking days to reach the 'cinema' on wheels. However, as the French regained the cities, this was discontinued, and the film unit, like every other wing of the Viet Minh, retreated into the mountain fortress of the Viet Bac.

Guerrilla units liked, whenever they could, especially in Cochin-china, to record their ambushes and other strikes at the colonial power. Developing remained a problem, but eventually a method was found, in the Eighth Zone, which involved a wooden tub with a man shut tightly inside. In the warm climate of the Mekong Delta, however, it was too hot for the technique to work. The way round this was to pack the outside of the tub with ice. But ice was only manufactured in Saigon. At first attempts were made to bring ice to the delta site, but too much of it melted. Instead therefore the tub was loaded on a boat and taken within easy reach of the city, greatly adding to the risk of detection.

The decisive breakthrough came after the Chinese Red Army had swept Mao Tse Tung to power across the border, and French control of the frontier was compromised. With the Viet Minh firmly established in the north-east of the country, supplies of equipment and stock, from Russia as well as China, became plentiful. The film unit was now, famously, given its own 'village', at a place called Palm-Tree Hills. In May 1953 Ho Chi Minh decreed the State Enterprise of Cinematography and Photography, under the supervision of the Ministry of Propaganda (as the Ministry of Information was then called). The following year, the Battle of Dien Bien Phu was turned into something of a cinematic epic, with Viet Minh cameramen holding their own at key points throughout the fighting.

Thu's office is lined with photographs of 'fallen cameramen'. The studio's heyday was in the American war, when its propaganda presentations undoubtedly did contribute to North Vietnamese morale. The immediate post-war years, 1976–8, were, by contrast, testing and unsatisfactory. Vietnam had been at war so long her film-makers didn't know what else to make films about, nor how to go about it.

Now, under Lu'u Xuan Thu's guidance, the studio makes films that 'help ordinary people live better lives' and at the same time 'pave the way for friendly relations with all peoples of the world'. He reels off a list of titles that won both domestic and international prizes (at venues like the Leipzig Film Festival). Then he heaves mightily. He can do the best-foot-forward propaganda bit, but . . . 'In 1985 we received a Heroes' Working Unit award from the government. That's been a heavy burden for us. Frankly we've had to suffer official approval.' I look at Zoom, Zoom looks at me. 'A heavy burden?' I repeat. Zoom nods. Yes. The heavy burden. Of official approval.

'The government,' continues Lu'u Xuan Thu, 'is requesting cutbacks in production. We have enough money to make ten films, when we were scheduled to make eighty. Heroes? Desperate heroes more like. I don't know. The latest thing is we make videos for the provinces. The provincial People's Committees seem to be getting money from somewhere, so we relieve them of some of it, in return for which we supply a sixty-minute documentary about the province in question. If you're travelling around you'll certainly see some examples of this work. We've developed a fixed format that goes down extremely well and looks a little more expensive than in fact it is. With any luck, if we do enough of these we'll have enough money to make a decent film again. It'll have to be feature films in the future though. Or rather, feature videos. In fact we've just completed our first two features. The first is called *Women*

190

Robbers. It's set in the 1930s and lasts four hours fifteen minutes. The second is called *Rain and Wind Life*. This one's also set in the 1930s. It's about a lady infatuated with European fashions. She escapes from her mandarin family and becomes westernized. A far cry from our classic documentary *Dien Bien Phu*, but it seems to be what the people want. Or at any rate what they're prepared to watch. I tell you though, it isn't easy. It isn't easy at all. We are directly answerable to the Ministry of Culture, and frankly speaking this creates big pressures. And as for our equipment – come, let me show you around.'

Lu'u Xuan Thu takes us on a guided tour of the studio, which includes a processing laboratory. He sees to it that I admire nothing. Almost he kicks some of the editing equipment. Everything is very old and comes from either Russia or China – some of it from pre-revolutionary China at that. 'Whenever our socialist brothers want to get rid of something, they send a gift to Vietnam. And try getting any spare parts afterwards!' His only solace is a Bell & Howell print-maker.

'Well now you've seen it,' he concludes as we prepare to say goodbye in the forecourt. 'You can perhaps understand some of my problems. I was never born to be an administrator, but here I am, administering a . . . a nightmare! I don't know why. We are not a violent people. We've fought the wars we had to fight. All we want now is quietly to enjoy ourselves. But that it seems is not to be. At least not in my lifetime.'

We return to Zoom's office, where, helped by the divine Ms Binh, I raid the safe for a fistful of hundred-dollar bills. I then spend much of the afternoon converting some of these into *dong*. Zoom tells me I probably won't be able to change currency again until I reach Saigon, but I musn't change too much because in Saigon the rate is much better than it is in Hanoi. I call in at the Gallery and at the Bac Nam restaurant, which today offers 4,200 *dong* a dollar. Miss Hoa, when I tell her this, immediately raises her rate to match. Then I pack. In the evening, a last dinner in Hanoi with Stein. Who knows when or even if we shall meet again? Nigel Cawthorne, who complains he is getting nowhere in a hurry with his researches, tags along. Afterwards I tell Stein about the Oxford Plan, as outlined by Tim Page. Stein gives it more room than I do. In turn he tells me about an interview he's had with Phan Anh, a jurist and former Politburo member. Phan Anh has told him that the National Assembly is about to set up a commission to study the possibilities of a new constitution that will propagate a multi-party democracy. More to the point, the basis of such a constitution would be the December 1945 Constitution, which 'ignored' the Communist Party.

'Can this really be?' I ask. 'Are you sure Phan Anh's not just using you to air some views?'

'Possibly,' replies Stein. 'In which case I would have to say I am very happy to be a pawn.'

'You are a liberal after all,' I say, and apologize for last night's 'remark'.

At once Stein becomes his most serious (which is also his most delightful). 'You mean when you told Tim Page that I was the only Marxist you'd met in Hanoi? I've been thinking hard about that. I think really I should define my position. I used to consider myself a Marxist-Leninist, but I'm not one now. Now I would call myself a socialist. Although of course as a historian I still employ Marxian analysis.'

And so, with Stein on Stein, my first period in Hanoi draws to a close.

Tuesday 7th November: Hanoi–Vinh (Nghe Tinh Province) At 6.35 a.m. Zoom is pounding on my door. I have slept well, am sleeping well; but in ten minutes I'm up and ready for anything. Zoom's mood is forcefully buoyant. The reason for this is soon given. Is it okay if we give a lift to three of Nam's relatives as far as Hué in the back of the minibus? They'll be no trouble. Really.

'What kind of relatives?'

'His aunts, I think.'

Nam, the minibus and Truc are waiting for us outside. Now that I see him again, I realize I have met Truc (pronounced midway between Chuck and Chook) before. He is one of any number of youngish cadres I've shook (rhymes with Truc) hands with on my various visits to the Company offices. He is shorter than Zoom, better fed and a few years older. His straight black hair is cut in a fringe across his forehead, giving him a '60s Beatles look. It will be some time before we are able to come to terms with each other. If he lacks Zoom's panache, he has a more serious, thoughtful, questioning side to him, but this takes a while to come across. His trip to the south with me is to be his first solo outing as an interpreter. There will be frustrations on both sides.

For now, Nam drives to the office, where we deposit my heavy suitcase. I am determined to travel as lightly as possible, which means two small shoulder-bags. It should be one small shoulder-bag, but there are certain essentials that cannot be jettisoned, for example a Travel Well portable water purifier that, at the end of the day, probably saves my health a dozen times.

From the office to an inner suburb, to pick up Nam's three aunts. As it turns out, they number five. Five old crones with an average age of seventy, plus what looks like all their personal belongings. The vehicle is loaded with all manner of boxes and foodstuffs wrapped in cloths. Touchingly, as I shake hands with each, they address me as *ong*, which roughly translates as 'sir'; *Ciao ong*, five times over now, and five times over many times during the coming days. I try to learn their names, but quickly discover the honorific *ba* is preferred. *Ciao ba* I say, also five times over. Four of them are withered and thin. The fifth, who seems to be their leader, is portly, and dressed in weathered greens. She wields a parasol that appears to somewhat confound her companions. All five have a tendency to cackle hard, but never for long. Periodically they press items of fruit upon me. As we travel along one of them is usually slicing up some or other kind of Asian gourd. The others meanwhile sleep. Nam's aunts indeed have a genius for sleep. No matter how bumpy the road, no matter how loud the male *boc phét* in the front of the van, Nam's aunts can snore through it all. Sometimes, turning around from my seat beside Nam to chat with Zoom and Truc, I study their faces, searching the wrinkles for the key to what must be a hidden wealth of experience. Had their lives been conducted in series instead of in parallel, then their combined longevity would stretch back to the beginnings of the English Civil War or the founding of Harvard University.

'What if I had said no?' I tease Zoom.

'Oh don't worry, Mister Zoom would have persuaded you. I know what a good heart Mister Justin has!'

But when I refer to Nam's aunts as Zoom's 'girlfriends', Zoom becomes visibly rattled.

Thus the minibus, laden with a complement of nine, rolls onto and along Highway One. Our first stop is at a wayside pagoda, an hour or so into our journey. Nam's aunts wish to propitiate the gods of travel by burning joss-sticks. Soon after we make another stop, so that I can propitiate the gods of travel by drinking *caphé xua*. I learn a little about Truc, although worryingly Zoom has to help him with his English, correcting more than the odd word. The reason why Truc was Zoom's contemporary at the Foreign Languages College is because he spent longer than normal in the army. He joined in 1973, soon after the withdrawal of the last American combat troops. In the war against the Saigon Army he spent one month on the Ho Chi Minh Trail before the fall of Hué. Thereafter his artillery unit joined the main communist front as it pushed down Highway One. His uniform, rifle and dried rations were Chinese, while the heavy stuff – field-guns, rockets and rocket-launchers, tanks, APCs – were Russian. After the fall of Saigon he stayed in the army until 1981, having reached the rank of sergeant. He knew that if he didn't quit, sooner or later he'd be posted to Cambodia. By then he'd had enough of the military life.

Our third stop is at a second pagoda, dedicated to the Trung Sisters, who, in 40 AD led a rebellion against the then Chinese rulers of Vietnam and briefly set up an independent kingdom. They have long since been incorporated into the heroic mythology of Vietnamese nationalism. By some they are seen as the original *toc dai*, or 'long-haired ones'. The pagoda itself, built in several tiers on the side of a hill, is grander than most. At the innermost altar I am cajoled by Nam's aunts into making an offering. A bundle of joss-sticks is pushed into my hands and I am told to murmur a prayer as I plant them into a bowl of sand before an array of Buddha images. A shower of sparks falls on my skin, my hand whips back, and some of the sticks fall on the floor. Nam's aunts, hastily picking them up, screech with delight.

'I still haven't got the hang of this,' I whisper to Zoom.

'Never mind. It's the prayer that counts.'

'But I prayed that this time I wouldn't burn myself.'

'You were supposed to pray for an uneventful journey.'

'Uneventful? But I want my journey to be as eventful as possible.'

'Then the Trung Sisters are responding to your wish. You see, we've hardly left Hanoi and already you've had an accident.'

Outside, in one of the yards of the pagoda, music strikes up, what might be termed a spritely dirge. I think to myself that there must be at least four musicians, but in reality there are only two: a man, who plays the equivalent of a banjo, and a woman who half-sings, half-wails the lament. She also plays two percussion instruments with two sticks; one a wooden block, the other an overturned bone-china saucer. The sound they produce is as importunately beautiful as it is unexpected, and for a while I am lifted up or transported out of myself, or whatever it is that good music of an exotic twang does to one.

The dirge continues as Zoom calls me down to the next tier where the pagoda's beadle is preparing green tea in an exposed room. We sit at a rough-hewn table and drink. I cannot help noticing that two Chinese calendars have been posted on one of the walls. Like most Chinese calendars these depict Chinese girls in immodest poses.

Zoom has observed them as well.

'In a pagoda?' I query.

'Yes. Why not? Perhaps they are just for you. You see, already you have everything. Nice music, nice tea and very nice girls. What more do you want?'

The aim today is to get to Vinh, the capital of Nghe Tinh Province. Soon we are back on Highway One, and soon the delta peters out. Increasingly the flatlands are spiked by hills. To our right, in the west, the central Indochinese mountain range begins to loom. For most of the way, the tracks of the Friendship Railroad, connecting Hanoi the capital of the North to Saigon/Ho Chi Minh City the capital of the South, run beside us. There is a long, slow-moving freight train that dogs us for two or three hours, during which time we stop off for lunch in Thanh Hoa, just after Ham Rong Bridge, a vital pass the USAF loved to bomb. Having overtaken the train once, we overtake it again, then a third time, after a level crossing where we are obliged to wait for *it* to pass.

Up until this point, the scenery has alternated between the gorgeously pleasant and pleasantly gorgeous, but thereafter, as the road, serviceable until now, becomes intermittently diabolical, it's typhoon country. We have encroached upon the long, irregularly watered coastal strip that stretches fifteen hundred kilometres between the two great delta pans. Although there are places where rivers that are much smaller than either the Red River or the mighty Mekong descend from the central mountains to paint the land with all the greens of the jungle, there is a prevailing aridity, and with it a terrible poverty. When the sun is out, the soil-bound peasant looks the same as anywhere else in SE Asia, but when the rains fall you see how frighteningly exposed he is, and how frighteningly slender are his means of survival.

Mid-afternoon the rains fall. The landscape becomes abruptly monochrome, as do the faces in the landscape. Everyone in the minibus falls quiet. Nam's aunts are all asleep, while Zoom, Truc and I stare broodingly out of the windows. Only Nam is energetic, negotiating the stones and little rocks that bestrew the way ahead.

'It's good for massage,' Zoom cries as his head hits the roof for the umpteenth time, in a vain effort to make light of our discomfort. 'Really.' But really, the piece of Soviet vehicle suspension to give anyone any kind of massage from any kind of surface has yet to be invented.

Even so, though the going is progressively harder, we reach Vinh by nightfall. The People's Committee being closed for the day, we put up at a guesthouse run by the Ministry of Energy. I pay 67,000 *dong* (say, $16) in advance, for two nights' stay. By careful cross-examination I will later discover that this modest fee includes lodging for Nam's aunts, but Nam himself is so excellent I can hardly complain. When we take dinner, the first glass of Saigon 33 is raised to him. Cheers, Mister Nam, *chuk xu khoe*, well driven, old pal. Afterwards, I and my two interpreters take a brief stroll around town, but there is little to be seen. Out of the dark children's voices cry 'Lien Xo! Lien Xo!' – Russian! Russian! – but I am too exhausted to protest my true nationality. I turn in at

196

nine. There are several cockroaches in my room, but I have learned long ago to suffer them without anguish. There is also running water, which surprises and pleases me. I was told by Tim Page that if I thought Lang Son filthy I'd consider Vinh a cesspit. On the other hand, my room is scarcely designed for privacy. The wall on the corridor side is windowed, and the lights shine through the thin gauze of the so-called curtains. But worse than this, the corridor itself comes to life around midnight, when a party of Vietnamese revellers return to their quarters, next door to mine. The building was originally constructed as an office block. There is shouting outside my door, then a tap-tap-tapping. Angrily I show my western face. This brings an immediate apology. The uproar subsides, but begins a few minutes later, followed by another knock. Again I show my face. Two drunken cadres proffer beer. Men from Danang, travelling north.

Wednesday 8th November: Vinh–Kim Kien   A long day, a day of the Revolution, and a day of relatives. Although Zoom wakes me up at half past six, it is 9.00 a.m. before we leave the guesthouse to begin our business. Confusion and acrimony are rife. A squabble has broken out among the various departments of Vinh City. The Bureau of External Relations is not speaking to the Party bureau and the People's Committee is annoyed that we are not staying at its guesthouse. Nghe Tinh, it seems, is about to be split in two, and so every office is trying to protect, promote and aggrandize its interests. For two hours Zoom scuttles about in search of peace and harmony. Eventually he returns with one Nguyen Xuan Lai, from External Relations. Mr Lai is intensely apologetic, and hopes that by lunchtime the city will have got its act together sufficiently to accord its honoured guest the welcome he deserves. In the meantime he will take us to Ho Chi Minh's birthplace. Further time is lost as Truc trundles off – despite his low stature, Truc is a master trundler – to ascertain whether Nam's aunts wish to join us. Nam's aunts do so wish, and we have to wait while they prepare themselves for what may or may not be a religious experience.

The drive to Kim Kien village takes forty minutes. Zoom stays behind – 'plenty more organizing for me to do'. The countryside is relatively rich. The hamlet of Tru, within Kim Kien, even verges on the idyllic. Uncle Ho's birthplace, two simple thatched-wooden buildings set in a well-brushed garden, is instantly recognizable from photographs I have seen in biographies. There is a two-room hut, and a three-room hut. But they are not peasant structures; they are graceful lower-mandarin dwellings, refreshingly cool inside. The two-room job, the one in which H.C.M. was born, is in fact a facsimile of the original, which burnt down a while ago. The uniformed guard however assures me it is exactly the same as the building in which the Great Patriot spent his first few years. It is made from the finest ironwood and bamboo wattle, though what should have been a clay bed-floor is in fact concrete. Most of such furniture as survived the fire has been taken away to the Ho Chi Minh Museum in Hanoi, although one or two original pieces have stayed behind to keep the replicas company. I am rather taken by a hanging bookcase, suspended from a cross-beam, and a wood-framed loom.

The loom belonged to Ho Chi Minh's mother, Hoang Thi Loan, a gift from her father, Hoang Sinh Duong, a teacher and man of some standing in the district. The larger dwelling, which also has a loom and two hanging bookcases, was provided (from the same source and by the village) for Ho's father, Nguyen Sinh Sac, also a teacher, with a keen interest in traditional medicine.

I take photographs. Having brought my camera it would be a sacrilege not to. Nam's five aunts stand in a line and I snap them too. This simple act gives them untold pleasure. Having offered joss-sticks at a small altar behind the houses, they offer me oranges. For a while we hang around, watching a factory outing tiptoe in and out of the property. It's a pretty, tranquil place, but there's a limit to how long one wants to spend in a pretty, tranquil place at ten in the morning. When the site's curator joins us, I suggest, through Truc, that if H.C.M. was really born here then he must still have relatives living in the village. After an inter-cadre discussion I am told that H.C.M.'s nearest surviving relations live within walking distance. If I want, I can visit them.

I do so want. We walk down a lane that looks like something out of an Italian rustic opera set. Our path is covered with hay.

198

Enormous cartwheels are arranged picturesquely in the hedgerows. Small boys chew grass as they stare at my party. Sweating bullocks nonchalantly incline their heads. It is warm, but the sun today is not a baker. Then along the edge of a paddy and another bucodyllic lane, which takes us into the courtyard of a single-storeyed, two-roomed brick house. There is a veranda, and on the veranda is the only occupant presently to be seen: an enchanting girl of five or six years, dressed in the manner of a Victorian urchin. This, I am told, is Vuong Thi Hoai, the great-granddaughter of Ho Chi Minh's aunt, Hoang Thi An.

Even if she were not so august a personage I would still have taken her photograph. But before I can do so, Nam's aunts, who have been following at a distance, seize the child, comb her hair and smooth out her dress. But the dress won't do. The aunt with the parasol dives into the house to find something more appropriate. Reluctantly Hoai puts it on. Then she stands for my Pentax. But now the sun has gone in, and I know I won't be pleased with the results. The session is saved however by the arrival of the father, Vuong Van Chung, H.C.M.'s first cousin once removed. I scrutinize his face for familial likenesses but can discover none. The sun comes out. Chung holds his daughter in his arms, and I have what I hope will be a tolerably decent addition to the album.

Chung, a man of roughly my own age, just about has time to tell me that, in my country, he would be a royal and live in a palace, whereas in Vietnam, despite his connections, he is only a peasant and must work hard to survive, before I am hustled away by Mr Lai and the curator. I cast a backward glance at the compound, which is animaled in every corner: chickens, dogs, a pig and God only knows how many beetles. The aunts follow at a distance, but even so I can hear them cooing with pleasure. I am now being taken to H.C.M.'s father's house, about four kilometres away at Sen or 'Lotus' village, where H.C.M. lived from the age of six. To get there we all cram back into the minibus, although I'd far rather walk.

This second site is not entirely unlike the first. Although there is only one three-roomed house, this has been enlarged by the addition of a kitchen-dining area. Again, all is ironwood, bamboo wattle and thatch. Most noticeable is an inside altar, dedicated to the memory of Ho's mother. Hoang Thi Loan died when her third child was eleven. Her husband did not remarry, nor did he employ any servants. Nguyen Sinh Sac was a poor scholar who had greatly benefited from his father-in-law's patronage. With his help he was able to go to Hué and take the mandarin examinations. But having passed, he decided not to become a mandarin, for that would have been unpatriotic. Under the French the mandarin system had survived, but a mandarin was nothing more than a running dog, an imperialist lackey. Instead he chose to resume teaching in his native village. The house was looked after by Ho's sister, Nguyen Thi Thanh, and by little Ho himself (or Nguyen Sinh Cung, as he then was). Ho and his elder brother, Nguyen Sinh Khiem, were both their father's pupils. The main lessons learnt, it seems, were patriotism, nationalism, perseverance and abstinence. In due course Khien became a revolutionary, followed by his younger brother. Interestingly, none of the three children was ever to marry.

A woman of forty-five, maybe fifty, with a tissue-soft voice that draws me into her richly lachrymose features, tells me that when Uncle Ho returned to Nam Dan Distict (where we are now) in 1958, after many decades' absence, he could still speak the local dialect. More than that, he also remembered the names of all those he had known as a child. 'And I must tell you something else,' the woman adds. 'When his brother died, he did not attend the funeral. Instead he sent a telegram explaining how he had to give all his time and energy to the nation. You see what a great man he was!'

Nam's aunts pose outside the paternal, patriarchal domicile. Click. I'm growing accustomed to their face. Click. It begins to rain, only a feather-light shower, but we all hurry across to the nearby Ho Chi Minh Museum, a rather grand affair only slightly typhoon-battered. Here two more guides await me, another soft-toned woman of the same generation as her predecessor, and a young thin fellow, Nguyen Sinh Tien, who also claims to be a member of H.C.M.'s extended family, from twelve generations back.

The museum itself is primarily a collection of photographic portraits. Ho's father, Ho's grandfather, Ho's brother, Ho's mother, Ho's sister, Ho in Paris, Ho at the socialist congress in Tours, Ho in Hanoi (1945), Ho with Vo Nguyen Giap during the Battle of Dien Bien Phu, Ho broadcasting to the nation, Ho doing a spot of gardening, Ho holding hands with the children, Ho exhorting women workers and, perhaps the most familiar of all, Ho in old age, dressed up in his whites, smiling and waving his timeless hello-goodbye to the world. All of which I've seen before in Hanoi, and all of which I'll see many times again as I journey south.

On the way back to the guesthouse we pass down some long avenues lined with substantial office buildings and tenement blocks. Mr Lai explains that Vinh is twinned with East Berlin. Berlin had Karl Marx, Vinh had Ho, so the one must help the other. At lunch, a sticky event, we are joined by a Mr Loc, from the Propaganda and Education Bureau of the provincial Party Committee, a man in his fifties still with a virile shock of gleaming black hair and maverick eyes. He says very little to Mr Lai, and Mr Lai says very little to him. There follows a ninety-minute delay while the city's various factions sort out who should take charge of me and my programme. Zoom is apologetic and angry. Finally, at a little after three, Mr Lai comes back to escort us to the Museum of the Nghe Tinh Soviet. Once again Zoom's place as interpreter is taken by Truc.

The museum is on the outskirts of the town, and has recently suffered storm damage. Part of the roofing is in tatters. Most of the exhibits have been moved for their safety into one room. Some photographs and facsimiles of posters and newspapers are drying out. The historic artefacts – weapons mainly, and the obligatory drum – have withstood enough of time's ravages to be unaffected by this latest degradation. There are also several jars of exotic snakes preserved in formalin.

However it is not the museum's contents that have brought me across Vinh. Rather I am to learn about the Nghe Tinh Soviet itself. It is time for another history lesson. I am introduced to the museum's director, Le Si Tuan, as well as his deputy, Doan Van Nam. Another reception room, another long table, another portrait of Uncle Ho, staring down at my notebook with his ripe onion

201

look. The teapot and teacups wait in everlasting readiness. I sit with Truc on one side of the table, the official delegation on the other. Elaborate formalities are exchanged. Very rapidly I have to think of something nice to say about Vinh. Then the insemination begins.

Le Si Tuan dives straight into the late 1920s. The Nghe Tinh Soviet was the brainchild of the (Leninist) Annam Communist Party. This was in the days just before the various communist parties that had sprung up in the three parts of colonial Vietnam (Tonkin in the north, Annam, and Cochin in the south) had been welded into the single Communist Party of Indochina by Ho Chin Minh and his colleagues. The point that Le Si Tuan seeks to establish is that Nghe Tinh Province, by fathering the first Leninist uprising against the French, can fairly lay claim to being the cradle of the Revolution itself. On 1st May 1930 a vast, well-co-ordinated demonstration of workers, students and cadres assembled in Vinh to demand 'freedoms': in particular, more pay, better working conditions and shorter working hours. The French duly wheeled out the guards, and the demonstration was broken up. Then again, on 12th September, another crowd, this time numbering 20,000, gathered in Hung Nguyen District, a few miles outside Vinh. On this occasion the French reacted more strenuously. The air force was called up, and the defenceless people bombed from the skies; 170 died immediately, another 47 from their wounds later. Nonetheless, or because of this outrage, the movement continued, and for a while French control of the province collapsed. The colonial administration was suspended, the mandarins fled. The Nghe Tinh Soviet, modelled closely on Russian-style collectives, came into being. For a few months, under the aegis of workers' councils, 'every village lived in peace'.

The French soon came back. Once their power had been restored by force, the Sûreté, or secret police, moved in. Many of the rebellion's leaders were arrested and shot. Hundreds of others were arrested and imprisoned. Those who remained at large however continued working for the cause. The Party organization survived, and in time was augmented, albeit in a clandestine fashion. Its headquarters were moved from village to village, month after month, year after year, until 1945, when, with the French and

Japanese at each other's throats, it struck for the second time, as part of the general national uprising.

Proudly Le Si Tuan tells me how several hundred French troops were taken prisoner on 9th March 1945, and how power was then wrested from the Japanese. Proudly too he gives me the names of the various local Party leaders who kept the torch alight during the dark years of 1930–45, some of whom were caught and murdered in a round-up of 1941.

As the roll-call of heroes is read out, a woman enters the room with a plain brown cardboard box and three photograph albums, which she places on the table beside Le Si Tuan. The albums, seized from the French police station in 1945, contain mug-shots of cadres and other revolutionaries arrested and detained by the colonialists. Each album has hundreds of pictures, and each picture contains two images: a profile of the convict, and his or her head-on face. About ten per cent of the convicts are women. In nearly every case the sitter, usually aged somewhere in his or her late twenties or early thirties, appears uncompromisingly glum. Names, where names are known, are written underneath. Otherwise there are just the French-supplied numbers. The register containing the key to these was never found.

It is a bit of a chore, but I leaf through all three books. It is almost like looking at skulls: you've seen one, you've seen the lot. Such is the uniformity of expression. What does impress me though is the curiously poor quality of the photography. Many of the faces already look like ghosts.

The cardboard box contains further incontrovertible evidence for the prosecution. Its contents are emptied out in front of me. There are half a dozen items: a wooden ink-pot, used by one of the Nghe Tinh Soviet leaders for writing messages; a quill that wrote those messages; a lamp with a hollow base, for secreting those messages; a small wooden drawer that, as far as I am able to glean from Truc, had something to do with printing; half a pair of handcuffs; and a nasty wooden cudgel.

But there is one exhibit to come, too big, or rather too long, for the box. A truly horrendous exhibit, an exhibit that clinches the case against the perfidious French: the vertebrae of a crocodile threaded onto a steel rod and used as an instrument of chastisement by the prison warders.

This, referred to simply as 'the crocodile', was also liberated in 1945.

The day is not yet finished. We must call on a home for some of the old revolutionaries of the Nghe Tinh Soviet period. Just as my entourage is leaving the museum Mr Loc arrives on a bicycle. He will accompany us to the hospice. And since he will accompany us in the van, he hands over his bike to Mr Lai. Party takes precedence over People's Committee. But Mr Lai is not altogether unhappy. Mr Loc could have put his bike in the back of the minibus and left him to walk. It seems that peace has broken out among the warring cadres of Vinh.

The home, called the Trai Diem Duong, is twenty minutes away, at the end of a dark and dusty lane. Here there are twenty-six 'residents', all of them participants of the 1930 rebellion – all of them therefore very very old. The average age I think is 86. They are looked after, at the People's Committee's expense, by a staff of seventeen, five of whom are nurses. The building is a long, kinked two-storey job, which I suspect may also have been built by the East Germans, though I am assured, almost passionately, by Truc that it was not. In the downstairs corridor I shake hands with several septuagenarians and octogenarians. The director, a rather young man, greets us and invites us to take tea in a little room that scarcely has space for the shorter than usual long table, and where the portrait of Uncle Ho is correspondingly reduced. In a while we are joined by two of the residents. The idea is they will personally give me their personal histories, even though their personal histories are all recorded and filed at the museum. One is a very old man, the other a very old woman. But before they can begin a third resident, dressed in pyjamas and leaning on a stick on one side, and on a nurse upon the other, more or less forces his way in. His name is Mai Van Kinh, he sports an H.C.M. goatee and is 95. He seems a touch muddled about where he is and who I am, but once he starts talking he does so with great resolution, and with great clarity. His revolutionary memory is cut too deep to be ravaged by senility. A member of the Nghe Tinh Party since 1930, he was, he tells us, imprisoned twice – in August 1932 and again in 1941. In between he escaped, and became a member of the Nghe Tinh

Central Committee. He describes himself as a patriot who adopted the Leninist programme in January 1930. He came from a 'proletarian' family in Thach Ha village, in Ha Tinh Province. He spent his time going from village to village, setting up Party cells and sometimes organizing protests and demonstrations. He also helped establish women's and youth organizations, again at the village level, in both Nghe Tinh and Ha Tinh, all the while disseminating the truths of Leninism . . .

(. . . The room is suddenly plunged in blackness – they have power cuts in Vinh as well. A tiny oil-lamp is produced, giving off no more light than a match. Reassured that the world has not yet come to an end, the old campaigner continues with his life . . .)

. . . After 1945 he worked in the personnel department of the Nghe Tinh Central Committee. He continued as a Party activist until his retirement in 1960, whereupon he was presented with the Ho Chi Minh Medal for good and loyal service. But that was thirty years ago, almost . . . Mai Van Kinh's face puzzles. The recent past is so less real than the distant past. He talks about his family and his marriage. His speech becomes slurred. But he wants to go on, he would like to go on all evening. Gently he is led away. Is he the oldest resident? I ask. Oh no. By no means. The oldest resident is 105. Later, perhaps, I will see for myself.

Another resident takes to the chair across the table. By the light of the lamp the face looks like a face in one of the French police albums, but miraculously aged, as in a horror film. Yet Nguyen Hu'u Tien, at 77, is a mere babe among Nghe Tinh revolutionaries. He too spent time in jail, six years of it. From 1945 he was chief of his 'village uprising section'. Then he became secretary to a 'peasant organization', then, in the war against America, a member of the Nghe Tinh Central Committee. He retired in 1969, having struggled against all four of Vietnam's enemies: France, Japan, the US and the Saigon regime. He thinks he has earned his room.

His place is taken by Nguyen Thi Sing. She wears a little blue beret and might just as well be one of Nam's aunts, except that when she shakes my hand she grips it like a vice. She is 79. Her husband was born in the same village as Ho Chi Minh. In the Soviet movement, she was a member of her village women's section. Later on she became its chief. On 1st May 1930 she was

205

one of those taken prisoner. She spent four years in prison. Although she was very weak by the time she was released, she
immediately resumed her Party work. 'But I never rose to any
exalted rank. I was also a family woman.' Her son died fighting
the Americans.

'Tell me about the prison,' I ask. 'Was it in Vinh?'

Nguyen Thi Sing nods. Yes, in Vinh.

'Were you tortured? Did the French use torture on women?'

Nguyen Thi Sing almost smiles.

'Oh yes. They tortured us women. I myself was tortured many
times. There was a Monsieur Robert, and he did all the dirty work.
Sometimes he used to give us electric shocks. And sometimes, if
Monsieur Robert was in a bad mood, he beat us with a rod. We
called it the crocodile, because it was threaded with the bones of a
crocodile's back.'

When Nguyen Thi Sing has finished I am shown the residents'
rooms. They are all much the same: a small bed, a wardrobe, two
chairs, tea-set, a thin rug and a balcony. Then I am taken to see the
oldest resident, the one who is 105. In the corridor I am able, just
about, to make out the features of Mai Van Kinh. He is lying in a
flat wheelchair, apparently exhausted. He revives enough to clasp
my hand. Then I go into the room. The oldest resident is rolled up
under a blue quilt at one end of the bed. A hand appears, followed
by a confused face. The oldest resident is a female. She is Mai Van
Kinh's wife.

What will happen when all the Nghe Tinh Soviet revolutionaries
have passed away? I inquire of the director on my way out. Will
the home then close down? Not at all. Later on it will be used for
veterans of the August Revolution and the war against the French.
Then it will be used for veterans of the war against Diem and the
Americans, and for veterans of the war of reunification, the Ho
Chi Minh Campaign. After that, veterans of the war against the
Khmer Rouge, and of the 1979 war with China . . .

'You see, in Vietnam, we have all the veterans we want. We may
not be very rich in anything else, but for veterans, our supplies will
last well into the next century . . . if not forever.'

       *   *   *

Thursday 9th November: Vinh–Dong Ha (Quang Tri Province) If I don't sleep well again it's not only because there are more drunken *can bo* at one or two in the morning, havocing a fair disturbance outside my room. It's because my head's too full. Yesterday had a shape to it. A birthplace in the morning, tales of action and defiance in the afternoon and then the worthy ancients in the evening, in their evening. And having to work rather hard all day. As an interpreter Truc suffices, but only just. Sometimes he doesn't understand my questions, but asks them nevertheless, so that the replies I get are *non sequiturs*. Sometimes too he abbreviates the replies to the point where they are not replies at all. He doesn't translate so much as negotiate. He will embroil himself in a long conversation with the person on the other side of the table, and then give me a three- or four-word précis. If it's going to be like that every day he'll run me to despair. Although I am aware of the strong propaganda element to my programme, whether in general terms, or as it is arranged on a daily basis, I am interested in Vietnam's past, in the Revolution and in those extraordinary men and women who staffed it. If I'm to have history lessons, then I want the full benefit of them. It shouldn't be up to my interpreter to decide what is and what isn't important. And I am, after all, paying for the service.

Nonetheless, yesterday had a shape to it. And it is the shape of yesterday that keeps me awake, far more than the shape of today. The shape of today is amorphous. For a start the rain has come, and the rain is relentless. Rain militates against shape, against colour. The long overdue winter, the northern monsoon, has finally shown its face, and its face is pale, bleak and miserable. And then I spend twelve hours of the day glued to my seat in the front of the minibus. Our target is Quang Tri, further from Vinh than Vinh is from Hanoi. We drive down through the remainder of Nghe Tinh, and then through Quang Binh, of all the coastal provinces probably the poorest. The sky is grey, and so is the land. The paddies, now flooded, take on the look of gruel. The peasant hovels appear particularly hovel-like. I do not understand how people can live in them, yet live in them they do. And the road: the road is fundamentally rotten. Only as we pass from Nghe Tinh into Quang Binh is there any excitement. The mountains to the west suddenly encroach upon the plain, the road rises, and we shoot for Ngang Pass, which marks the provincial border. In the swirling clouds that envelop us it's as if Nam has become an aviator. Up and up and up, the engine roaring, and all his aunts for once simultaneously awake.

'Your girlfriends are enjoying this,' I shout to Zoom.

Zoom scowls, the first time I have seen him scowl.

The rain lashes against the windows. At the summit there is momentarily a window in the weather. Fleetingly I catch sight of a stretch of coast, curved like a scimitar, way below. The South China Sea at its most bellicose. And then this giant glimpse vanishes, the van splutters its relief, and we begin the descent. At Dong Hoi, Quang Binh's capital, we stop briefly outside the External Relations Bureau. We are supposed to visit some tunnels, but of course, it's far too wet. Zoom jumps back in the minibus, a roseate smile on his face. 'Good news,' he says. 'We can drive on. Otherwise we'd have had to spend the night. You know what it's like, once a People's Committee gets hold of a visitor.' Then why, I ask, didn't we just drive straight through? 'Because I had to show them our papers. That's what I've been doing in Hanoi. Every province we enter we have to seek permission.'

'*Have* to?'

'Well, not have to. But it's better. It's more polite.'

Such formalities! We drive on through the wasteland of Quang Binh. We cross the Giang River and Zoom points to some houses through the rain. An Xa village, the birthplace of Vo Nguyen Giap. A little further another village, the birthplace of Le Duan.

'Many many big potatoes born around here,' Zoom cries, thankful there's something to enthuse about.

'Yes. I know. Can't you see? It's a big potato field.'

Sitting beside Zoom, Truc laughs. It's the first time he's laughed at any of my jokes. This makes me marginally better disposed toward him.

We are approaching the end of Quang Binh, and we are also approaching the Seventeenth Parallel, formerly the frontier between North Vietnam and South Vietnam. Perhaps because Zoom tells me this, I begin to notice the unusually large number of circular ponds beside the road. Bomb-craters. In its time, this has been one

208

of the biggest battlefields in Asia. Today it looks like the Somme must have looked seventy-five years ago . . . without the Bosch.

A change of plan. We'll spend the night in Dong Ha, not in Quang Tri. In any case, Dong Ha is now the capital of Quang Tri Province, so it behoves us to stay there.

It's getting dark. Peasants in their hovels are lighting their paraffin lamps. Very few of the hamlets we pass have electricity. Suddenly I'm aware of a bridge.

'Where's this?'

'Oh. I should have told you. The Hien Luong Bridge. We're on the Seventeenth Parallel. Now we've crossed it. We're in the South. Congratulations.'

Nam smiles and presses hard against the accelerator. There is a sudden improvement in the road surface. Even so, night has fallen by the time we reach Dong Ha, where there's electricity, and somewhere a People's Committee guesthouse.

Friday 10th November: Dong Ha–Hué (Thua Thien Province) Dong Ha is strictly a staging post, and because the next destination, Hué, is a mere sixty or seventy kilometres further south, I'm allowed the absolute luxury of sleeping late, until 8.00 a.m. Zoom, Truc and Nam have already breakfasted by the time I'm up. They're never so happy as when they've managed to start the day with a bowl of noodles, whereas for me *caphé xua* and a small loaf of bread will always suffice. To satisfy this slender need we pause at a roadside restaurant in Quang Tri, eight miles further south. Zoom asks whether I'd like to see the 'ancient citadel', dating from the early nineteenth century. Yes, I say . . . since we're here. It takes some time though to find the way. Nobody seems quite sure where the citadel is. The explanation for this is provided when eventually we find it. Two bits of crumbling, broken wall and that's your lot. There is no ancient citadel in Quang Tri any more. It was destroyed, like most other buildings in the city, in 1972, when the NVA (North Vietnamese Army) launched one of its heavier attacks.

As we twist and turn back to Highway One it becomes easier to see why the provincial capital has been transferred to Dong Ha.

Quang Tri today is nothing but a shambles. The more I look, the more I see the scars of war. New houses have gone up beside the shelled carapaces of old houses. Sometimes, between the houses, bomb-craters have been left unfilled. And yet, from the perspective of someone travelling south from Hanoi for the first time, not everything is bleak. Street stalls have an abundance of tropical fruits one simply doesn't see in the north. Also, the small urban and inter-urban buses are painted gaudily. There is, for the first time on my journey, a distinct splash of southern dash.

For all that, the true south is still a long way off. Hué, which we reach toward the end of the morning, is as different from Saigon as Saigon is from Hanoi. It has its own geography, and its own important history, reflecting the divisions that intermittently have always plagued Vietnam.

It is thought that a settlement of some kind or other has existed on the banks of the Song Huong, or Perfumed River, for well over two thousand years. For a while Hué was the centre of early Chinese rule in Vietnam. Situated in a fertile river valley on the narrow coastal strip between the two passes of Ngang and Hai Van, it enjoyed a double strategic advantage: it could be defended against the non-Chinese, non-Vietnamese people who inhabited the south, and it could also be used as the launch-point for the conquest of the south. In the fourteenth century Hué became a Vietnamese city, once the Viets had successfully expelled the Chinese from their lands in the north. Indeed it became the capital of Annam, at a time when Annam and Vietnam were synonymous. As the Viets pushed their way southwards, overcoming the Chams and other Mekong Delta peoples, Hué prospered, commercially and culturally. It was the centre of the silk industry, and it was also a centre for Buddhism and Buddhist learning. But no sooner had the whole of what today we call Vietnam been conquered and unified under one emperor than divisions began to appear. Then as now, southerners resented northern control. Also, local warlords resented control by anyone. From the middle of the sixteenth until the end of the eighteenth centuries Vietnam gradually degenerated under the deadweight of warring factions. The emperor became no more than a figurehead. Two dominant clans emerged: the Trinh in the north, and the Nguyen in the south. In 1673 a hundred-year truce was concluded between the two families, a stand-off that did little to safeguard Vietnam against outside interference, but rather enshrined internal divisions. The Dutch, the Portuguese and finally the French sought advantage for themselves by siding either with the Trinh or with the Nguyen. Eventually, in 1802, with French help, the Nguyen reasserted themselves. A new dynasty was founded. Nguyen Anh, changing his name to Gia Long, became the first line of emperors that lasted until the final abdication of the Bao Dai in 1955. From 1862 however the Nguyen emperors were effectively French puppets. In that year Tu Duc, the fourth of the new line, signed a treaty which was, in time, to render the whole of Vietnam a protectorate of the European power.

From these developments Hué prospered. The Nguyen emperors had chosen Hué as their capital, and the French were content to leave them there. Hué was also the administrative capital of Annam, one of the five *départements* of French Indochina (the others being Tonkin, Cochin, Cambodia and Laos). The Nguyens built themselves a fine palace in the Chinese Han style and, once real political power was denied them, turned their attention to patronizing the arts. Hué therefore became the cultural centre of Vietnam, a title to which it still pretends. But because of this, it also became a centre for pre-revolutionary nationalists, a place where at least the concept of a free and independent Vietnam was discussed by members of an educated elite.

After 1945, Hué lost its way. In July 1949 the French officially declared Saigon the country's capital. Annam and Cochin were scrapped. After 1954, and the partitioning of Vietnam along the Seventeenth Parallel, Hué 'belonged' to the south. Its administrative significance was reduced to that of a provincial capital. Because of this, because of a feeling of displacement among its citizens, because of its proximity to the parallel, which made the city especially susceptible to communist infiltration, and because of its strong Buddhist tradition, Hué became something of a hotbed for dissidents who opposed the Catholic regime of President Diem in Saigon. Nineteen sixty-three and 1965 witnessed violent anti-government protests in the former imperial capital. Several Buddhist monks immolated themselves in fire. But Hué's political ambiguity did not spare it the ravages of war. Rather, the opposite. Early in

211

1968, coinciding with the Tet Offensive, communist forces stormed and took the city. Furnished with lists of those who either worked for or sympathized with the Saigon regime, the cadres went on a rampage. Several thousand citizens were butchered. The communists too were capable of atrocities. But that was not the end of the affair. As the Americans and the Saigon army recovered from the initial shock of Tet, the counter-assults began. In Hué the fighting was particularly intense, and particularly close-quartered. Stanley Karnow calls it 'the most bitter battle of the whole war'. The city was eventually retaken, but at an unimaginable cost, in terms not just of lives lost, but also of material destruction. Within a few short weeks much of Vietnam's cultural heritage had gone up in smoke.

When, in *The Gentleman in the Parlour* (1930), Somerset Maugham described Hué as 'a pleasant little town with something of the air of a cathedral city in the West of England', he was being either exceedingly facetious or exceedingly silly. I have yet to discover a cathedral town in any part of England that has tropical canals, tropical weather, tropical architecture and tropical people, not to mention cyclos. And I'm sure things haven't changed that much in sixty years. But then that's Somerset Maugham for you: always eager to laud the East, and always casting his net far wide of the mark. Poor sod. Probably he was tanked up on gin slings at the time.

I wouldn't argue with 'pleasant', though. That's one thing you can say about Hué: it's pleasant. As Nam delivers us along the northern bank of the Perfumed River, past the Linh My pagoda, which doesn't look at all like an English cathedral, and towards the imperial gate, which is about all that remains of the Imperial Palace, I am struck by a certain peaceableness. I am also struck by the horseshoe of purple-mauve mountains that, at a distance, surrounds the city, and by the long iron bridge across the Perfumed River, designed by Georges Eiffel.

We cross the river, and turn into what was once the European quarter, a network of spacious streets that, at a pinch, you might just about expect to find in the west of France with both eyes half-closed. Zoom has arranged in Hanoi for us to stay at a 'villa', number 18 Le Loi Street, that belongs to the local tourist authority. In reality this is a suburban bungalow of some comfort – which is as well, given that we are to remain in Hué several days. A central double room, sitting area and dining place, with bedrooms leading off either side. My own is a suite that includes a good-sized shower room with hot water and a large, bulbous orange spider.

'You like it?' inquires Zoom, poking his head round the door with a face that's flooded with cheerfulness.

'Absolutely I do.'

'You see, we could have stayed in a people's guesthouse, but then I said to myself no, Mister Justin should have somewhere quiet and beautiful. Mister Justin should discover what life's like in a Hué villa.'

'Thank you, Zoom. I think we'll all be happy here. How much will it cost?'

'Oh not a lot. A little bit more than the guesthouse, but less than a hotel. Maybe twenty dollars a night. And small money for our food.'

But best of all is the staff, a manageress and three maids-cum-waitresses who sleep and prepare our meals in small outbuildings at the back. They are, all of them, attractive, graceful, demure women who confirm immediately Hué's reputation as a repository of unusual female charm. Keeping themselves just beyond arm's reach, they project an aura of intimacy that is as binding as it is unmotivated.

Nam removes his aunts to wherever it is in Hué that Nam's aunts reside. Zoom makes a first attempt to contact the People's Committee, without whose blessing I can, it seems, have no programme. Truc, as is his wont whenever the opportunity presents itself, falls fast asleep. Later, he comes with me across the river to the main shopping area. It has been decided that I need new trousers for an upcoming interview. Zoom has had word from Mr Hong that Le Duc Tho, the man who negotiated for three years with Henry Kissinger in Paris, is prepared to receive me in Saigon. Since I had no idea Le Duc Tho is still alive, and therefore didn't request an interview with him, this comes as a double surprise. A pair of trousers seems a small price to pay for such an honour.

213

In fact it is a very small price. Having checked out half a dozen clothes shops, and having unsuccessfully attempted to squeeze my legs into any number of ready-mades that have all the volume of elongated socks stitched together at the top, I stumble on a tailor's. Truc sniffs cautiously, but I assure him it is just what we are looking for. And so it is. The tailor's assistant takes my measurements and then introduces me to several bales of perfectly acceptable Polish cloth. How much?

'Fifteen,' Truc translates.

'What, dollars?'

'No. Thousand *dong*.'

'But that's absurd.'

'No. Really. It's cheap.'

'That's what I meant.'

The trousers, I am advised, will be ready within twenty-four hours. By paying in advance I am given a 500 *dong* discount.

In the evening we eat so well at the villa it becomes difficult not to conclude that my hostesses have not attended finishing school, or indeed that their attention and skills are not part of a ministerial master-plan to make me an everlasting slave of Vietnam. King prawns, fish, beef, tender chicken that for once does not disintegrate into pieces of string that have to be pulled from between the teeth at the end of the meal, frog's legs the same and fresh vegetables, all washed down with Russian mineral water and Heineken beer – the odd thing is, the closer I approach Saigon, the less Saigon 33 I encounter.

Afterwards Nam drives us to Hué's own Thong Nhat Hotel, at the upper end of town on the same side of the river. This is a modern establishment for tourists, and the idea is to view the Perfumed River by night from its broad terraces. In the old days, long before the hotel was ever thought of, courtesans drifted up and down the water in semi-covered barges. On nights when the moon shone, their voices, elevated in song, could be heard vying with the crickets and nightjars for several miles. But there was danger as well as pleasure. If an amorous mandarin or *colon* let his mind and body drift too far, and the barge drifted up-river or, more to the point, was thus propelled by the conniving bargee, balanced on narrow boards at the back of the vessel, then he was

214

liable to sudden attack, from accomplices squatting in smaller, swifter boats.

But tonight, in 1989, there are no such transports of delight. Nor for that matter is there any moon, and after an hour or so we return to the villa. But I am not ready for bed. It is not yet ten o'clock. I propose a walk to stretch my legs. Zoom and then Truc do their utmost to dissuade me. I must be tired, surely I have some notes to write up, who knows whom I will meet, etcetera. But I am loath to listen. Walking the streets of strange cities by night is something that has always appealed to me. It is an innocent pursuit, but one which I cannot long do without when I am abroad.

'Okay,' I say, 'you're both tired, then stay here. I'll go by myself.'

In fact I'd rather go alone. Much as I love my minders, after four days of their continuous company I crave a little solitude.

But my protests are all to no avail. Truc suddenly discovers he is not so tired and volunteers to come. So, leaving Zoom behind to make *boc phét* with Nam, we set off once again for the river.

Truc wastes no time in telling me that although he is now a married man, and has lately become a father, he must still obey his mother, in whose house he lives. For example, if his mother expresses the wish that everyone should be in bed by eight, then everyone is in bed by eight.

'You're not my mother,' I reply. 'Try again.'

Truc tries again. He has been asked by Mr Hong, he says, to keep an eye on me, and make sure that no harm befalls me. This is the solemn duty he has been entrusted with. To get me down to Saigon, and around the Mekong Delta, and back up to Hanoi all in one piece.

'Then have no fear,' I counter. 'I am an inveterate coward. The first sign of danger, and you won't see me for the dust of my heels.'

'But sometimes, you know, a thing can happen very quickly.'

'Sure. Especially indoors.'

There is silence between us for a hundred metres or so. Something tells me it is important that, as far as Truc is concerned, I establish my habits, my *modus vivendi*, at an early date. The business about mothers particularly needles me. Yet there is a

215

measure of ambivalence involved. Truc I suspect is not merely or even being devious. For all I know, his filial piety does indeed run that deep. There is also the matter of group co-operation. One would be expected to give ground from time to time, to make life simpler for the group, whatever its project happens to be. Yet what if different members of the group, viz. myself on the one hand, and the employees of the Services Centre of the Ministry of Information on the other, have radically different notions of what the group project is?

'I'm here to study Vietnam,' I mutter tersely, as much to myself as to my companion. 'In all its aspects. Vietnam now. In accordance with the principles of *doi moi*. Oherwise I would never have come.'

'Of course,' replies Truc. 'And I am helping you.'

'Then why the resistance to walking out at night?'

Out of the very small matter of my wanting to take a post-prandial stroll through the well-lit streets of Hué, a storm is brewing.

'Shall we go back now?'

'You go back if you like. I'm going to have some coffee.'

Truc, the loyal cadre, the one-time sergeant, nods and wearily sticks to my side. Clearly this is as much a test for him as it is for me.

'Look,' I begin, 'I know it's right and proper to obey one's parents and all that stuff, and I know you have your instructions, I won't call them orders, but please consider the following: if I were the perfectly obedient sort then almost certainly I wouldn't be here. I'd be back in Britain, doing something that involved as little risk as possible. But I'm not like that. It's not the way I'm made. Can you understand?'

Truc nods. But whether he understands or not I have no way of knowing.

'I'm not like you, either,' I add. 'I've never fought in a war. So I still have a little appetite for risk. I realize, for your sake, and Zoom's sake, I shouldn't take any very great risks, but no way does that mean I'm not going to take any.'

Again, without speaking, Truc nods.

Oh God, I think to myself, am I making his life that much of a misery?

216

'Look. Here's a place. I'll buy you a coffee.'

We turn into what's either an open-air coffee shop that sells beer, or an open-air bar that sells coffee. The only customers are six or seven younger Vietnamese sitting round a table. As soon as they see me they shout greetings – 'Lien Xo! Lien Xo!' – and invite us to join them. Truc instinctively suggests we sit elsewhere, at a table that is as far removed as possible.

'That's okay, Truc. We'll sit with them.'

'But you don't know who they are.'

'I don't know who anyone is. But let's at least try to find out. Vietnam now, remember.'

Again, Truc is obliged to give way. The problem, it seems, is that these youngsters are not instantly recognizable as cadres. Nor are they Hanoians. In fact they are a group of rail-workers having a night off. The conversation that follows is, to put it mildly, flaccid. Once they've discovered I'm not Russian, their main interest is to test my opinion of Vietnamese women. Since I'm no expert in the subject the best I can proffer is fulsome platitudes. And that, with Truc translating with all the enthusiasm of a stuffed dormouse, is about as far as we get.

'A nice bunch,' I comment breezily as we stride back to the villa.

Truc's silence, offered either as a reproof or as an expression of a deeper perplexity, irritates me in the extreme. The reason for this is because he gives me nothing to help me decide whether his responses tonight are a manifestaton of his own character, or whether they are programmed, systematic, that is, symptomatic of The System. And because I can't decide, my feeling toward Truc becomes vindictive. Rather than give him the benefit of any doubts, I begin, in the privacy of my thoughts, to accuse him from both directions – as one who threatens to impede the freedom of my movements from both personal and impersonal motives.

In short, on my part an animus develops. In short, I become, in my attitudes toward the fellow, wholly and unreasonably unjust.

A part of the problem is that I am sorry to be losing Zoom, whom I have come to regard as indispensable. Zoom the specialist in gratifying my every wish, Zoom the seasoned socialite, Zoom the master organizer, Zoom the life and soul. A hard act to follow, and even harder when the audience, having risen to its feet in its applause, is making for the door.

'Thanks,' I say to Truc, when we reach the house. 'I enjoyed that. We must do it again soon.'

Saturday 11th November: Hué A leisurely twenty-four hours, or supposed to be. Two types from the Bureau of External Relations show after breakfast, and I am introduced to a Ms Cuk, who will join my party as a local guide on my sightseeing excursion tomorrow. Then I am left to read and write at my will. Zoom has errands to perform around town, Truc reads, sleeps. The manageress and one of her minions prepare a beautiful lunch. Afterwards, to my considerable satisfaction, when I announce I'm going for a walk, nobody objects, and nobody volunteers to accompany me. For Zoom, Truc and Nam a siesta, on the few days it is possible, is not to be refused.

I walk along Le Loi Street away from the centre, away from the river. Pausing to observe landmarks that will enable my return – a bridge, a Catholic church, a rickety old power-station – I take a turning right, a turning left. After twenty minutes or so I have passed beyond the edge of the city proper and into its rustic suburbs. Kids run up to me from all directions, to touch my hands, or pull the hair on my arms. Their attention and their company beguile me. Vietnamese children are among the friendliest, most enchanting on the planet, and as I travel south it will always be a bad day when I am not mobbed by at least a hundred of them. In a real way they compensate for the vexations I experience at the hands of my minders, the problems that arise from the unending game of cat and mouse I must involuntarily play with the Ministry. Whenever I feel the Ministry has won the latest round, I look for the kids, and indulge their frivolous interest as if my life depended on it: a happiness therapy, a draught of innocence.

The procedure is invariable. I am walking along when two or three of the bravest run out in the street or road or path in front of me. 'Lien Xo! Lien Xo!' they shout. To which I reply: 'Toi khumh phai Lien Xo! Toi la Anh' – meaning, I'm not a Russian, I'm English. And this, it seems, is always sufficient to establish an eternal rapport.

Thus I walk out of a hot afternoon into the environs of Hué.

218

Lien Xo! Lien Xo! Khumh phai Lien Xo! But after a kilometre or two, after I have crossed a couple of superbly green tropical canals, or water lanes, I am accosted by an adult calling himself, like every second male in the country, Nguyen.

Nguyen speaks in a babble of French and English. Standing in the middle of the road, he tells me, before I can ask, that formerly he was an employee of the Saigon regime, although in quite what capacity remains unclear. Something to do with the army, but also something to do with priests. Fifty-odd, silver-haired, mild of manner, dapper in his daytime pyjamas. As best I can I keep him at arm's length. He invites me into his house. I look at my watch and make an excuse. He repeats his invitation, whinges a little. I reconsider. Oh, very well then, but I mustn't stay long. A quick cup of tea. As he leads me rather hastily through his garden I look round to see whether I am being observed by any cadres, but as far as I can tell there are none.

Nguyen's bungalow, by the Vietnamese standards I am so far accustomed to, is by no means a modest establishment. There are various items of modern electronic equipment – hi-fi, television, cassette player, etc. In the centre of the living area is an altar, adorned with a crucifix and many photographs of his daughter and his daughter's family. The daughter lives in America, which I presume to be the reason for her father's apparent affluence. For, as Nguyen repeats several times, in both languages, he is un-employed, and fully intends to remain that way until such time as the government gets rid of itself.

I am thinking how best to make my escape when Nguyen unexpectedly comes to the point. How would I, he asks, like to see the remains of four American soldiers?

This is almost exactly what I don't want to hear. I'm not yet halfway through my stay in Vietnam and I know that if I start involving myself in clandestine body-viewing and am found out then I may very well become *persona non grata*. Also, only a couple of days ago someone (I think Zoom) has told me about a report carried on *Voice of America* that President Bush or one of his spokespersons has agreed to accept Vietnam's argument that there are certain rotten elements in the south who have hoarded US corpses precisely with a view to selling them for a profit when

219

the occasion presents itself. It fleetingly occurs to me that I am being set up. I am about to become one of several persons coming out of Vietnam with confirmation of such stories about bones for sale.

On balance, it is probable I am not being used. When I left the villa in Le Loi Street no one, least of all myself, had any idea where I was going. Also, Nguyen acts the role of furtive a little too convincingly. He has become nervous in the extreme. Moreover, he does not ask for money, or in any way suggest that money should be part of the scenario, though again he may have reasoned there is no reason why an Englishman should wish to give money for dead Americans unless he were palpably mercenary, which (I've always prided myself) palpably I'm not.

To impress upon me that he isn't kidding, Nguyen now shows me a piece of paper he keeps secreted in an eighteen-inch length of hollow bamboo. The paper bears the impress of a GI's disc:

KING/ORVILLE D./348 44 9152/A NEG/BAPTIST

Somewhat reluctantly, when Nguyen urges me to take the paper with me, I agree. He also writes down his name and address on another piece of paper. I put both into my camera case. I promise I will do what I can to contact King's family. I then tell Nguyen that it would be unwise for me to spend any futher time in his house. And so I leave the premises with the kind of casual saunter that would stick out a mile on the promenades at Nice on a cool day in March.

After a while I slow my pace. When more children come up to me I give them exactly the same attention as their predecessors. I do my best to behave as though nothing untoward, nothing remotely interesting, has happened. The children also provide a pretext for me to turn round, and look back down the lane behind me. But again, as far as I can tell, nobody is following.

Nonetheless, to protect myself, I later give Zoom an outline of my meeting with Nguyen, without revealing either his identity or his whereabouts. If I was seen – and in Vietnam domestic espionage is still rife, viz. the noodle-seller outside the Sofia – then this I figure is the best way to prevent any repercussions. Possibly I can pre-empt any request for a full statement by offering a partial statement in advance. Zoom, I know, will be anxious for me not to be bothered: my status as a guest of the Ministry of Information should afford the necessary immunity. Yet telling Zoom is also hazardous, since I'm not entirely sure how pressured he will feel to pass on my information. It is with some relief that I observe his agitation. He really wishes that I hadn't met this man. It is entirely possible that I was seen, because the houses of the likes of Nguyen usually are watched. He also ventures the opinion that the next time I go walkabout I should take either himself or Truc with me.

Still later, Truc expresses the same opinion.

This though is at the end of the day, after a sumptuous dinner during the course of which a bottle of 'vodka' (rice-alcohol) is opened to celebrate our being in Hué. Between now and then I borrow a bicycle from the manageress and make my way across the Perfumed River to collect my trousers. The cut and fit are both excellent. On my way back however the bicycle breaks down. The chain comes off its cogs. Rather than attempt to repair it myself, I hand the machine over to a street mechanic who has his stool and tools in front of a state-run general store. Whilst he mends the bike, I go inside. There I meet a middle-aged woman called Dr Trang. I ask her what she does, and she tells me she's a paediatrician at Hué General Hospital. The main health problems in the area are malaria, malnutrition and dysentery. She asks if I would like to visit her at work. Enthusiastically I agree. In Hanoi I have requested a hospital visit, but the request has gone unheeded.

'So you see,' I tell Zoom and Truc, after the plates have been cleared away by a hauntingly gorgeous Miss Lam, 'I'm helping you. I've managed to organize a bit of my own programme!'

Finally, after discussing Nguyen and the four dead Americans, I sneak out of the villa for a late-night walk round the block. I have hardly gone ten yards when a young man who is obviously a cadre draws up alongside and engages me in conversation. Since there's no way I can shake him off, I soon return to my room. But I shouldn't complain. It's been a fruitful day, despite or because of the lack of an official agenda.

Sunday 12th November: Hué   It's time to be a tourist. The Nguyen

221

emperors, progressively stampeded by the mighty French, were aware that their government might not go down in history as one of unrivalled might and majesty. To compensate, they built themselves large mausoleums on the outskirts of Hué, in the Chinese manner. In death they would achieve all that they had failed to achieve in life. Today I am taken to three of these tombs.

We are joined, after a dawn breakfast, by Ms Cuk and Nam's five aunts. The first tomb is about ten miles up the Perfumed River, and was built by and for Tu Duc, the fourth of the Nguyen dynasty, who ruled from 1847 to 1883. Tu Duc was the emperor who effectively sealed Vietnam's fate when he signed a treaty with the French giving them direct control over several provinces around Saigon in the South. Of all the Nguyens he was perhaps the most autocratic, certainly, within the limitations permitted by France, the most despotic. Also, he had one hundred and three wives, but none of them could provide him with a son and heir.

Tu Duc spent a great deal of his time at his mausoleum, which doubled as his summer pavilion. Initially it was called his Ten Thousand Year Home, but this was later changed to Modest Tomb, in deference to three brothers – Doan Hu'u Trung, Doan Hu'u Ai and Doan Tu Truc – who led a rebellion of all those poor sods obliged to build the place. The Doans wanted to replace Tu Duc as emperor with his elder brother's son, Tu Dui. When the uprising failed, Tu Dui and his father were expeditiously executed. By that time (1866) the tomb was all but completed. The cost in lives and gold was great, but at least the emperor had the decency to give it the new name: a lesson perhaps to future generations of Vietnamese in how relatively easy it is to rewrite history from the top.

'King Tu Duc was very conservative, very cruel and physically very weak,' Ms Cuk tells me as, for a modest fee, we enter the precincts, 'but he was also a literary type.'

I have been to more impressive sights, but then a steady drizzle may have something to do with my disappointment. The mausoleum is divided in two: a larger, palace-like structure, which Tu Duc used when he was alive; and the tomb itself, an overgrown stone-walled mound a little way away from the rest. Externally the most striking feature is a lily pond, where the emperor fished and boated and listened to music. The palace, mounted on the side of a hill, is set back from this. You cross a moat and climb up a healthy spread of steps. In the centre of these is a narrow band of marble stairs, reserved at the time for the exclusive use of Tu Duc. Then you enter the emperor's day-room, a substantial hall constructed out of rather fine ironwood beams and pillars. Some of the emperor's belongings are exhibited in glass cases, for example his heavy seals, his authentic French clock. Bronzes and ceramics, dragons and chimeras. A huge wooden bed with a finely polished surface. (The emperor sat on this all day, amid a heap of cushions, listening to music and poetic recitals.) Bird-cages, candlesticks, incense burners. Then through to a courtyard at the back, housing Tu Duc's night-quarters, the kitchens and a small theatre. Most invitingly, a gateway leading to a stone staircase and another gateway: beyond which, the village of concubines. Here some four hundred of the monarch's mistresses lived; and here they had to go on living, after his death ... just in case a royal finger should beckon from the tomb.

Trailed by Nam's aunts in all their finery, and flanked by Zoom and Truc, I return to the central open courtyard. A wet breeze slaps my face. Ms Cuk tells me that when the wind blows through the pine trees music can be heard. I listen intently, but all I can hear is the plop plop plop of some unusually large raindrops on the decaying lily-pads. It's a strange place. When you are outside you want to be inside, and when you are inside you want to be outside. This I think may reflect Tu Duc's psychology. When he was alive he thought continuously about being dead. Perhaps now he's dead he thinks continuously about being alive.

'It's very pretty,' I say, slightly dismayed at what I read in my official Vietnam tourism guidebook (*Vietnam My Homeland*, printed by the Su That, or Truth, Publishing House): viz. that what is in front of me is 'the most beautiful and dream-evoking of all mausoleums and royal tombs in Hué'. If that is the case, then shouldn't it have been saved for last?

In fact the best is to come, but not immediately. Mausoleum number two, another ten miles south, belonged, or belongs, to Khai Dinh, the twelfth and penultimate Nguyen emperor (1916–25), a man said to suffer from a crushing inferiority complex. And

223

it's quite a thing. Begun in 1920, it was not completed until 1930. One hundred and twenty-seven steps take you up the face of a mountain to the tomb rooms on top. No living quarters here I'm afraid – Khai Dinh, a hopelessly vain fellow, spent most of his reign abroad, playing the culture vulture in Europe – but a quite extraordinarily emetic blend of oriental and late European baroque architectural styles, with plenty of rare marbles to make the ascender's dizzying head spin. Cham and Chinese elements blend with the spirit of Vaubon to produce a monument of unmitigated kitsch – a word I have much fun and some difficulty in explaining to Zoom as we near the summit of this queer pile.

The tomb rooms are even more of a caper. Of these there are three: a front altar room, the tomb itself and a back altar room behind. It is the first of these however that captures an unwilling imagination:

> The art of interior arrangement [recites my guidebook] reached its apex in the harmonious combination between decoration and sculpture and painting. This can be seen in the mosaics made of multicolor pieces of ceramics, porcelain, terra cotta and broken bottles, featuring many traditional subjects such as decorative motifs representing the Chinese character 'zhian' (royal stamp), trees and plants, leaves and flowers, and animals, according to the themes of *bat batu* (eight weapons), *tu linh* (four noble animals) and *tu quy* (four seasons).

Yellow is the dominant sensation, and being inside this classically proportioned space tells one a little of what it must be like to be a globe-trotting canary addicted to cassis.

'Harmony,' says Truc *sotto voce* at my side, and almost wagging a finger in my face – sometimes he takes his role of instructor a little too much to heart. 'You see? Harmony!'

In addition, the marriage of Chinese lanterns and French candelabra, unreflected on a black-and-white chequered floor. In the tomb room, as well as the tomb, a bronze statue of the gadfly emperor himself, cast in France and weighing over two tons.

Zoom has only to catch my eye to know what I am thinking. He

224

smirks and I smirk, and we agree that the only possible solution is lunch.

Lunch is taken in the corner of a desperately filthy market even further south on the banks of the Perfumed River. I dare eat only that which has been boiled before my eyes. We then negotiate, at a price, a boat to take us across the waters to a place where there is a path leading to the third and final mausoleum, the Emperor Minh Mang's.

Minh Mang (ruled 1820–40) was the second Nguyen emperor, and arguably the best of the crop. Although he had 78 sons (four of them, according to legend, the fruit of one night's exertion) and 64 daughters, he is regarded as being of the sober and serious school. He was what none of the other Nguyen were, with the excepton of his father, Gia Long: a capable administrator. He cared equally about literature, education and defence, and had an interest in science. His tomb, imposing without being lavish, is suggestive of what might have been. Unlike the others, it is constructed on level ground. It consists of a series of low, rectangular yards leading to the tomb itself. Between these open spaces are various barrier constructions: the emperor's stele, a prayer hall, a raised pavilion with fan-shaped windows. There are also, along the central path, Han-style ornamental gates. And then, at the far end of a path eventually flanked by ornamental ponds, a great black moated circular structure, containing the mortal remains of Minh Mang somewhere beneath a low, broad mound covered with jungle weeds, a stark and uncomprising homage to Death.

A simple austere compound, following a processional form of architecture.

'I like this place,' I tell Zoom. 'Particularly the tomb. It has great dignity. I'd like to hang about a while.'

My entourage finds a place to sit. Nam's Number One Aunt dishes out bananas and apples. I watch them from upstairs, through one of the fan-shaped windows of the raised pavilion. Around me, a great carpet of bird droppings. I even feel inspired to make a quick sketch of the nether-end of the mausoleum in my notebook – a thing I do only once or twice a decade. Curiously, about this place my guidebook offers less than half a dozen words: 'Stately, closed and well-guarded.'

*　　　　　　　*　　　　　　　*

We still have time on our hands. On the way back into Hué we visit the city's premier pagoda (out of a hundred and fourteen): dedicated to Thien Mu, or the Heavenly Lady. Its distinguishing feature is an ancient, seven-tiered tower, in which used to reside seven golden Buddhas, only these have now been replaced with bronze replicas. There is a huge bronze bell, one metre forty centimetres broad at its base, that you'd need to be a martial arts fanatic to sound, and in the main altar room six objects that excite my interest. The first three are Buddhas, representing the past, the present and the future; the fourth is a fat gold Buddha; the fifth is a star-stone, a frankly astrological gimmick; and the sixth – well, the sixth is Stein.

Stein has just arrived, having come up from Danang (where he flew from Hanoi). He has a new guide, Loc, whom he introduces me to with near-frantic urgency. His problem, he says, is he hasn't found anywhere to stay yet. Or rather he has, an expensive hotel he doesn't like. I introduce Zoom to Loc, with the firm instruction that he's to move heaven and earth, with or without the aid of the star-stone, to see to it that Stein and his party transfer to the villas in Le Loi Street.

My party transfers to what little remains of the old Imperial Palace, for a preliminary viewing. But the real joy is back at the villa: next door, Stein has already moved in. Everyone agrees to a slap-up banquet.

And a slap-up banquet it is, only who gets slapped up and who doesn't is not altogether clear. Initially Zoom and Truc are in the highest spirits. They have received a message that Sau Dang, the man who will drive me down to Saigon and beyond, is already on his way and will be with us shortly. Stein is in high spirits because he has been listening to the BBC World Service, and has just learned of the incredible events in Berlin: the Wall is coming down, chunk by chunk, even as we eat. Loc is in high spirits because that is his character. Nam is in high spirits because soon he will be driving back to his family in Hanoi. And I am in high spirits because why the hell shouldn't I be if everyone else is?

Such a collection of high spirits however can only be fraught with subtle dangers, and so it proves. I learn from Loc that he is a Cao Dai-ist, and after a few bottles of beer decide to take him on.

226

Cao Dai is among the stranger phenomena of the religious world, and one which, never having had any direct exposure to it, leaves me entirely baffled. In most encyclopaedias it is described as eclectic, highly eclectic, syncretic or highly syncretic. The sect was founded in 1926 by Ngo Van Chieu in somewhat unlikely circumstances. Ngo was attending a seance one night when he received a message from 'Cao Dai' himself. Subsequently Cao Dai became the supreme deity in a galaxy of deities, over whom he presided. The others included Christ, Confucius and Buddha, with the likes of Victor Hugo, Jean d'Arc and Sun Yat Sen putting in guest appearances. Ngo became Pope. In the 1950s Cao Dai developed a paramilitary wing which, in keeping with Saigon politics, from time to time changed sides. At first it supported President Diem, then it opposed him, obliging him to dismantle its army, and exile its then leader, Pham Cong Tac. However, as a church, Cao Dai, with its 2,000,000 congregation, continued to exert influence. Many of its members later joined the National Liberation Front, the official 'opposition' to Diem and his Saigonite successors, clandestinely set up by the communists in 1960.

Now is my chance to get to the bottom of Cao Dai. I go for it in the Socratic manner.

'A Cao Dai-ist, you say,' I say looking at Loc.

'Yes I am. I belong to the Church of Cao Dai.'

'And what exactly is the Church of Cao Dai?'

'It's a church of saints to promote peace and understanding between all peoples of the world.'

'By saints you mean people like Jesus Christ and Confucius and the Buddha and Victor Hugo.'

'Yes, certainly.'

'And is the Prophet Mohammed included among your saints?'

'Yes he is included.'

'But how can that be when Mohammed preached war against infidels, against those who followed some others of your saints?'

'Well, we only choose those parts of the Koran that we think are good.'

'But how do you decide what is good and what is not?'

'According to the principles of Cao Dai.'

'Ah, I see. But what are those principles?'

227

'They are derived from the teachings of its saints.'

'For example, Jesus Christ and the Buddha?'

'Yes. That's right.'

'And, for example, the teachings of the Prophet Mohammed?'

'Yes of course. I think you begin to understand Cao Dai very well.'

'But can't you see that what you've described is a vicious circle?'

'No,' says Loc, 'it's the truth, as practised differently by different people at different times.'

'But what if one person's truth conflicts with or contradicts another's?'

'It couldn't happen.'

'And why not?'

'Because the truth's not like that.'

'Who says?'

'All the saints of Cao Dai say.'

Arrrrghhhhhh!

I desist from further inquiry, even though I'm curious to know how this religion for all seasons has fared since Reunification. Zoom has been giving me a peculiarly black look. Instead, Stein and I begin, in our usual fashion, trading notes. During the course of our conversation I tell him about my meeting with Nguyen, and the four US bodies. Again, Zoom looks discomforted.

'But we are all friends here,' I say.

'Exactly,' says Stein. 'We are all friends. And it is good to talk about these matters.'

The dinner ends in rather lower spirits than it began. Stein and I take a stroll. Since we are accompanying each other, no objections are raised. No sooner are we out of earshot however than Stein tells me he too has heard about President Bush's alleged acceptance of the Vietnamese government's position that there are some bad elements in the country who have hoarded American corpses since the war in the hope of selling them back to their families for large sums of money.

'In short, my friend, I think you have been set up.'

I tell Stein the same had occurred to me, and then I give him my objections.

'You shouldn't underestimate these people,' says Stein.

228

'Do I ever? But I don't believe either that they have plants on every back street.'

We continue our walk and we continue our conversation, albeit along other lines. Stein fills me in on Hanoi gossip during the brief period he outstayed me there. One idle item concerns Nigel Cawthorne. Or rather two items. Firstly, Cawthorne, in his quest for living Americans, has been arrested for attempting to climb over a wire fence into the Hanoi Hilton. In fact he could have gone in by the front entrance. Secondly, having finally succeeded in obtaining an interview with the Foreign Minister Nguyen Co Thach, no sooner have they shaken hands than Cawthorne collapses on the floor and has to be taken to hospital to have a gallstone removed. (Later, when I return to Hanoi, I will hear that it wasn't Thach, but the Defence Minister. Also that when Cawthorne eventually returns to his room at the Thong Nhat, he finds Tim Page has flown out with all his money. Even more improbable is the final embellishment: Page leaves a note on Cawthorne's table that reads: *Sorry, mate, your money has gone MIA.* Page denies this when I get back to England, though he adds: 'Wish I'd done it though. Nigel owed me some money.')

At the villa, another conversation, this time with Zoom. Zoom is not altogether his usual happy self. In fact he is distinctly alarmed by my having mentioned Nguyen (though not by name) and the American remains over dinner. Zoom is of the opinion that Loc is a security agent.

'As in security lock?' I quip. 'Come off it. The man's a Cao Dai-ist.'

'So he says.'

'Are you sure?'

'I'm not sure,' he shrugs. 'But I think so. In any case, one should be careful.'

'I'd better have a word with Stein.'

I cross the darkened garden to the villa next door. Observing that there is a light on in Stein's room, I tap on his window. Stein comes to the frame. Our final conversation today is held through a grille; and because there's a power cut, the oil lamp at Stein's elbow causes our faces to flicker in the most cloak-and-dagger manner.

Stein has been listening to another World Service broadcast. His whole being is agog with serious excitement.

'These are great moments in our lives,' he almost whispers, looking down at me. 'The whole of East Europe is in revolt. Communism is finished.'

'Sad or glad?'

'Oh very glad, I think. This is a great opportunity for socialism.'

Stein gives me the details, then drops his voice even further: 'By the way, I must tell you. Your interpreter is a security person.'

'Don't tell me. Thus spake your man Loc.'

'Yes, but how did you know?'

'Because Zoom just said the same to me about him.'

Stein ponders the implications of this, and then delivers his judgement:

'I think, my friend, in future we had better confine the more interesting parts of our discussions to when we are alone.'

'Perhaps. Though what does it matter? Neither of us has done anything wrong.'

'Even so . . . In the meantime I have been thinking over once again your encounter with the man with the bodies. I am sure it wasn't a coincidence. Bush makes his statement, and then you, a journalist, immediately light upon a confirmation of what the Vietnamese government wants everybody to believe.'

'I don't know,' I say. 'I think if one stops believing in coincidences one stops believing in life. In any case, what would you call our meeting like that at the pagoda today? If that wasn't a coincidence then I might reach out for the conclusion that you too are working for the Vietnamese security services.'

Stein, the ultimate chess-player, ponders this as well, and there is only the thinnest trace of a smile on his lips when he replies: 'Yes. I hadn't thought about that. I suppose you would have to consider that possibility.'

Stein closes the inside shutters of his windows and I creep back to my own villa, more for fear of hurting than of drawing attention to myself. When I get under the mosquito net I cannot help recalling G. K. Chesterton's novel, *The Man Who Was Thursday*. Perhaps

Loc and Zoom are both security. Perhaps Truc is too. And Mr Nam. *And* Nam's five aunts . . .

I begin to giggle, and it is quite a while before I can stop.

Thank God no one can hear me.

Monday 13th November: Hué   It's Ho Chi Minh time again. Accompanied by Mr Thu from the External Relations Bureau (whom I have to buy breakfast at his favourite downtown restaurant) and by Ms Cuk, I am taken to the Quoc Hoc, the National Education School for sixteen- to eighteen-year-olds preparing for university. More specifically, it is required that I attend the once-a-week school assembly. Fifteen hundred pupils stand in form lines in the central compound while the National Anthem crackles out over an ancient Tannoy system. They are then addressed by the school's director, Dang Xuan Trung. Attention is less than absolute, and in no sense do I feel these many young people have been, are being or will ever be brainwashed. There is though a certain uniformity about the girls. They are each and every one of them dressed ravishingly in dazzling white *ao dai*. I take many photographs. A thousand pretty eyes follow my movements as I stalk between the files, attempting – or pretending – to obtain the 'correct' angle. I have never before been in the presence of such collective prettiness. Away from the teachers' rostrum, at the back of the lines, there are whispers, pinches, muted cries. There are also suggestions as to whose picture I should take next. My camera gives me the perfect excuse to examine, at length and in detail, the supple shapes suggested beneath the tightly fastened flowing garments. Vietnam now, sweethearts. Click! I become hyper-aware of my legs. They are confused as to which way they should turn next.

The director and the vice-director, Tran Van Dung, receive me afterwards. As well as Ho Chi Minh, Quoc Hoc's alumni include Pham Van Dong, Vo Nguyen Giap, Le Xuan and a dozen other worthies. But it is of course as Uncle Ho's *alma mater* that the school's reputation is assured. It was opened, I am told, in 1896, by the French, as an academy for future puppet mandarins. To his eternal credit Nguyen Sinh Cung was expelled in 1908, having

231

joined other students in a demonstration against the 'poor teaching standards'. All the teachers were French, and none of them were interested in learning for its own sake. Subsequently, during the war against the French, the Quoc Hoc was used as a colonial barracks. After 1954 it was reopened as a place of education. In the two decades leading up to Reunification it frequently exercised the concern of the Saigon government. Periodically some staff, even students – 'patriots' – were taken away and imprisoned. The Quoc Hoc always was a seed-bed for dissidents.

And now?

'After 1975 there was a review of the staff. Some were replaced. New teachers from the north were introduced. This was essential, as an exercise in quality control.'

I am shown round the buildings, still the French originals. It's a nice place, comparable to Chulalongkorn University in Bangkok, only stripped of the gilded gables. In some of the classes I recognize some of the faces I saw earlier through the viewfinder of my Pentax. The girls – a slim majority of the students – are still dressed in their *ao dai*. I nod, smile cautiously, and do my utmost to appear the disinterested visitor I'm supposed to be. The male students however are ahead of me. As soon as I catch any of their eyes their faces explode into foot-wide grins. At the Quoc Hoc today I detect a distinct dearth of politics.

I pass out under the watchful gaze of Uncle Ho himself: the hand-raised-waving portrait which is suspended under the eaves of a renovated pink building close to the gates. I graduate to the Teacher Training College, a mile away on the same southern side of the Perfumed River. Here a reception committee awaits me: two vice-directors and half a dozen lecturers. The college prepares graduates for a life ahead in education, either in Hué itself, or in any one of the ten central provinces. I open my notebook. Truc sits beside me and makes an utter hash of translating. Fortunately, included around the table are two or three English teachers: as in Hanoi, English is the in subject, and the college is struggling to meet increased demands for qualified practitioners from the provinces. 'In accordance with state planning,' someone hastily adds. Once through the statistics, something like a real debate develops.

232

There has been real progress since 1986. Students are freer to choose their special subjects. Also, the students are increasingly of a higher standard. Before *doi moi* preference was given to those who had served in the army. It also helped if you came from a 'revolutionary family', if you were the offspring of a 'fallen hero'. Now students are selected according to merit. There is also a streamlining system: the best pupils are put into special classes so that they have more chance of reaching their potential. Yet when I inquire of what is taught, a certain stickiness develops. I am anxious to discover whether Buddhism and Confucianism have any bearing on the syllabuses. Heads nod and shake around the table. Somebody says, 'Ho Chi Minh paid much attention to Buddhism and wanted it taught.' Somebody else says, 'The proper place to acquire Buddhist teaching is in the home.' Ditto Confucianism. The political philosophy classes are still confined to the orthodox indoctrination of Marxism–Leninism.

'But surely since Confucian ideas have played such an important role in Vietnamese history and culture, Confucianism is studied in Hué?' I plead.

But no, Confucianism is not studied, neither here nor at the university.

Yet, on my way out of the room, when the meeting finishes, one of the lecturers, a young woman, grabs my arm and whispers in my ear: 'But of course, we all read Confucius at home!'

Is this said just to placate me? Had I asked a similar question about J. K. Galbraith would the same have happened? Somehow Confucius as a clandestine, neo-subversive text doesn't sound right.

Mr Thu vanishes. The head of the English department, a young and terrifically intelligent man called Tran Xun Thao, takes me across to his neck of the concrete. Briefly we sit in his office, where he tells me of the sheer difficulties in obtaining teaching materials, particularly the works of standard authors. He wrote his own doctoral thesis on Ernest Hemingway, but has only ever managed to lay his hands on four of Hemingway's books. Then I am taken to be introduced to a class.

It happens again. Before I can refuse I am left alone with them. Well, not quite alone. Truc sits at the back of a large, airy room in which forty or so young men and women are seated at bench-desks. He looks at me with a slight air of defiance. I have been giving him a hard time for his bumbling attempts at interpretation earlier, and now he's eager to see how well I will fare. The class is too big for me to repeat the tactics used at the Foreign Languages College in Hanoi. There are too many to create an intimate, personalized circle. For a moment I am flummoxed. But then, inspiration! I remember *Good Morning, Vietnam!*, and Robin Williams's handling of an English class in Saigon *circa* 1968. I give it to them. Simply by slipping out of my own persona and into someone else's I succeed in raising the atmosphere I want: a laugh a minute for at least an hour. At the same time though I use the laughter as a cover for something more serious. I introduce the topic of 'student technique'. Always be nice to your teacher, I tell them, a teacher is as human as you are, but also don't be afraid to see to it that you get the best out of your teacher. If he doesn't speak up, or goes too fast, or fudges anything – and I give examples of all these pitfalls – then the student owes it to himself to harass him.

I also make a point of attacking down the lines. Determined that all should be involved, I rocket up and down the desks spraying questions in every direction. Plainly they're not used to this, and I believe, once they've accustomed themselves to my shocking teacher technique, a certain temperatuire is generated. At any rate, when the class disperses twenty minutes after the bell, a body of them implore me to return.

But there is one young woman who is not at all bewildered. On one of my forays past where she is sitting she gently tugs my arm and gives me a note. Signed 'Cherry Blossom', this tells me that I am truly a human being and that she hopes I will become her 'special friend'.

For two days this will, at odd moments, tickle my vanity no end, until, showing it to Stein, Stein produces from his pocket an almost identical letter. Stein too has been to the Teacher Training College, and Stein too has been assured that truly he is a human being.

Truc, Zoom, Nam and I take lunch at 'Hell Restaurant', a truckers' joint where we are served with pork wrapped in coarse rice-paper.

The afternoon includes a brief visit to the local Ho Chi Minh Museum, where I am given a potted version of Hué's revolutionary history (which does not include the Viet Cong reprisals of 1968), and a longer visit to what remains of the old Imperial Palace. Except for the monumental gate, the palace proper was largely destroyed in the American war. A few buildings have however survived, including an ornate ironwood resting pavilion inlaid with a great deal of mother-of-pearl built by the third Nguyen emperor Thieu Tri (1840–7). The collection of traditional Vietnamese artefacts that this now houses is genuinely impressive: ceramics, ceramic bronzes, lanterns, marble tables, beds old and new, a gold-fringed palanquin, a set of stone cymbals (*dan da*), opium pipes (iron as well as bamboo), various turtle-shell boxes, ivory jugs, ivory glasses, white jade ornaments and at least one cruciform betelnut holder. An elegant wooden sculpture shows a crane (beauty) standing on a tortoise (longevity), apparently giving him a foot massage he is ill equipped to appreciate. Four Hungarian generals, attended by their overweight wives, trail forlornly around the exhibits. Truc, whose day it is not, translating Ms Cuk, painfully relays the vital information about Thieu Tri's eating habits. The emperor was accustomed to select his dinner from a spread of 150 dishes prepared by 150 cooks. To make life easier, each dish was named after its chef, so that if it didn't meet with the monarch's satisfaction the man could be summarily dismissed.

Outside, the imposingly famous nine dynastic urns. Then it's back to Nam's van for a ride to Duong No village eight kilometres away, to see the house where Ho Chi Minh's father lived when he stayed in Hué. About this charming but otherwise insouciant edifice there is just a breath of scandal. For Ho's mother died in Hué. More to the point, she was not (or so the rumour goes) living with his father at the time. Rather she had taken to drink, and Nguyen Sinh Sac *had turfed her out*. Either that, or she had left voluntarily to pursue a gayer life. At any rate, there are reasons to suspect that the Holy Family may have been less inviolate than its Marxist-Leninist promoters have ever since cracked it up to have been.

I am also shown, to give my venerative faculty its final outing for the day, the single-storeyed dwelling where H.C.M. himself stayed in Hué after he had enrolled at the Quoc Hoc. Thereafter I am able, with the benefit of one of my hostesses' bicycles, to enjoy relative freedom, touring the green back streets of the old Vaubonesque citadel for an hour or so more or less on my own. Then it's back to the villa for another, somewhat early aggregated dinner, during the course of which Ms Cuk demurely plucks her vocal cords to give Stein and me a dreamy rendering of two Hué moon-songs.

The dinner is early because Zoom and Truc are due to have a second dinner elsewhere. The reason for this is the equally premature arrival of Mr Sau, who was not expected until tomorrow.

Nguyen Minh Dang, to give Mister Six his full and proper name, is a cut above his fellow mortals. To begin with, he is inordinately good looking. His face, though capable of many delicate expressions, reminds me, when I first see it, of the features of the classic Japanese *samurai*. His hairline forms a deep V over a generous forehead, his short sideburns are stylized, like velvet cones. His nose, in profile, is very slightly hooked: an Italian touch, aristocratic, at times arrogant. The body follows: a well-kept, supple bull's torso. Legs. A southerner, with a southern temperament: quite unlike the Hanoians I am used to. Capable at times of real noise and an overweening passion. Not altogether without some of the qualities of a prima donna. But these Sau is entitled to, by virtue of his provenance, of his seniority (he tells me he is fifty-three) and because he is an accomplished actor.

Sau has appeared in over thirty movies. He tends to play the womanizing gangster, the Saigon regime officer who falls prey to all the corruptions of the flesh. In reality Sau, or Captain Sau Dang, as he used to be, was and is a cadre – as well as being an inveterate ladies' man. Originally he was a VC who regrouped north to join the NVA. Beneath the flamboyance of his everyday personality is an enduring commitment to the values of the Revolution, even though the Revolution is often at odds with his lifestyle.

He is, as I soon discover, immensely popular, and this for me is one of his assets. To walk down a street with him is no longer to be gazed at by everyone: everyone is gazing at him. He takes the heat off. He also possesses a magical *what's-in-it-for-me?* grin that

236

Jack Nicholson would be hard pressed to best. Put at my disposal, this grin becomes *what's-in-it-for-us?* As my guide to the south, he has the further advantage that all the world, or nearly all the world, knows him. And because of his age, he is on an equal footing with all but the very highest potatoes. There are very few doors that do not yield before him.

As well as being an actor and an old revolutionary, Sau runs the Saigon office of the Services Centre of the Ministry of Information. The acting is a side-line. This though is an aspect of the southern system. To succeed in any activity not directly related to government it is almost essential to work for the government. That way you will have friends who will let you do what you want when you're not in the office. Sau also owns a coach, which he rents out as a private business. Several times Truc will tell me that he is 'rich', though how rich is purely a matter of conjecture.

All of which poses a conundrum. I can think of no other country in which a man of Sau Dang's standing, experience, age and personality would willingly give up six weeks of his time to chaperon someone who is more than a dozen years his junior, whom he has never met before and whose language he speaks not a word of. And yet that is precisely what he has undertaken. For the next forty-odd days he will be my guardian, my organizer, my negotiator . . . and my driver! And all these things he will do not simply with a good grace, but at times with a fervour.

On some days, the fervour I could do without. Sau has his instructions the same as any other cadre, but in Sau's case they have to be fulfilled to the letter. This means that his great powers of determination are occasionally at odds with what I think I should be seeing and doing. Yet, he is never so happy as when I am happy. That, I dare think, is where he derives his job satisfaction.

Conversely, in opposition he is a formidable force. And because meekness is not an abiding part of my own make-up – though I can display it when I want to, when I have to – real clashes are portended between us: moments when in the consummate purity of his heart Sau Dang believes he knows my best interests, and I believe he doesn't, and we are both reduced to gnashing our teeth, with poor Truc bearing the brunt of it from both sides. I though will gnash my teeth the harder, because, in simple human terms,

I'll always know that in resisting Sau I am resisting someone better than myself.

He is there at the villa when I return from my short cycling expedition. Zoom, hyper-excited, all but pulls me into his room. 'Sau Dang's arrived! Really!' Sau, after a non-stop drive up from Saigon in the thirty-year-old battered blue Mazda that soon will seem the nearest thing I know to home, is stripped to his underpants. We shake hands, but that for the moment is as much camaraderie as either of us can muster. Sau does not join the dinner table. Zoom apologizes on his behalf. 'Mister Sau has some relatives in Hué, so he has gone to have dinner with them.' The 'relatives' turn out to be two women, about my own age. For a good deal of the forthcoming journey to Saigon they will accompany us, squashed into the back seat of the Mazda with Truc nestling sheepishly between them.

For now, they have hired a private dining room in a nearby hotel, whither we all – Stein included – repair. I sense at once that Zoom and Truc would prefer an all-Vietnamese party, so we decline the politely offered invitation, and having been introduced to Madame Phuong and Madame Thu, Stein and I disentangle from the group. We will, we say, find our own way home.

First though we opt for a beer. The only bar we can find doubles as the reception desk of a massage parlour. I tease Stein into having his back pummelled. While he is gone I fall into conversation with a lieutenant-colonel at the next table. The man tells me he saw me earlier in the day. He was escorting the four Hungarian generals around the antiquities museum at the palace. He opens up surprisingly quickly. His family come from Saigon. His father, an early Party member, was killed fighting the French in 1946. He himself went to Hanoi in 1953, to study English at the university. In the war against America he returned south, working as an intelligence officer. He interviewed over thirty US prisoners of war. These included Bobby Garwood, the last American to leave Vietnam. (Garwood is supposed to have stayed on 'voluntarily', until one day he decided he'd had enough. In America he was tried as a deserter and given a four-year jail sentence. Rumour has it that his Vietnamese minders and girlfriend were subsequently shot: the

238

government al legedly considered they might have been corrupted by the inconsistencies of his attitudes.) The morale of the American fighting man, the colonel tells me, was never high.

Now he is an infantry commander in the Fifth Zone, based at Danang. The army is currently developing its 'business interests': it owns several rubber, coffee and tea plantations, and some of the younger officers are being trained in business management.

As casually as I can I ask about MIAs. The colonel seems not at all surprised that I should ask. Yes, he says, some of the old southerners have deliberately kept bodies, hoping to sell them when the time is ripe. He knows of at least ten cases of this in Danang alone.

Stein emerges from his massage not nearly as refreshed as I'd hoped. He complains about the filth on the floor, although the massage itself, the first he has ever had, excites no complaint. The colonel, after writing down his name and inviting me to stay at the Army Guesthouse in Danang, goes through the doors and into one of the cubicles. Before leaving the hotel, I suggest we call in on my entourage. Getting lost on the way to Madame Phuong's private dining room we are accosted by two prostitutes. We are just politely evading their overtures when Truc materializes behind us. He is unnecessarily inquisitive, and suddenly I feel angry. What are *you* doing? I ask. Truc dissembles, but doesn't leave us until we are out on the road.

That night there is, apparently, a kerfuffle. Two prostitutes, presumably the same women, come to the villas in Le Loi Street. They present themselves to Stein's guide, Lok, and his driver. Lok, a puritan in the Thang mould, is not at all amused. Did they go to the wrong villa? Or were they intended as a present of some sort? A practical joke perhaps. Though later I quiz Truc, exactly what happened is never established.

Tuesday 14th November: Hué   Zoom has fixed for me to visit the Central Hospital, following my chance meeting with Dr Tran Thi Doan Trang on my first afternoon in Hué. Built by the Americans, it is a sizeable, refreshingly modern place. I am introduced to several of Dr Tran's colleagues. Respiratory disorders, seasonal

239

malaria, malnutrition and diarrhoea are the daily problems they have to cope with. Primary health care consists of attempting to apply the GOBIFFFA programme. G is for Growth monitoring: records are kept on every child in the province. O is for Oral rehydration therapy: glucose and salt to combat dysentery. B is for Breast-feeding, another weapon in the fight against infantile bowel disorders. I is the six-part Immunization scheme: TB, whooping cough, tetanus, diphtheria, polio and measles. F: Food supplement (for mothers and babies); Female education (first aid, symptom recognition, ordinary hygiene); and Family planning (contraception and pregnancy spacing). And A, vitamin A, reflecting an endemic deficiency in the Vietnamese diet.

Although the programme is still being evolved, it is, I am assured, working. There has also, since the advent of *doi moi*, been an improvement in social economic conditions both in the city and in the province. In addition, private medicine is now available to those who can afford it. Whereas two years ago on average two hundred patients arrived at the hospital every day, now the numbers are down to fifty. Certainly, when I am taken through the wards, a very high percentage of the one thousand beds are standing empty. Yet the equipment I see is antediluvian. Even something as basic as serum separation cannot be done in the rudimentary pathology laboratory. Dr Tran's colleagues tell me about other shortages too, particularly drugs. Post-op anaesthetics, for example, are wholly unavailable, so instead surgeons have to make do with acupuncture. In the maternity wing I am shown a battery of incubators that date back to French times. Only one of them works.

What is not explained to me is that neither central nor provincial government can any longer afford to run the public health service. In the Thatcherite spirit that prevails, health care too is expected to be self-funding. For this reason prescription and hospitalization charges have been introduced. While the rich may be going to the private doctors, the poor are simply staying away, reverting to 'traditional medicines' instead. The empty wards therefore are not wholly explicable in terms of the efficacy of the primary health care programme.

This is told me much later on my journey. For now, it is all smiles. I am taken to have tea with the hospital's vice-director. As we are talking, a representative of the 'US Committee for Scientific Cooperation with Vietnam' enters the room. Every inch of Dr William Fritz is the Good American. In the war he served as an engineer in central Vietnam. While still on his tour of duty he decided that one day he would return to Vietnam to help repair a little of the damage his country had caused. With this in mind he studied medicine when he got back to the States. Today he is a successful surgeon. Once a year he comes back to Vietnam, at his own expense, and operates wherever he is most needed.

'So what have you been doing this morning?' I ask.

'Oh the usual thing. Mostly resetting bones that were broken years ago and have never properly mended. A couple of appendectomies. And . . . But come, you must see for yourself.'

Dr Fritz takes me back into the hospital proper, to the intensive care unit. I enter a room in the corner of which a patient is moaning under a blanket that has been pulled right up over his head.

The reason the blanket has been pulled up over the patient's head is that most of his face has been blown away. Both ears and one eye are missing. Also gone: the feet, one leg and one arm.

Briefly a nurse uncovers him: the patient, a man probably somewhere in his sixties, looks at me with the eye that remains. He shakes uncontrollably, and emits a ghastly high-pitched whimper. I think he sees me. I also think he thinks he's already dead, and that in some recondite manner I am one of his killers.

The nurse gently replaces the blanket. The whimpering subsides to a moan.

'What happened?' I ask.

'What always happens,' Dr Fritz replies. 'His plough hit a leftover landmine. It was probably one of ours.'

'Will he live?'

'Nope.'

After that, the rest of the day is out of tune. At lunchtime Zoom and Nam set off on their journey back to Hanoi. In the afternoon I return to the Teacher Training College to give a repeat performance of my Robin Williams impersonation, but it doesn't work. The class has grown since I was last there. Instead of forty students I am confronted by well over a hundred and fifty. Word it seems has got round. Instead of student technique, I endeavour to open up a discussion about religions and ideologies. When everyone in the world thinks differently, what's the solution? I ask. To my intense disappointment the young man in the front row, whom so far I've considered as the brightest of an enthusiastic bunch, sticks up his hand and says, 'We must all become Catholics.' Previously, when I'd asked the class for an example of a word that describes something that doesn't exist he'd shot his hand up and said, 'Utopia.' In the end I fall back on aping Hollywood manners. Only then do I raise more than a polite laugh. When the class falls out however, a group of students, led by Miss Cherry Blossom, stay behind and invite me to take coffee with them at the Children's Culture Centre at the other end of town. At closer quarters the students become overly self-conscious. What they really want, it transpires, is a group photograph. We remount our bicycles and find a photographer who lines everybody up outside the gates of the Thong Nhat. I scarcely have the energy to say *com chien*, fried rice. Then in the evening there's a formal dinner at the villa: a game of compliments with a professor from the university, Mr Thu from the External Relations Bureau, and Mr Thu's superior, Nguyen Van Dieu, the bureau chief.

Mr Dieu, who actually does in a small way think he's God, I don't take to at all. He tells us (Stein is in on the occasion too) that he is a member of the national lawyers' association. Halfway through the meal Cherry Blossom comes to the gate, ostensibly to request my address, so that she knows where to send the group photo once it's ready, but actually to cry a little on my shoulder. Her problem is her family's on its way out, going to America hurrah!, only Cherry Blossom doesn't want to leave Vietnam, she wants to stay in Hué with her friends and continue her studies.

'Then stay,' I say. 'You're old enough.'

'No, I cannot. Not without my family. I could not survive. A person without a family is like a person without her clothes.'

The compliments, the formalities are still going on when I return to the table. Suddenly I've had enough of them. Since so far I've been denied the opportunity of meeting anyone from the Ministry of Justice, I decide to tackle Mr Dieu. The Amnesty International

242

Central Hanoi: replica of the Paris Opera House surmounted by an air-raid siren.

Mister Nam in his Russian van.

Zoom has his head attended in Halong Bay.

By the waters of Lenin Stream: Zoom and Tam.

Zoom with cadres and army men outside the cave at Pac Bo.

Cao Bang worthies: the author with, to the right, Vu Ngoc Bo
(chairman of the People's Committee) and Mr Vuong.

Mister Nam's aunts, all five of them, outside Ho Chi
Minh's childhood home.

Ho Chi Minh's great-grand-niece Vuong Thi Hoai with
her father Vuong Van Chung.

The loveliness that is Hué: two of the house-mothers at the villa in Le Loi Street.

Have Mazda will travel: Sau Dang's wheels on their way back from Phu Chau.

Truc on the left, Sau Dang on the right.

Nguyen Anh Vu: southern hospitality personified.

Kissinger's nemesis: Le Duc Tho.

Ho Chi Minh's mausoleum in Hanoi.

The right-hand man of the Revolution: General Vo
Nguyen Giap, with the author.

report on human rights abuses should be out by now (in fact publication has been delayed until February, but this I cannot know). Carefully I congratulate my hosts on all the areas where Vietnam has been given a clean bill of health. Then I come to the judicial system. Are there going to be reforms in that department as well? I ask. The atmosphere freezes. The university professor (a geologist) almost shouts, 'No, that cannot be true, there is nothing at all the matter with our laws.' Mr Dieu and Mr Thu, casting angry looks in my direction, confer between themselves. The opinion is expressed that such matters are better left undiscussed at dinner. This in turn arouses Stein, who staunchly supports me. No, he says, in his ultra-pedagogic manner, such things must be aired. The spirit of internationalism, and all of that. But no progress is made. A phoney amicability is restored, but the dinner ends soon enough.

Probably, as far as Hué is concerned, I've burned my boats, but since I'm leaving for Danang tomorrow, what the hell?

On his way out Mr Thu presents Stein's guide with a bill for his services. It's only 20,000 *dong,* but even so Stein is angry. All that Mr Thu has done is eat and drink at our expense whenever he's had the opportunity.

'What do you make of that?' I ask Truc. 'Can I expect the same tomorrow morning?'

'Probably. You see, Mr Thu is retiring soon, so . . .'

Stein and I take a walk. The streets are full of intimidating barking dogs. Also, the public Tannoy system has come to life. On every third lamp-post a loudspeaker blares forth propaganda. Suddenly the city has lost its charm. These are not the last impressions of Hué I want to take with me, but nonetheless that's what they are.

Stein tells me, with guarded triumph, how he has spent the day visiting the tomb of the first Nguyen dynasty emperor, Gia Long. Not a place on the tourist circuit, but out in the real jungle where a boy was needed to walk ahead and clear the non-existent path of snakes. 'I have to tell you, I really felt what it was like to become an explorer.' I am made to feel a little envious. With Truc to keep an eye on me I seriously wonder what opportunities for adventure will come my way in the month ahead.

We say goodnight. Goodnight in all probability is also farewell. It is the end of Stein. And that doesn't make me happy either.

Wednesday 15th November: Hué–Danang The feeling that I'm leaving all the people I like behind persists. Mr Sau is only in the offing, I do not know him yet. Truc has yet to win his spurs. Zoom and Nam have vanished. Stein is gone . . . I must say farewell to the girls who have looked after me so well at the villa in Le Loi Street. Even the appearance of a delegation of students from the Teacher Training College just before breakfast cannot lift my spirits. They too have come to bid adieu. And sure enough, Mr Thu drops by, to see me out of town and collect his twenty thou. I have it ready for him though. In Hanoi I bought a supply of hand-painted greetings cards from a stationer's near the Thong Nhat. Mr Thu gets the drawing of a pig.

Danang, the fourth biggest city in Vietnam and renowned as the place where the first US combat troops landed, is not so far, just sixty or seventy kilometres down the coast. To get there though we must hike ourselves over Hai Van, another mountain pass that if anything is even more colossal than Ngang (between Ha Tinh and Dong Hoi). At the top a rain storm rages. To the south however is the sunlit gleam of watered plains. Sau clutches my knee and grins. From here on the weather, increasingly wintry until now, will dramatically improve, if baking tropical heat can be called an improvement. It's as simple as that. At Hai Van, at this time of the year, the meteorological layout of Vietnam is creased down the middle like an open book. On the left (as you look toward the sea) rain, and a damp that makes the limbs ache. On the right, a humid heat that considerably increases your appetite for any kind of liquid refreshment.

Reaching the shoreline we stop at a village for coffee. Sau's female 'relatives' investigate large packets of dried seahorse. From the boot of the Mazda Sau himself produces a crate of Heineken, which he sells to the café owner. In the days to come there will be not a few such transactions. Madame Phuong, Truc whispers, has gotten rich by trading jade. He also tells me that Sau is called Six not only because he is a fifth child, but also because he once saw

244

off six attackers in a fight. Hearing his name, the hero adds to his own mythology by producing, from his pocket-book, a carefully folded article that appeared some while ago in an Australian film magazine. 'Sau Dang, the Charles Bronson of the Vietnamese Screen'. The interviewer relates how she asked Sau whether 'he always got his girl', meaning did he always play Romeo parts. But Sau mistook this for a question about his actual life. His answer: 'Quite often, but I always love my wife too.'

I hand back the article. Sau smiles and pumps my knee again. Truc, who has obviously been carefully briefed by Zoom in the art of keeping Mister Justin happy, says: 'You see? We are all gangsters on the road.'

We reach our destination in time for lunch. Danang does not appeal. After Hué it's gratingly hard. My first appraisal is: the best that can be said for it is it's not as bad as Haiphong. The streets are scruffy, and lack character. The People's Committee guest-house, close by a canal that forms a part of the port system, in particular is sepulchral. The doors are kept locked, and the staff to open them are often impossible to find. My room, though big enough, lacks a window. Added to which, when we first arrive I am told I must pay $30 a night for the privilege of such an imprisonment.

'Why don't we stay at the Army Guesthouse instead?' I say to Truc, 'I've got the address.'

'I'm sorry. But we are guests of the People's Committee and they want us to stay here.'

'Guests?!'

The other thing to be said in Danang's favour is that it provides the perfect excuse for my escalating dudgeon.

There are some things to see however, and see them I will. Today, the Museum of Cham Art, run by a Mr Ky. Cham art consists exclusively of Cham sculpture, which at its best, blending Hindu and Buddhist motifs and forms, is as good as anything in SE Asia. As I run my eyes and fingers over thousand-year-old stone breasts, however, a nameless figure pops out from behind the farouche countenance of an enlarged Shiva. 'This country will never be any good until the government changes,' he spits in my ear, and disappears. I look round quickly to see where Truc is, but

245

Truc is standing some distance away, blearily contemplating a goddess who holds what appears to be a toasting fork in her left hand.

Having paid a courtesy call on the External Relations Bureau of the People's Committee, we return to the jailhouse. I find a warder and, while Sau and Truc rest, obtain temporary parole. The people in a long, winding market half a mile away are all exceedingly friendly, but still Danang remains beyond my liking.

On my way back I pass a shop that surprisingly sells bottles of Johnny Walker whisky. I inquire the price: 30,000 *dong,* or about $7. I buy it. Why not? Sau Dang I'm sure will appreciate the gesture.

I've already clocked Sau's liking for drink. This is confirmed in the evening. Madame Phuong, who evidently must be well off, treats us all to dinner at a restaurant near the centre of town (where she is staying at a hotel). The cans of San Miguel pile up on the table and around the legs of the chairs. Here I observe, for the first time, the southern way of eating. Everything that can be tipped onto the floor is. Bones, gristle, beer cans, bad vegetables, any rice that spills from the rice-bowl.

We walk the main street in search of coffee. Now Sau comes into his own. Everybody recognizes him. People stop and stare. Truc nudges me, as though to say *There! you see! everything you've been told about the man is true!*

Even so, it's early to bed. As soon as we enter the guesthouse the doors are secured behind us.

I ask Truc what do I do if I want to get out. Truc tells me that I mustn't want to get out, that what I should want is relaxation and an early night.

'That's the best thing. Don't you remember? I told you. In Hanoi if I stay out late then my mother doesn't give me any breakfast.'

Thursday 16th November: Danang–Hoi An   I suppose it's worth trying. Lock me up at night, then I'll appreciate the daytime tourist excursions more. So after an early breakfast of coffee and bread taken at a roadside stall it's off to the old trading port of Hoi An — better known to the outside world as Faifo, from the times when the French called Danang Tourane. The journey takes an hour. On the way we stop at one of the new joint-venture prawn farms the Australian community in Hanoi had told me to visit. To my chagrin, the large new prawn tanks are each and every one of them empty. Sau pulls a face, as if to say: No good! No good! Truc, who seems sometimes to have difficulty in knowing what to think himself, scowls agreement.

At least though Hoi An is worth the trouble getting there. It teaches me a thing or two. Perhaps this is because it's an anagram of Hanoi. At the tourist office I am greeted by one Mr Nhan. Mr Nhan does his level best to bury the intrinsic prettiness of the place beneath the customary pile of statistics. Hoi An enjoyed its apogee in the seventeenth century, although its continuance as a port lasted right up until the early years of the present century, when the shipways finally became so silted that cargo vessels had to be re-routed elsewhere. The Chinese, the Japanese, the Portuguese, the Dutch and the French have all used it at one time or another. The town's distinctive feature is its layout. There are three main streets. Along these the merchants built their houses. Parallel with the streets are, or were, canals, so that merchandise could be loaded straight onto boats from the back of the houses. But to be exact, there are nine – nine! – different forms of building in Hoi An. Mr Nhan lists these as: private houses, family chapels, community halls, communal houses, temples, pagodas, bridges, wells and tombs. The average age of each building is 200 years, although the oldest goes back at least a millennium. Today the population has shrunk to around six thousand, of whom 26% are ethnic Chinese. In the past, the principal exports were swifts' nests (for birdsnest soup), incense, quartz, silk, amber, silver, ivory . . .

I am taken through the narrow streets to examine one of the bridges, Chua Cau, originally built by the Japanese in 1593. The base is stone, the covered superstructure ironwood, jackwood and other hardwoods. The purity of the constructional lines however has been sabotaged by an overlay of Chinese and Vietnamese ornamentation. Next I am ushered inside one of the merchant houses. This I like, this does something to me. It is not wholly unlike a Georgian chapel. The interior is narrow and lofty, with a barrel-vault ceiling high above my head. There is a shop room at the front, where presumably the merchant displayed his wares to potential customers, beneath a raised storage loft; and then a back room, where he, his family, his apprentices and his servants lived. All is deeply polished. Ironwood columns are hung with decorated poems, the words and floral patterns inlaid with shell. There are lace curtains, candlesticks and old silver lamps. The furniture is heavy, prosperous, reassuring, the atmosphere unlike anything else I have seen or will see in Vietnam. I am impressed by the way it has been preserved, as well as by the fact that it has been preserved at all.

Finally, in Hoi An, a Chinese community hall, part what it says it is, part temple, a place of ancestors, shrines, figurines, inscriptions and conference tables. Plus a lovingly detailed model of a trading junk.

At the rear, an altar dedicated to the three important gods of health, wealth and longevity. At the side, smaller figurines for specific remedies: for example a goddess who will stop your baby crying, if you leave her a sufficient tip. I have never been especially enamoured of Chinese religious iconography, chiefly for aesthetic reasons: there's usually a bright plasticity about the *objets* that does nothing for the soul. Also, a multiplicity of curls and squiggles that tend to irritate rather than transcend. In Taoist or Confucian places of worship the tone rarely succeeds in getting beyond superstition. But here, in the Fu Kien Community Hall at Hoi An, I see the other side: that health, wealth and longevity are the most anyone can hope for, and that to seek to go beyond superstition is excessive. The strength of the Chinese is in their practicality, and their practicality is strong because it is confined to the basics. Since health, wealth and longevity can never be absolutely guaranteed to anyone, it is only natural that superstition should be allowed free play.

The practicality of the Vietnamese is exhibited on the drive back to Danang. Off the main road, I am led up and into the Marble Mountains.

In very broad terms, the Viet Minh, in their struggle against the French, and the Viet Cong, in their struggle against the Saigon regime and the Americans, controlled the heights, while their enemies exerted tenuous control over the coastal and alluvial plains. Danang, being a coastal port with a network of waterways, is surrounded by plain. It was therefore a good site for a concentration of US forces. On the outskirts is the enormous Hoa Vang airstrip. But also on the outskirts, three or four miles to the south, is a small range of limestone hills. Although these stand in splendid isolation, they were nonetheless, in accordance with the great pattern of the Vietnam wars, infested with guerrillas.

What made infestation possible was that the Marble Mountains were largely hollow. First I climb up the craggy slopes, then I climb down again, into a series of truly huge caverns. Here the VC had a camp, which included a field hospital for cadres wounded in guerrilla campaigns in and around Danang. Truc points out rifle-bullet and mortar-shell holes on some of the walls of the caves. Periodically the Marines moved in, in an attempt to flush Charlie out. But Charlie, with or without the help of the women's artillery unit, nearly always held his hollow.

We stop off too at the beach, near where the first US Marines landed. The shoreline is a beautiful breezy tropical postcard. At a sandy restaurant I am introduced to a gaggle of writers. I must meet Nguyen Khac Phuc, they tell me. It's a pity he isn't with them. Nguyen Khac Phuc is the number one author in Danang. He is writing a seven-volume novel about the war. The whole is called *Flying over Death*, while individually the separate parts have titles like *Tuition Fees Paid with Blood, The City against the Wind* and *The Colour of the Dead*. The basis of this monumental saga is the life and times of one particular hero-cadre, Le Cong Co. Le Cong Co is real and living. Originally he was the organizer of the youth and resistance movements in Hué. Now he is vice-president of the provincial Fatherland Front, a deputy to the National Assembly and a director of the Danang Province Tourist Company. Maybe *Flying over Death*, when it is finished, will turn out the *War and Peace* of modern Vietnamese literature.

Maybe. Or, I cynically tell myself, Nguyen Khac Phuc knows which side his bread is buttered. Or perhaps both.

But I too must sing for my supper. My room rate at the guesthouse has yet to be settled. In the afternoon I am wheeled along to the People's Committee for a fulsome re-education session with the vice-chairman, Nguyen Ding An. The reception room is bigger, the central table longer than any I've encountered before, and Mr An's wad of notes thicker.

Nguyen Ding An has the face, manner and persistence of a junior accountant. He slays me with figures. The first point about Danang, he kicks off, is that it is equidistant from Hanoi and Saigon. The population of the city is 400,000, of the province 1,700,000. The province has an area of 12,000 square kilometres, seventy-five per cent of which is mountainous. Wet-rice cultivation, bronze, silver and ceramics have been on the go since the most ancient of times. Until the thirteenth century, Danang was a part of the Cham people's kingdom (Champa). From then on it gradually but inevitably became part of Vietnam. In the seventeenth century it became the focal point for 'international economic expansion'. Silk, sugar, pepper and spices. But not only was Danang the place where the first US Marines landed, it was also the original point of entry for the French, and Quang Nam Danang was the first province to offer them resistance. Later it was the first province to organize its own local Communist Party committee. The Americans concentrated one-fifth of all their forces in the area, and so not surprisingly Danang became one of the fiercest battlefields of the US war. 'Most' of the countryside was destroyed. The peasantry were either brought into the city (whose population swelled to over a million), or concentrated in villages along the highway where they could be supervised. Even so, the total number of Danang Vietnamese killed in the fighting was 200,000. All this created an unenviable post-war heritage. There were for example 130,000 long-term wounded to look after, and the province's agriculture had been smashed. But by 1980 annual production had risen to 500,000 tons of rice, or paddy equivalent, and the people had been led back to the land. Soldiers and the youth were mobilized to clear the minefields. New irrigation works were constructed.

The way ahead was to consolidate agricultural produce and germinate industrial ventures with a view to finding export markets. Exports and would-be exports include mulberry, peanuts, bananas, pineapples, melons and peaches. ('Exports' do not necessarily go abroad: in province-orientated Vietnam, exports also include anything sold to another province.) And then of course, there's wood.

There are approximately 30,000,000 cubic metres of wood waiting 'to be exploited'. Already, 50,000 cubic metres are sold out of the province every year. And this is after local demands have been met.

'But please, don't worry! Deforestation is not what we are doing, it's what the Americans with their napalm and Agent Orange did. We are actually replanting as and when we can. We have plans for the re-arborification of the whole of the coastal strip.'

New forests will provide rattan, wood for paper-pulping and the 'correct' environment for the many plants required by traditional medicine. There will also be fresh coffee, cashew and pepper plantations. The army is helping with these projects a great deal. And then of course, seafood. Danang has the benefit of 150 kilometres of coastline. The current 40,000 tons of fish landed annually are only a beginning. 'We are driving for shrimps.' The whole of the handicraft industry has been rebuilt since the war. Now it is the second largest in the whole of the south. Advanced technology comes next. One problem though is the supply of electricity. The present capacity is only 25,000 kilowatts per hour. This is three times what it was in 1975, but there is still a long way to go. But never mind, the national grid is on its way. Only for now must we go it alone. The future, when it comes, will consist of shipbuilding, textiles, chemical processing, glass, oil . . . all on the grand scale.

Has he overstated his case? Well yes, he has a little. As well as electricity, Danang needs technology, skills and money. Unemployment is very high. So the doors are open. Anyone can come and help us. Know any multinationals? Yes, there are investors arriving almost every day from Saigon, but somehow they are reluctant to invest their new-found wealth in industry. Mainly their money goes into the service sector. 'In Danang now are many new restaurants. But perhaps our excellent king prawns will entice the larger sharks from overseas.'

It is the familiar story. The achievement is as great as the needs, the needs are as great as the achievement. Right now my achievement is to have taken down most of what Nguyen Ding An has told me – of which the above is only a synopsis; and my need is a shot of whisky. Back in my room I open the Johnny Walker Red Label purchased yesterday. But before I can taste it the smell sends me reeling across my bed. If it's not actually coloured methylated spirits, then it's a brilliant imitation.

Sau takes a sniff and utters an oath. This comes out sounding like a nasal 'Door-mat!' In its shortened form, 'Mat!' or 'Ma!' suffices, as good a stand-in as any for the French 'Merde!' It becomes the phoneme by which I will always remember Mister Six.

Truc, on the other hand, is as pleased as Punch.

'You see,' he counsels, wagging a finger two inches in front of my face, 'you've been cheated. This stuff is fake, *zaum*. We call it Saigon whisky. You shouldn't buy things unless I'm with you. It's not safe.'

'As I recall you were asleep at the time.'

But Truc affects not to hear this. His triumph is too great. He agrees to accompany me to the shop and ask for a refund. When we get there the woman who sold it has disappeared. I ask when she'll be back. Her family, or what I take to be her family, shrugs. Truc agitates, begins throwing his Hanoi weight around, shouts. He has decided to become really angry. A brother or a cousin or a son appears, a big fellow. Not wanting the situation to get out of hand, I suggest we return later when the original vendor is there and lead Truc off. Truc expostulates against southern perfidy, then expostulates again with me. Beneath it all he still can't help crowing, and there's a thin urge toward violence in me that I struggle to contain.

'By the way, do you know yet how much I'm supposed to be paying for our rooms?'

Truc shakes his head.

'Don't worry, Sau Dang will sort it out.'

But because I haven't yet had to chance to benefit from Sau's formidable capacity for negotiation, I'm not so easily pacified. I counter-attack from the other flank.

'I do think, Truc, that in future we should establish the price for our accommodation before we take it and not after. That's the way it's done everywhere else in the world.'

Perhaps we would have continued smouldering at each other all

252

evening, but as it is Sau has organized a treat. We are to dine at Madame Phuong's brother's house, on the outskirts of town. This is strictly a family affair. In other words Colonel Quai's wife keeps us well supplied with a veritable feast of dishes, including a brilliant version of Peking Duck, and keeps herself (along with her daughter) out of sight in the kitchen of her gardened bungalow. This, I am assured by Truc, is normal. The womenfolk do not usually sit at table with their guests, although Madame Phuong and Madame Thu on this occasion prove exceptions to the rule.

The colonel I like immensely. He is a serious, slightly lawyerly man, now retired. A northerner, he joined up forty years ago, and took part in Dien Bien Phu. Indeed, he participated in all the major campaigns, except the war with China. In the '60s he regrouped south, becoming the commander of a guerrilla, or VC, unit. He tells me at some length about General Giap, about Giap's switch to a 'slow-and-steady' strategy after initial failures against the French in the Red River delta. Interestingly, he also refers to the war against the US as 'Giap's war'. At least up until 1972, he says, Giap was completely in charge. Western historians have long been uncertain as to when Giap's overall command of the NVA began to wane.

All too soon however we have to leave. The People's Committee has arranged a night-time appointment with its recently retired president, Pham Duc Nam. We sit in the guesthouse exchanging compliments. The atmosphere is distinctly sticky, mainly because I've already been told more than I need to know about Danang by Pham Duc Nam's subordinate, and because, on the larger issues, such as *doi moi*, Tiananmen Square and Cambodia, Pham Duc Nam sticks to platitudes. Also – and I don't blame him – Truc is visibly weary. Only when I delve into Pham Duc Nam's own revolutionary past does the man venture out of formalities. He spent much of the war in the mountains directly to our west. The great problem, he says, was salt. Partisans in the plains tried to smuggle salt into the foothills, but all too often they were captured or killed. But the irony of it was that, up there on the heights, he spent half his time gazing at the sea.

'The sea was full of salt. One of my comrades wrote a poem about this, about needing what is directly in front of you.'

253

Surprisingly, the Ho Chi Minh Trail didn't penetrate to Danang until 1972. In the meantime many families had lost up to six or seven of their children in battle.

'Did they tell you, in Danang Province alone two hundred thousand people lost their lives because of the Americans?'

Yes, I nod, they told me that.

'But we bear no grudge. You must remember that as well.'

Friday 17th November: Danang–Quang Ngai Before going to sleep last night Truc came to my room for a little chat. He tells me that it is his 'duty' to get me back to Hanoi safely and in one piece after touring the south. Presumably he wants my co-operation in this matter. By way of reply, I tell him that I also have a duty, to myself and to my publishers, which is to come up with the goods on 'Vietnam now'. Therefore if sometimes I do foolish things like buying a bottle of phoney whisky or being offered four American corpses he shouldn't mind too much because at least they teach me some of the things that are going on which the People's Committees in all probability will not bother to mention. Yes, it's good to know how many hectares are under mulberry cultivation and what the annual paddy production equivalent is, but it's the whole story I'm after.

'Vietnam now. That must be our motto.'

Truc nods, and repeats the phrase. Then he asks, what do I really want?

The short answer is, whatever it is I'm not getting in anything like a regular supply. The long answer is, everything!

'It's okay,' I answer. 'I'm enjoying myself. I suppose though I'd like to meet more people, more individuals. People who are doing things but who aren't cadres. Also, I'd like more things left to chance. These People's Committees are all very well, and it's very flattering to be given so much of their attention, but . . . but there must be more to life than People's Committees!'

Again Truc nods.

'Is there anything else?'

'No. There's nothing else.'

He leaves me with the impression that perhaps none of what I've said has taken root. In fact there's quite a lot else I could have said to him, but to have done so would merely have been petulant. In particular I would like to have asked him to modify his manner of address. Truc has the habit of barking orders at me. When we drive somewhere and we get to our destination, his first words are, 'Get out!' If I'm feeling charitable, I put this down to his yet-to-be-consolidated mastery of the English language. If I'm not, then I put it down to his army background. Already, in my notes, I've shorthanded him to MLS: My Little Sergeant. Also, he has the habit of snarling at children whenever they crowd me in the streets. I very much want to tell him that the children are my allies. But, particularly after the whisky episode, I'm aware that exemplary dignity is the best, the only stand to take. To admonish him over such details would surely be to lose a little face. Yet maintaining one's exemplary dignity, or trying to, only adds to the strain.

'Get out!'

Nonetheless, when the day comes, we do make some headway. Before leaving Danang I meet three people, all of whom unquestionably are individuals.

The first is Nguyen Khac Phuc, the seven-volume novelist I missed yesterday at the beach. Very early Sau drives us round the back streets of Danang until we come to a gated yard and Truc tells me to get out. The gates are unlocked and I am shown into a 'writer's camp'. It is not like the writers' camp in Halong Bay however. The offices are large and empty. Vinh Quyen, the camp's director, and himself an author, provides tea and compliments. Phuc arrives a few minutes after. He is thoughtful, shrewd, cautious; somewhere in his early forties. He confirms the things I have already been told about his monumental project. And then, lo! – even at this hour – we have what might be termed a proper dialogue. I do not take notes, but afterwards I recall several striking phrases and analogies. Perhaps it's because I see him on his own, because there isn't any committee of fellow authors breathing down his neck. Parrying my attack he admits no apology for concentrating his work on the war. The war is his background, he has been both cadre and soldier. 'A man in a revolution grows like bread in the oven.' But he doesn't set out to extol the conflict, even though he compares the writer's life with the fighter's. 'They are

255

much the same,' he says. 'The Revolution is literature in arms. In the old days writers spoke of the spirit of Vietnam. In my time simple words were not enough.' But his stance is that of the humanist. The South-East Asian mind likes 'to overcome reality'. Its central characteristic is to yearn for peace. In his own work he would like to emphasize the Buddhist strands in Vietnamese thought: the opposition of male and female, the five elements. Western writing tends toward the obvious, the didactic. Eastern writing prefers subtlety, ambiguity. If he writes about the war, it is not to 'remind' his readers of those events, it is to 'share' his experience. He is not interested in ideology *per se*. If anything the opposite. Politics he thinks are ultimately ephemeral. Politics are like a snake coiled around the writer. But, through humanism, the grip of the snake 'may sometimes be relaxed'.

The second, Phan Van Hang, is an artist; a painter and a sculptor. We visit him at his 'Garden of Statues'. His house is self-designed, almost aggressively modern. Inside, an open-plan living space, adorned by a beautiful soft-spoken wife. Outside, carved shutters I'd quite like to take away with me: entwined and twisting naked nymphs partly inspired by the Cham dancers I saw at the Cham museum.

Hang sports a wild west-coast beard and is distinctly Bohemian. He is also prepared to speak his mind. But then he can afford to. He is something of a celebrity. In 1970, in Saigon, he staged a famous happening. At an exhibition sponsored by the International Red Cross he unveiled a work called *Chung Tich,* Evidence of War. It consisted of coils of barbed wire onto which he had stuck an assortment of limbs. What made his work bite was that the limbs were real. Hang had collected them from battle sites and preserved them in formalin. On one side were the breasts of women, on the other hands of children. 'You see,' he says, 'all my life I have been concerned with peace.' Needless to say, the police destroyed his masterpiece, before President Thieu came to the show. 'I was not surprised, but when articles about me were censored in the regime's newspapers, I couldn't work any more. And again, after 1975, it took me a while to adapt to the new regime. At present I'm not a member of any official body. Even so, the government will sometimes employ me.' For example, the time last year when General Secretary Nguyen Van Linh visited Danang. Hang was asked if he could model the Leader's head in clay in thirty minutes. He thought the request unreasonable, but nonetheless complied. 'But it was difficult. There were too many people milling around. It was only because my wife carried the water that I was able to finish the piece in time.'

Hang shows me around his garden, which is full of heads of all sizes in all styles. In the centre a large frame, a kind of altar, on which rest the features of various 'cultural heroes' of Hang's own choosing: Tolstoy, Dickens, the composer Trinh Cong Son, several local artists. The incipient features of Ho Chi Minh can be seen emerging from a large block of white marble under an awning in one corner of the garden. Hang looks at it without expression. Another official commission.

When I leave he presents me with a piece of paper. It is his 'testament', which he has had translated:

> A SOLILOQUY
> I was born in Nam O, of Quang Nam Danang.
> Mother died early. Then Father was no more when I was
> a little over ten years old.
> Brothers and sisters were as poor as the country.
> At the age of thirteen I had to prepare me for life myself.
> For thirty years or more I had been a drifter trying at
> various jobs: bread-selling, street-singer, and other
> manual labouring . . .
> The place I used to frequent was my school. The people I
> used to meet were my friends and my teachers, my foes
> and my lovers.
> That was the way I entered life yet with my confidence in
> Man. In the World. And in Life itself.
> Though once a photographer, film actor and journalist, I
> finally took more passionately to arts than anything else,
> for I learned that
> > *VINCENT VAN GOGH* WAS TORMENTED
> > TO GET HIS ARDENT FLAME OF LIFE AND
> > CREATIVENESS,

257

MARC CHAGALL USED TO BE A MAN OF
INNOCENT DESIRES,
SALVADOR DALI WAS A MAN OF REASON
AND A MYSTIC.
Then with the help of HERMANN HESSE's 'Two
Intimate Friends' I followed the call of Sculpture guided
by the shining stars of

AUGUSTE RODIN
HENRY MOORE
ALEXANDER CALDER
ALBERTO GIACOMETTI

I had never had a single lesson in sculpture, still I would
be grateful to those pioneers.
Let me offer my thanks to the Age of Cultural
Development and Exchange, and the light of Peace.
Let us bear in mind and heart the images of all our
beloved ones whose plight, endurance and even sacrifice
have engendered what appears as it is before our eyes
now. All this has been the blood, sweat and tears of a
man hungry for arts.

Let me leave the right to enjoy and evaluate it to each
and every contemplator.

PHAM VAN HANG

The third is Vo Thi Lien. I have seen her before, in two or three
television documentaries about My Lai. She is one of only five
survivors of the massacre. Her performance is electric, but it is
always the same. She tells of the destruction of her family by
Lieutenant Calley's men in a high, twittering voice that might
almost belong to some rare species of bird as her sweet, pretty face
smothers in tears. In a sense she is perfect. She is the angel of the
air who has fallen among the daemons of the earth.

My Lai, somewhat against my will, is on my programme. In fact
I will go there tomorrow. I am nearer than I think. My reasons for
not wishing to visit My Lai are simple. It's been covered often
enough, and I am wary of the ghoulish. Also it symbolizes, as
perhaps nowhere else can, Vietnam Then, as opposed to Vietnam
Now. But for the last couple of days Truc and Sau have been

258

insisting. No one who comes to Vietnam can drive straight past the My Lai turning. So I will go. But I have made a stipulation. On no account is that poor woman to be dragged out for my benefit. Who knows, perhaps she is just a wonderful actress, but the times I have seen her on the screen the pain has seemed real enough, and I have no wish to have her put on the rack once more. It would be unnecessary. But when we arrive in Danang we discover she is living in the city. Would I like to visit her at her house? My curiosity gets the better of me. Yes as a matter of fact I would. I want to see not the televised Vo Thi Lien, but the other Vo Thi Lien. I want to see if any kind of normality is possible after what she witnessed when she was five years old.

We drive to her house, a one-storeyed, three-room dwelling in the suburbs. Truc tells me to get out. We pass through a pleasant garden. The household is impoverished but tidy. Lien is married now. Her husband, as it happens, is also a sculptor. He is a small man, about my age. His eyes though are large, and full of love. We sit at a table in a corner by the window. Lien comes in. She is instantly recognizable, the exceedingly pretty face before it crumples, before the tears flow. She serves me tea. We talk about this and that, about anything that comes to mind except My Lai.

What was I expecting? A padded cell with searing scratch marks on the walls? Lien slays me with her naturalness. There is nothing very much on her mind except motherhood and housekeeping. A little girl runs in and out of the garden, which is planted with various kinds of fruit. Lien keeps one eye on her daughter. After a while she talks about what she has done since My Lai. When she was thirteen she went on a world tour. Among other places she visited England. She was paraded in a campaign to publicize American atrocities in Vietnam. I ask whether having visited so many countries she doesn't now feel a little restless. But no. What she would really like is to return to the countryside, to live near My Lai, near her family, even though they are all dead. The country she liked best was East Germany, because one afternoon she was allowed to play with children of her own age. Children, she thinks, should always have a lot of friends. Without other children to play with, a child is likely to grow up, well, wrong somehow.

Lien seems to be perfectly adjusted in her present incarnation.

259

The camera crews should leave her alone. Meeting her informally, away from My Lai, is somehow cleansing. Her capacity for ordinary happiness is what has survived. In a land of sorrows, she is a tiny shining beacon that repairs one's faith in humankind. When I leave she comes to the gate with her own and other children and waves me down the lane. I too have intruded upon her, but by being her ordinary self Lien has absolved me.

Sau bangs the wheel of the Mazda as it bumps on the unmade road. 'Maaa!' He is angry. He remembers the last time a crew came to film at My Lai, a British one I'm ashamed to say. They took Lien there in a limousine, but because they were driving straight back down to Saigon they made her take the bus back to Danang. She had to wait a long time before the bus came. She was pregnant at the time. 'Maaa!'

Also, they never bothered to send a copy of their film to Vietnam.

We take lunch in a newish café. The girl who serves me is Amerasian. Her features are neither one thing nor the other, though her hair is a light brown. Her mother, she tells me, died exactly one hour after she was born. She has two older sisters, both by the same father. Soon they will be going to America, on the Orderly Departure Program. She hopes one day she will find her daddy, whom she has never met. But she concedes, simply as a matter of fact, that the chances are slim. She is already eighteen, she says, and knows all about men.

The plan is to set off immediately for Quang Ngai, our next port of call, but we have to wait forty minutes at the guesthouse for the 'accountant' to arrive. (We use the time to revisit the whisky shop. They have no money. Grudgingly they give me a few packets of cigarettes instead.) Eventually a pale young woman arrives on a bicycle. Sau negotiates with her. A tariff of $17 per night is agreed upon. For the facilities we've had this is high by other SE Asian standards, but less than I'd originally feared. Probably it would have been cheaper to stay at the Army Guesthouse, but at least now I'm reassured that under Sau's wing I'm in capable hands.

Quang Ngai, the next provincial capital town, is 150-odd kilometres away. Madame Thu remains behind in Danang, so from now on it's just Truc and Madame Phuong in the back. Madame Phuong, on the few occasions I think about her, puzzles me. It seems she has money and it seems there is something between her and her 'relative' Sau Dang. Sau on the other hand rarely pays her more than civil attention. Sometimes they appear to share a room, sometimes they don't. Past her prime, she is not perhaps the perfect ornament for Sau's well-developed vanity. On the other hand, she seems never to mind how much beer she buys.

The journey, through a dry landscape that intermittently bursts into a full-blown tropical blaze, is largely uneventful. We do however, at my own request, pause at Chu Lai, the site of the former US Air Force base. Today, very little of this remains. An eight-kilometre fence along the left-hand side of Highway One marks the extent of all that used to be. The hangars, the control tower, the workshops (Chu Lai was essentially a maintenance depot) and the administration buildings have all been cleared away, the materials recycled into who knows how many smaller projects. In their place, half a mile from the road, a small barracks for a detachment of the Vietnamese Army.

'Come on, let's stretch our legs,' I say to Truc. 'Get out!'

At the gatehouse a sleepy guard looks at me with some apprehension before resting his rifle. He cranks up his field-telephone and then waves us through. After a hundred metres Truc wants to turn back. I want to go on. As yet I don't know that the buildings in the distance are a barracks. Eerily, Tannoys are loudly casting a Voice of Vietnam radio programme across the wind-swept rotting runways. The wind comes directly from the sea and I can hear the pounding of waves on the shoreline. The programme is something educational. A clear woman's voice enunciates simple Vietnamese sentences which are then repeated by her class of four- or five-year-olds. There is no sign of anybody. Fellini would have felt at home here.

'There's nothing,' says Truc.

'Nonsense. Where there's radio there's life.'

Truc follows at a snail's pace as we come to the compound. Two NCOs peer at us with smiling disbelief, before one of them slouches off to the living quarters to raise the company officer, a friendly lieutenant who at once offers us tea. It is so nice of me to visit him, he tells me. Often weeks go by without a visit from anybody. He has no idea what the air base will be used for in future. When I suggest perhaps a mulberry plantation he nods. 'Perhaps. Yes. It's possible.'

Before making our way back to the Mazda he shows me around the camp. In the main building is a small library and an even smaller Ho Chi Minh Museum.

'You see,' I tell Truc, 'Ho Chi Minh again. We might have missed him.'

We reach Quang Ngai a little after dark. Ominously the Mazda has begun playing up. The problem seems to be the fuel injection pump. Twice we have to stop as Sau does on-the-spot repairs. Again, we are to stay at a People's Committee guesthouse. Yet, as such places go, this one is superior. Inside the concrete walls have been panelled with dark inviting woods. For no very good reason, to arrive there feels like checking in at a skiing chalet.

Sau flashes his what's-in-it-for-us grin and sets out my case to the receptionist. Then he retires to his room with a bad stomach. Truc gives me the good news over dinner. There will be no charge. An astonishingly comely waitress called Thuyet agrees to sit with us for a little *boc phét* after a meal that includes unprecedentedly generous portions of fresh vegetables. Although it's early to bed, I retire a happy man. Quang Ngai, I've already decided, is nice.

Saturday 18th November: My Lai The duty call to My Lai is made in the morning. We drive twelve kilometres back up Highway One, then turn off toward the sea. My Lai, a hamlet in the village of Son My, is then another seven or eight kilometres down a not particularly good road. The massacre occurred on 16th April 1968. Five hundred and four children, women and old men were mindlessly and pointlessly slaughtered by Company C. The doings of Company C that day, commanded by Captain Ernest Medina (Calley merely led the worst-behaved platoon) are probably the best-documented military atrocity on record. Even at the time the Americans took a lot of pictures of their victims. In My Lai itself there is now a museum where the photographs, blown up, are arranged in such a way that the story tells itself – starkly, simply, terrifyingly.

262

When you've seen the shots you take a tour of the surrounding paddies. The massacre did not take place all at one spot. Rather the killings were enacted at different sites over an area of two or three square kilometres. Mostly they were concentrated in the adjacent hamlet, Tu Cung. In Tu Cung, 306 children, women and old men were killed.

The scenery is excellent. You walk along the edges of the fields beneath unusually large jungle fronds. There are pleasant smells emanating from various kinds of orchard. Peasants ride on the backs of their wobbly bullock-drawn ploughs. The ripples lap almost at your feet. And every so often you encounter another memorial plaque. Here, on 16th April 1968, died 97. Here, 8. Here, 170. In some cases, individual memorials have been raised. Low on the ground, they are shaped a little like US private mailboxes. In the end, it is these that get to you. You try to tell yourself it's senseless, but in fact you know it's not. What happened here was very intimately connected with the senses.

I return to the museum, and thank my guide-for-the-hour, Miss Trinh, another of the five survivors. I am given a large pamphlet that sets out the facts and provides a fair sprinkling of the shots I have seen a hundred times before. 'My Lai–Son My since then evokes irresistibly the satanic profile of that monster called US imperialism.' Almost. I spend a little time taking photographs of the gleaming white, social-realist statues that have been erected outside in the gardens. There is also a wall covered by a cluttered mosaic. Then we pile back into the Mazda and head back for Quang Ngai. On the way we pass a wedding party: a straggling group of guests, some of them on slow-moving motorcycles, dressed up in carefully ironed suits that might have been left behind by the French. They all bear presents wrapped in brightly coloured cloths. On Highway One we pass two groups of marching schoolchildren, their leaders flourishing the national flag, the old gold star on the old cadmium background. Sunday, Truc tells me, is Election Day. Everyone will cast a vote, deciding who is to become a member of the councils that in turn will decide who sits on the local committees. The National Homeland Front, the Party at large, the organization you join if you're not qualified to join the Party itself, is out in force.

Lunch. And then another long seminar. Singing for my supper. And, in Quang Ngai, singing for my bed as well. My informant is Hong Nhan, director of the Culture and Information Bureau of the People's Committee of Quang Ngai Province. An educated man, he has been in his time a history teacher, and knows how to present his facts and figures. The atmosphere is markedly friendly. Mrs Thatcher has just questioned the right of the Khmer Rouge to a seat at the United Nations. For once she is willing to distance herself from Washington. There is also a certain buoyancy afoot: Quang Ngai, which used to be an autonomous province until it was amalgamated with Binh Dinh to make up Nghia Binh, has become itself again. The Quang Ngai People's Committee are once again masters of their own house.

I am served with tea and a local delicacy, *keo guong*, or 'mirror sweet': a combination of sugar, sesame seed and peanuts, rolled out into a thin glaze that actually is one of Indochina's tastier confections.

Hong Nhan introduces me to the vital statistics of Quang Ngai Province. The population, the length of the coastline, the hectares under cultivation, the paddy product. Not an outstandingly rich area of the country, one would have to say. Then it's the revolutionary history, from the earliest times. Early insurrections against the French, and how the French tried to isolate the Vietnamese in the plains from the Ko, Re and Kadong tribespeoples in the mountains. The impetus derived from Ho Chi Minh's Communist Party of Indochina, and Quang Ngai's participation in the Nghe Tinh Soviet movement. The local patriot, Nguyen Nghieu, who, moments before his execution, shouted out: 'My blood will mix into the soil of the Tru Khuc river: every grain of sand will become a revolutionary.' How, after 1930, the Revolution 'went underground', until the spring of 1946, when the whole province 'became a battle zone', as the French and Japanese fell out amongst themselves. Then the war against the French, 1946 to 1954. 'At night, nobody wanted to sleep. We only wanted to pursue the fight.' And then the Diem regime, and how schools were turned into concentration camps and the executions continued and women were subjected to the water torture and men had snakes inserted in their trousers, or else had their ears cut off. For Quang Ngai was never Catholic, and resisted the Saigon regime to the hilt.

Indeed it is Hong Nhan's contention that the second Indochinese

264

War began in Quang Ngai, at Tra Bong, in the north-east of the province. There, on 29th August 1959, the first 'insurrection' against Diem was launched.

Later, when the Americans came, Tra Bong resistance base was bombed for over a month. Again the whole province became a battle zone, but now on a scale hitherto unimagined. The coastal strip was reduced to scrub, the mountains defoliated, the people decimated. 'But our suffering only strengthened our hearts and minds.' Local guerrillas learned how to operate effectively out of the uplands, with tendrils of the Ho Chi Minh Trail supplying their rear. In May 1965 'an entire Saigon Army division was wiped out'. In 1975 the province was liberated on 24th March, *before* the arrival of the North Vietnamese Army.

Mr Hong describes in detail the 'strategic hamlet programme': the endeavour, from the early 1960s, to contain guerrilla activities by relocating villagers along the highway in compounds where they could be more easily controlled.

'There were so many incidents,' he tells me. 'The massacre at My Lai, for example, or the one at Binh Hoa. But these were simply bigger versions of what happened everywhere, every day.'

Binh Hoa?

I've never heard of the Binh Hoa massacre. I press Hong Nhan for the details. Mr Hong rummages in his notes. He's not sure, but he thinks perhaps four hundred children, women and old men were killed.

'Four hundred! And when did this happen?'

'At the end of 1966.'

'In other words, *before* My Lai?'

Hong Nhan nods.

'Yes, beforehand. But this time it was the South Korean troops who did the killing, not the Americans. So nobody in the outside world is very interested.'

Are there any survivors? He believes there are, but isn't sure. He will have to check. Can I go there? Hong Nhan prevaricates. He'd like me to go, but tomorrow is Election Day, all the cadres will be busy.

'I don't mind. I can wait until Monday.'

Is it possible I've stumbled on the blueprint for My Lai?

265

At this juncture we are joined by Le Thanh Tam, the vice-chairman of the People's Committee. He is a burly sort whose old revolutionary eyes twinkle beneath an artistic blue beret. A big, jolly potato. Hong Nhan confers with him, relaying my request. After a brief discussion I am told I can visit Binh Hoa tomorrow.

In the evening there are many toasts. A banquet is given in my honour in a private room at the guesthouse. Not many writers/ journalists who visit Vietnam tarry long in Quang Ngai. Le Thanh Tam presides. A considerable amount of rice-alcohol is drowned by an even more considerable amount of beer. Sau Dang holds court, regaling the party of seven or eight Quang Ngai cadres with tales of Saigon scandal. After a while however Mr Le makes his apologies and leaves. Today he must also welcome a group of Americans: a body calling itself the International Mission of Hope is coming to lay the foundation stone of a new hospital in My Lai. Some of these I meet afterwards, after they too have been banqueted. They are a motley crew of charity workers, led by a courageous woman who once served as a nurse in Saigon. For me however the most interesting is a veteran, a former Marine who talks about the Vietnamese family he has 'adopted', here in Vietnam. I quiz him about the ROKs, the Korean mercenaries. He is not inclined to speak highly of them. There was a tendency among the officers to shoot non-coms whenever they had drunk too much. 'Generally, we endeavoured to put as much daylight as possible between them and ourselves.' They were well-trained soldiers, but they were not companionable buddies.

On a personal note, the veteran claims that he is 'overwhelmed by the forgiveness' he has encountered since returning to Vietnam. (But he is also a born-again Christian, and such people do tend to be overwhelmed by forgiveness . . .) He tells me too that he knows about the unexploded landmines that are still taking lives.

'I'll tell you. I know of a case where a boy lost his leg even before he was born. His mother died, of course.'

Sunday 19th November: Quang Ngai–Binh Son–Binh Hoa–An Phuoc Election Day! – though from the activity you'd never have guessed it. Dull, overcast, for which, later, I shall be thankful. Truc wakes me at 6.45 a.m. Get up! At eight o'clock we leave the guesthouse, Sau Dang, as ever, energetic at the wheel of the Mazda. We are joined by Doan, Hong Nhan's assistant at the Quang Ngai Bureau of Culture and Information. We drive north-wards, back up Highway One, well past the My Lai turning. It takes thirty minutes to reach Binh Son, the small capital of Binh Son District. We stop at the People's Committee headquarters. There is no one to meet us, despite the promise made last night. No big potato, no medium potato, no little potato even.

Across the road is what counts for the local police station. A group of three or four non-uniformed men are standing, gazing at us. Doan leads us across for a truncated interview with their leader, a short man with a dangerous face in a leather jacket. He is, he says, chief of police in these parts, and it is clear from his manner that he doesn't want us around. Sau expostulates with him, but for once without results. The members of the Binh Son People's Committee are all busy with the election, there is no one to go with us to Binh Hoa, and we shouldn't go there by ourselves. And in any case, the little thug assures us, there will be no one at Binh Hoa to provide a welcome. The Binh Hoa People's Committee is also busy with the election.

I ask whether I can come back tomorrow. The reply is ambiguous, evasive. For now, there is nothing for it but to return to Quang Ngai. Sau, angry, tells me he will sort matters out later in the day, with a real big potato. Truc, translating, also huffs and puffs.

But where are all the big potatoes this morning? I query. Yes, I know they are tied up with the election, but *where* are they tied up? Knowing also that the election is a mere formality, I sense that if we don't get to Binh Hoa today then probably we'll never get to Binh Hoa.

Sau thinks some of them may be in My Lai, attending the foundation ceremony of the hospital being built by the Mission of Hope. Then let's go there, I say. So we drive back south, and take the My Lai exit.

At the hospital site there is no sign of the Americans. The foundation stone has already been laid, and work has started. But they are at the museum, being shown the atrocity photographs by Miss Trinh. Miss Trinh, I notice, is wearing a white *ao dai* today. And in the party are Le Tranh Tam (the big, jolly potato) and Hong Nhan.

Sau tells them about the refusal at Binh Son. There is no debate, no discussion. Hong Nhan just tells us he will accompany us back to Binh Son and sort things out. In fact he promises to go one better. He will give up the rest of the day to us. He is sure his presence will be effective. Most of the members of the Binh Son committee were his 'students' during the war.

So, back to Binh Son. The committee building is still deserted, closed, we are now told, for an early lunch. But a few words to the janitor from Hong Nhan, and the chairman and the vice-chairman are soon found. My party is led upstairs and offered tea in a square, shabby room where the wind plays havoc with the shutters. The chairman appears, flustered, falling over his words. Compliments are exchanged, apologies accepted. A telephone call is made, someone is sent off to Binh Hoa to see to it that we are properly received. Meanwhile, what about lunch? – at the committee's expense of course! Sau grins for the first time since breakfast, and slips me a wink. We repair to a local restaurant, the best that Binh Son can offer: a friendly super-shack where the flies considerately lay off until I have finished eating.

At one o'clock my entourage sets off for Binh Hoa, swelled now by a jeep-load of local dignitaries and their henchmen, following behind. For the tenth time it is explained to me that the police chief's reluctance earlier in the day had to do with his fears for my safety. I am the first foreigner to have travelled down the Binh Hoa road since the war finished in 1975, so I must understand that naturally the police erred on the side of caution.

Thus, four hours later than I anticipated, and having negotiated a road that is pitted and cratered all along, we arrive at Binh Hoa. It is a poor sod of a place, an outpost in a province not renowned for a high rice yield, or a high anything else yield. Much of the surrounding countryside is wild, scrub more than jungle. We are relatively near the sea, and salt winds have made this land their own. But the village's People's Committee is ready and waiting, about twenty of them. It is immediately obvious that my visit is as unusual as, an hour or so before, it was unexpected. For these people, my coming is an event without precedent. The election work, if there is any, has been shelved.

Everyone crowds into the committee building, a one-storey, one-roomed job without electricity – no more than a glorified concrete shed festooned with two or three red banners and the obligatory photograph of Ho Chi Minh, looking, in this instance, almost frighteningly avuncular.

I am introduced to Mr Ngoc, the chairman, and Mr Kiem, the secretary, of the local Party cell. Immediately I am asked if I mind having my photograph taken. A gaunt young fellow then begins taking photographs of all and sundry. If I am not mistaken, he and his camera have come in on the jeep from Binh Son.

I sit almost at one end of the long table that fills the room. Soon two slightly built older men, who spend much of their time glancing at each for mutual support, take the two chairs opposite me. These, I am told, are 'witnesses' of the Binh Hoa massacre. With some assistance from the committee, they will tell me the story. Neither belongs to the committee, nor are they Party members. It is only right, therefore, that they should have some 'help'.

These old men touch me. Introduced as simple souls, it is difficult to see them as anything else. They have had no 'time' to prepare their statements, unless twenty-three years can be counted time. When either speaks, he stands, overwhelmed by the attention not only of myself but of those, I am sure, who in his daily life fulfil the role of masters.

Mr Bui De speaks first. Of the two he is older, and considerably the more frail. He falters, is flustered, but he speaks absolutely from the heart. His eyes quickly soak. He simply cannot grasp why, after so many years, a complete stranger has arrived to ask him questions.

In answer to those questions, Mr Bui tells me that all the men in the Binh Hoa village had been revolutionists. They had responded well to the call to liberate the homeland. For each of the enemy forces – the corrupt Saigon regime, the United States Army and the South Korean mercenaries – Binh Son had been a tough nut to

269

crack. Then he tells me about Binh Hoa, and what happened at Binh Hoa village on 5th December 1966. A detachment of South Koreans, from the Green Dragon Division, arrived shortly after daybreak. They herded everyone they could find into a bomb-crater not two hundred metres from where he was now sitting. Thirty-four persons in all, old men, women and children. The younger men of the village, himself included, had all become guerrillas, VC, and were nowhere to be found. And so, having taken those they could find to the crater, the Green Dragons pushed them into its pit and shot them.

All thirty-four were killed. For the next three days the Koreans kept guard, preventing anyone from retrieving the corpses for burial, hoping perhaps to lure the VC out of the surrounding bush. By the time they left, the bodies, soaked in mud and water, had begun to decompose. When they were found they were largely unrecognizable. It didn't help that the Koreans had mortared the human remains on their way out.

It was decided to leave the bodies where they were, fill the crater in and designate it a grave. As well as the human mutilation, the rats had been to work, and the stench, says Mr Bui, was unbearable.

At the time Mr Bui was forty-five, a farmer by trade. He did not in fact witness the killing, but he did see the bodies afterwards. I ask whether any of his own family were included among the victims. For a moment Mr Bui is silent. During this pause I examine his hair, which is white and close cropped. Then he nods. Yes. He lost five children that day, four daughters and a son. One by one he gives me their names: Bui Thi Xiem, Bui Thi Lam, Bui Thi Moc, Bui Thi Xi (the daughters) and Bui Van Duc (the son). With Truc's help I inscribe each in my notebook. Mr Bui watches me as I write. I suspect he is illiterate, but he doesn't need to be told what I am doing. He says nothing more. Truc whispers in my ear, 'You see, he is so moved.'

It is now the other man's turn, Mr Pham Van Cuc. Mr Cuc is younger than Mr Bui, darker, more alert, but equally deferential, toward both myself and the officials around him. He describes a different incident, at another hamlet in Binh Hoa village, An Phuoc, about six kilometres away, which took place on 6th

270

December 1966, the day after the Binh Hoa episode. Again the Green Dragons arrived at dawn. This time they surrounded the entire place, so that no one could escape. Some of the inhabitants (old men, women, children) were already out working the land, but they were soon brought home. The victims were then divided up into three or four groups, and taken to different points around the hamlet. The killing began at around 10.00 a.m. Some were shot, some were mortared, some grenaded. A few of the women were stripped and tortured first. The Green Dragons clenched their hands and drove fists into vaginas. Five women were raped. Then they in turn were shot, mortared or grenaded. In all, some 456 individuals were butchered, including pregnant women and new-born babies. There were however seven survivors, all of them children, whose living bodies were discovered at the end of the day, after the Koreans had left.

Mr Cuc, with some help from the committee, then goes on to tell me about a third incident, in Tri Hoa hamlet, that took place some three months earlier than the Binh Hoa and An Phuoc episodes. On this occasion the Koreans had rounded up twelve persons, pushed them into an 'underground room', and lobbed hand grenades down the hatch. All were killed. By the time their remains were discovered they were so badly decomposed that once again it was impossible to identify them.

34 + 456 + 12 = 502: two less than the official tally at My Lai. Why, I wondered again, had I not heard of this? And it was not my bad memory. When later I check the indexes of the war histories, Binh Hoa is nowhere to be found. Indeed, not only am I the first westerner to have come to Binh Hoa, I am also the first journalist of any kind. Not even the Vietnamese have sent reporters here. Why?

Probably, as Mr Hong intimated yesterday, because the Americans were not directly involved, because it was not a matter of westerners slaughtering Asian innocents, but of Asians slaughtering Asian innocents. I detect a distinct whiff of dog eat dog about the matter. So I begin asking questions about the Koreans. It is reaffirmed that they were infantrymen from the Green Dragon Division, a crack unit. In addition, their average age was mid to late twenties. In other words they were not kids, neither were they conscripts. They were highly trained regulars, not at all like Lieutenant Calley's men. They were, if the phrase has any relevance, professionals.

As far as anyone in the room knows, no Americans were present. It is however 'inconceivable', I am told, that the Americans did not get to know about the massacres. For one thing, the Americans monitored every move their Korean mercenaries made, and for another they had their own not altogether inefficient intelligence system. Also, Binh Hoa 'changed hands' routinely. Sometimes the war against the Viet Cong was pursued by the Green Dragons, sometimes by the US Marines, sometimes by the Saigon Army. Nobody in Binh Hoa could ever predict exactly who would jump out of the back of the next APC that passed. The massacres were much talked about throughout the district, and nobody in the district could have been unaware that they had taken place.

Addressing myself to Mr Bui and Mr Cuc, I ask why, in their opinion, the South Koreans did what they did. There follows a five-minute confab. Everybody in the room joins in. Truc explains: they want to give me the right answer, nobody should give me a wrong answer, the thing's too important. The correct answer must be agreed on first. Even so, collective as it may be, the answer given me is not, I believe, a fudge. The reason the Koreans murdered the villagers, I am told, is that they kept on returning to their villages. Binh Hoa and its hamlets had repeatedly been cleared. The inhabitants had again and again been regrouped along the highway, where they could be better watched, better controlled. But each time they were moved, the villagers came back. They wanted to live where they had always lived, on the 'land they had always loved', close to the graves of their ancestors.

I am then told that, after the massacres, the Koreans systematically destroyed the villages, razing each to the ground. The buildings were fired, the animals either killed or removed, and the paddy dikes breached.

Next question: why no monument?

After 1975, they tell me, a small monument was erected, a simple structure of unmorticed stones. But this has long since been destroyed by typhoons, a plague of the area. The truer monument is 'in the hearts of the Binh Hoa people, who can never forget'. But yes, of course, they would like to build a proper monument, and place memorial tablets like the ones in My Lai. Only, there's no money. The Korean conscience, it is implied, is not as amenable as the US conscience. Also (and this they articulate), the world's media are largely western media, and therefore less likely to be interested in what is (wrongly) perceived as an exclusively intra-Asian affair.

Lest I should think badly of the people of Binh Hoa, Mr Ngoc, the committee's chairman, emphasizes that each family keeps and maintains a private altar dedicated to the memory of the massacred. In four days' time will take place the annual ceremony at which the whole village gathers to commemorate the dead.

And there is another thing which I should be told. After the massacres had taken place, those who escaped, mainly women fortunate enough to have been away or out working distant fields, sent their black armbands to the resistance groups, together with letters outlining what had been done. As a result, in February 1967, a section of the Green Dragon Division was wiped out at Quang Thach, in Son Tinh District. And a few weeks later, in another reprisal, a whole company of South Koreans were taken out at Onh Ran Hill, in Binh Son District itself.

It is now time to visit the sites of the two principal massacres. A short walk brings me to the 'crater', the grave of thirty-four. A shallow declivity, 25 feet or so in diameter, marks the spot, on the slope of a gentle hill. I get everyone to stand around the perimeter and take photographs. (Unknown to me my camera's winding system has fouled up, and the pictures will not develop.) It is a curious scene. The committee members stand to attention, in a large ring around nothing in particular, like modern-dress Druids at Stonehenge a while before Stonehenge was built.

At the top of the hill is a conventional war memorial (paid for by the state) dedicated to the 'fallen heroes' of Binh Hoa. There are thirty or forty graves, earth mounds and nothing else. But there is one grave that has a white headstone, and Mr Bui is crouching beside it. I take Truc over, and learn that the grave contains the body of the only child of Mr Bui's who wasn't murdered. He was killed in action later, fighting for the independence of his people.

I take another photograph, and walk a few paces with Mr Bui, leaving Truc to trail behind. He is so old, so lonely, and I know perfectly well that if I apply too much pressure on his shoulder, where my left hand rests, he will crack up. Already I feel overwhelmed by what I have seen and heard today, but my feelings must be as nothing compared to his. Nothing that anybody, least of all myself, can do or say could make amends for the suffering that has afflicted Mr Bui for the last twenty-three years.

At least, though, I don't think he resents my presence, my intrusion. He is almost eager when I suggest he accompanies us to An Phuoc. Six of us pile into Sau's Mazda. (The jeep has returned to base, my safety is no longer in doubt.) It's a rough drive along a terrible dirt track, and any other driver must surely have given up. From time to time we must all get out, to lighten the load. Off the track, the terrain is equally broken, uneven. Humps and hillocks abound. Such paddies as there are have a derelict, inconsolable appearance.

Finally the car can go no further. We continue on foot. A hundred metres or so and we come to a compact sugar-cane field, the crop reaching up above our heads. This is one of the sites of the An Phuoc massacre; but there is, it seems, nothing to be seen. Just a small field of tall cane, eight or nine feet high.

We walk on, down into An Phuoc hamlet itself, another three hundred metres. Again, there's not much to see. A sort of destitute sterility hangs over the place, set off by the antics of a toothless old woman in the middle of what, for want of a better term, passes as the village green. Obviously deranged, somewhere in her eighties, she howls and cackles as soon as she sees us, flapping her arms in imitation of a hen. Her neighbours emerge from their bamboo-and-leaf dwellings and regard her impassively.

The chief massacre site lies on the far side of An Phuoc, a ditch running between more derelict paddies. For a moment my eye is caught by a scatter of black stones lying in the ditch, but these are natural objects. They have nothing to do with the atrocity. My reduced entourage waits while I balance my way between two paddies to take yet another photograph that will never come out. There is nothing of particular interest in the viewfinder, and my finger springs the shutter mechanically.

We wait long enough not to be seen to be beating too hasty a retreat, and then turn back in the direction of Sau's car. But then, as we pass the sugar-cane, a fellow almost leaps out at us. He is unkempt, in his early fifties, and terribly anxious to talk to me. Truc has a few words with him, then tells me that he is another 'witness'. There is something he wants to show me. Would I mind stepping into the cane?

I follow him in. In the middle of the field, completely hidden by the surrounding walls of plant, is a clearing measuring perhaps 40 feet by 8. On the floor of this clearing is a row of eight or nine unmarked graves.

The man's name is Ha Mau. He is excited, agitated, desperate. To put him at his ease I ask questions. It emerges that six of the graves are occupied by his wife and children. Once again I find myself inscribing names. His wife, Truong Tri Su, his eldest daughter, Ha Thi Dong, his eldest son, Ha Van Chi, his second son, Ha Van Thanh, his second daughter, Ha Thi Be, his third son, Ha Van Tung. All massacred, and all buried here, in the place where Ha Mau continues to grow his living.

And some there be that have no memorial. I leave with a promise that the names of Mau's lost family will one day be printed in the West. Sau meanwhile has performed further heroics. Quite unnecessarily he has brought the Mazda another two hundred metres down the track. We still have to get in and out of the car every fifty metres, but the man's determination to furnish transport touches me.

The light is just starting to go when we arrive back at Binh Hoa. The committee has found a 'survivor', and of course I cannot leave until I have spoken to him. Doan Nghia is in his early twenties, and he is blind. He was an An Phuoc baby, just seven months old, when the Green Dragons carried out their biggest operation in the district. He was shot, he tells me, in the back, and left lying on the ground. His father, a VC, came to An Phuoc very soon afterwards, and recognized his son among the corpses. Nghia's mother, sister and grandmother were there as well, but each had perished. An older brother, however, was also rescued. But there was no saving

Nghia's eyes: they had taken the impact of a grenade, and had been caked, several hours, in an admixture of muddy soil and blood.

Nghia goes on to tell me that today he lives alone. His father was soon afterwards killed in action against the Americans. He cannot help but feel bitter about what happened. The state gives him what it can, but that amounts to less than $4 a month. He would like to work, to learn a skill, but in this part of the country there are no schools for the blind. Even more he would like to find a wife. Unless he can find a wife he thinks his life will be a permanent emptiness. When I ask if there's anything I can do for him, he pauses, then says: 'I wish that the international community could help me to lead a better life.'

I say goodbye to the committee outside the committee building. There are still around twenty of them. Mr Cuc is also there, but Mr Bui has vanished. To shake them all by the hand would take too long. Instead I lead Nghia forward a little. Suddenly he drops his trousers to his ankles and, feeling with his fingers, shows me the scar of the bullet wound in his buttock. The wound is almost as old as he is, yet he has never seen it. I hug him, as hard as I dare, then wave adieu to the onlooking committee.

Back at Binh Son I am introduced to another survivor of An Phuoc, Truong Van Chuc. Chuc is thirty, and he can see. At the time he was seven and saw a lot of what happened. He tells me that the Koreans arrived sometime before 8.00 a.m. At 10.00 a.m. they gathered the villagers in a field – presumably the ditch I saw during the afternoon. Then, slowly and meticulously, for all to view, they cleaned their weapons. At 1.00 p.m. they began the shooting. They also used grenades and mortars. At 4.00 p.m., or thereabouts, when they considered everyone dead, they walked to the houses and set fire to them.

Wounded in the back and in the leg, Chuc hid under a tree. Before doing this however, he had made a search for his little brother, but his little brother, when he found him, was dead. Chuc took his brother's shirt, which was green, and put it on. Probably it was this, he says, that saved his life, because it afforded him a degree of camouflage. The Koreans shot at him as he ran away. Hit twice, he fell to the ground. Then, undetected, he crawled to

276

the safety of a tree. There he stayed for a very long time. His great fear was that the Koreans would come back. The worst thing he had seen was how they had bayoneted a two-year-old baby. At the time, the baby was crying for milk. The mother had been unable to satisfy his demand because, even though she was only a few feet away, she was dead.

He watched the village burn to the ground. Slowly he became confident that the Koreans had left. He then crawled back across the field, to see whether he could find anyone else alive. He couldn't. All he could discover was corpses, hundreds of them.

It was at this point that he started to feel afraid, more afraid than it is possible to imagine. He noticed many severed limbs – hands, arms, legs, heads – peppering the ground all around him. They even hung from the branches of such bushes as there were.

Chuc is a pleasant, soft-spoken, clean-shaven young man. I look at him across the table and ask whether, in his opinion, any of the women had been molested before being killed. He replies that he was too young at the time to know the answer for sure. What he does remember is that all the bodies, when he emerged from his hiding-place behind the tree, were clothed. But while he is aware that that might not signify anything one way or the other, he ventures to suggest that the Green Dragons, unlike the Americans at My Lai, were not disposed to acts of rape. But they did not stop short of torture.

For a few moments we relax. Chuc tells me about his present situation. He is married, he has one daughter, and he works as an accountant for the Binh Son District People's Committee. He also has two living brothers, not present at An Phuoc on that day in December 1966. His mother however was, and perished. His father, a VC, was already dead. So, I ask, what does Chuc think about it all now? His eyes immediately drop, and he locks into silence. I look at Truc, to make sure my question has been put. Truc says: 'Yes, he understands. But he is too moved to answer.'

I explain why I have come to ask questions which I know must be painful. If the world is told about Binh Hoa, then someone in the world might do something for Binh Hoa. Chuc nods. He knows all that, and says he trusts me. He is just so surprised that after all this time a foreigner should come and ask any questions at all. Then he tells me that on balance, but only on balance, he considers himself fortunate. He survived, and that is why he continues to live in the district, so as not to desert the dead. Otherwise . . . otherwise his leg, shot by an AR15, still plays up. But only when there is a sudden change in the weather.

Everybody is quiet in the car on the way back to Quang Ngai. Nobody can answer the biggest question of all: how can people be such shits? But as we reach the outskirts, Hong Nhan leans forward from the back seat and touches my arm. He requests that if I do write anything about Binh Hoa then I should emphasize that I mean Binh Hoa in Quang Ngai Province. The point being that there is another Binh Hoa in the next province south, Binh Dinh, and Hong Nhan is not altogether sure that there wasn't a massacre there too.

Dinner is subdued. Thuyet lets me hold her hand a while without knowing why I should want to do such a thing. Afterwards Truc and I walk around the town. There's not a lot to see. It's dark and ghostly, but the ghosts are benign. We drink coffee in a shabby place that also serves, at 50 *dong* apiece, rice pancakes. Suddenly it dawns upon me.

'You did well today,' I say to Truc.

Truc looks at me suspiciously, not knowing what I have lined up.

'I mean it.'

'Thank you.'

'Your translation was fluent. A lot of the time I wasn't aware of you, if you see what I mean.'

He looks at me, surprised now, pleased but quizzical.

'You know, an interpreter should be like a piece of polished glass and all of that.'

'Oh yes. Like a cassette tape on a good machine. That's what we were taught.'

'You were taught well.'

I want to go on. I want to apologize. I've given Truc no leash at all. This is his first outing on his own, his first solo performance, and I've given him no help, no understanding. He is not as young as Zoom. He has come to interpreting at an age when many interpreters think of giving it up. To do this job, he has had to abandon his wife and young child for six weeks. For nine years he was a soldier. He wants a different life for himself, and has worked hard to achieve it. Probably I am the first westerner he has spent any real time with. Probably too he finds my idiosyncrasies every bit as hard to take as I find some of his. Yet at times I have treated him with near derision.

I should apologize, but in the event I say nothing. It is Truc who breaks the silence.

'You see,' he says, 'I was so moved. Especially by Mr Bui. Because of that I stopped thinking about translating and just did it. I forgot my nerves.'

Henceforward I have more time for Truc. I grow to like him, much more I think than he will ever like me.

Monday 20th November: Quang Ngai–Nha Trang (Khanh Hoa Province)   Driving driving driving. A very early start for a very long journey, all the way to Nha Trang, all the way through Binh Dinh, Phu Yen and into Khanh Hoa. Four hundred kilometres if an inch. Breaking the back of what the French used to call the Balcony of the Pacific. An infinity of tropical rain, cascading down from a not very dark sky. No time to stop at Quy Nhon. Extra days in Hué and Quang Ngai mean our schedule is in arrears. The Mazda bounces, creaks, sways, groans, pants. Disturbing noises crescendo from the engine. At a small rocky pass where a battle was fought against the Koreans, Cu Mong I think, Sau Dang spots life on a barren hill, stops, produces a rifle and blasts away. He is a hunter as well as everything else. He misses. *Ma!* The bird flies off. Lunch at Song Cau. Madame Phuong fans herself non-stop. Truc sleeps. I am drowsy. Only Sau remains alert. Driving driving driving. Until, an hour out of Nha Trang, the Mazda loses its bottle, halts of its own accord. *Maaa!* The damned injector pump. Sau scrabbles beneath the bonnet. We start again, we stop again. Finally he ties a piece of string around the offending mechanism. All it needs is an occasional tug. He brings the string in through the driver's window. We start again. The Mazda stalls. Sau yanks the string. The Mazda

279

picks up speed. A convoy of lorries ahead. The way to honk the horn is to touch the ignition with the loose wire that hangs from the wheel. Honk the horn and tug the string. We'll get there in the end.

We get there in the end. Nha Trang. A place of promenades and large white hotels. Also, the chief point of supply for the US forces in the Third Zone. The grandest resort in all Vietnam. But the People's Committee is closed. We are directed to a hotel away from the sea, another Thang Loy (Victory), originally built by the Chinese for the benefit of Americans. Hard to tell whether it's a people's guesthouse or something else. How much will it cost? The room is clean and spacious. I yawn under a cold shower. In the restaurant the head waiter speaks perfect French-English and produces a beefsteak. I notice how bright the lights are, how here in the south the wattage is up to par. I yawn again. Sau grins and rubs my knee. He's happy, I'm happy, Truc I think is happy.

Tuesday 21st November: Nha Trang By daylight Nha Trang looks very nice. The sea is a palette of rich blues, ranging from the turquoise to the cobalt. The bay is smothered with brightly painted rocking fishing boats. Many of the buildings are whitewashed, and there are waving palm trees everywhere. The focal point of the city is a gleaming white colossus: the good Lord Buddha. But somehow it's a place that doesn't get through to me.

The morning is wasted, which is to say I keep to my room in a vain endeavour to catch up with my notes, which have fallen a long way behind. Sau scours the city looking for a reliable garage to repair the Mazda. He also makes contact with the People's Committee. In the afternoon I am briefly introduced to a bag of potatoes at the Bureau of Culture and Information. The director, two vice-directors, the chairman of the Khanh Hoa Province Writers' Association. I am spared the indoctrination session until tomorrow. I do have time however to establish that nobody has ever heard about Binh Hoa. Then I am taken off to inspect the number one tourist attraction: the ancient Cham temple built on a hill just below the colossal Buddha. The three mitre-shaped buildings are cut from the same cloth as the much grander monuments at Ankhor Wat and Ayutthaya. It is curious though that the altar of the largest of the three is still 'alive'. In the grotto-like sanctum, candles and offerings surround the statue of the goddess Ponaga ('Mother of the Homeland'), who gives her name to the miniature complex. Her head, originally cast in gold but removed by the French, has been replaced, but her body, draped with various cloths, is original. The young man from Culture and Information invites me to feel her breasts. They are very large, very firm and very cold.

We climb up to the Buddhist pagoda, Long Son, that dates from 1966. The best that can be said about it is that it must have cost a lot to build. The large prayer hall is immaculate and soulless. The head monk, Chi Tin, advises me to adopt his faith. He has served the Buddha for fifty years. One of his fellow monks publicly burnt himself during the war. Phra Tin I sense is more of a survivor. Nonetheless, when I offer alms in the form of a 5,000 *dong* note, he jumps back in holy horror, before pointing to the offertory box.

Then we climb to the colossus itself, which is also somewhat soulless. In its base is, or was, the library. This was sealed up after the Tet Offensive however, when it was discovered that a Viet Cong cell was using it as a base for terrorist operations in the city.

And that, for today, is my lot. In the early evening we attempt a swim among waves that are hard edged and inhospitable. Madame Phuong sits in a deckchair drinking beer, the mother of us all. We eat in a cheap restaurant where Sau Dang once again is recognized and acclaimed. Later, Truc and I stroll the promenade. We wind up at the Seamen's Mission, for the best and cheapest massage in town. For less than a dollar, and more than an hour, a girl who is so small and so thin she looks as though she couldn't lift a cooking pot beats my back like a Black & Decker hammer-head. She too though retracts in horror when I offer her a second dollar: although by now I am fully clothed, she mistakes my intentions entirely.

Wednesday 22nd November: Nha Trang–Cam Ranh   Before breakfast a trip in a motor-boat to a sea-farm a mile or two down the coast. The object I think is to impress upon me the astonishing natural beauty of mauve mountains rising out of the ocean. Exotic tropical fish glide in open, saltwater tanks. But it's too early to do more than behold. On the way back we look over the Emperor Bao Dai's summer villa, built on the best location on a promontory overlooking the sea. Later it was requisitioned by Presidents Thieu and Ky for their personal use. More or less it has been kept in good order. The tattiness of an art deco bedroom was probably part of the original design. Now the house belongs to Nha Trang Tourism. For forty dollars a night visitors can sleep on the royal couch and wake up feeling lordly: probably Asia's premier tourist bargain.

Culture and Information is waiting for me. Having been advised of my matinal needs, a female cadre stands behind my back perpetually ready to serve more coffee. Four bigger potatoes sit opposite with alarmingly fat bundles of written papers. Sixty-five per cent of Khanh Hoa Province is mountainous. There are two flights per week to Saigon. The railway works. Nha Trang is officially designated one of the country's top ten tourist destinations. The average mean temperature is 26 degrees centigrade. The city has seventeen old quarters, and out to sea there are nineteen islands. The province is famous for *tram huong*, a perfumed wood that has many medicinal properties. On the world market it is highly valued, as are the appropriately named *yen* birds, whose pellets are exported to Hong Kong where they are eaten by wealthy Cantonese and Japanese gourmets. Another good medicine is the hot springs at Diem Khanh and Ninh Hoa. The water is hot enough to boil an egg and will do your skin no end of good.

Nha Trang is prosperous. One reason for this is the tolerance extended to 'economic returnees' – Vietnamese who fled the South in 1975, but are now returning with fortunes acquired in the West. And not just the West. The case of one Nguyen Hung is cited, a fat cat who has made his pile in the Philippines. Now his son is joint-venturing back in the homeland. (And it's true. The tale I will hear again and again goes like this. In 1975 there were two brothers, both Saigon regime men. The one flees the country with the family gold and prospers in Paris or San Francisco. The other, unwilling to leave the land of his birth and his ancestors, stays behind. After all, he is Vietnamese. He is slung into a re-education camp, he is stripped of his rights, he is no longer allowed to work. His children

282

are not allowed to attend college. The years go by. Suddenly, it's *doi moi*. The exiled brother returns home, is welcomed with open arms. His wealth is what the Socialist Republic needs just now . . .)

Another reason is that Nha Trang sits at the crossroads. To the north Danang and Hué, to the south Saigon, to the east Dalat. Hence the concentration of US forces in the '60s. But try as hard as it can, Culture and Information struggles to bring very much glory to its city's and its province's war history. Between them, the Americans, the Saigonese and the Koreans just about had Nha Trang sewn up. Nha Trang was not taken during Tet. Nor, it seems, was the city in the vanguard of the fight against the French. 'We would tell you about the French war, but time does not permit.' Instead I am told about the concentration of enemy forces, perhaps in the hope I'll think that such a concentration was necessary because of the rebellious nature of Khanh Hoa, and not because of Nha Trang's strategic position.

There was activity in the countryside however, and in the mountains. The strategic hamlet programme broke down in Khanh Hoa as it broke down everywhere else in the South. Beginning in 1963, the regime planned to create 281 'secure villages', but in the event only succeeded in building fifty. Along the lines of the *kampongs* erected by the British in Malaya in the war against the Chinese communists, each new settlement was surrounded by wire. The gates were opened at 7.00 a.m., and closed at 5.00 p.m. Each house had a label stuck on its door, listing the members of the family who lived within. Families were also grouped in units of five, 'in order that they might control each other'. But unlike Malaya, where the Malays quickly saw that it was to their advantage to be protected from their ethnic enemies, those inside had as much, if not more, in common with the guerrillas outside as they did with their 'protectors'. The terrorist incidents continued.

The first crisis came in 1963. A band of approximately 150 Viet Cong operated out of the hills. They were supplied and supported by the minority hills people. In an initial operation two hundred Saigon troops were killed. Sixty of these were slain with poisoned arrows. Reinforcements were sent, and an unsuccessful attempt made to locate the VC base. Another 500 Saigonese were squandered.

283

The VC had gained an important psychological victory, even though Saigon's response was to call in the USAF to begin carpet-bombing the uplands. It was also the kind of victory that led to the commitment of American ground troops.

The second crisis came in March 1969, a year after the Tet Offensive, when combined American, Saigon and Korean forces located and attacked a major VC hideout in a cave system at Dong Bo, just five kilometres outside the city. In a month of fierce fighting fifty guerrillas held off 'vastly superior' numbers. At least a hundred enemy were killed, often 'in hand-to-hand fighting'. But their success was to no avail. When they couldn't storm the caves, the Americans withdrew and sprayed them with Agent Orange and other deadly herbicides. Today the caves are still 'too dangerous' to enter.

We leave Nha Trang for Cam Ranh. It's only a forty-kilometre drive, but it takes an age. Again and again the Mazda stops in its tracks. I have plenty of time to observe the increasingly luxuriant foliage, against which red flags and red banners, so strident in the north, hardly stand out at all. And when we do lug into the small town, there's no immediate joy for us. All the rooms at the primitive guesthouse have been booked by a party of Filipino sailors. The manager shows us an attic in which there are three pieces of furniture that might pass for beds in the dark, but one look at the thick pile of rat droppings on the floor dissuades us. Clearly the room has not been used for a decade. But no problem. On the other side of Cam Ranh is a motel built out over the water. The individual bungalows are decidedly decorous. There is a risk from water snakes, and there is also a section of the motel, between the bungalows and the dining room, that calls itself a 'special commercial area'. This turns out to be a massage parlour and a steam-bath facility. What do they do? Dangle their filaments between the floorboards into the water six inches below?

Having dumped our bags, Sau again goes off in search of a mechanic. With the wooden shutters of my room flung open wide and an electric fan spinning slowly I spend an hour lying on my back staring up at the upper contours of Cam Ranh Bay, listening to the water as it laps around me. It's the first time since I've come to Vietnam that I've spent any part of the afternoon relaxing. The feeling is that of a low-key idyll, disturbed only by thoughts of what havoc a typhoon would do to it, and a sense of the pointlessness of my being here anyway. Cam Ranh boasts the finest natural anchorage in Vietnam, but the chances of my seeing any of it are zero. It used to be the biggest American naval base in SE Asia; now it's the biggest Soviet naval base.

Little by little the idyll subsides into boredom, until Sau returns. As well as having hopefully fixed the car, he's discovered an excellent restaurant down the highway. To my great delight we dine on fresh oysters. With paper-wrapped fish, soup, prawns, rice and a quantity of Heineken, for little more than $12 we furnish ourselves with the absolute in private banquets.

Thursday 23rd November: Cam Ranh–Phan Thiet (Thuan Hai Province) The Mazda is not repaired. Even before we set out Sau realizes the faulty pump will never hold. He takes the vehicle back to Cam Ranh town, and it is close on 10.00 a.m. before we leave. We are going to Phan Thiet, the capital of Thuan Hai Province, about 160 kilometres south. When we've been to Phan Thiet we'll double back as far as Phan Rang, and then head up to Dalat in the highlands. Why we're going to Phan Thiet is not altogether clear to me. It was not on my list before I came to Vietnam, and nothing I've heard since has made me think again. I suggest we go straight to Dalat. Both Truc and Sau resist this. No, I must certainly go to Phan Thiet. Mr Hong has said that I should, and what Mr Hong says . . . It is the beginning of my first contretemps with Sau, the first pitting of our wills. It doesn't quite come to the boil, but for the next three days the relationship smoulders at its edges.

The Mazda doesn't help. Six times it breaks down, six times Sau Dang performs mechanical heroics. The third time it ceases to be a joke. The luxuriant tropical vegetation also runs out quickly. Bare mountains and scrub become the order of the day. After Phang Rang, a kind of desert, twenty kilometres of it, no houses, no people, just graves. Mile after mile of graves, some of them isolated, some of them grouped together. Villages of the dead. Necropolis.

The vegetation thickens. We arrive in Phan Thiet, a small

provincial city that straddles a pretty river. An unusually large statue of Ho Chi Minh, but not quite of the same order as the Nha Trang Buddha, catches my eye. We late-lunch on chicken and coconut juice. At the People's Committee we are welcomed cordially by yet another Mr Hong, grey-haired like every other Mr Hong. He knows all about Sau Dang. Soon he knows all about me. Sau Dang raps hard on my behalf for several minutes. I hear the phrases 'Nuoc Lenin' and 'Binh Hoa'. Mr Hong begins to smile. Will we excuse him for a minute? After conferring with his colleagues, he invites us to stay at the People's Guesthouse free of charge. Outside Sau grins radiantly, though Truc cautions that I must expect another economics/history lesson.

The first part of the lesson comes in the afternoon, in the form of a practical. There is a reason for the added size of the statue. I should have known. In 1910 Ho Chi Minh spent seven months teaching at a school here. The school, which I am taken to, is stunning in its simplicity. It is all wood, beautifully cool and lighter inside than its modern replacements. Its founder, Nguyen Qui Anh, was the son of a famous scholar, Nguyen Thong. Both were nationalists. The future Great Leader taught literature, French and gymnastics to little boys and little girls. He also helped out with the garden.

The school is close by the statue, and the statue is in front of a Ho Chi Minh Museum. By provincial standards the latter is unusually opulent. It is also very advanced, being all glass and concrete and decently air-conditioned inside. The shape I am told represents a lotus, but if that is the case then it is a peculiarly cubist lotus. The exhibits are the usual photographs, although in the centre of the building, in a species of well, there is a slightly magnificent mural: a masterpiece of the Revolution, it depicts a guerrilla anti-aircraft unit. It is reminiscent of a Stanley Spencer Resurrection or Crucifixion: all of life is there, but none of the figures represented quite has the brains to see it.

Signing the visitors' book (in Vietnam visitors' books are taken seriously) I add a required message. Forgetting where I am, I extol the virtues of the traditional architecture I have just seen across the way. 'Who needs glass and concrete and electricity,' I write, 'when wood was enough for Ho Chi Minh?'

286

If I have caused offence, my hosts are too polite to show it. I am still the honoured guest. In the evening we are invited to the Phan Thien Culture Palace. This too has a Spenceresque character. There is a great plethora of activities for young people to test their brains and brawn. Everyone is busy. Video games and video shows, billiards, martial arts, table tennis. A nascent rock band stomps hard on the boards of a makeshift stage outside in the compound, which is dominated by the looming outline of a Saigon Army fighter jet.

The director of the Culture Palace would be incredibly pleased if I would watch two films. My swelling entourage regroups in the video hall. Video No. 1, made in Japan, shows off Thuan Hai's premier dance group. There are six or seven routines they plough their way through. First, Cham style: dressed as gilded air-hostesses, they come on in a kind of musical fashion show. Holding pots in their hands they try some gentle acrobatics. Or is it a variation of *Swan Lake*? Then they sing a 'traditional' Cham village song: 'Our Love for Uncle Ho'. Next comes the golden bikini dance, with both sexes participating. Were it not for the seriousness of their faces – has anybody got some paracetamol? – this surely is something the Thai Tourist Authority would be proud of. Then there is the Returning Soldiers' Welcome Dance (fully clothed version of); a Cham Head Dance, performed mainly on the knees; and an Ah-Here-Is-My-Fan Dance. In the final routine the fans, which are coloured a green that is more liverish than livid, become butterfly wings as the assembled Thuan Hai lovelies do the ancient Cham Butterfly Parade.

Now the main feature: *Thuan Hai – Loyal Area*. Of Generals and Lotuses. Another visit to the H.C.M. Museum, opened to mark the tenth anniversary of the liberation of the province. Visits from the Politburo: the late Le Duan, Pham Van Dong and others. An orgy of self-congratulation among the local big potatoes. The early provincial Party members. Shots of the railway station. A guest appearance by Le Duc Tho. American helicopters. Poetic rubble. Families of the Revolution, the fathers, mothers, sons and daughters of 'fallen heroes'. The place in the jungle where the Party hid. The loyal peasants (celebration music). The shot of the minority hero who shot down a US plane with a pre-war rifle.

Crossbows and booby-traps. The Party goes to the mountains, ostensibly to taste mountain brandy. The strong cordial of the Revolution! A butterfly hunt near Phan Rang. Caves where the VC hid out. The war mother who lost eight sons against the beast of American imperialism. More joss-sticks than there are stars in the heavens. Subliminal insert of a social-realist war memorial. Dancing on the Cham towers. The inevitable agricultural sequence. Here come those big potatoes! The garment industry. Cotton-farming. Fish. Apricots and onions. Sheep. Followed by pigs. A touch of heavy industry. The hydroelectric power-station that keeps the fish-sauce factory operating. A salt mountain at sunset. Nurses with medicine chests. Further tribal dancing, filmed from all the unsensuous positions. Thousands of schoolchildren doing the butterfly dance with red fans. The dancing school. Another look at the Cham towers, and another visit from Pham Van Dong. Those golden bikini girls again. Camouflaged ack-ack guns up in the highlands. A glimpse of the seaside. A military parade. The presentation of a Gold Star medal. The H.C.M. Museum for the last time. Children enjoying themselves at a fairground. Around and around and around ... The Hanoi Documentary Film Unit. I would recognize the style anywhere. It dawns upon me that this is what 'they' want my book to be like.

Later, I take Truc over the bridge to hang around the central market area. In some Vietnamese towns I get a feel for the people, in some I don't. Phan Thiet belongs to the former category. There is something infinitely engaging about those who seem prepared to spend all night squatting on their heels chatting in the shadows. We take coffee at a stall in an oval piazza. We make *boc phét* with all and sundry. Now that Truc has grown accustomed to my curious habit of wanting to go walkabout at every available opportunity, he has become relaxed about it. He smiles and orders himself a bowl of noodles. That is his habit, his need. No matter how much he's eaten, he always has room for noodles last thing at night. Sometimes I think that if I told him the only bowl of noodles in the whole of Vietnam was sitting on the other side of a minefield he'd walk straight across and eat it.

*   *   *

Friday 24th November: Phan Thiet–Phan Rang   Here we go. The teachers assemble in the reception room on the ground floor of the guesthouse – for their solitary pupil and his minders. As well as Nguyen Van Hong, from the External Relations Bureau, there is Dang Ngoc Long from the Planning Bureau, My Ngoc, the chief of army history in Thuan Hai Province, as well as a vice-director of Culture and Information (only in Phan Thiet it's Information and Culture). But also waiting for me is Tran Ngoc Trac (pronounced Jack), until recently chairman of the provincial People's Committee, and always an old revolutionary. His presence turns the lesson into something rich and strange. He has a gift for me. He also paints a more vivid picture of what it was like to be a VC than I will hear anywhere else.

Trac, aged sixty-six, dominates proceedings. He begins, correctly, by telling me how Ho Chi Minh came to be in Phan Thiet. Having been expelled from school in Hué, he was sent by his father to Quy Nhon, to learn the art of schoolteaching from Pham Ngoc Tho (the father of one of Ho's comrades, Pham Ngoc Thac, later Minister of Health in the Socialist Republic). The French Governor of Annam, however, refused to allow Ho Chi Minh's name to be added to the approved list of teachers. Ho therefore decided to travel south, leaving Quy Nhon by boat. In Tuy Phong District, at the end of 1909, he rented a small dwelling from Trung Gia Mo, a high-ranking mandarin. But Mo was also a patriot, and a friend of Ho's father. Indeed, he had just been released from prison. Wealthy enough to fend for himself, he encouraged Ho to hide in the local pagoda by day, where he would be safe from the ever-watchful eyes of the Sûréte. Mo then sent him on to the Duc Thanh school in Phan Thiet. There he arrived in February 1910, just before Tet (New Year), and there he stayed until just after the mid-autumn children's festival in September.

'During this time,' Trac solemnly reminds me, 'Halley's comet appeared.'

From Phan Thiet, Ho travelled to Saigon by train. He spent three months at a mechanical college, and then set sail, on 5th June 1911, to begin his globe-trotting adventures.

By coming to Thuan Hai, Trac continues, Ho demonstrated his patriotism, because even at that early stage there existed three 'revolutionary' organizations within the province: the Lien Thanh Thu Xa (1906), a fund-raising body to promote the dissemination of patriotic propaganda; the Lien Thanh Thuong Quan (1906), a commercial concern; and the Duc Thanh school itself.

The alias Ho used at this time was Nguyen Tat Thanh. His students, some of whom are still alive, remembered him as 'an excellent gymnast and a true patriot'. Sometimes he took them 'visiting', excursions into the countryside where, far from French ears, he could fill their minds with Thoughts for the Future.

In the French war, the people of Thuan Hai Province were 'among the first to use Ho Chi Minh banknotes', printed in Annam for the first time in 1947. In time these notes became known as 'the money of Uncle Ho's beard'. The printing blocks soon faded, and all that appeared on the later notes was the print of the growth under Uncle Ho's chin. 'But the people willingly accepted these from the Viet Minh in payment for rice and other goods, for by possessing such a note it proved they were patriots.'

As well as Uncle Ho money, there was also 'Uncle Ho salt' – *Muoi Cu Ho*. After the 1954 Geneva Accords, every effort was made to create salt reserves in the mountains, both for the benefit of the *montagnards*, and for the benefit of future guerrillas, if, as anticipated, the southern regime reneged on its agreement to participate in nationwide elections.

'And this was vital, for salt is the most precious of all traditional medicines. How could we have lived without it? I can tell you, in Bac Ai there were men who kept their salt all the way through, from 1954 until 1975.'

Trac returns to the first years of the Revolution. On 24th August 1945 a revolutionary government was established in Pham Thiet for 160 days. But at the end of January, French troops arrived from Dalat, coming through Phan Rang.

'We Viet Minh, armed at the best only with rifles, at the worst with sticks and crossbows given us by the mountain minorities, were like a rat trying to attack an elephant.'

A detachment of the Sancerre-trained colonial army duly came to Trac's native village, Long Huong in Tru Phuong District. One of his friends was stopped and searched on the road leading into Long Huong. He was found to be carrying a stick and a petrol-bomb. His comrades tried to force his release, but in the event they had to flee.

'Our guns didn't work. But that was not the reason for our failure. The reason for our failure was our lack of military knowledge. If you have military knowledge, almost anything will suffice for a weapon. Even so, despite our ignorance, we fought the French.'

Trac waves his arms and looks at everybody round the table.

'Let me tell you about the French. As long ago as 1885 they began massacring us. It happened at La Gang, near the sea. The people there didn't like the French taking everything away from them, so they protested. So the French organized a massacre. And sixty years later nothing had changed. Early on in the war La Gang became a base for the patriotic Viet Minh. So the French destroyed the village three times between 1946 and 1951, killing 339 of the inhabitants, most of whom were women and children. Often babies were wrenched from their mothers' breasts and thrown into the flames of their burning homes.'

Another centre of resistance was Bac Ai, in the mountainous north of the province.

'I myself lived up there. At the time I ran the propaganda section, but I often had to fight as well. In 1954 most of us left for the North. We gave the people the victory sign as we departed, and said: See you in two years, after the elections. But the elections were never held. Instead the Diem regime began terrorizing the people. There was a campaign to destroy everyone who had been a Viet Minh, everyone who had fought for his country against the foreign invaders. Every day there were burnings and killings. Just to be a suspect was to be as good as dead. Wives who had husbands living in the North were forced to divorce and remarry Saigon officers. Or not to marry them, if you follow my meaning. The regime even harassed the *montagnards*, resettling them in the plains, where they had nothing they were used to, and where they were kept like animals.

'But it was not just the *montagnards*, it was everybody, all the non-Catholics. So of course, sooner or later there had to be an uprising. This happened at Baram Carum, on 7th February 1959. It was the first time weapons were used against Diem. Between 1954 and 1959 there was no use of weapons, anywhere in the South. But at Baram Carum, well, we used weapons. The Central Committee have now confirmed that this was the first uprising in the second war, the war against Saigon and the Americans. Previously the official first uprising was in Ben Tre. But that was in 1960, after the fifteenth plenum of the Central Committee had sanctioned armed struggle at the end of 1959. But our uprising happened before this, so until now it has been kept a secret.

'Saigon however sent reinforcements. There was a witchhunt throughout the plains. Soon we were forced deeper into the hills. Often we were short of food. We were obliged to discover new vegetables. I remember one that was called *thang ngan*, a leaf. Supposedly this was poisonous, but we were so hungry one of us volunteered to taste it. Since he didn't die, we all started eating it. It kept us alive, and we named it after our courageous comrade: Thang Ngan.

'We lived on cassava, sprinkled with salt when we could get it, and bamboo shoot. These were the three Ms: *mi*, *muoi* and *mang*. Later the three Ms became six Ms, as we added *mo* (pork fat), *mam* (solid shrimp sauce) and *mì* (monosodium glutamate). We relied for our supplies on the ordinary peasants in the plains. They made sure we never starved, though we came close to it at times.

'At Bac Ai, we lived in the caves. As the war progressed our main task was to shoot down enemy planes. We dug foxholes so that we wouldn't be killed when the bombs dropped. But we had to stay out in the open too, so that the planes would spot us and come down and we could shoot at them.

'Our first success was in March 1965, when we hit a reconnaissance aircraft. A short while after, we got an F105. By the end of the war 246 aircraft had been brought down. We bagged every type, except F111s, which flew too fast, and B52s, which flew too high. In time, the USAF became very wary of the air space above Bac Ai, which was later credited with the title Hero's District.

'Our hearts always sang when an enemy plane fell. Life was so difficult. An enemy plane in the jungle enabled us to make a few consumer goods. Rings, combs, things like that. We were short of everything. We had to use bamboo bark for paper, leaf and coal for ink. Often there was a shortage of water too. Sometimes the only way to wash was to stand out in the midday sun and sweat. We called this fire bathing. And in the early mornings, if there had been a frost, we would stand under the trees and shake the trunks, just for a few drops of the stuff. Often water was like blood to us.

'But we didn't want for female company. There were several women Viet Cong. They too sometimes shot down enemy planes, using their rifles. If the enemy captured them, they were particularly cruel. They reserved their worst tortures for the women. But the women were always brave, braver than us men sometimes. I recall that one of them, Xa Ai Du, was taken prisoner by some Saigon soldiers. They tortured and tortured her. They wanted to turn her, to make her spy for them. Eventually she relented, and agreed to do what they wanted. She said she would lead them to one of our secret camps. But what she actually did was lead them to a place where we could easily ambush them. She took them up the wrong hill. When they realized they'd been tricked, she laughed in their faces. "I'll never be your slave," she shouted. "I'll never be unfaithful to Uncle Ho." And with that she jumped into a ravine and killed herself.

'And I recall Mrs Nia. Mrs Nia lived with us in the caves. Recently she had given birth to a daughter. But this child would never stop screaming. One day a Saigon Army search unit came dangerously near. Fearing that her daughter would reveal our position, she killed her. It was a terrible thing to do, but then that was the war. It limited your options, it even made you inhuman.'

Trac concludes. As he does so, he opens his wallet and carefully extracts a tissue-thin banknote. It is forty-three years old and bears the familiar beard. Its face value is 100 *dong*. It wouldn't buy me much today, but in 1947, when the *dong* had parity with the *piastre*, it would have purchased a ton or two of rice. Trac has been keeping it all this time. Now, as a token of solidarity between humans, he presents it to me, accompanied by a hug.

God knows what I've done to deserve either.

Dang Ngoc Long from the Planning Bureau briefly fills me in on the ordinary statistics of Thuan Hai Province. The population, the per capita electricity supply, the hectares under cultivation, the fish production advantage. But my mind is elsewhere, captivated by the coherence of Trac's memory. In any case it's time for lunch. The People's Committee has organized a farewell banquet across the river.

Vodka and beer glasses are raised in frightening succession. Once again Sau Dang holds court. A military commander fixes me with his eyes. He wants to see how much I can hold, how much I can't. *Chuk xu khoe* and down the hatch. Henceforward there'll always be one of them. Prowess in alcohol is prowess in manhood. Always somebody who'll want to see what kind of comrade, what kind of *dong chi* I would have made. Thus, even before we arrive at the Mekong Delta, the habits of the delta have struck. Four gruellingly inebriate weeks lie ahead.

We leave Phan Thiet. The plan is to stay the night in Phan Rang, and then drive the 120 kilometres to Dalat in the highlands. I am apprehensive. I suggest to Sau we should skip Dalat and go straight to Saigon on Highway One. I can't seen how the Mazda will cope with the mountains, and so far my experience of mountains in Vietnam is that they are not the place to break down in. Sau scowls. He is determined to take me to Dalat. The Mazda will make it. Trust him. Also, he has been having an argument with Madame Phuong. For two or three days now both Truc and I have noticed that Madame Phuong is getting on Sau Dang's tits.

The Mazda behaves itself back to Phan Rang. We stop twice, once for Sau to take a pot-shot at a brace of white, heron-like birds hanging about in a paddy, once to swim. The waves are negotiable. I discover I can swim considerably further out to sea than my minders. Truc watches me forlornly from the shoreline. To hell with any sharks, this is freedom at last. But the effects are mutually beneficial as well. Afterwards I can face the Mazda, I don't mind if it does break down.

Phan Rang is undistinguished, except by a group of Soviet pilots who are training Viet airmen at what used to be the American air base in this neck of the woods. The guesthouse-hotel is set pleasantly within a miniature park, though the rooms are small and airless. Also, I must pay for them, since in Phan Rang I have no 'programme'. For once, when I take a postprandial stroll, I am neither stared at nor mobbed. It is assumed I am Russian. There are enough of them about.

Truc and I continue to make progress. I persuade him that 'Get out please' is politer than 'Get out!' and in return he provides me with a few lessons in Vietnamese etiquette. One, at formal banquets, I should always offer my first *chuk xu khoe* to the oldest man present, whatever his position. Two, I should never chew my sunglasses when receiving compliments. Three, I should keep my name-cards in my jacket or shirt pocket, never in my back trouser pocket. You can keep money there, but anything else is *verboten*. To present someone with a warm name-card from the posterior is equivalent to breaking wind in his face . . .

Saturday 25th November: Phan Rang–Dalat First thing Mr Sau performs his tricks and gets us a reduction on our bill. The man really does have the knack. I am therefore reasonably relaxed when, after just ten kilometres, the Mazda grinds to a halt, precisely in the middle of nowhere. But Sau refuses to turn back. He spends an hour tinkering with the engine. At last we're ready to go. In front of us looms a wall of mountain. There are also mountains to our left and to our right. It's not a happy sound the Mazda makes, but at least it's a sound. Soon we begin the painstaking climb toward the 'high plateau'. There is a steep pass, then another, then another. Butterflies proliferate. We even overtake a white Lada. Then the white Lada overtakes us. Sau is overjoyed: there are friends of his inside. After another mile we come across them having a picnic of hot tea and boiled peanuts. Extra cups are produced, our thirst quenched.

Whilst the others chat I walk on ahead, for a panoramic look at the valley we have just left. The view, eastwards toward Phan Rang and the sea, is staggering. Something happens to me. The effect of Mr Trac in Phan Thiet is still percolating. Leaving the road, I squat on my haunches, gazing at the highway below, no bigger than a piece of string, and the tiny dots in the gleaming paddy-fields that represent peasants at work. A great expanse of silver-green, ringed by mauve, with the blue beyond. Suddenly I begin to feel what it must have been like to be a guerrilla, a Viet Cong, stuck up here, year in year out, biding his time, patient like a rock, looking every day on the land of his ancestors, able, perhaps, to detect the grass roofing of his own village, spotting an American or Saigon army APC patrolling the highway, patrolling the network of smaller roads that connect the hamlets to the villages and the villages to the district towns.

His ears pick up the sounds of a helicopter gunship almost before it leaves the ground. Instinctively he withdraws for cover, or retreats to warn his comrades of a possible attack. Sometimes he has seen airplanes swoop across the valley and take out this village or that village, even his own village, with deadly accurate rocket fire. Sometimes the aeroplanes fly toward the mountains, to drop napalm where their pilots have been told his base camp is. And for the moment there is little he can do, except wait and wait, until the next operation, when he will descend stealthily by night into the valley to launch a lightning attack on this or that enemy installation. But mostly he squats on the heights, perhaps thinking about his family, whom he hasn't seen for several months, wondering whether his father is still alive, and whether his mother is still in good spirits, and asking himself what has become of his favourite sister. She will be eighteen now, and more beautiful than ever. Has she been noticed by a neo-imperialist GI?

By night he is cold. He has been attacked continually by mosquitoes, all manner of other insects, sometimes by bats. Once he trod on a poisonous snake. But he was luckier than Comrade Anh, who trod too lightly on a snake and died. Usually he is hungry. His group must raid another enemy detachment, for it often relies on captured rations to survive. No tendril of the Ho Chi Minh Trail has reached here yet. Perhaps it never will. It's too far from the Laotian border, too far from the all-important Mekong Delta. And behind him in any case, the enemy holds Dalat.

He sights another APC roaming the valley. Having nothing more urgent to do, he fixes his mind on it. He wills its removal, and imagines the day when the whole plain will finally belong to him and his . . .

Truc disturbs my reverie. Get in please. Sau has finished with his friends and has brought the Mazda up the road. As we drive on I welcome the change in temperature. Each time we reach the summit of a pass it becomes distinctly cooler. The landscape also

296

metamorphoses, once we have attained the plateau. Now the hills are too low, too delicate, to be called mountains, though, if they could be seen from the plain, that is certainly what they would be called. There are fruit orchards everywhere, and the soil is darkly red. It is as though I were passing through another country. And this surmise is vindicated when we enter the outskirts of Dalat. Astonishingly, the road is now flanked by houses built in a variety of European domestic architectural styles. The chalet prevails, but there is at least one attempt at a mock-Tudor thatched cottage. The beams though are a mite too thin, and the pale yellow plaster of the walls does not ring true either. I also notice how, though the temperature cannot be anywhere above fifteen or sixteen degrees centigrade, the women walk around beneath coloured parasols. Against long sections of low, white-painted wooden fencing, their attempts to appear dainty are enormously successful.

In a sense, Dalat is all outskirts. In its colonial heyday, it was the premier hill resort in all Indochina. All the richer *colons* had houses here, which they lived in during the hottest months. As I soon discover, there is a small 'downtown' area which throbs with small-scale commerce at night. There are also three or four large-scale hotels, built by the French. But the overwhelming impression is that of a well spread out composite of half a dozen upper-middle-class European suburbs.

We lunch at an 'old' restaurant in the middle of this centre-less city. Cauliflower, shrimps, mange-tout. The proprietor is a friend of Sau's, and there is beer to make us welcome. Then we pay our duty-call on the People's Committee. The committee members wear thick sweaters and cloth jackets. The younger cadres don leathers and are sharp-faced. I am not altogether surprised when the first man we talk to tells us no papers concerning my visit have been received from Hanoi. This arouses my fears. I have been warned that Dalat is one of the places in Vietnam that is likely to cost me money. But Sau Dang sweet-talks energetically on my behalf. Soon the committee chairman comes from his office to look us over. A small figure, with a glazed china face that gives nothing away. But Sau, when we climb back in the car, is confident.

My fear is, surrounded by so much elegance, we'll have to stay in some bleak people's guesthouse. But of course I'm wrong. The old European-style house we remove to, in an estate of old European-style houses, is a little chill, and my room has neither bathroom nor shower – instead I must make do with a communal washroom of the most primitive kind – but the place has bags of dignity. Soon Truc announces that it's been decided I need pay only 12,000 *dong* a night. And soon after this he returns to announce that in fact I need pay nothing at all. Sau has met someone else who knows him. Indeed, whenever I leave my room, a courtesy pack of cigarettes is left on my table.

I begin to like my room, which occupies a large corner of the ground floor. Outside the shuttered window, a young cowherd is grazing his bullock. I also begin to like Dalat. It is a civilized place, not because it was built by Europeans for European requirements, but because it still exists. It is a little shabby now perhaps, too many of the houses need renovating, but . . . I imagine what the Khmer Rouge would have done to Dalat, had they ever laid their hands on it. In Vietnam, the Cultural Revolution has been postponed indefinitely.

I take a painfully cold shower. Or rather, I stand in a tiny concrete cubicle in the communal washroom dousing myself with freezing water that gushes out of a tap only eighteen inches off the floor into an iron bucket. By means of an ancient plastic mug, I scoop the contents of the pail over my head. Yet the spartan bother of this can only make me feel good. My head is still full of the hardships endured by the Viet Cong, so that almost everything about Dalat comes as a kind of paradise.

A sleepy, sheepish young man arrives at the house from the Bureau of External Relations. His name, I think, is Chi. He assures us that my programme in Dalat is under active consideration. Meanwhile would I like to see the Emperor Bao Dai's palace? Since it's only a short distance away, at the top of the hill we're halfway up already, we walk. The 'palace' in fact is no more than a modern hunting lodge. It has the size and texture of small hotels you find in the outer suburbs of London erected either in the 1930s, or just after the Second World War. The corners are rounded, the windows have metal frames with horizontal panes of rectangular glass. There are just the two storeys. But if the outside is anodyne, the inside is *louche*. As a private dwelling, it crystallizes what every *petit bourgeois* from Kōbe to Cologne has dreams of living in. All is expense, with few concessions to taste. Or perhaps I am prejudiced, perhaps I've begun identifying more than I'd care to admit with the privations of the VC. There is a film-set quality to it. A large vestibule gives way to a drawing room that has deep, all-of-a-piece art deco armchairs and sofas, coloured gold. I am struck by the fawn-shaded wall-to-wall carpeting, something I have forgotten exists. In the middle of the room, a stuffed tiger, and on the walls several sets of antlers. Bao Dai fancied himself as a hunter, as well as a womanizer. Then there is the 'cabinet room', with a long, highly polished table. The French allowed Bao Dai to play at politics long after they had stripped his throne of all its real powers. His study, again, is thoroughly un-Vietnamese. Behind a desk that must have been the last word in modernity in 1929 is a bookcase full of books. All of them are French. On the desk, whether by design or by accident, a tome on elephants lies open.

I ask to go upstairs, to look at the bedrooms, but I am told upstairs is out of bounds. The building belongs to the provincial Party Committee and is still used to entertain 'special' guests. The bedrooms are occupied. Instead I am invited to try the gardens. These too are preserved, in good order. I could be somewhere in Austria on a summer's evening.

The actual evening turns out to be not very Austrian. Although we have been told that food as well as cigarettes would be provided at the house, by seven o'clock there is still no sign of the cook, nor indeed of any of the staff. We decide therefore to go downtown, returning to the 'old' restaurant for a *sukiyaki* accompanied by sliced pig's heart and unsliced chicken hearts. Sau Dang is in good spirits. To begin with he has succeeded in getting me to Dalat. Secondly, Madame Phuong has, somewhat unceremoniously, been put on a bus for Saigon. Thirdly, we have rechristened him Sau Dai, in ironic comparison with the last of the Nguyen emperors. It's time, he thinks, we had ourselves a Saturday night. First we visit a bar on one of several pretty lakes that are a feature of Dalat. The bar is empty, but Sau orders a bottle of superior 'vodka' and we begin to make merry. 'Perhaps,' says Truc, 'tonight we'll find some snake.' We move on to the Palace Hotel, by comparison with Bau Dai's villa a real palace, built to last by the French. It's also where, in 1946, Vo Nguyen Giap met with his French counterparts in the pre-talks that preceded the Fontaine-bleau Conference. A piano that has actually been tuned sometime in the last ten years invites my fingers. We talk to an effeminate Russian diplomat.

In the lobby, I am mesmerized by a three-faced figurine on sale in an antiques booth. It is one of those Hindu-Buddhist objects that might have come from almost anywhere – Burma, Thailand, Indonesia. An assistant tells me it is a Cham sculpture, seven hundred years old, and that I can have it for $200. I examine it more thoroughly, and seek both Truc's and Sau's opinion. A repeat of the Danang whisky mishap is the last thing any of us wants. Not fake is the general verdict. I offer $150. The assistant tells me she will have to 'ask the owner'. The piece belongs to a distinguished local family which is in the process of realizing its assets. Another assistant is dispatched, and soon she returns with the owner's son. A price of $160 is agreed. Sau grins triumphantly as the head is wrapped in paper.

We move on to another, newer tourist hotel where there's a discothèque. The place is jam-packed with smartly dressed youth. Truc affects not to be remotely surprised. 'This is the bourgeoisie,' he comments. 'There are no cadres here.'

We bag a table and are at once joined by two or three not very young women. I make a point of dancing with a group of students from the next table. Real whisky is served. We are next joined by an elderly man, almost rigid with courtesy. He speaks excellent French. After a while he asks me if I'd care to dance. I look at Truc, but Truc says go on, it's not what you think, in Vietnam men do dance with each other. A little reluctantly I am led to the floor, which immediately clears. The old man, happy as a lark, spins me around and around. When the music stops the room bursts into applause. Another gesture toward international amity has been made. Sau grins and massages my knee. The music finishes. It's closing time already. We pile into the Mazda with two of the women. Before the engine can start a third materializes from nowhere. A girl you'd have to call a beauty. On the way to the villa we stop to purchase a crate of Heineken. The party continues in

300

Sau's room. The beauty sings some traditional Vietnamese songs. Truc, gleaning his information from one of her companions, tells me she is married, but her husband has taken to alcohol. For a hundred dollars . . . A hundred dollars! I ask Truc to explain that I am a poor white. Complimenting her on her voice, I retire to my room. Lovingly I fondle my three-faced figurine. For just sixty dollars more I have bought a thing of beauty that will last forever.

Sunday 26th November: Dalat For the ordinary visitor to Dalat probably every day feels like a Sunday. The sights to be seen are all of them gently recreational. Chi escorts us to a nursery where the full range of highland blooms and a few monkeys can be viewed in tranquillity. Then we drive eight kilometres to 'Love Valley', number one romantic spot with a kinked lake and boats and ponies for hire. On the way we pass – gosh! – a golf course. My only complaint is that the pony men, wearing outsized cowboy hats and brandishing rifles, are just a little too anxious for one to hire their animals. Their overtures are physical, as is my response. 'Mountain types,' says Truc. After lunch, a visit to a waterfall, cascading majestically through a ravine that is also something of a heat trap. Again we meet some of Sau's friends. A film crew is shooting a sequence from a historical costume drama. A handsome young man dressed in all the colours of a peacock flashes a bejewelled sword in the face of a handsome young woman clad in flowing white. As the camera rolls, the director scowls. Taking me to one side, he explains: really there is no point in making films in Vietnam. The Party doesn't censor the finished product, it censors the script before it is shot. And always the Party man has his own ideas for extra scenes. This, the director says, will be his last movie for the Saigon studio that employs him. Next year he's off to America, Orderly Departure Program or no Orderly Departure Program. Have I been to Hollywood?

The evening is more predictable. The cook has been found, and a formal dinner is prepared. I am received by the two biggest potatoes of Lam Dong Province: Nguyen Xuan Du, the Party secretary, and the china-faced chairman of the People's Committee, Trinh Khiet. The Party speaks first. Nguyen Xuan Du is a hard-

301

minded patriot who spent twenty-four years of his life in the jungle. His finger frequently stabs the air for emphasis. A native of Binh Dinh Province, he first came to Lam Dong in 1949, after joining the Viet Minh resistance. After 1954 he stayed, becoming a Viet Cong in the second war, on the political side. In 1960 he became leader of the provisional provincial Party Committee – a post he has never relinquished.

Nguyen Xuan Du tells me about the Revolution as it affected Lam Dong. Lam Dong is one of the three plateau provinces, the other two being Dak Lak to the north and Song Be to the west. (Kontum, in central Vietnam, is classified as 'mountainous'.) In south-western Lam Dong no fewer than eight tendrils of the Ho Chi Minh Trail snaked their way toward the delta. For this reason, and because the uplands formed a natural refuge for VC guerrillas, and later NVA regulars, the province 'was subject to many enemy operations'. But Dalat itself was a tough nut to crack for the communists. As well as a military academy it boasted a police training college, and an organization for preparing the 'political wing' of the ARVN. There was in addition a religious factor. Because the city was essentially French in its evolution, there were many churches and many Catholics.

The Viet Cong lived with and off the villages and hamlets. To begin with, the Saigonese mounted 'jungle search' operations, but the jungle was simply too big. Later, carpet-bombing tactics were employed, but again the guerrillas escaped annihilation by sheltering underground. Initially, they were divided into two wings: jungle VC and city VC; but these in time were amalgamated, and Dalat was 'liberated', almost a month before Saigon, on 3rd April 1975. The suburbs had been taken by force, but inside the city there was no fighting. After a 'people's uprising', the Saigonese simply withdrew.

In these events, Nguyen Xuan Du assures me, Northern regulars played next to no part. Dalat was liberated by local men, by guerrillas and the communist militia.

He beams. Since 1975, everything has doubled at least: agricultural produce, the number of hectares cultivated, coffee exports . . . the population too! Lam Dong, as the French realized a hundred years ago, enjoys great natural advantages. It has some of the best farming land in all of Indochina. The only problem is finding investment capital and finding markets. Markets, both domestic and international, are sometimes hard to come by.

I ask whether central government is doing enough to provide a market structure. Nguyen Xuan Du frowns. 'Of course! Between the province and the government there is much co-operation. You must understand. Our problems are also Hanoi's problems.' The US embargo has much to answer for.

Abruptly, he gets up and leaves. Have I, or has Truc, said the wrong thing?

Trinh Khiet takes over. Tourism, he thinks, is the key to Dalat's future. As well as thirty hotels, there are a thousand villas 'waiting to be exploited'. But before he can go, I ask for the usual biographical details. He was born, he says, in 1927, in Binh Son District, Quang Ngai. Abruptly the interview changes course. Binh Son, Binh Hoa, the massacre. I ask Trinh Khiet for his version. It corresponds very closely with what I have already been told, although he adds a few new details. Binh Hoa was in fact a 'liberated zone', in the French as well as the American war. In the latter there were 'several hundred' guerrillas living, mainly in underground bunkers, in the area. The Green Dragon units of the South Korean army were sent in expressly to eradicate the guerrilla bases. Many of the villages in Binh Son were 'sealed off': that is, surrounded by mines and machine-guns. When the Koreans couldn't locate the bases, they turned on the villagers instead.

Trinh Khiet tells me that the number of victims given me in Binh Hoa is, in his opinion, on the low side. 'Seven hundred and twenty would be more accurate.' Then, with his face still retaining its mask-like composure, he 'confesses' that he himself lost twenty-two members of his family in the butchery. 'Only my sister survived.' His nearest and dearest were among those buried in the crater. It is a matter of personal regret to him that no lasting monument has yet been erected.

Nguyen Xuan Du returns, bringing with him a gift of five large packets of Dalat coffee (which I would recommend to anyone). I ask Trinh Khiet whether, in his opinion, the Americans would have known about Binh Hoa. Trinh Khiet asserts that most certainly they would have done. Nguyen Xuan Du however goes one further. He has visited South Korea, and talked with Park Chung-hee, the former President. Park 'apologized' for Korean 'activities' in Vietnam, but told Nguyen Xuan Du that the ROK had been 'pushed into them by the United States'.

If I am less than fully persuaded by this passing of the buck, I keep it to myself. My interest in Binh Hoa has earned me new friends tonight. I learn that beneath his implacable exterior Trinh Khiet nurses a profound humanity, which he shares with Nguyen Xuan Du. They have done their bit for their country, but, on a lighter note, they look forward to the day when a shuttle service, run for the benefit of carefree holiday-makers of all nationalities, hops between Hong Kong, Hué, Dalat, Bangkok, and back again.

Monday 27th November: Dalat–Saigon (Ho Chi Minh City) At last Saigon, even though Saigon will be little more to me than a base for further journeyings. The 300-plus-kilometre ride from Dalat takes less time than I anticipated. Perhaps because the road runs downhill nearly all the way, the Mazda behaves impeccably. Also the road, by Vietnamese standards, is excellent. We leave the house at eight, stopping at the city's main market on our way out. Sau Dang, now christened Sau Dai in honour of the exiled emperor, fills the boot with vegetables for his wife: mange-tout, potatoes, a cauliflower that weighs in excess of two kilos. I throw in some carrots and a bunch of blood-red hyacinths.

As long as we are on the plateau, rolling hills spread with a brown-tinged coverlet of orchards and occasional concentrations of floral magnificence serenade the eye. Such serenity also provides the right occasion to sort out an important source of altercation with Truc. Ever since setting out from Hué, Truc has been in the habit of surreptitiously locking my door almost as soon as I am seated beside Sau in the Mazda. There is a push–pull button on the window-ledge. Clearly he has taken to heart Mr Hong's instructions to do everything in his power to protect my person. But this one small detail of overzealous client care bugs the hell out of me. Waving my arms at the passing hills, I tell Truc that I suffer acutely from incarceraphobia. Anything that remotely resembles a lock is anathema to me. Understand? Truc nods his head. Nonetheless, the next time we stop I hear the all too familiar click behind my right ear.

'Truc?'

'Yes?'

'Pass me Sau Dai's rifle.'

'Why?'

'I'm going to shoot you.'

Truc laughs. He gets the message though. It doesn't happen again.

Lunch is taken at a large establishment in Bao Loc, the last conurbation in Lam Dong. Sau Dai meets yet more of his friends. The plateau peters out. But instead of the paddy table I am expecting, there is simply an agglomeration of every kind of plantation: coffee, tea, rubber, cotton, banana. I begin to understand why the French were so keen to retain hold of Cochinchina. This is fertility on the grand, Asian scale, and continues all the way to the southern metropolis.

As the Saigon number-plates proliferate both Sau and Truc become measurably excited: Sau, because he is nearing home, and Truc, because he remembers the first time he ever went south, in 1975, during the Ho Chi Minh Campaign. His artillery unit, from the Second Army Corps, was among the first to enter the city. In his time he too has been a conquering hero.

We pass an eerie forest, over ten kilometres of it, on both sides of the road. This, Sau explains, was planted in 1960 by the infamous Madame Nhu, President Diem's gun-toting sister-in-law. The idea was that after fifty years, when they had reached maturity, the trees would be cut down and used to build a new palace for Diem's heirs. Given the size of the forest, the projected household was also to be on the grand, Asian scale. Now, the dynasty has gone, and only the arborific afflatus remains. Yet, as they flicker in my gaze, a renegade thought enters my head. The trees have another twenty years to go, before they are ready. Who can be certain that, when the time comes, they won't be used to erect a palace for another dynasty, one not yet configured in the expectations of a nation that always has been prone to convulsive change?

We also pass two townships of special note. The first, Phuong Lam, is full of spires, and half-spires. Every two hundred metres or so, on either side of the highway, stands a church. Again Sau explains. Here is where many of the Catholics who fled from the North in 1954 were settled by the Saigon government. They were to form an outer defence, a bastion against guerrilla encroachment from the hills. What interests me is that two or three of the churches are new. Indeed, one is still under construction.

'That's right,' Truc concurs grudgingly. 'You see, still the Catholics are very rich. They can afford temples when others cannot even afford rice.'

The second township, Thong Nhat, restores the balance. Reunificationville, created by Hanoi after the fall of Saigon, behind enemy lines as it were. Here there are no churches, but an especially large People's Committee, and an especially large local Party headquarters, with red flags and banners everywhere.

A third township we motor through is where, he proudly tells me, Truc was quartered for a month following the final communist victory. What were his duties? I ask. His main task, he replies, was to help control the looting. But whether the looters were the disbanded ARVN, or peasants coming into the city from the country, or even members of the NVA, he cannot recall. All he can say is that looters there were, and that such people were swiftly dealt with.

Already we have rejoined Highway One. At the Bien Hoa turning (another formidable American base) we are just twenty kilometres from our destination. But we do not follow the same route as the Ho Chi Minh army. The main bridge over the Saigon River is closed for repairs. Instead we must make a fifteen-kilometre detour, and enter Ho Chi Minh City via a side door. Having been told by all and sundry in the north that, materially, Saigon is infinitely richer than anywhere else in Vietnam, I am bewildered by slums that are as slumlike as any I have seen. But then Saigon, even in its heyday, always did have a fetid underbelly, the wherewithal to mock at its own pretensions.

Just after four we arrive at Sau Dang's office. His branch of the Services Centre of the Ministry of Information is but one bare concrete room in a dingy complex of bare concrete rooms belonging to other government agencies, at one end of Soviet Nghe Tinh

Street. I had expected, at the least, the walls to be covered by photographs of Sau from the movies he has appeared in. Instead the only enlivenment is a Chinese calendar. To make the solitary strip-light work, Sau must stand on his empty desk and fiddle with the starter mechanism. Then he throws open the horizontal shutter overlooking the yard. Through this aperture, reminiscent of a Roman shop-window, he converses with colleagues and friends he hasn't seen for the past fortnight. Among them is Madame Phuong, who, it transpires, as well as putatively being a dealer in jade and other precious materials, works here as a 'guard'. Whatever argument she and Sau may have had is forgotten. Today she is all smiles, eager with her dinner invitations.

Our first task is to establish where I am to stay. The magic formula 'private villa' has been dropped several times on the journey south, but now this must be confirmed. To do so, Sau must make a telephone call. He picks up the receiver. At once his face puzzles. *Ma!* Someone has cut the wires! Then he grins. *He* has cut the wires, as a precaution against other cadres in the building using his line whilst he was away.

'But does Sau Dang have to pay for his own office telephone?' I ask Truc.

'Not at all. But the Company does. And everyone these days wants to minimize their expenditure.'

My accommodation, when I get there, provides my first intimation that Saigon may not be all bad. It consists of a well-furnished room in a comfortable bungalow off Ky Dong Street, in the centre-north of the city. The highly patterned floral bed-linen, only gently perfumed, and brand-new water heating system are conspicuously imported. The villa, which is owned by a retired economics professor and his doctor wife, and is surrounded by a reasonably high security wall, has three or four such rooms, which are rented out, with official approval, for an average $20 each per night – by SE Asian standards an appropriate tariff. The Japanese air-conditioner for once provides the correct flow of cooling air.

Sau and Truc decamp. Sau will stay at home, Truc either in Soviet Nghe Tinh Street or with some cousins. (Everyone has cousins in Saigon: the effect of the family insurance scheme during the wars, by which some members gave their allegiance to the

307

North, others to the South. Thus, for example, Zoom's grandfather had two wives: one here, and one in Hanoi.) Left on my own, I luxuriate in my new-found freedom. Later I eat at the only halfway hygienic restaurant I can find in the immediate vicinity – a large covered place that sports a band. I could be anywhere in provincial Thailand. Two young girls belt out western songs. The hit of the moment seems to be a number whose frequent refrain is 'I want to find you by my side' (next morning, when I wake up) – or words to that effect. Another song that rides high in the charts consists of 'Saigon, Saigon, Saigon', repeated over and over, endlessly. The singers' metallic, nasal tones somehow complement the simple food I order: fried beef and plain boiled rice. Afterwards I walk around some. I've been told it's unsafe to go out alone after dark in Saigon, but in Ky Dong Street I fail to learn why. Everything and everywhere is very shabby and very friendly. Nor am I approached by any hookers – something else I've been warned about – although I do spy a hunky Russian with a brace of Amerasians. *Glasnost* and *doi moi* feeding on the leftovers of the American feast?

Tuesday 28th November: Saigon   My once-a-week (if I'm lucky) long sleep, nine hours of it, is terminated by the screams of children in a school playground directly behind the villa. Truc, who has said he will come at nine, is late. In fact he is five hours late. The morning is largely wasted. I take lunch at the same place I had dinner. There I am buttonholed by one of Saigon's many disaffected. This is a feature of the city, at least for the western visitor. Never a day passes but someone steps forward to proffer an analysis of his country's ills. The young man who sits uninvited at my table is courtesy incarnate. 'May I?' he asks, before helping himself to the cigarettes that are lying at my elbow, and before considerately advising I change to another brand. Pre-1975 his father was a businessman, but has stopped trading ever since. 'Under *doi moi*, it is impossible to know what is and what isn't permitted. The government just refuses to tell people what the rules are.' Even so, Saigon is 'rich'. There are many dollar millionaires, and an ordinary person, if he is smart, and has friends among officials, can earn $15 a day. The big problem is the state-run industries. 'They are run by old revolutionaries who know nothing about economics, but who insist on telling their subordinates they know everything.' Also, state factories tend to be staffed by relatives and comrades. The right jobs for the right people is an idea that has yet to occur to the Revolution. Only in the private sector are you hired and fired on merit.

My interlocutor is less jaundiced than some. He concedes that Marxism-Leninism as tailored by Ho Chi Minh probably was the only way Vietnam could win its independence, but it is totally inappropriate for national prosperity. The real trouble is, Confucian values have if anything been reinforced by the Revolution. 'The young must respect the old, because of what they achieved for the country. But the old should acknowledge that the liberty which the young seek is also something that they themselves fought for.'

'And what do you do?' I ask.

'I work for the government of course. I have to. I am a film editor. Working for the state enterprise gives me contacts with people who pay me to work for them privately. There is no other way. But it is a lousy, corrupt system.'

Sau and Truc pick me up from the villa at two. Most of the post-lunch period is spent at the barber's. We all three need haircuts. But what we get is no regimental short back and sides. Rather it's the closest I've come to visiting a beautician's. The shop, called 'The Hong Kong', is off a busy main street. It takes the stylist, a pinched, moustachioed middle-aged man, forty minutes to journey from one side of my head to the other. He pays particular attention to the crown, which is bald. And that is just the beginning. Having scraped the nape of my neck with a real barber's blade, he shaves behind and above the ears, and then the ears themselves. The ears are followed by the face. My stubble receives his absolute attention. In the most scholarly fashion he examines my cheeks, my jowl, my chin. Then it's time for the shampoo. I am led into a darkened back room and placed upon a reclining chair. A girl of real, if somewhat petite, loveliness begins creaming and massaging my scalp. Because she is quite short our two faces are, and remain, about three inches apart. The effect is unexpectedly intimate. On the wall behind her is a poster of a rose. This invites me to study Miss Vuong's face objectively, as one might indeed study the petals of a flower. The nose is flat but exquisite, the eyes curry-leafed, the lips full, painted and pouting. The skin is pure, fragranced. Miss Vuong asks whether I can take her back to England. I tell her I most certainly will. We both know that the relationship will end the moment the shop's mama-san deems my hair is clean enough.

Mama-san is all apologies. She is sorry, but to have my hair shampooed a fifth time would really be a little excessive. I am returned to the salon proper. My stylist makes his final calculations, then vigorously massages both my hands and my back. He pummels me and he slaps me. Then he works me over with a vibrator: not a purpose-made machine, but a small motor that he holds by a makeshift strap. It feels good though, and I am sorry when he thinks I have had enough.

After that, what's left of my hair is blown with an antique French drier. A net is placed over my head, and at the last stage a small quantity of oil applied.

Sau and Truc meanwhile have been put through the same decadent process. Sau though has also had his tits vibrated, and Truc, a little truculently, has been seated under a standing drier, so that for a moment he becomes Madame Truc.

Sau Dang beams with non-stop pleasure. A large part of that pleasure seems to be derived from the pleasure I am having. Saigon is his city, and he is determined I shall enjoy it.

Thus is the afternoon dissipated. I pay the bill, a mere three dollars, and we return to the office in Soviet Nghe Tinh Street. The purpose of this is to meet 'Mr' Nguyen. Nguyen, freshly arrived from Hanoi, is the Services Centre's vice-director. Although I have met him only briefly once before, a hand shaken among a cluster of outstretched hands, he greets me as a brother. He is the most engaging and most dynamic of fellows. Lean, hoarse voiced, younger than I, he can also be quite deadly, and in a variety of ways. His ambition makes him 'dangerous'; but it is a minacity tempered by grief. Two years ago his sister was killed in an automobile accident in Thailand. That, apparently, knocked his teeth out for a while. For six months he lost interest in everything except rice-alcohol. And although it is reputed he has now re-covered, I notice, at odd moments, he has to drive himself. His ambition is no longer sufficient to ride him all of the time.

Madame Phuong and Madame Thu appear at the window. We have not forgotten, they hope, our promise to join them for dinner. We all climb into the Mazda. I am given a rapid, phantasmagoric tour of central Saigon by early evening. Rue Catinat, the Presidential Palace, the former US Embassy, the Customs House, the old Bank of Indochina – a montage that depresses as much as it excites. We stop at a café owned by Nguyen's deceased sister's husband's family. Nguyen makes a present of several bundles of joss-sticks. Then to the restaurant run by a friend of Madame Phuong, a thin, mildly elegant woman in her fifties who repeatedly asks me for a date. Her husband was a Saigon regime man who left in 1975 and has never been heard from since – a not untypical story. Nguyen blatantly tells me to ignore her, because 'afterwards we'll go somewhere special, for bananas perhaps'. Quails' eggs, spring rolls that seem to be alive, crab, dried chicken and superior rice pancakes storm our hunger. A mountain of dead Heineken cans piles up on the table. Nguyen, one moment the leader of the pack, slumps forward the next. I express my concern, but Truc assuages me: 'Don't worry, he's always like that.' In due course we help him back to the car. Sau Dang hits the wheel with his fist. *Maaa!* Someone has suggested that he too is drunk, and this has raised his fury. If he isn't drunk though, he should be, from the amount of beer consumed. I am. Dropped off at the villa I roll onto my newly re-perfumed floral nylon sheet and crash straight out. So ends my first full day in Saigon. And so end many Saigon nights.

Wednesday 29th November: Saigon　My Cochinchina programme begins. By request I am introduced to Trinh Thi Ngo, who meets me in Sau's office. Trinh Thi Ngo, also called Thu Huong ('Fragrance'), is better known to us as Hanoi Hannah, the Tokyo Rose of the Vietnam War. Hers was the beguiling voice that sought to persuade hundreds of thousands of Marines and grunts to lay down their weapons and either change sides or go home. Now she is fifty-nine, poised and the first woman in Vietnam I'm aware wears high heels. She looks remarkably as she did twenty-five years ago. She does not however make for an especially telling interview. Unlike western broadcasters and presenters, she is reticent, shy, anything but full of herself. I warm to her immediately. Her affair with the English language began in the 1950s. Ironically she wanted to understand the American movies that, immediately after Dien Bien Phu, were still being screened in Hanoi. She'd attended a French *lycée*, but the *lycée* did not equip her to follow Hollywood. Then, in 1955, she began working for Voice of Vietnam. When VoV set up an English service, she became its chief announcer. It followed naturally ten years later that she should also be the one to front propaganda broadcasts to the US forces then swarming into the South.

She listens every day to the BBC World Service. In the early days of the Democratic Republic (as the North formally called itself) many Hanoian broadcasters had been trained in London. Hannah recalls a morning when Pham Van Dong visited the radio station. He said to the assembled cadres, 'Follow the BBC way.' Still she tries to. She tells me she sometimes listens to Voice of America as well, but 'it is not as good'. The BBC at least tries to see things impersonally, 'just like the Voice of Vietnam'.

I ask about her family. Why is she living in Saigon? Because her husband, an engineer, lives and works there. I put it to her that it may not be a coincidence that so many families are split up north and south. Rather to my surprise, she agrees entirely. Only two or three per cent of cadres, she tells me, did not have relatives who worked for or supported the Saigon regime in some capacity or other. In other words, if she is to be believed, 97% of the Party faithful have a southern connection. This is the statistic I have been looking for. That it should come from a veteran propagandist makes it even more startling. Yet there is a message in that too. Such is the Vietnamese love of a statistic that once it is established everything else must give way, including any ideological implication.

We drive Hannah back to her flat. Sau deposits me at the villa. In the afternoon it has been decided I should visit the port area, and in particular the Ho Chi Minh Museum. I chat for an hour or so with two Canadian Chinese, who have taken the room next to mine. Their interest is in exporting seafood. Broadly they confirm the things told me yesterday by the anonymous film editor. There is a lack of clarity about business law. No code of practice has been promulgated. Agreements and contracts require lawyers, but still there is no established private legal practice. Entrepreneurs are often nervous that the government, which has maltreated them in the past, may suddenly change tack any day and repossess anything and everything. Many rich families are still sitting on their hoarded gold. Otherwise, communications are bad, transportation is bad, local business skills are bad. On the positive side, there is an abundant, cheap and largely willing labour force, and potentially a vast abundance of natural product.

'I think,' says Lenny Wong, 'that what Vietnam needs right now is for one top-notch multinational to make a significant investment here. Then others will follow. It would inspire confidence at home as well as abroad. Sure, there have been plenty of joint ventures set up, but in global terms they're all small money. One billion-dollar project, or even one quarter-billion-dollar project, would transform the scene entirely.'

At two o'clock Truc arrives on a potentially lethal Honda to tell me my programme's already been changed. Instead of the Ho Chi Minh Museum I'm to come to Soviet Nghe Tinh Street to watch a 'Cambodia film'. What, has the Hanoi documentary cinematographic unit been to Phnom Penh as well? But no, the film in question is a regular feature, the first to have been made in Cambodia since the Khmer Rouge took power in 1975. We go to Sau's office, and then upstairs to the 'video room': a small room with a dozen chairs and two screens on one tiny table.

Both are running. The Cambodian film, called *Shadow of Darkness,* has just started. Nguyen, for reasons best known to himself, softly assures me that no Vietnamese technical assistance whatsoever was given. The storyline, somewhat distended, focuses on the various fates of three or four individuals caught up in the Reign of Terror. Made with old equipment, non-existent resources and modest editing abilities, some of it has the feel of a 1930s classic. The opening sequences, shot in black and white, depicting Khmer Rouge brutalities, are genuinely powerful. Still twitching bodies lie where they have been thrown in a ditch. It crosses my mind that perhaps in some awful way this is live footage. A child is hurled against the rocks and left to die a miserable death. Even more effective is a cut-in of Pol Pot. The actor's jerking, splendidly chiaroscuroed head masquerades as the complete marionette of evil as the Khmer Rouge leader addresses his cohorts.

It's a scene Fritz Lang would have been proud of, though I'm not quite so sure what he would have made of the unintended juxtaposition: on the other screen, running concurrently, a party of bikinied Saigon lovelies roam in a well-drilled pack up and down the white-sanded beaches of an unidentified coastal resort. Propaganda courtesy of Saigon Tourism.

The little boy's parents are taken into captivity. The mother is raped by a wicked warlord, the father tortured to death in front of her. From then on the film becomes exceedingly complicated, as the mother escapes and joins an incipient resistance force. In the end, after all the cast have changed sides a dozen times, the wicked warlord gets his come-uppance. There are also several romances. At one point the hero, a peculiarly beefy young Valentino, bursts into song. The movie threatens to become a glossy musical. The swamps are alive with the sound of it. But then the scriptwriter remembers where his lovers are and continues the story. There is more fighting, more duplicity and a lot more falling in love. Finally, just as the hero and the girl he really will love forever think they are safe, they are surrounded by a horde of Khmer Rouge. As machine-guns are primed and rifles aimed all the couple can do is embrace. Rat-a-tat-a-tat-a-tat-a-tat. But what's this? Something has gone dreadfully wrong. All the Khmer Rouge have fallen down dead. Not a moment too soon the Vietnamese liberation army has arrived over the hill. The hero's kisses mingle with close-ups of the familiar lone-star-spangled flag.

'Well, that was good, wasn't it?' I say, turning to the man sitting next to me.

'Oui, peut-être. Je l'ai fait.'

The man is Ivon Hem, the film's director. I ask him whether the opening scenes were based on actual events. Yes, everything was based on the truth, from the beginning to the end. 'I wrote the story as well.' Weak chinned, his face is strikingly glum. Like every Cambodian I've met he lost most of his family during the terror.

314

Hem himself though avoided it all. When Phnom Penh fell he was in Karachi, and he stayed away until 1979. He put the four years to good use however. In India he learnt the art of film-making. He had already decided that one day he would lead the revival of the Cambodian film industry from the front.

After much handshaking and many compliments Hem distributes posters for *Shadow of Darkness* before being driven away in a limousine. In Sau's office, Sau, Truc, Nguyen and I decide that I should treat my loyal entourage to a special dinner. For a while we roam around Saigon in the Mazda, principally in search of new hats. I see all the buildings I saw yesterday. But there is something new as well: the Floating Hotel, a joint venture with an Australian company. The Saigon People's Committee have provided the berth, the Australians have provided the hotel, originally built to be moored on the Great Barrier Reef. Rooms start at $150 a night. It is large, white and rather like an apartment block in the Barbican I once chose not to live in. Hundreds and hundreds of Saigonites crowd the quay to look at it, their eyes full of silent wonder. It opens next week or the week after, but no one who hasn't got a fistful of greenbacks will be allowed access. It occurs to me that, after fourteen years' absence, Saigon's soul has come home to roost.

The restaurant we eat at is nothing special, except that the waitresses all wear shockingly short skirts and bright pink blouses that have numbers pinned on. Perhaps they are for sale, perhaps they're not. Their smiles are a touch more lascivious than the norm; but then one notices this is true of each and every one of them. At our table, decorum is preserved. Quails' eggs and *sukiyaki* are swept away in a steady flow of San Miguel. Nguyen avails himself of the occasion to conduct a little official business. Without formalities, and in front of Truc, he asks whether I'm satisfied with Truc's interpreting. If not, then he can be sent back to Hanoi. Before Quang Ngai, if the proposition had been put to me more delicately, I might have jumped at it. But now I'm completely behind Truc. He has developed a new habit. Often he asks me to help improve his English. We have an unspoken agreement that, when he does return to Hanoi, he'll be a fully fledged guide.

'Truc is doing brilliantly, Tiger,' I reply. 'I want him to stay.'

Chuk xu khoe! Nguyen has got the only answer that, in the circumstances, he was likely to get. The official business has been dealt with swiftly and directly. We can all relax again.

Sau suggests we move on somewhere where the girls are 'really beautiful'. In the event we wash up in a coffee shop where there are no girls at all. Sau has remembered that he too has an official capacity. Or perhaps it is just his caprice. In any case, dropping one hand on my knee, and another on Truc's, he launches into a long diatribe. Whatever else I may think, he says, I must bear in mind that the strategic hamlets created by the Diem regime and the Americans were not the same as the British-directed kampongs in Malaya. Absolutely they were different. The strategic hamlets in South Vietnam were really prison camps. Isolation, not protection, was the name of the game. In Annam, in the midlands, yes – some people were persuaded to resettle of their own volition, but that was only because they were short of food and the Americans enticed them with rice.

And there is another thing Sau Dang wants me to take on board. Should it happen, in my freer moments in Saigon, that I meet anyone with stories about re-education camps, then I should also remember, and never forget, the many crimes committed by those who served the regime, all the crimes perpetrated by collaborators against the people of Vietnam.

Yes, Papa Sau, yes. It is not indoctrination, it is not propaganda, it is one man's passion, the residue of when Sau was Captain Nguyen Minh Dang, the anger of one who fought the fight. And though I cannot tell him, I envy him and love him for it. Whatever the larger rights and wrongs, a man who has once in his allotted span found something he believes worth the living and the dying for is better than one who hasn't.

Thursday 30th November: Cu Chi Sau is his debonair self again as we drive forty kilometres north-west to the famous Cu Chi tunnels, an extraordinary warren of underground passages and chambers mined by the communists that is set to become one of SE Asia's stranger tourist attractions. Originally begun by the Viet Minh in the war against the French, the tunnels came into their own against the Americans. They afforded protection against carpet bombing, they were used both as living quarters and as storage systems, and they spread beneath the countryside like dry rot in untreated timbers. Although underground shelters and hide-outs were constructed in many parts of South Vietnam, almost anywhere the ground permitted in fact, the Cu Chi complex deserves its notoriety. Laid out end to end, it would stretch for almost three hundred kilometres; and because of its proximity to Saigon, it had a unique strategic importance.

The Americans were aware of the tunnels, or at least some of them. They did not however at first realize that most of the tunnels linked up into one vast system. In time they developed squads of 'tunnel rats', trained to enter the underground labyrinths in search and pursuit of Viet Cong. But they never penetrated very far. Charlie frequently laid booby-traps, and there were natural hazards as well: for example, venomous snakes. And always, inside the tunnels, the enemy was on home ground. He knew where the secret trapdoors were, which tunnels led to a dead end and which didn't. He was the master of the subterranean shooting alleys.

Sau takes me to the very centre of the web, the Viet Cong headquarters, where the current national leader, Nguyen Van Linh, then a senior political officer and secretary of the Saigon branch of the Communist Party, spent weeks, sometimes months, underground. At surface level, sunken pits covered by low, camouflaged roofs, made tolerable conference rooms. At any moment though they might have to be evacuated. The thatch was prepared from a special, non-inflammable leaf, so that nothing but a direct hit could destroy them.

Here then was the nerve centre of insurgency operations in the Second Military Zone. Already every effort has been made to preserve and renovate the tunnels in the immediate vicinity. A former Viet Cong captain is on hand to show me over. We make a subtle progress. At first he leads me, above ground, from one covered pit to another, showing me a kitchen, a meeting point, a dining hall. Then he takes me down into a pit. Then he invites me to try a tunnel for size. Finally he dares me to pass, underground, from one pit to another. Just two hundred metres or so. It won't take you more than five minutes.

317

That five minutes is a species of hell. The tunnel is about two and a half feet in diameter. Too old to scramble on all fours, I advance bent over double, crouching. My back instantly begins to ache. I also break out into a profound sweat. The air is both unbelievably hot, and intolerably stale. But these discomforts are as nothing to my fear. My fear is of bats. Bats! Tim Page, bless his English heart, told me in Hanoi of a guide who took a client down the tunnels and was attacked by a swarm of bats. He spent the next nine months in hospital and was lucky to survive.

Yesterday the guide, today the client. Truc has elected not to join me. The former VC brings up my rear. I mention my fear. He passes a torch. There are no bats, he assures me. Take a look for yourself. I shine the frail beam down a cross-passage. Immediately I see two or three of the things flitter towards me. The effect is uncanny. They fly straight at you, but the impact doesn't happen. They seem to evaporate just when they should be hitting your face.

'Only little ones,' says my chaperon.

The torch reveals several more bats hanging on the walls and rounded roof like semi-transparent ravioli. But it's too late to turn back. We have passed the halfway point. I am aware that I am breathing at thrice my normal rate. I am unable to decide however whether this is due to lack of oxygen, or naked panic.

I make it. Even after so short a time the sunlight is blinding. When the tunnels were operational, men and women who had spent more than a day underground had to spend ten minutes adjusting their vision in half-light before climbing out, otherwise they really were blinded.

The soldier congratulates me. The failure rate among visitors is high. Many cannot endure more than one minute in the tunnels. Some Viet Cong lived in them for periods of years. The average population was 5,000. Before the Tet Offensive, this rose to 10,000. It took one man one working day to advance a tunnel by one cubic metre. Living conditions were never good. I have only visited the first level down, where the air is relatively breathable. But below are another two. Or, as the poet Duong Huong Ly, addressing the Earth, wrote: 'Your entrails, O Mother, are unfathomable.'

Yet finally, the grotesque claustrophobia will not be the strongest impression will take with me from Cu Chi. What has struck me

318

most is the neatness of the tunnels, their regularity, the uniformity of their light brown-grey walls. In a way they epitomize not just the Viet Cong war effort, but the Vietnamese mind itself: excelling in the small-scale, intricate and seemingly endless. And I am also struck by the curiously monastic quality of what I have seen: the demands made by communal living in a social structure that differs from the normative family; the common purpose; the shared privations; the belief in attainment of the larger goal. The Viet Cong were the very monks and nuns of war.

We find Sau Dang stretched out asleep in a hammock. Before arousing him, I take his photograph. At a small hut I am invited to buy an 'I've Been to Cu Chi' T-shirt. I decline, but purchase instead a chequered VC headscarf. Like the Khmers, the VC used his garment for a multiplicity of purposes. As a towel, as a kerchief, as a rice bag, as protection against the sun, as a protection against mosquitoes, as a pillow even. It will, I am sure, come in handy. And that's why I buy it.

A few miles away we lunch at a village restaurant-cum-recreation hall. A large billiard table, pinched perhaps from some abandoned barracks. The owner is a recently retired army man. Sau tells him enthusiastically about me, and my going down the tunnels. I hear the magic formula 'Nuoc Lenin', and at once the man offers me his captain's cap. The trophy tempts me, but better sense prevails. Keep it for your grandchildren, I tell him. In any case, it doesn't fit. It's a size too small for my swollen head.

After lunch I pay the price. A visit to the Ho Chi Minh Museum can no longer be postponed. Housed in one of the old French buildings in the port area, formerly a shipping agent's office, it boasts one of the fuller collections of H.C.M. photographs in the country. I traipse through room after room of that which I have seen many times before. Number one exhibit though is unique. Uncle Ho's watering can, a sort of recycled baby milk-churn. Also, a copy of his payslip. The son of a mandarin had to work his passage out when he left Saigon for Europe in 1911. He was employed on board the *Latouche-Tréville* as an assistant cook and waiter.

Then the day winds down. At the office Nguyen is negotiating with a Korean businessman for the purchase in Singapore of some recording equipment the Services Centre needs. His business style is fast, furious and free-wheeling. Appearing to agree to everything, he waves his hands and cries out hoarsely, 'Yes, yes, why not?' But when he reaches his résumé it is clear his head works like an abacus. Several details have been stored and redefined. The Korean though is no fool either. A second round of negotiation ensues. Then a third. By sheer persistence Nguyen secures the advantage.

We leave him to it, and visit Sau Dang's home – the top two floors and roof of an old, crumbling, narrow tenement block. I meet two of his children, and his wife, who is shy, retiring, sweet. Sau immediately offers me a glass of home-made snake-wine. I think he half-hopes I will delicately refuse, but is thrilled when I accept. It is true, he says, I am becoming more Vietnamese by the hour. I take a second glass, and feel a slow powerful heat ripple out through my body from the stomach. Within ten minutes my back, savaged at Cu Chi, feels like a sheet of malleable steel.

Another Saigon evening is under way. Nguyen is collected. Another 'special' restaurant, this time an outdoor place whose speciality is baby oysters grilled in their shells at the table over a charcoal fire. Squid in breadcrumbs. The mama-san, dressed in a low-hanging football shirt, is another Saigon desertee. But though she is friendly to a degree, she doesn't press me for a date. We take coffee and a bottle of almost real whisky in a glitzy new hotel, where waiters and waitresses alike sport searing make-up. The Youth Movement of Tomorrow, perhaps. We finish the whisky. Nguyen keels over. 'Never mind,' says Sau. 'Now we must go somewhere really special.' But once again on the way to the car something upsets him. Has someone else said he is drunk? Who knows? *Maa!* Exactly like a kicked sheep. Once Sau's cool is blown, he forgets everything. The somewhere really special turns out to be my villa. Goodnight. See you tomorrow.

The Canadian Chinese are still up, drinking cognac in the garden. Why not have a glass? They are waiting for a caller, a man, they allege, who runs a re-education programme. When he shows with a sidekick, I have my doubts. Palpably he is not a cadre. I also notice how one of the Canadians speaks remarkably fluent Vietnamese. Jokingly he tells me that they are discussing whether those being re-educated can be used as a cheap labour force. Please tell him I am a journalist, I say – a sure way to avoid an unwanted conversation. The man eyes me, neither gingerly nor approvingly. But he doesn't say a word more.

Friday 1st December: Saigon Ah, December! The temperature is a little up on yesterday. The morning is free, but the un-dull moment is never far away. I strike south for lunch, crossing two big roads, and order fried rice at one of Saigon's ten thousand coffee parlours. The shop doesn't sell fried rice but the owner is so excited at my choosing her establishment in preference to the other nine thousand nine hundred and ninety nine that she promises to procure whatever I want. Small girls are sent dashing in several different directions while I sit sipping a lemon soda. But before they can return a truckload of forty or so youths, all of them wearing white baseball caps, white T-shirts with black Chinese calligraphy, plum-coloured culottes and sandals, crunches to a halt immediately outside. At once a formidable din sets up. Cymbals crash, a very large drum pounds, a gong gongs. Out of nowhere two dragons appear.

The reason for this commotion lies across the road. An old three-storeyed building is being renovated as a hotel; a Chinese/ People's Committee joint venture. The hotel is nowhere near ready to open yet, but inside an advance celebration is being held. The troupe of martial artists are the first course. They convene in the somewhat narrow forecourt and mount their show. The two dragons fight. Inside each is an eight- or nine-year-old boy. The percussionists generate sounds of enormous gusto. One of the dragons is slain. Now the older members of the troupe are put through their paces. A twelve-year-old dances a beautifully choreographed battle dance. Several guests fling money onto the sandy, stony ground in front of him. Two fifteen-year-old combatants stage a fight that looks anything but mock. They hurl each other body and soul around the floor. The dust unsettles, a small trickle of blood appears. Larger notes are scattered around the arena. The drum beats faster, the fighters begin to hate each other. And the actual midday temperature is already in excess of 30°.

Forty minutes later the tumblers are still tumbling. The discipline, the precision and the energy expended are all devastating. By now I have had my lunch, but I am about to have another. Returning to the forecourt I endeavour to find someone who speaks a language I know, to ascertain more clearly what it's all about. At once I am invited inside, where a thunderously boisterous banquet is in progress. A bespectacled, suave Chinese takes me in hand. I give him my card. Ah-ya-ha, a writer. Immediately I become the moment's guest of honour. Seven tables rise and salute me. There is a round of prolonged applause. My mouth is packed with shrimps, my stomach filled with beer. My inclusion at the party, my host tells me, is a good omen: the hotel is bound to prosper on account of me. Why don't I come and stay when I get back from my trip round the delta?

The fact that the Four Seas Trading Company is working with the local government doesn't entirely persuade Truc, when I tell him about the invitation.

'We'll have to ask Mr Sau and Nguyen,' he says.

'You mean I'll have to get permission?'

Truc flusters. No no, he doesn't mean that at all. But in fact he does.

We visit the Four Seas downtown trading office later in the afternoon to confirm the contact. They invite me for dinner, but Truc declines on my behalf. Sau Dang has already lined something up. There are friends of his he wants me to meet.

Chinese friends, as it happens. We drive to Cholon, the lively Chinese quarter, and make our way upstairs at an untypically stylish restaurant. The group that awaits us has probably never joint-ventured with the government at any level. There are about ten of them, all businessmen, along with three women who are almost certainly taxi girls. The table is large and round, and already chock-a-block with empties. All eyes fill with glee and anticipation as we enter the room. Each wants to do a 100% with me. My tankard of Tiger Beer is drained and refilled with awful regularity. The Chinese with the biggest stomach – an inflated life raft tied round his middle – is particularly menacing. Again and again he pulls to his feet and points his finger at me. *Chuk xu khoe! Tram phan tram!* The dreadful thing about him is a certain kindliness of face, making it hard to refuse.

322

'Do they drink like this every night?' I whisper to Nguyen on my right. Nguyen, who has wisely filled his glass with Coca Cola, shouts back: 'Yes, every night. They are all very rich, and in Vietnam . . . beer is what you spend your money on.' Sau meanwhile has his own hundred per cents going, but starts giving me nervous looks. Confident that I can drink any Chinese under the table, I decide to respond to the challenge. Okay guys, if that's the way you want to play it . . . I start issuing my own toasts. On your feet, fatso. And you. And you.

The merriment ends. The leader of the pack tells me he wants to take me dancing. Sau and Nguyen quickly intervene. If I go off dancing that means they must go with me, and clearly they have other plans. Sau makes a little speech, and then everybody starts making his excuses. The leader grabs my hand. He really wants to take me dancing, but he's just remembered: there's urgent business to attend.

Back in my room by eight, I sober up on Dalat coffee. The Canadian Chinese knock on my door and ask me to join them. They are accompanied by the re-education man. Tonight though his identity has changed. He is and isn't voluble. Far from being in charge of a re-education programme, he hints that he is an escapee. He has, he informs me, a tale to tell, a tale that is seven or eight times better than *Papillon*. Why don't I buy it from him?

A somewhat routine conversation ensues. I say I'd have to know what it is before I bought it. He says, fairly enough, that'd be cheating. I say there's no other way. He says as it happens there's a film-maker in Paris who is already very interested, but Paris is a long way away and in any case he needs the ready cash. I say I'm sure you do. He agrees. Although he has escaped, he is still a prisoner. What he needs is some dollars. So why don't I give him some, and then he'll tell me his story which is a hundred times better than *Papillon*.

But I am not that kind of writer. The best stories shouldn't cost anything. So I advise him not to sell himself short. Wait until Vietnam–US relations are normalized, then introduce yourself to the first person from Hollywood who comes to Saigon.

'Be patient, and ten million dollars will be yours.'

'Ten million? But I want twelve.'

'Well, perhaps they'll give you eleven. I'm afraid I could only give you eight and a half thousand *dong*.'

For a split second Re-education Man is tempted. But his pride at once asserts itself. Pah! Eight and a half thousand *dong*. What do I think it is he's trying to sell me? His sister?

Saturday and Sunday 2nd and 3rd December: Vung Tau A little holiday, a well-earned rest. Vung Tau. Five of us pack into the Mazda: Sau, myself, Truc, Nguyen and a woman called Nha. A friend, or so at first I'm told, of Sau Dang, Nha is too old to be called Miss, too young to be called Madame. She sits between Truc and Nguyen, as silent as she is fetching. The journey, including a stop for coffee, takes three hours. We take lunch in the centre of Vung Tau town, and then head for one of the outlying beaches. It is lined with restaurants doubling as hotels. Three or four openly advertise massage parlours, and there is a noticeable lack of cadres.

We go to the last restaurant-hotel in the row. While Sau, Truc and Nguyen negotiate terms with the manager, I am left alone with Nha. Discreetly she opens her handbag and takes out a small round purse. Inside this purse is a clutch of photographs. They are all of herself, and each has been cut out from a larger photograph. Choosing one, she hands it to me, smiling the smile. Then, seeing Sau come out of the building, she hastily returns the purse to the bag and the bag to her side.

The impending dilemma is temporarily solved when I am shown over the rooms inside. The object of the weekend becomes even more obvious when one of the waitresses who has accompanied me up the stairs begins clawing my arm. The rooms, costing less than $2 a night, presumably plus extras, are less than basic. Or rather, very basic indeed. Large beds occupy small windowless spaces lined with sexy pictures from foreign magazines.

I do however have a choice. It is explained to me that three hundred metres away from the beach is a proper guesthouse where the rooms have air-conditioners as well as windows, and where I can stay for $7 a night. Sensing that my entourage would welcome a little privacy, I gratefully comply.

The guesthouse is a characterless, peeling concrete job where it seems I am to be the only guest. A woman gives me a choice of three rooms. I choose the one in which the air-conditioner makes the least noise. It is also the biggest and the cleanest. Deserted by Truc, I try to explain to her that what I'll need is soap, a towel and a flask of boiled water. She nods and disappears. An hour later she is nowhere to be found. Instead I am besieged by a small army of children. In no time at all I have the things I require.

At four I wander back to the beach. Sau and Nguyen are already in the water, battling vast waves. I am tempted to join them, but decide against it. What I need is a proper swim, not an unarmed combat. In a while Truc comes down from his room, followed rather quickly by the same waitress who earlier wanted my arm. I leave him to relax and stroll southwards along the beach, which is full of Saigonites, with or without wives, children, taxi girls and waitresses. It is a pleasant-looking place with good sand, curving palm trees, whiffs of bluish smoke. Perhaps because it looks so nice I am overcome by a stong sensation of sadness. There is no other reason for it. Not irritation, not homesickness, not even boredom. Simply a feeling of unspecified sadness creeps up and overwhelms me. When I return to the restaurant, conviviality fails me. Sau and Nguyen are out of the water and drinking beer now. Why don't I have some? Probably I should, but after five days in Saigon I am hoping to rest my liver. Inside the sadness transforms into a full-blown gloom.

Sau frowns, is not pleased. He wants to know why I am not happy. After a while we decamp to a second restaurant, for dinner, a kilometre or three away. This is also run by a Saigon regime abandonee who makes too great a fuss of me. She supplies *pommes frites* when what I want is rice. The snake-wine circulates. We are joined by more people Sau knows. One of them is a Pakistani Vietnamese, a likeable big fellow called Ali Khan who runs a general store in the town. Another is the owner of the beach place where my entourage is staying. He makes no bones in telling me the score. He employs twenty girls as waitresses in shifts, and they are all very good at their work. He knows, because he has got each and every one of them to work on him. Free.

Mama-san invites me to chat with her in French at a separate table. I am wholly unable to disconnect her from the conviction that I am an American who has come back to Vietnam to help restore the Saigon regime. Nor indeed can I manage to dissuade her from believing that, in years gone by, I was once her lover.

She tells me her story, which is exactly as I had predicted. Her husband left her fifteen years ago. He took with him most of the children and all of their money, promising that one day he'd return and collect her. She still thinks he will. Probably she'll always think he will.

By the time I am permitted to return to my own table Nguyen has already slumped. The empties are stacked up and counted. Sau grimaces. We've not had nearly enough to drink. We return to the beach hotel. Around a round table a fresh party is made. From somewhere, a bottle of cognac. My mood recovers, as does Nguyen, who becomes boisterous and domineering. Nha sits and smiles at everyone. Then she retires to her room. The drinking continues.

Sau gets up, leaves. In a flash Nguyen is on to me. 'Now is your chance,' he tells me, filling my glass.

'My chance for what?'

'For Em Nha of course.'

'I think Em Nha belongs to Sau.'

'But she is waiting for you!'

'And if Sau returns?'

'He won't.'

I look at Truc, but Truc is twiddling his fingers in a self-contained reverie. Nguyen returns to the attack. 'Really. Go to her. She is waiting for you.'

'Well, if that is the case, then I must go and tell her not to wait.'

I am very drunk. I knock on Em Nha's door and a little voice tells me to come in. Em Nha is sorting through her handbag. If she has been waiting for me, she doesn't show it. Nonetheless she invites me to sit beside her on the bed. We struggle to exchange pleasantries. I am just pondering whether in fact I should kiss her after all when the unmistakable timbre of Sau Dang's voice is heard through the paper-tin partitions. *Maa!*

Em Nha assumes a rigid, virginal aspect even before I stand hastily to leave. This however does not prevent her, with lightning movements, from slipping a piece of paper into my hand.

The paper has her Saigon address on it. Or so I infer, before disposing of it in the unlit hell-hole that passes for a toilet. My plan is elementary. When I return to the table I caress my stomach as though my absence had one reason and one reason only. I even make a point of waiting until I'm in the room before doing up my flies.

Sau, though he is too proud to show it, is scarcely taken in by this. Probably Nguyen has told him anyway.

The irony is that Sau's own departure from the table was on a mission undertaken on my behalf. He has reckoned that my afternoon gloom must have to do with a want of female company. In a short while, as though by magic, another pretty woman, dressed in a striped red vest, is sitting at my side.

It is a situation Nguyen finds immensely comic. To even up I force him into battle. *Chuk xu khoe* you bastard! Truc and, to a lesser exent, Sau join me in the assault. Soon Nguyen keels over again. My secondary motive however is to incapacitate myself. Sorry, dear, I've had too much. But of course it backfires horribly. I become so inebriate I have no idea whether I am incapacitated or not, and it is possible that I do not return to my guesthouse room alone.

Or perhaps I do. At all events my waking is unaccompanied. I head straight for the sea. The waves are even bigger than yesterday, and back out several hundred metres. There is no chance of fighting through them to the calm beyond. The only sport is to stand there while one wall of water after another buffets and batters you.

'Good massage,' shouts Nguyen, who is already in the sea by the time I show. Or is it a question he is putting to me? I wait until we are ashore before explaining what I think of him. The bastard is chuffed. The little mix-up last night, Nguyen says, cements our relationship. Now we can be brothers forever.

Sau is in a filthy temper, though the cadre in him does everything to hide it. Truc confirms that the fault is largely mine. Sau is not a man who likes having any of his numerous women almost pinched from under his nose. Even so, he is above revenge or retribution. In the afternoon he drives me to such local sights as there are: the main resort area, stuffed full of grand hotels and which will – given time, tourist inclination and a load more *doi moi* – become another Pattaya; a gaudy pagoda, replete with Reclining Buddha, where I observe two Russians and a French woman offering joss-sticks; and another Bao Dai villa, which Nguyen thinks would make a good casino. Casinos are currently prohibited in Vietnam, but with the right injection of capital through a joint venture, anything is possible.

We collect our bags and turn toward Saigon. At once the Mazda, on its best behaviour for the past few days, acts up. On the one hand it seems to reflect its driver's ill humour, on the other its antics make Sau even more irritable. The pump and the electrics run completely amok. Sau drives with one hand permanently upon the ignition key. In his anger he wants to overtake everything in sight. But no sooner has he overtaken than the car begins to slow. *Ma!* And then the explosions start. Not the ordinary bang of a vehicle backfiring but cannon fire. Cyclists, dogs and chickens abandon the road in terror.

Sau triumphs. We reach the city just as darkness falls. Winning heals his spirits. Having dropped off Em Nha, we repair to yet another restaurant with one of Khan's friends, who has hitched a lift from Vung Tau. Sau swallows his beer and clasps my knee. Again, I am deprived of any excuse not to drink. The renewal of our friendship demands liquid celebration. At the seventh *chuk xu khoe* I feign a slump. But no matter. A waitress materializes at my side. If I am too far gone to lift my glass, then she will do it for me.

She also sees to it that the oysters, the breaded chicken and the fried noodles find their way into my maw. To help me digest, she massages my neck and back. She is a pretty lass, although her face is cruelly disfigured by a birthmark the size of a cigarette pack. At the end of the meal, at Truc's bidding, I tip her $2, slipping the money discreetly into her hand. She returns the gesture by slipping her address into my hand. Please will I write? It may help her in her quest to emigrate.

Monday 4th December: Saigon   We are supposed to set off for the delta provinces at midday, but at ten Truc telephones. Our departure has been delayed a day. Instead he will come to the villa at noon. By one there is no sign of him, so I slope off to eat. When I

328

return I am surprised to find the figure of Le Tien waiting for me. He is all good humour and smiles, but nonetheless he threatens me with all sorts of meetings with various writers' associations. Truc comes soon after. Do I mind if I amuse myself until dinner? He has some work to do. Also, he has heard that his mother is very sick in Hanoi and wants to phone home. On the back of his borrowed motorcycle I ride with him to Soviet Nghe Tinh Street, where Sau takes over and drops me off at the Caravelle Hotel. I spend two hours crawling up and down the old Rue Catinat inspecting the antique shops. Mainly I am anxious to compare my Cham head with what else is on sale. To my relief, although there is no shortage of fakes, they are all manifestly just that: fakes. Also, they are mainly sold as reproductions, nothing else.

The state-owned shops nearest the Caravelle have the most reproductions. They are also the least interested in selling one anything. Further up the street the private vendors make a proper go of it. As soon as I inquire about Cham sculpture I am taken into back rooms, where heads, arms and busts are carefully unwrapped. At first I am shown palpable fakes, but, when I exhibit my scorn for these, what I take to be the genuine articles are produced from even greater quantities of wrapping. Sometimes there is a similarity to the fabric and style of my own Dalat purchase. But there is no parity in the prices asked. To my delight, the Rue Catinat, which presumably is where the western market begins, is thoroughly exorbitant.

Between shops I am befriended by a cyclo driver who claims he has seen me many times in Ky Dong Street. At first, since I have never once seen him, this arouses my suspicions. Saigon cyclo drivers are notorious for their misdemeanours. But then, just because of this, I change my mind. If he knows where I am staying then that is probably because he has been told. And who but one of my minders should have told him? Probably he is a cadre, but if it saves me money and perhaps my skin, then so what?

I tell him where to meet me and when. Then I wander off around the port area, Saigon at its classic best. At the top of Rue Catinat I am accosted by a whole bevy of cyclo drivers, one of whom, in a voice identical to Humphrey Bogart's, tells me that he knows Tim Page well.

329

'See you again, pal,' he says, when I decline his offer of a ride.

The crowd in front of the Floating Hotel is still there. Perhaps these people think it is bound for Hong Kong and they can cadge a ride. I walk back slowly past the Continental. On the pavement a woman lounging in a deck-chair makes a twin gesture that is so lewd it almost counts as art. Simultaneously she rubs two fingers in the time-honoured shorthand for dollars, while with her other hand she rubs her crotch. I am reminded of an old print I have at home, entitled by its eighteenth-century English engraver 'Economy of Time and Labour Exemplified by a Chinese Waterman': the waterman is so balanced that, using his feet as well as his hands, he can operate the rudder of his boat, a string attached to its sail and an oar at the same time as he smokes his opium pipe.

An older woman invites me to 'take coffee have my sister'. I take coffee at a safe distance away, by myself, and then seek out my friendly cyclo driver. He is waiting for me. For a very modest fare he takes me back to Soviet Nghe Tinh Street, where Nguyen, with dollars piled up before him, is doing a little more business with the captive Korean. Then we all repair to an Indian eatery of unimaginable squalor. This however is entirely my doing since in Vung Tau I made too great a point of telling Ali Khan how much I enjoy subcontinental cuisine. Sau, ever anxious to please, picked up the hint. Alas, there is no other Indian restaurant in Vietnam. However, a generous cup of snake-wine at his apartment afterwards just about heals the injury to our mouths. I sleep, as in view of the days ahead I need to sleep, extremely well.

Tuesday 5th December: Ben Tre Roadshow Part Two begins. As the crow flies it's not a great distance to Ben Tre, a hundred kilometres or so, but getting there takes all morning. The reason for this is the distinctive feature of travelling the Mekong Delta: the ferries. Even if the queues of vehicles all-sorts can be jumped, the ferries themselves are slow grannies. Purpose-built in the days when Vietnam was occupied, they support a lively subculture. The cars and trucks pack into the decks, and then the people, either pedestrians or cyclists, pack into the interstices between the cars and trucks. For ten, twenty, thirty, forty minutes, however long it takes to get across the next broad estuary of the Mekong, you live, if live is the word, in a jungle of faces, hair and arms, a fair proportion of which belong to hawkers.

The hawkers are of all ages, although children and young women predominate. In their hands the ferries become floating supermarkets, although little of the proffered merchandise is packaged. There are all the fruits of the tropics, with papaya and oranges the best sellers. There is sugar-cane and coconut. There are soft drinks in Cellophane bags, and sticks of bread coated in grime. There are also trayfuls of cigarettes, little plastic toys, postcards and pocket-sized calendars depicting naked women rolling on the sands of not very clean beaches. And of course, there are tins and bottles of beer: Saigon 33, Heineken, San Miguel . . .

If it weren't so hot the sensible thing to do would be to roll up your window and sit tight. But because it is hot, really hot, this would be a recipe for, at best, heat rash or, at worst, death by boiling suffocation.

Yet the ferries are not unwelcome. They break the monotony of delta driving, and provide, at irregular intervals, the chance for a fleeting, meaningless flirtation. When the younger female vendors discover you, the prettiest is always pushed forward until she hangs over you as you sit in the car: can Mister take me to Can Tho? Can Mister take me to Los Angeles? Or there is the chance to observe, at very close quarters, the different Mekong types. The chauffeured, uniformed big potatoes in their peeling limousines, the shady men in too-small Homburgs pulled down over their faces, the dispossessed followers of the former regime, travelling from nowhere to nowhere, the baseball-cap hopefuls, the farmers, the farmers' womenfolk taking their produce to market, wives of all ages and sizes going about their families' business.

From Saigon the three of us – Sau, Truc and myself – pass through Tan An, the provincial capital of Long An, and My Tho, the provincial capital of Tien Giang. Neither town is very much more than an agglomeration of concrete, bamboo, sweat and bad dentistry. From My Tho we take the last and longest ferry across two kilometres of water and deposit ourselves on the northern shore of Ben Tre Province. Whether we are still on the mainland, or whether we have arrived on an island, is a moot question.

331

Because we are now so near the sea, because the estuaries of the Mekong at this point are so broad, and because of the sudden abundance of the coconut palm, the answer tends toward the insular.

The coconut is the symbol of Ben Tre. In what I take to be the centre of Ben Tre town – a small affair that seems to have given up the struggle for city status – is a large, social-realist statue of a coconut cast in iron. Half open, it seems to want to become a social-realist hamburger.

The Mazda churns around this twice before we glean directions to the People's Committee complex. The committee is out to lunch, but rooms are awaiting us in the adjoining guesthouse, behind a fortification that contains two-tiered pill-boxes. We lunch well on a moored river-boat. We spend the early afternoon kicking our heels and generally hanging about. Then cadres appear, and I am taken off to the Ben Tre Revolutionary Museum. The walls are covered with photographs that, until 1975, were kept undeveloped in cartridge cases. A principal exhibit is an oil drum and a strong stick, instruments of Saigonese torture. Interestingly there are also pictures of the immediate post-1975 period. In Ben Tre the Revolution did not culminate with the fall of Saigon. Counter-revolutionary groups continued to operate out of the jungle until 1978.

I am introduced to a 'heroine', Doan Thie, now a major, a regular army woman, and a director of the museum. In 1968, at the time of the Tet Offensive, she was a nurse. She had joined the resistance five years before, aged thirteen. All her family were VC. But her big moment came during Tet, or rather just after the Saigon counter-attack. She was at a field hospital, looking after seventy-odd wounded with just a staff of four other nurses. Suddenly the hospital came under attack. Bombs fell, artillery shells exploded. Two of the nurses were killed. The remaining three, led by Doan Thie, decided to evacuate their patients to safety. This meant getting them across a river and into a tunnel, a distance of 500 metres. Many of the wounded had to be carried, but somehow Doan and her assistants, even though none of them were either very large or very strong, got them across. Not one patient was lost.

Soon afterwards the Saigon Army overran the field hospital. But by then all of Doan Thie's patients were safe. The Saigon unit couldn't find the tunnel, but even if they had it would have been too dangerous. Doan Thie herself had surrounded the entrance with mines, and she was waiting for the enemy with a box of grenades at her side.

We dine early on eel stew at the guesthouse. The cadres appear. I am invited to a film show.

Two video tapes are to hand, but a video player is not. We spend half an hour touring offices in downtown Ben Tre. Eventually we climb three floors to a small room above a noodle parlour near the river. The room is chock-a-block with equipment, but none of it seems to work terribly well. Or perhaps, mercifully, it is something to do with the tapes themselves. The first film is essentially about pylons. The Vietnamese attitude towards pylons is different from our own. For them a row of pylons stalking across the landscape is not an environmental blot, but a sure sign that the Revolution is doing its thing.

In Ben Tre the Revolution needs to pull its weight. Being so near the sea, the back-kick of salt water into the canal and river irrigation systems is the cause of permanent hardship. Only twenty-six per cent of the land is freshwater-irrigated the year round. Desalination plants exist, but they are too few and there is not enough electricity to supply them. The solution, according to the film, is the up-coming national grid. With Soviet help, electricity is being brought into Ben Tre Province all the way from Dong Nai, on the other side of Saigon. In the meantime the people must bear with their recurrent stomach disorders.

The pylons are presented in all their glory, as are the local big potatoes, and as is the everlasting fraternity between Russian and Vietnamese construction workers. Sau is not pleased. He realizes this is boring the pants off me, mainly I suspect because it is boring the pants off him. He scowls so hard at the screen that the tape breaks down. After a short argument it is replaced by the second, a Hanoi-made extravaganza of typical Ben Tre entertainments. An epic version of the Ben Tre coconut dance, performed in Hanoi's Lenin Park, is followed by Ben Tre folk songs, accompanied by a koto-like instrument and a massive fluttering of false eyelashes.

Then there is a solo performance. A rather lovely female with real eyelashes gives her rendering of the coconut hymn. Several pertinent points about coconuts are woven into the lyrics. Coconuts are good to eat, once provided nourishment for the glorious resistance, and can be used to carry water, while the leaves of the coconut palm furnish villagers with thatch for their houses. But the chief, the remarkable, the singular virtue of coconuts is that they give Ben Tre's gloriously talented revolutionary singers something to sing about.

This time Sau Dang doesn't wait for the tape to snag. He simply leans forward and turns the machine off. *Ma!* We return to the guesthouse where, at an impromptu party in Sau and Truc's room, I am introduced to a local old revolutionary, Vo Van Long.

In fact Vo Van Long enchants me. Touching sixty, taller than the average and with a face that is simply too finely featured for the passions it masks, he is charm incarnate. Also, he is not a particularly big potato.

A native of Ben Tre, Vo Van Long joined the resistance early. Between 1956 and 1959, as a former Viet Minh, he was imprisoned by the Diem regime. At his court hearing, he wanted to expound his feelings about Diem in detail, but his lawyer restrained him. Mitigation reduced his sentence from twenty years to three. In the war against America he worked as an administrator, a co-ordinator, an organizer. One by one he lost all his family. As a guerrilla he suffered every kind of hardship and often nearly starved. 'But not for one moment did I ever doubt what I was doing, or the cause I was fighting for, even though, if I had my life to live over again, I would rather have studied literature and written poetry.'

The fighting in Ben Tre, he tells me, was particularly bitter. Between them the United States and the Saigon Army laid waste two-thirds of the province. Chemicals were sprayed on every town. 'But our enemies forgot our spirit. Originally the people of Ben Tre came from Annam, over three hundred years ago. Ben Tre is a collection of islands, and so we have the independence of an island people. We are like the Mekong river itself. We are incorrigible.'

Is he boring me? Vo Van Long thinks it proper to ask. Life is so difficult. On the one hand, he very much wants me not to be bored, for that would be rude, inhospitable, un-Vietnamese. On the other hand, there is so much he wants to tell me, so much he could tell me, if he had the time. His fear, his great overriding dread, is that one day he and a hundred like him will die, and that once all his comrades are dead then the memories they have will pass over to a place where they cannot by any means be recovered by the living.

For example, there is the story about something that happened right here, in Ben Tre city. The Saigon Army had encamped in the city proper, on the north bank of the river. On the south bank was a guerrilla camp. The guerrillas included among their numbers some *toc dai*, long-haired ones, women cadres. By night the Viet Cong general got his *toc dai* to sing songs, so that the words would float across the river into the ears of the Saigonites. 'But these were not revolutionary songs. They were traditional Ben Tre songs, because we wanted to demonstrate to the Saigon Army to whom Ben Tre really belonged.'

Vo Van Long talks on. I am not taking notes. On the table between us is beer, rice-alcohol and Russian brandy. Every story told, every detail recalled, merits a toast. It is no way to remember anything. Yet I do remember, toward the end of the evening, his aunt. His aunt lost so many family, so many children, that the day came when she stopped crying. She had run out of tears.

Wednesday 6th December: My Thanh–Long My–Giong Trom
There is no time to sleep it off. Truc wakes me at 6.30 a.m. I have a busy programme ahead of me, some of it inside the gentle jungle. Our cicerone for the day, from Culture and Information, is a relaxed good-looker whose rose-tinted glasses at times even threaten to put Sau Dang in the shade. We trundle eastwards down a dirt track corridored with lush green fronds. Our first stop is at a village called My Thanh where I am invited to view a perfectly unexceptional market. Our second stop is at Giong Trom, to exchange compliments with the Giong Trom District People's Committee. Our numbers swell as we press on to another seemingly unexceptional market in a village called Tan Hao. I am told that Tan Hao was 'liberated' in 1972, and that a unit of NVA regulars were stationed there. Subsequently the place was bombed by the

USAF, killing four hundred soldiers and a thousand civilians. But there are few, if any, scars to show. Nor for that matter is there any coconut juice. For that we have to wait until we reach the final village, Long My.

Long My is a massacre site, although by Vietnam War standards the massacre was slight. On 11th June 1964 napalm rained down out of the clear blue sky, scoring a direct hit on the village school. Five children were killed, and thirty-seven others wounded. Another American victory.

I am received by Mrs Thuy, the headmistress of a new school in large measure funded by UNICEF. I ask whether the old school was used as a refuge by the Viet Cong. She assures me that it wasn't. On the day of the napalm strike there were only pupils and teachers in the building, the same as on every other day. But Long My had been liberated as early as 1960, and the school itself was run by the 'Provisional Government'. Hence American and Saigon interest in it.

Mrs Thuy, having provided my entourage with two coconuts' worth of coconut milk each, shows me over. The school boasts 662 pupils, aged three to fifteen, organized in two shifts, and a dozen simple classrooms. As I pass the open windows the classes politely stand and applaud. Sau suddenly remembers that he knows a family of farmers down the lane. Leaving the others behind he takes myself and Truc a mile or so into the interior, where we find a large, ramshackle house and plenty more coconut juice. Multi-coloured dragonflies prance amiably in an astonishingly beautiful jungle garden. What used to be a crater is now an ornamental pond. Then we head back. Lunch is a midday banquet at Giong Trom. There is no beating southern hospitality. For an hour one must be riotous. Afterwards we retire to a rest room for a half-hour siesta. I stare at the ceiling, Truc stares at the ceiling, Sau stares at the ceiling. Then it's boat time.

Sau wants to take me to another farm, a farm that grows everything. As this however is four or five kilometres down-river on the opposite bank we must first return to My Thanh, where a man with a reasonably powerful decaying launch owes a favour to one of the People's Committee that is looking after me. Once aboard, I begin to appreciate how boating is the life and soul of the

336

delta, even at this outpost. Whatever can be transported by water is. Also, every family owns a sampan of sorts, to supplement its diet with shrimps and whatever fish can be caught. And then, just as young Hanoians do their cruising on cycles, so the rural young of the south take to the water. A boatful of girls passes one way, a boatful of boys passes the other. As they approach each other, paddles are left to dangle over the sides. Looks are exchanged, comments made. Then one of the boats rows away; or not, as the case may be.

Sau Dang points to a place where Viet Cong were wont to lie in wait for passing river patrols. Over there, amongst the reeds, was once a mortar emplacement. Then we land, clamber ashore. A path leads us to a small sugar-processing plant, and then on to the farm itself. The farmer, a minuscule man with a not very minuscule wife, is overjoyed to see us. Out comes the beer, out comes the vodka. I look at Truc, Truc looks at Sau, Sau nods. 'No, really, you must,' interprets Truc. *Chuk xu khoe, cham phan cham*, all over again, many times. The farm, full of orchards, becomes absurdly idyllic. The light is unexpectedly delicate, the greens all pastel. Dragonflies ponce in serried formation. I congratulate the farmer on the size of his pods. The farmer congratulates me on the girth of my belly. Only with a number of subtle arguments am I able to persuade him that the way I like my rice-alcohol is to mix it with copious amounts of coconut milk. The farmer at length responds. Coconuts are sent for, coconuts arrive, coconuts are opened. Suddenly the amount of rice-alcohol left in the rice-alcohol bottle looks pitiably little. So let's have another bottle! *Chuk xu khoe! Cham phan cham!* The farmer begins to tell me how happy he is. He sits on some of the best land in Ben Tre, and since *doi moi* he has been able to sell his produce at a price. Already he's up to $150 a month. So he can afford all the rice-alcohol in the world, particularly as he makes the stuff. How would I like to taste some of the house vintage?

We make our getaway at five. The boat wobbles back toward My Thanh. At least I think it's My Thanh. The names of the several villages I have visited today become hopelessly scrambled, and they become even more scrambled when we bid adieu to the Giong Trom People's Committee members, or what's left of them, over beer in a restaurant.

By the time we return to the guesthouse we have about half an hour to sober up. The big potatoes are coming, statistics and history are in the offing. But never mind, says Truc, there will be another banquet afterwards. 'Then we can forget everything.'

Opposite me are Le Huynh, the vice-chairman of Ben Tre Province People's Committee, and Vu Hoang, the director of the Bureau of Culture and Information. Mr Hoang sets the coconut rolling. The hectares, the geography, the waterway mileage, the population. In 1954 there were five times as many palm trees as there were in 1975, after the Americans had done the land over. Now full cultivation has almost been restored. That is the size and the smell of it. After the Geneva Accords many Viet Minh regrouped north, but 2,000-odd remained in Ben Tre. Their sincere ambition was to help fight the election on behalf of the Communist Party by peaceful means. But the promised election was never called. Instead 'the Diem regime transgressed its powers'. Many of the 2,000 were imprisoned, some were executed. The repression was particularly brutal in Ben Tre because Ben Tre never had had a big Catholic population. Even so such cadres who remained at liberty followed Hanoi's orders to show restraint, to resist only non-aggressively.

The period 1954–9 was 'bleak beyond belief'. In October 1959 however the situation became even bleaker. Diem promulgated new laws. All Viet Minh/Viet Cong were to be executed, and so was anyone connected with them – friends, relatives, associates. This left the people of Ben Tre with no choice. Unless they responded militarily they stood to lose everything – their land, their chattels, their loved ones, their lives.

The Ben Tre communists were visited by Le Duan. Le Duan listened to their problems and reported back to the Politburo in the North, submitting fifteen 'fundamental resolutions'. By accepting these the Politburo, through a plenary meeting of the Party, effectively transformed what had been a political struggle into a military conflict. Further, the dissidents in Ben Tre were told they now had formal permission to take up arms against Diem. Thus began the Second Indochina War.

The Ben Tre Uprising began on 17th January 1960 at Dinh Thuy village, in the district of Mo Cay, on the Ham Luong river. The rebels were at several disadvantages. Their armed brethren had regrouped north, and many of their leaders were in prison. There was therefore a lack of weapons and a lack of personnel. But there was no lack of spirit. It was do or die. New weapons were fashioned out of ploughs, hammers, knives, anything that came to hand in the peasant farmyards. With these a band of 160 cadres launched their attack. The police station and administrative offices of Dinh Thuy were stormed and taken. Now the Viet Cong could add a few rifles to their arsenal.

The revolt spread through the surrounding villages. More buildings were stormed, more weapons were seized. Soon the whole of Mo Cay District was under guerrilla control. The Saigon Army mobilized swiftly and earnestly. Twelve thousand well-armed troops were dispatched to the province. But this only encouraged local resistance. The guerrillas enjoyed 'massive' popular support. Ben Tre city itself was subjected to a wave of demonstrations demanding the withdrawal of the Saigon Army. And it was around this time that the *toc dai*, or 'long-haired' soldiers, made their first appearance. In no other province did women play as big a part in the Revolution as they did in Ben Tre. One of their number, Nguyen Thi Dinh, even, in time, became a general.

The women organized many of the demonstrations. They also appealed, with some success, directly to local Saigon soldiers either to hand over their weapons or to desert. To gain any kind of advantage all kinds of tricks had to be employed. When the Viet Cong could lay their hands on any gunpowder, it was used to simulate artillery fire. On one occasion cadres, dressed in 'regular' uniforms and bearing fake weapons, surrounded a Saigon detachment and persuaded it to surrender. Drums and bugles were sounded vigorously off-stage. Having moved into Mo Cay, the Saigon forces were quickly obliged to move out again.

Thereafter Ben Tre was never properly pacified. Try as hard as it might, Saigon could never regain control of the countryside. The province was peppered with fortified positions, but these only acted as a bait for the Viet Cong. Every fortified position attacked and overcome meant enough weapons to assault a further two. Eventually Saigon, with strong American support, fell back on the even cruder tactics of carpet bombing. In all the delta, Ben Tre was the most intractable province. If you can't beat the enemy, annihilate him.

Vu Hoang looks up from his notes. Am I ready to inscribe? Between 1945 and 1975 in all 250,000 Viet Minh and Viet Cong were killed in Ben Tre. In addition the communists suffered 60,000 wounded. Further, 300,000 people were affectd by herbicides . . .

Le Huynh, a solid man with seemingly little fun in him, takes over. I have begun asking questions. Yes, it is true, Ben Tre's was not absolutely the first armed uprising in the South, but it was the first to be explicitly sanctioned by Hanoi, and it was the first to take place after the Party adopted Le Duan's resolutions. And yes again, of course there were some Catholics in the province who supported the Diem regime, at least initially. But Le Huynh discounts the Catholic factor. There were not a lot of them, Ben Tre always had been 'independent minded', and in any case, during the fighting, most of the churches were destroyed – by the enemy.

He reiterates much of what his colleague has already said. There were three distinct aspects of the uprising: a mass movement of support among the people, a military campaign and a political struggle. It was, Le Huynh says, the combination and orchestration of these three thrusts that kept Ben Tre beyond the Saigon pale, just as, in the final analysis, they accounted for the success of the Revolution itself. 'Through their hatred of Diem the people were united by the Party into an effective power for resistance.'

But the hardships persist. The People's Committee must spend half a million *dong* a month on looking after herbicide victims and other long-term wounded. This creates an ongoing drain on family as well as public resources which inhibits the work of repairing other war damage. The roads are still unsurfaced. There are seventy bridges that need to be renewed – and the average cost of a new bridge is two thousand million *dong*. There is the problem of salt contamination, not to mention water pollution from the upper Mekong.

Le Huynh fixes me with his eye, as if to ask: what can *you* do to help us cope? And his eye remains fixed on me during the banquet, served a short while afterwards. He is one of those. He wants to know the mettle of my gut. In vain I protest that I have gotten drunk three times today already. Three times is not enough. There must always be a fourth. We are all *dong chi,* comrades together. And so I raise my glass, and raise my glass again, until, rather rapidly, I reach the point where the only hope of survival is to fight fire with fire. But there's no beating Le Huynh. He's more than a match for me, and probably he's more than a match for Sau Dang, who can sink twenty cans of Heineken any place, any time. But just when I think the room is about to curl up and cannonball into outer space, the session ends. Le Huynh, even in his cups formal to a degree, stands, extends the courtesy of a stiff hug, and liquidizes into the night.

Thursday 7th December: Long Xuyen (An Giang Province) Sau Dang's hand lands hard upon my knee for a morning rub as I sit beside him in the Mazda. Through Truc he asks whether I've enjoyed Ben Tre. I loved Ben Tre, I reply. Sau beams. If I loved Ben Tre then I'll adore An Giang. An Giang is a western delta province, whither we are now bound.

We make our way back to My Tho, and then strike westwards, along the northern bank of the Tien Giang River. We recross near Vinh Long and drive south to Can Tho, the capital of Hau Giang, and the largest city in the south after TP Ho Chi Minh. Then it's north-westwards, along the southern bank of the Hau Giang River. We arrive in Long Xuyen, the capital of An Giang, late lunchtime.

We take three ferries. Today it's lottery tickets and chewing gum that are proffered most strenuously by the hawkers. On all three there are swarms of children who do their best to disperse my hangover – despite Truc's efforts to shoo them away. The landscape itself thins out. The foliage is less dense, less oppressive than in Ben Tre, though the road continues to be lined with gigantic fronds. Increasingly the dwellings are made of wood and leaf-thatch. The people are of another race. Their faces are broader, swarthier, less anxious than I am accustomed to. Pigs and bullocks are chased everywhere by small boys, and thick tropical smells pervade. Through the fronds I see everywhere ditches, ponds, streams, canals, rivers and hundreds upon hundreds of boats. The Boat Country! Most of the dwellings seem to be surrounded by water. It is a land where you don't have to go to sea to catch fish. You just drop your line or a net over your front doorstep.

It is all very hot.

At Long Xuyen inevitably our first port of call is the People's Committee. Sau, who has had his own hangover to contend with, swings into action. Twenty minutes and he comes bouncing out of the building, his thumbs riding high. We are to stay in a 'first-class' tourist hotel. The People's Committee will cover all our expenses except alcohol. We drive quickly to the Thach San Long Xuyen, before anybody changes their mind. And a pretty decent place it is. My room is clean, air-conditioned, spacious and accoutred with new furniture that includes a refrigerator. A regular $30-a-night bivouac.

Even so, I nearly foul it up. Downstairs in the lobby is a canary-yellow-shirted football team, grannied by a gaggle of high-ranking army officers. I make inquiries. It is the Laos Army team, come to play the Vietnam Army team. The Comecon Shield, or whatever – a four-yearly tournament. There are supposed to be fifteen teams playing but in fact there are only five. Eastern Europe has withdrawn from the competition virtually *en bloc*. Now there is only the Soviet Union, Vietnam, Cambodia, Laos and Hungary.

I talk to a Viet colonel who invites me to watch the match. Kick-off is in half an hour. I ask Truc if that's okay, and Truc nods. He'd like to see the game himself. We ride to the ground in the Laotian bus. Inside the bus, the Laos players all don dark glasses. It occurs to me that most of them have been selected for their looks. One in particular has worked hard on the prima-donna role. He would leave Diego Maradona crawling. Preening his fingernails he refuses absolutely to have anything to do with his team-mates.

We sit in the official enclosure. What looks like a healthy sampling of both countries' chiefs of staff sit at a long table facing the field, which is flanked by two surprisingly solid concrete grandstands. There are about 5,000 spectators. Crowd control however is never likely to be a problem. Dotted around the field are men with sub-machine-guns.

I ask Truc why this match is being played here, and not in Hanoi or Saigon. Truc tells me partly it's for 'political reasons', partly because Long Xuyen is about the only place in Vietnam anybody is still prepared to watch a local team. Three or four years ago football was number one national sport, but since the

342

advent of video sets the fans have been able to watch high-class European football and have lost interest in the home brew.

The game itself bears this out. The play lacks precision, although several of the Laotians cavort beautifully off the ball. Perhaps they have already clocked that in Indochina there's a brighter future in ballet. The Viets are less stylish but more diligent. They form a pack and make a habit of crowding the Laos penalty area. After fifteen minutes a goal is duly scored. One–nil remains the half-time score, and at full time nothing has changed. The rest is diplomacy. Marines ('national defence operatives') escort the teams back to their coaches. The colonels and the generals toast their opposites with Heineken.

For me though it's been fun. Inside the official enclosure I have made several new friends. The nearest sub-machine-gunner has run out of cigarettes and becomes my lifelong brother when I offer him mine. I also make friends with a little old woman who sells me more cigarettes when I run out sooner than anticipated. I make friends with the doctor, who tells me that he graduated from Saigon University two years before Reunification. After Reunification he spent two years being 're-educated'. It must have worked because he can't think of a single thing to say against the Revolution. And finally I make friends with five sisters who belong to an 'acknowledged' Long Xuyen sporting family, hence their presence in the enclosure.

I am invited to their house after dinner. Truc says 'maybe'. The match ends and we walk back to the Khach San Long Xuyen. There, Sau Dang is fuming. Where the hell have we been all afternoon? The People's Committee wanted to meet me. *Maaa!* He takes it out on Truc. But things are smoothed out later. It transpires that the reason the People's Committee wanted to meet me so soon was to take me to the football match. Zero sum. My official An Giang programme will commence tomorrow.

Sau though is less than ebullient at supper. He tells us he has some 'business' to attend to afterwards, so we must amuse ourselves. I press Truc into accompanying me to visit the sports family. We find a cyclo driver who doesn't have the first clue where the house is when we show him the address. Nonetheless he takes us to where he thinks it is, can't find it, then demands to be paid double. Truc loses his bottle entirely. The little sergeant in him rears its beret. I realize that in a country where wages are minimal, haggling about the odd twenty cents is what it's all about. Eventually the little sergeant subsides, and we walk to our destination, which, as it happens, we have already passed. The house proper is at the back of a garage-like structure that doubles as a workshop of some kind. The five sisters make a palaver of being surprised by our bothering to remember them, blush, hide their faces behind their hands, giggle. But soon enough they are entertaining us with their vivacity. I begin falling heavily for the third oldest, Phuong. It is not however a *boc phét* situation. Two brothers appear, and then the father. The father, a well-preserved ex-army man, takes us in his stride. There's none of that what-the-dickens-have-you-brought-back-from-the-stadium-this-time? routine. On the contrary, he is at pains to tell me about his family's achievements. The walls are adorned with a galaxy of sporting medals. One of his daughters is a swimmer, one an athlete. His real hopes are pinned on the youngest, a gymnast. There is a chance she will go to the 1992 Olympics.

Glasses are put on the table. But for once, no beer, no rice-alcohol. Instead, Coca Cola. Or rather something resembling Coca Cola in Coca Cola-like bottles. The family business is manufacturing soft drinks. One of the sons is in charge of preparing the cordials, another makes the bottles.

For the thousandth time in this country I am overwhelmed by the hospitality and friendliness of ordinary people. Later, one of the sons takes us back to the centre of Long Xuyen on his motorbike. For a while I walk around. Long Xuyen is unlike the other towns and cities of the delta. Its streets are wide enough to be called boulevards, the buildings are crisp and generally white, and there are several square, or squarish, piazzas. It is unusually regular, and also curiously deserted. Such Vietnamese as I see appear to be lost. There is no intimacy for them. There is too much street lighting. I could be in a new town in Spain or Greece. It's as though something big has happened a week or two ago, but now it's over, and the crowds have packed up and gone home. The bullring is closed.

＊　　　　　　　　＊　　　　　　　　＊

344

Friday 8th December: Long Xuyen–Chau Doc–Phu Chau–Vinh Te An Giang, as it happens, is rich in different worlds. For a start, it is the only delta province that boasts any mountains. There are seven small 'ranges'. An Giang also has a hundred kilometres' worth of border with Cambodia, and there are seventy-five thousand Khmers living inside the province. So at least I am told by Nguyen Anh Vu, head of Culture and Information, in a dawn pep-talk before setting off for the province's western reaches. We will stay the night at Chau Doc, right up on the border itself. We are to be accompanied by two of Mr Vu's henchmen: Dan, an incredibly tall gangling beanpole of a fellow, and a photographer, Nguyen.

The journey to Chau Doc involves no ferries. It is straight and dusty all the way. But we have scarcely progressed to Long Xuyen's perimeter when I realize, to my horror, that I have left my dollar-rich secret shoulder-holster under the mattress in my room at the hotel. Sau dutifully turns round. The long-haired receptionist smiles bountifully as soon as I walk in the door. A little disdainfully she holds up that which I had feared lost. It has been nestling in my armpit two months now and has developed a certain protective odour. She makes me open it and count my money. It is all there. Sau sighs with relief. Truc chuckles. He cannot wait to wag his finger at me. 'You see,' he says as soon as we are in the car again, 'someone like you needs his helpers.'

We arrive at Chau Doc and halt briefly at the People's Committee, to advertise our presence. We then set off immediately for a smaller town ten kilometres to the north called Phu Chau. This time there is a ferry, no more than a motorized barge on which there is just room enough for the Mazda, my entourage and a handful of hawkers. To get the car on board we must all climb out. I sit on the ferry's side. The Hau Giang at this point is only two or three hundred metres across. As I look at the milling water-people, I notice that photographer Nguyen has gone to work. Every time I look at him his camera clicks. After the sixth time I ask why he is taking so many pictures of me.

'To put in our museum.'

'But why?'

'Because you're famous.'

'No, I'm not. I absolutely promise you.'

'But when we have your picture in our museum you'll be very famous indeed.'

The reason why we've come to Phu Chau, other than to observe the rounder, darker features of the many Khmers pushing carts along the way, does not become apparent until after we've lunched on banana-fish at a restaurant that overhangs the much broader waters of Tien Giang River, 150 kilometres upstream from Ben Tre. Toward the end of his life, in the 1920s, Ho Chi Minh's father journeyed to Chau Doc (then an autonomous province) to live and study at a Buddhist pagoda, Dong Thanh. Thither we now wend. To my mild astonishment Dong Thanh is built, in the midst of a jungle clearing, in the manner of a superior Indian mansion. The Hindu input.

I am received by the *dai duc*, or head monk, Thich Tinh Duyen. Dong Thanh, he tells me, has been newly classified a national monument by the Ministry of Culture. He is the fourth abbot. The first abbot built the original pagoda out of leaf and wood a hundred years ago. The second abbot replaced this by a brick-and-tile job. The third abbot, Thich Chan Nhu, who died in 1973, created the present structure. As for Thich Tinh Duyen himself, he is rather inclined to leave it as it is. In fact he is obliged to. Once a pagoda becomes a national monument there is not a lot that any abbot can do to leave his mark.

Our conversation is on the brink of becoming interesting when Sau Dang, for no discernible reason, begins agitating for our departure. Really we should be going now, he says, displaying scant respect for the old man talking to me. But why? Having taken all this trouble to bring me here, it seems odd to want to drag me off so soon. Conceivably actually communicating with the monk was not on the agenda. Conceivably too Sau Dang, who has had to put up almost daily with requests to meet representatives of the Cao Dai and Hoa Hao sects, suspects I nurse religious tendencies, and that in some not altogether mysterious way I am to be kept away from anyone who might encourage such reactionary tendencies.

Yet I must doubt it. From Phu Chau we drive back to Chau Doc, and then on five kilometres to a place called Vinh Te where there are temples and pagodas and nothing else, a veritable Mecca of the delta region. Here all tastes, all reactionary perversions are catered for. It grew up from the times when the border with Cambodia was ill-defined, non-existent. Surrounded by An Giang's mountains, it is officially classified as 'a place of scenic beauty'. The central shrine consists of a pagoda within a temple. A vast dark goddess, the big sister of Ponaga in Nha Trang perhaps, sits enthroned and enrobed in purple cloths. She also sits enrailed. So sacred is she that no visitor must approach too near.

Nonetheless Sau Dang performs his magic. A step ladder is produced and I am invited to slip my hands beneath the goddess's bodice. Once again I encounter breasts that are cold and hard but of such a magnitude that momentarily my head does swim. Have I, I wonder, been showing too much interest in the wrong deity? Is it Sau's intention to make me love the Mother, not the Buddha? At any rate, when I descend from my perch, Sau is smiling from one ear to the other.

Adjoining the main prayer hall is the goddess's dressing room. Every year each one of Vietnam's provinces sends her a new costume. Patently there is great competition to see which can dress her best. The result is a wardrobe that, if she ever saw it, would convince Imelda Marcos that heaven and earth can and do coexist in at least one spot on the planet.

Across from the Chua Xu Temple (as it is called) is a mausoleum, a smaller-scale version of the tombs I have seen in Hué. Here the mortal remains of a mandarin are enshrined, Thoai Ngoc Hau, the man who originally got Chau Doc started. And close by this a Buddhist pagoda, Chua Tay San, gaudy without, and dingy within.

Sau, to his immeasurable delight, has discovered, within the precincts of the mausoleum, a certain kind of seed which, when wetted, explodes. Like grenades, they have a delay mechanism, so that he can chew them first, and then place them in the palm of his hand. Bang! Or pop! Depending on the seed's innate virility.

We find a stall that has tables and order tea and beer. I begin wiping my face with my Viet Cong cloth. Sau shows me how to wrap it around my head in the authentic manner. Photographs are taken. And then rat-a-tat-tat-a-tat! Sau has deposited a fistful of magic seeds into a pool of water. That is what happened when the Viet Cong were around. Ha ha ha. Ho Ho Ho.

*   *   *

347

At dusk I am struck by the immensity of the delta. The road back to Chau Doc lies on a high dike. Other high dikes, with whole villages strung along them, stretch to far horizons and beyond. The dying sun burnishes the mirrored paddies. By contrast, Chau Doc is a mean huddle of a town. The streets emit a powerful stench. One possible reason for this stench I encounter in my room, windowless and as cell-like as I have yet to encounter. The water, although running, is grossly impure. Having washed myself, my skin takes on the sticky texture of fly-paper. That is to say flies, of which there are many, stick to it. And, as I learn from Truc, the water is called just that: sticky water.

We eat in a covered market, where the stench is most concentrated. A never-to-be-forgotten meal, and for all the wrong reasons. There is no light, I have no idea what I am eating, the tastes are new to me in an unpleasant way. And as we eat, eyes appear in the gloom around the table. These belong to beggars. They are waiting for us to finish, whereupon they will descend on the remains of our dishes. Only they can't wait so long. Hands brush our arms in the darkness. Anything that falls off the table, or is swept off in the southern style, never reaches the floor. Truc berates unseen fingers. Sau swears tempestuously. A child with an empty, filthy plastic bowl attaches herself to my thigh. I suggest buying extra rice and distributing it. Truc gives me a look of utter horror. Do that, he says, and we'd be crushed to death in the rush. There'd be an uprising. Sorry.

As it is we are almost crushed to death in the hotel. The staircases are aswarm with *pho*, prostitutes. The place has become a snake-pit. Chau Doc is not the back of beyond I have taken it for. As well as the pilgrims visiting the shrines at Vinh Te, there are the traders, legal or otherwise, coming out of war-torn Cambodia on their long overland journey from Thailand. Chau Doc is a sticky watering hole toward the end of that trail.

Saturday 9th December: Chau Doc–Ba Chuc–Tri Ton–Long Xuyen War-torn Cambodia, war-torn Vietnam. There's no fucking end to it. I mean there won't be an end to war until there's an end to fucking. My party leaves Chau Doc at dawn. Again there is much to be squeezed into the day ahead. We drive south, beyond Vinh Te, hugging the border on our right all the way. The mountains in the distance are Cambodian. So are the fields in the immediate middle distance. I see for the first time those peculiar palms which are the scenic hallmark of Cambodia: tall, bare trunked, lollipop headed. In the morning mists they resemble nothing so much as low-tethered barrage balloons. Football faces peer at our passing vehicle from their chequered wrappings. After thirty minutes we turn east, back into Vietnam proper. After forty-five minutes we arrive at Tri Ton, a district capital. Our purpose is to visit Ba Chuc. To do this we need the approval of the local People's Committee, housed in a French-made building. I am met by the vice-chairman, Quang Vinh Song. I receive a preliminary briefing. In April 1978 the Khmer Rouge 'invaded' western An Giang. They crossed the border and attacked five villages, burning and looting as they went, leaving four thousand dead in their wake. But come, we'll show you. We drive back the way we came, twenty-one kilometres, and then take the Ba Chuc turning. Ba Chuc was one of the five villages assaulted. The countryside is desolate. The land is pock-marked with bomb-craters, the vegetation still seems unwilling or unable to grow. I am reminded that the USAF were here before the Khmer Rouge were ever heard of. Nonetheless the villages are sprouting again. We pass village after village. Quang Vinh Song is at pains to point out that all of them have a school and a clinic. The socialist state is rebuilding Armageddon. Each village also has a People's Committee, swathed in red banners.

In this part of the world the land is like a classroom blackboard. It fills up with words written in the human alphabet. Then comes the cataclysm, and wipes the board clean. Fresh words reappear, words that perhaps are marginally different, but are composed in the same human alphabet. The deep peasant-rice-water structure remains the same. And the words remain until, after ten years, a hundred years, a thousand years, the next man-made cataclysm comes along:

> *Again I wrote it with a second hand,*
> *But came the tide and made my pains his prey.*

349

The poem that Spenser wrote about the effects of love is also about the effects of any kind of human endeavour.

We come to Ba Chuc. The centrepiece is a memorial erected in 1984. It is like no other memorial. It stands like a fashionable pavilion in the plain. The motif I suppose is that of a modernist lotus. A rigid red-painted flame burns eternally on the roof. Below the roof, an octagonal, glass-windowed cabinet containing 1,700 skulls.

The skulls belong to those slain by the Khmer Rouge in 1978. They are classified, in the eight double-panelled windows, according to age and sex. In this window, 'Adult females of Ba Chuc from 21 to 40 years old'. In that one, 'Mature females of Ba Chuc from 41 to 60 years old'. 'Children of Ba Chuc from 3 to 15 years old'. Behind them, in the centre of the monument, a pile of bones – ribs, pelvises, femurs, fingers – heaped up at random, unclassified.

The skulls I can look at. Seventeen hundred skulls do not in fact move me. How could they? I have handled skulls before, albeit only in biology classes. A skull is a thing that has no flesh on it, and for me humanity is flesh, not bone. A skull is the idea of man, a symbol only, not the man himself. Shakespeare said this in his line about Yorick. *Alas* poor Yorick. Nothing stronger. Alas – seventeen hundred skulls. But the point about a skull is that one pretty much resembles another. As symbols go, a skull is very common. Its only power is its hidden-ness: it is the symbol each and every one of us carries about with us, at all times unseen until 'we' cease to exist.

What does move me, what chills me even, is the photographs. Unlike My Lai, there is no museum, no gallery of horrors. But there is a pamphlet, in size and design remarkably similar to the one supplied at My Lai. The pictures are very largely of corpses. And there is no escaping their deadness. The flesh is not merely asleep. It is stongly decomposed. The Vietnamese did not recover the bodies of Ba Chuc until several days, sometimes several weeks, after the massacre. The flesh in the photographs therefore has had time to melt. And it is this that makes the images I hold in my hand so much more grotesque than the symbols behind the glass, even though, technically, the latter are more 'real'.

There is one photograph in particular that tells the story. A woman lies in the mud with her arms and her legs spread out. Very slightly she resembles a starfish. Probably she has been lying there a week. This you can tell because the flesh is tightened around the bones. The sinews of war. She is largely naked. Her clothing has been pulled up around her head. Her thighs, even in their decay, suggest curious strength. But evidently not strength enough. Between her legs lies a stake. This has been driven into her vagina. The effect is not unlike a gear-lever protruding from a gearbox.

The sharp end of the stake almost pierces through the hip. As I said, there won't be an end to war until there is an end to fucking.

The words of the pamphlet are all in Vietnamese. This is not as yet an international war-tourist site. Beijing is mentioned though. What happened at Ba Chuc was done 'with the backing of Beijing'. What I am looking at therefore is something more than a memorial. It is also a call if not to arms, then at least to vigilance. I have been brought here partly to learn, to be reminded that the Khmer Rouge attacked Vietnam some while before Vietnam invaded Cambodia. The Khmer incursions, so the pamphlet states, began in April 1977. The people of Ba Chuc were slaughtered between the 14th and the 25th of the following April.

The parading of corpses is one of the oldest means by which the justness (or otherwise) of an armed conflict is made manifest. These were our people, there can be no excuse for their demise. Probably, perhaps, the Vietnamese argument is 'correct'. The invasion of Cambodia may well have been retaliatory, a necessary device of 'state security'. I have no certain means of knowing. But the propaganda element, though present, is for me secondary. At the heart of the matter is that grim pathology unique to humankind, which outweighs specific causes and effects, specific retributions; and it is not in anyone's best interests to dwell upon those causes, those effects, except as they exemplify that pathology.

Close by the memorial is a complex of pagodas. These I am taken to, to examine the interior walls. The interior walls are studded with bullet-holes, and sometimes stained with blood that is now more than ten years old. The Khmer Rouge had no respect for any kind of authority other than their own. The spaces beneath the altars were no refuge from their guns, their knives, their stakes.

*   *   *

We return to Tri Ton, to lunch outdoors beside a lotus pond and a Khmer pagoda. On the way Sau Dang bangs and thumps the Mazda's steering wheel as he delivers the most impassioned of his monologues. There are tears of fury in his eyes. Later I ask Truc for a translation. For a moment Truc hesitates, then he comes out with it. 'The reason why Sau Dang was so angry was because of what he had seen. He thinks that the government should have acted sooner. He thinks we should not have waited until 1978 to invade Kampuchea. He thinks Hanoi should have sent our army there a year before. Then, maybe, Ba Chuc would have escaped its punishment.'

Punishment?

Oriental fatalism dies hard.

But Sau, the man of fibre, recovers quickly. There are more friends of his in Tri Ton, and they join us at our table. Lunch becomes another banquet. The local cadres do their best to furnish me with local propaganda, but the effort has soon to be abandoned. Mainly they want to impress upon me that the government is doing everything in its power to protect and develop the region's minorities, including resident Khmers. And because of An Giang's seven mountain ranges there are *montagnards* as well, and they are cared for with all the love the People can muster. But then, pressed up against a dangerous border, it's what one would in any case expect.

While Truc and Sau take a short siesta I investigate the Khmer pagoda. The sugared architecture and the dozy saffron-robed monks remind me strongly of Thailand. Then the Tri Ton People's Committee assemble across the road for group photography outside a more or less new culture palace that sits on the site of the old French prison. Afterwards I am taken to another pavilion beside another lotus pond where a novice rock band is rehearsing. Welcome to the Hotel California' is what these cultural guerrillas sing. What is lacking in accuracy is made up for in volume. They would like me to think they are as large as a symphony orchestra.

Between Tri Ton and Chau Doc we stop off at a 'pleasure park', set within space of almost scenic beauty between two mountains. In effect it is a holiday camp in the middle of nowhere. There are cafeterias, bars and a disco built round a lake. The place is

352

astoundingly empty. The manager does his utmost to tell me that Lam Vien is what socialism is all about. Jokingly I tell him a massage parlour might help to draw in the crowds. His face lights up. The massage parlour is opening next year, 1990, the Year of the Tourist.

At the wheel Sau becomes angry again. He thinks it was a waste of his time and my time going to the park. It will be a struggle to get back to Long Xuyen before dark. With some furious driving he manages it. We are given the same rooms at the Khach San Long Xuyen as we had before. We take dinner at an ordinary restaurant close to the market. Afterwards, Truc and I climb to the top floor of the hotel where there is a penthouse dance-floor. Even here in the sticks the young have learnt their steps, their foxtrots and their sambas and their cha-cha-chas. We withdraw to the balcony. Truc, clearly concerned about the health of his mother, opens up about his family and himself. He is not a Party member, he tells me, because he comes from a 'bourgeois' background. His father and his grandfather were property owners in Hanoi. His mother still owns several houses, although the yield, now, is next to nothing. The Party controls the rents. His brothers and sisters are all doctors and teachers or small merchants. Truc alone became a cadre. Every family should have one. The thing that frightens him most in life, he says, is ambition. The higher you climb, the harder you fall. In the past he has taken some risks. A year ago he involved himself in some kind of private-sector gambling project in Lenin Park. He was soon advised to discontinue. Now that he is a father, he craves security most of all. His position at the Ministry of Information has yet to be confirmed. On the other hand what attracts him to interpreting is the contact it will give him with outsiders. Man cannot live by rice alone. Listening to outsiders helps him think about his own society. If he can understand his own society, then he will be better placed to find the security he seeks within it.

Truc's is not an adventurous mind, but there is a kind of grinding method to it. He is also more vulnerable than I orginally supposed. At the end of our talk he asks whether we are brothers yet. Zoom's way would have been to slap me on the back and tell me, 'We are brothers now, Mister Justin!' But Truc's way is equally valid, and I tell him yes, of course, we are brothers and always will be.

Sunday 10th December: My Hoa Hung–Long Xuyen   The Revolution resumes. The tall, beanpole cadre, Dan, collects us at dawn. We have breakfast at the museum he is a vice-director of. Then it's all aboard for a journey up-river, to My Hoa Hung, the birthplace of Ton Duc Thang.

Ton Duc Thang, or Uncle Ton, became President of North Vietnam in 1969, after Ho Chi Minh's death. In his hands the presidency downgraded: the President was no longer the nation's father, but a figure wheeled out on state occasions. Real power was entrusted to the Party General Secretary, Le Duan. Although Ton was never a figure of the stature of Le Duan, General Giap, Pham Van Dong or Le Duc Tho, there were several advantages in his appointment. He was uncontroversial. He was solid. He was a southerner. And he enjoyed the favour of the Russians. He was a little like Krushchev without the fists. His finest moment came in 1919, aboard a French naval vessel in the Black Sea. Having been taken on as an engineer, he somehow managed to raise the red flag on the ship's mast, to express solidarity with the October Revolution. He was, of course, dismissed, and sent back to Cochinchina.

Ton was born in 1888, the son of a wealthy farmer. Schooled in Long Xuyen, he attended technical college in Saigon from 1906. Graduating as a mechanical engineer, he worked for a while in Toulouse before joining the colonial navy. After his disgrace he became a trade union militant and leader in Saigon. The idea of a single union for all Vietnamese workers was partly his. In 1929 he was imprisoned, and remained in prison right up until 1945, transferring to the notorious Con Dao island penitentiary in 1930. He did not meet Ho Chi Minh until 1946. During the French war he became a senior Party figure, rising to chairman of the Viet Minh League. In 1958 he was awarded the Gold Star medal. Just over ten years later he became President, a post he retained until his death in 1980.

The house where he spent the first eighteen years of his life has been preserved in much the same way that Ho's various domiciles have been preserved. It is though rather larger, sporting a long veranda and somewhat more spacious rooms. Close by is a Ton Doc Thang Museum, full of his photographs. The curator keeps a box of Ton Duc Thang badges, which he presents to visitors, and a book for them to sign.

Thinking of something to say that will enhance one's reputation as a bosom friend of Vietnam about a man whom one was never really aware existed before is, at nine in the morning, akin to a salt tax. Whatever I write has all the hallmarks of a fudge. The curator nonetheless is thrilled and wreathes me in smiles. Then my entourage marches single file back to the boat. It is not though, an outing I would have missed. The real joy of this morning caper is the river. At Long Xuyen the Hau Giang is broad and exceptionally slow moving. The light is Venetian. The boatman has brought his son along with him. Periodically the eight-year-old dives overboard into the completely opaque bottle-green water to disentangle the propeller from whatever it is that has entangled it. All around us other boats are having similar difficulties. Toward the shores there are rows, three or four deep, of floating homes. The tiny decks are piled high with perishables. The inhabitants stare at the passing traffic. Their expressions are uniformly farouche. They are like refugees in their own country.

The An Giang Museum, when we return there, has been opened, despite its being Sunday. Hints are dropped that this is on my behalf, although I am aware of other visitors. As provincial museums in Vietnam go, it is distinctly superior. Indeed it possesses at least one world-class exhibit: a wooden Buddha figure, at least a thousand years old, discovered only recently, whose tattered, weeping robes actually do seem not to be part of the body. There are three halls, of which the most interesting is easily the first. In this is gathered most of what has survived from the Oc Eo civilization (second to eighth centuries AD), a southern kingdom displaced by the Chams before the Chams, in their turn, were displaced by the Viets. The most interesting items are square burial pots the size of a domestic washing-machine. In one corner, sprinkled on cadmium-red cloths, are the lesser remains. Half of a Hinduesque bust, two whole pots, the shards of several others, a necklace, two or three wristlets, some small carved stones. It would all fit comfortably into a holdall, and is all that is left of the daily life of a civilization and its people.

The second hall is more conventional: the wars. One item is a tube developed by the early Viet Cong for spraying chilli powder into the face of an enemy. The third hall is given over to the post-Reunification achievements of An Giang Province: the agriculture, the light industries ... the sporting record. It is hard though to channel my attention. I am led through the rooms by a bevy of dazzlingly attractive women in gleaming white *ao dai*. Like a relay team, one passes the baton to the next. The baton is a long thin stick with which they point out the details of the exhibits. To the best of their ability they endeavour to maintain a schoolmistressly pose. But their loveliness, reflected in the visitor's eyes, keeps on overwhelming them, and it is a little upsetting to discover afterwards, in the backyard of the museum, a crèche for their several babies.

These cultural *toc dai* are, I suspect, the brain-children of Nguyen Anh Vu. Mr Vu — or Hai Vu as he allows himself to be called (*hai* = two, which means he is a first born) — takes the afternoon history class at the People's Committee. As I quickly discover he has a finger in every pie. As well as being the chief of the Bureau of Culture and Information, he is a member of the An Giang People's Council (the law-making body), of the People's Committee and of the Party Committee. To a very large extent he is An Giang Province. He is also a *doi moi* enthusiast. In his time he has been a propagandist, a journalist, the director of a radio station and an administrator. A compact man with curiously virile curly hair, he is still, at fifty-two, dynamic. Truc wastes no time in whispering to me that Hai Vu is just the sort of big potato to get things done. As if to prove this, no sooner, during the course of initial compliments, do I express my admiration for the Dripping Buddha but a messenger is sent to arrange for its photograph to be taken. By the end of the session the photograph, still wet, is delivered into my hands. It is, as it happens, the first photograph of the statue to be taken.

'When a woman is pregnant, who knows what skills her child will develop?' Hai Vu has a way with ideas, even if none of them are very new. 'The working people are the main factor in our success,' he continues. Because today's and tomorrow's leaders must be drawn from the masses, it is important that the masses are looked after. Creativity from below, instruction from above. In a word, *doi moi*. Since *doi moi* the province now produces a surplus. With the surplus the needs of the people can be met. Electricity can be taken to the villages. The barren war zones can be replanted and repopulated. People will have more space, and better roads to connect that space. As the old Vietnamese proverb goes, as the water rises, so does the boat. Give the people what they want, give them only the best-quality goods, and the people will defend and further the Revolution. Life is so simple, so easy, so perfectible, once you know how.

I ask about the Cham Muslim community, the biggest in Vietnam. Are there any whispers of Islamic fundamentalism yet? Hai Vu looks at me and smiles the smile. Of course not! The Cham Muslims are fully assimilated. They have lived in Vietnam for a long time, and they are 'conditioned' to Vietnamese thinking. Just recently the People's Committee persuaded the women to stop wearing veils. Now they are 'coming out' more. Also, the men have begun restricting themselves to just the one wife. Everyone in Vietnam is a progressive! Conversely, the government allows, and even encourages, traditional custom, for having 'ethnic respect' is also progressive. Thus, in An Giang, the People's Committee has part-sponsored Khmer as well as Cham festivals. Everyone can have their own New Year!

We are joined by a younger cadre, Ngo Quang Lang, a historian trained at the Marx–Lenin Institute in Hanoi. The heavy stuff is about to come. Hai Vu is merely the enthusiastic master of ceremonies. Ominously, Lang sets down a pile of notebooks and begins adjusting the maps on the wall behind him. I am given the revolutionary history of An Giang from the earliest colonial times.

Pre-communist uprisings occurred in 1867, 1880 and 1912. To a degree these were 'religious' in character, an attempt to defend traditional Vietnamese culture. 'Stone bullets' were used in home-made rifles, and the tactics employed were not unlike those used later by the Viet Minh and the Viet Cong. The rebels went first for the smallest enemy positions, in order to capture badly needed weapons, then for the bigger positions.

The French however had relatively little difficulty in containing these revolts, and there followed a 'quiet' period. 'But this was just on the surface. Below the surface, ideas of revolution were swimming freely.' One important idea was the notion that national salvation would only be achieved through national unity. Local uprisings simply played into the imperialists' hands. This gave birth to the Viet Nam Phuc Quoc Hoi, or 'Association to Regain Vietnam', a nationalist body made up mainly of teachers headed by Cham Van Liem.

Although the VNPQH was short-lived and non-communist, it showed the way for other pan-provincial groupings, particularly the Viet Nam Youth Revolutionary Movement.

For reasons best known to himself, Lang skips the period of the French war. The notebook is opened, but after a cursory glance, the notebook closes again. During the US war however 'An Giang once again came to the fore of southern resistance.' This is evidenced by the fact that on one small mountain alone – Tuc Dup hill – the Americans dropped two million dollars' worth of bombs and artillery fire, in an attempt to flush out a single VC unit comprising 'no more than fifty cadres'. Eventually it was so heavily napalmed and defoliated that 'to this day not a tree, not a flower will grow there'.

From 1963 onwards, the province developed a 'panther skin' character. The land belonged in more or less equal measure to the Saigon Army on the one hand, and the revolutionary guerrillas on the other. The VC were strongest around the mountains, and around Long Xuyen. Their biggest base was near Phu Chau. Their weakness was that they were too far south to benefit from the Ho Chi Minh Trail. To some extent, however, this deficit was made good by the 'keen' support of the Khmer people across the border in Cambodia.

But perhaps the most interesting An Giang episode came nine years after Reunification, in 1984. A former Saigon Army colonel, Mai Van Hanh, penetrated the frontier out of Cambodia with a force of a hundred men disguised as Vietnamese regulars. His aim was quite simply to march on Saigon and re-establish the Republic. Certainly he had the connivance, and probably he had the backing, of US and Thai agencies. The adventure ended in disaster. Mai

358

Van Hanh's bogus unit was spotted and attacked. Some of his followers were captured, others fled. Mai Van Hanh himself was taken prisoner, and duly sentenced to death. But on the intervention of President Mitterrand – Colonel Mai normally resided in France – his life was spared. Eventually he was returned to Paris, 'where perhaps he is plotting another coup'.

It is early evening when the lesson finishes. On my first day in An Giang, Hai Vu pledged that on my last our formal relationship would end and 'our friendship begin'. Now he keeps his word. He invites the three of us – myself, Sau Dang and Truc – to a 'private banquet' in one of Long Xuyen's better restaurants. On the way Truc explains that this is a little exceptional. Banquets are generally hosted by at least two committee members, with attendant cadres. We dine by ourselves in an upstairs room. The meal begins with a tremendous flourish of compliments and toasts; but these are less in observance of the formalities than as a pretext to hasten inebriation. Tonight, getting down to our emotional underwear is what it's all about. Hai Vu's features, though they are hard like the features of most older revolutionaries, convey great grace as well. He is a Party man, a loyalist, a manipulator even. But he is also the consummate oriental. The pleasures of life are not to be sacrificed to any ideology. He epitomizes the Vietnam I have come to study, the Vietnam that has presented itself to me. Our conversation, which is energetic, sharp, at times boisterous, takes the form of a triple rondo. For ten minutes he talks of the sadness of war, of the blood spilled and of relatives lost. Then abruptly he switches. Now we exchange men's stories, and extol the patient modesty of the Vietnamese woman. Hai Vu hints that in his time he has had many girlfriends. Ten minutes of this, and bang! he's off on another track. He wants me to know deeply that in Vietnam the people, the masses, are all important. But the people need guidance, and the Party is the best, the only means for securing this objective. And then it begins all over again. The war, women, ideology. Ten minutes, ten minutes, ten minutes; the discrete themes of his life reasserting themselves over and over, in competition with each other, but also seeking integration.

I do not agree with everything he says, he does not agree with everything I say. But at heart the point is established. We are not so very different. We eat the same food, drink the same drink and laugh at each other's jokes. The *chuk xu khoe* get very slightly out of hand. There is a coda to the rondo. Hai Vu tells me soon he must retire. I think he wants to be reassured, that the Revolution was right, that the cause was worthy. Vietnam has been isolated from so much of the world for so long that doubts are inevitable. What *does* everybody think about Vietnam? Out there? In the world which is not Vietnam? In the final reckoning, do Hai Vu and all his kind belong to the party of the angels?

My reply is necessarily tactical, because the question is only suggested. But it also comes from the heart. To combine the two, tactics and heart, is the whole art of grace, and Hai Vu's insistence on the presence of grace at our table can only be respected. I tell him that in their hospitality the Vietnamese have taken the wave method of attack into their soul. Since coming to Vietnam I have been assaulted by wave after wave of interest and generosity. (This is not entirely true, but in Hai Vu's case it is true enough, so why not? My feelings at the moment are toward the man, not the nation.) I am, I say with as straight a face as I have ever said anything, on the very brink of capitulation.

Hai Vu is pleased. He would like, he says, to take us to his house. Let us drink the night away. But Sau intervenes. An old friend of Mr Vu's, he knows that he has been warned by his doctor to go easy on the rice-alcohol. The grace, the hospitality conceal a frailty. Also, there is tomorrow's programme. We will instead visit him at breakfast, and say goodbye then.

Sau drives him home. Truc and I wander through the streets. We wander across the pretty, lighted river-bridge. We wander down a familiar road. We come to the house that belongs to the sporting family. A barking dog brings out first one sister, then another. We are invited in. Quite properly we decline. Tomorrow we are leaving Long Xuyen, tomorrow we are leaving An Giang. We have only come to bid adieu.

Monday 11th December: Long Xuyen–Soc Trang (Hau Giang Province) Tonight we will stay in Soc Trang, Sau Dai's native town, in Hau Giang, on the other side of the delta, further south and back near the sea. I have hardly put head to pillow when Truc is knocking on my door, bidding me rise. We make our way to Hai Vu's dwelling, a thirty-year-old villa in the suburbs. In front of the villa is a restaurant, his wife's business. Between the restaurant and the villa, a delightful garden. He is throwing bread into his pond when we arrive. Giant carp leap to catch the pieces. His mother, in her eighties, moves quietly on the veranda beyond, observing her son's curious guests. Coffee and loaves are served. There is a little tension in the air. Last night was so good, it is a hard act to follow. But it is not impossible. A little wickedly, Sau Dang suggests Hai Vu and I make each other a final toast. It is seven-forty in the morning. Vodka is prepared. We raise our glasses. We hug. It has nothing, or at least very little, to do with the Revolution.

The vodka though, combined with too many nights of too little sleep, wrong-foots the day ahead. Nothing goes very smoothly. On the way back to Can Tho the front right tyre bursts. There is an enormous hissing, an enormous screaming. Sau brings the Mazda to a halt just in front of – surprise surprise – a motor mechanic's shed. *Maa!* A typical southern trick. Business is sluggish, so scatter a few nails on the road! The hole in the tyre is as big as a shilling. But there is nothing we can do about it, other than accept the only 'help' available. Where is the proof – other than in the studied indifference of the mechanic himself? Even his children stare sullenly at the car, refraining from their typical exuberance. It wastes time as well as *dong* though, and Sau becomes bad tempered. He does not take kindly to being swindled. When the Mazda sets off again his sullen fury silences both Truc and myself. And nothing on the way to Soc Trang lifts any of our spirits.

We reach Soc Trang by one. Nicer than Chau Doc, it has nothing above average going for it. Like every other delta town, it straddles a congealed river. But the place lacks conviction in every aspect. The houses are tatty, the bridges are ugly, the people lacking in vivacity. For forty minutes Sau circles the town looking for his acquaintance, any acquaintance. Everyone it seems is out. Eventually we park in the high street, where Sau leaves messages at a shop selling socks and Taiwanese tennis shirts. Then we head out of town again, to lunch in a restaurant at the side of a scrawny park. The People's Committee directs us to a hotel on the river bank. Once again we are invited to stay free of charge. *And there won't be any history lessons.* Sau Dang has told them, I think, that he can teach me everything about Soc Trang I need to know.

I join Sau and Truc in a seventy-minute siesta. I have several vibrant dreams. Then, before I am fully awake, I am standing in the precincts of a Khmer Buddhist pagoda. There is something that Sau wants to show me, which is why he has brought me here. He directs my gaze upwards. A hurtful sunlight pours down through the upper branches of unusually high trees. I blink. Then I see what it is Sau Dang wants me to see. There are hundreds and hundreds of bats. Not the little things I saw in the tunnels of Cu Chi, but giants. Fox-bats in fact. Sau claps his hands. Thirty per cent of them leave their branches and make a swoop: like fragments of ancient, broken, black umbrellas.

Truc says they remind him of B52s. A weasel-faced fellow from the People's Committee tells me that the peculiarity of the pagoda is that although the bats live and sleep within its precincts, they never feed there. Conversely, they always return, to hang upside-down above the *nagas* of the vihara.

I look inside the pagoda itself: a darkened, gloomy place. At one end of the main prayer hall an elderly, bespectacled monk sits in a chair near a window. I approach him quietly. Is he asleep? Truc whispers to me that he is the abbot, that I should offer him some customary compliments. Putting my hands together to make a *wai*, I realize, a split second too late, that the figure in front of me is the most lifelike sculpture I will ever see. Nothing in Madame Tussaud's can compare. The abbot is all wood.

Truc and two saffron-robed monks laugh their heads off. The weasel-faced cadre, alarmed at my possible loss of face, explains. The figure is of the abbot who founded the pagoda a hundred years ago. The spectacles are those that he wore when he was alive. It is these that have fooled me. And in any case I have behaved 'correctly': it is right to compliment the venerable dead.

We pass out of the prayer hall and through a long shed which houses, like a parked bus, a ceremonial canoe, big enough to seat fifty-two oarsmen. All around, between the pagoda and the tradi-

362

tional Khmer tombs, hay is piled high. We bundle into the Mazda and drive on to a museum of Khmer handicrafts. Coffins, betel-nut baskets, ear-rings, sticks, animals made out of bamboo. The museum itself is new, installed in a small pagoda erected in 1940. To my chagrin I see the name of Prince Norodom Sihanouk heading the list of benefactors tabled on a wall. I cannot reasonably put the question I have been wanting to ask of the two ineffably courteous Khmer women who have shown me around the collection: what do they really think in their hearts of that self-serving piece of slime? Instead I have yet again to sign and inscribe a message in a visitors' book. For an awful minute I am totally stumped. I am pleased if at least some Khmer people have found security in this place far from their country, but I am also aware that in the delta museums like this are being promoted by the government largely to impress visitors that Vietnam is a tolerant, multi-racial, polyvalent society. And yet I know that not every minority has fared so well, and that there are many things that are not tolerated in Vietnam. For instance, freedom of the press, freedom of speech.

Weasel Face tells me that sixteen per cent of Soc Trang District's population is Khmer. They are not recent immigrants, but have lived here several generations. There is also a fair sprinkling of Chinese in the area. To make this point I am next taken to a Chinese temple, which in its essentials is remarkably similar to the Chinese temple I saw in Hoi An. I am not however taken to the Catholic pagoda, which we pass along the way.

Dinner is taken at the 'tourist' hotel, which is marginally more accommodating than the dump in Chau Doc. That is, the water is marginally less sticky. By now Sau Dang's friends – mainly Chinese – have materialized. The meal is oddly disjuncted. On the one hand Weasel Face, a perfectly sincere yet nervous young man, seems to think it is a formal banquet. On the other hand Sau's gang have set their hearts on a piss-up. Tonight is to be a hundred-cans-of-Heineken night. Weasel Face tries to tell me that Soc Trang is open to the West, that already there is a French joint venture afoot, but very soon he is drowned out in a wave of *chuk xu khoe*. It doesn't help that we are seated at opposite ends of the table, or that Truc appears as fatigued by propaganda as I am. When char-broiled pigs' testicles are served, Weasel Face gives up. Suddenly Truc suggests that if I like I can beg to be excused. I don't need prompting twice. With a flurry of compliments I rise to my feet and make for the door. Truc follows closely behind. He too wants out from Heineken.

Rebuffing the overtures of a prostitute on the staircase I make for my room. It is a rare opportunity to attend my journal. But as I sit at the desk writing what little there is to be said about Khmer pagodas and Chinese temples, I recall that my requests to visit Cao Dai and Hoa Hao churches are still unanswered.

As it happens I have no terribly deep interest in either of them. I am fairly certain that neither holds the key to Vietnam Now. But they become symbolic. They are the litmus test. They are what I've asked to see in the south. Whether I encounter them or not will determine the degree to which my 'programme' is simply or mainly propaganda; will determine the aperture of the 'open door'.

Tuesday 12th December: Soc Trang–Ca Mau (Minh Hai Province) Sau and his friends did get through a hundred cans of Heineken last night. Sau himself makes a great show of being none the worse for wear at breakfast. We leave Soc Trang at a reasonable hour. Weasel Face comes to the *khach san* to offer final compliments on behalf of the People's Committee. He looks more than ever like a man conscripted into the Italian priesthood on his mama's orders. We are headed for Ca Mau in the extreme south, the capital of the southernmost province, Minh Hai, and the last substantial town in Vietnam, the end of Highway One. There are no big ferries. The natural delta system peters out, although there is a grid of straight-cut canals some of which stretch over a hundred kilometres. To come across one, to go over one, is suddenly to rediscover the immensity of the land. For the land is dead flat. Between the canals the vegetation is scant. The lush foliage quickly gives way to scorched scrub.

In Hanoi Mr Hong voiced the opinion that I should go to Minh Hai not just for the formal purpose of seeing Vietnam 'from top to bottom', but also to learn of the extreme poverty of the toe. By eleven I already believe him. We pass through Minh Hai city, the former provincial capital, and arrive in Ca Mau just over an hour later.

Ca Mau is a scrappy clutter assembled on a bend of the Bai Hap. The Bai Hap is a river without true source. It is fed by the canals, and extends from coast to coast. Hardly it moves at all. We call at once on the People's Committee, where we are received by a sturdy Mr Hong. Truc impoliticly passes on my comments about the sticky water in Chau Doc. Sturdy Hong assures us that the water at the People's Guesthouse is as fresh as one could want. We go to the guesthouse. At last I have been barracked. Not only is the water as sticky as candy-floss, but it doesn't run at all. Try as hard as I may, I am unable to find a single tap in the entire building. The communal washing facilities consist of a row of concrete cubicles some of which have open tanks in them. It is not entirely clear which are the washrooms, and which are the toilets. My room is also exceptionally basic. The walls do not reach the ceiling and the mosquito net does not reach the mattress, which is crawling with fleas and other wildlife. A slow-moving fan merely advertises its senility. There is a desk, but no chair. Nor is there any glass in the windows, just dilapidated wooden slats.

A maid grudgingly brings me a Thermos of boiled water. I endeavour to make tea. The tea tasts of salt.

It is now that Truc tells me that we are to stay five days in Ca Mau. Five days! I gesticulate at my new surroundings. I can take five days of this, but there has got to be a good reason for it. Five days is longer than we have stayed anywhere since leaving Hanoi except Hué.

Lunch teaches me that there is nothing special about Ca Mau apart from the endemic poverty. Truc tries to tell me that the poverty is temporary, that it has been caused by a scandal. Two years back it was discovered that a majority of the provincial big potatoes were in the pocket of a former Thieu regime minister who had subverted them with consumer goods. But it doesn't wash. Minh Hai is poor because Minh Hai always has been poor and always will be poor. It's too hot, it's too flat, and the water doesn't work.

'Now come on. Tell me what it is we're supposed to be doing here for five days.'

Truc confers with Sturdy Hong. The answer seems to be that we are to spend three days in a mangrove swamp at the southern tip. It will take three days because the only way to get there is by boat. Off Highway One there are no roads that are serviceable.

'But we've had this conversation before. I've told you already that mangrove swamps are a complete waste of my time. I've visited mangrove swamps in Thailand and I've visited mangrove swamps in Indonesia and my appetite for mangrove swamps is satiated. They're all the same.'

There are worse fates than to be stuck in a mangrove swamp for three days, but my strong feeling is those three days would be better spent on extending my programme in Saigon. I'm not, as I remind my guide, here simply to enjoy myself.

Truc thinks for a moment, then replies:

'But Mr Hong would like you to do this.'

'Which Mr Hong?'

'Mr Hong in Hanoi.'

'Then he should have told me.'

'Anyway, it's too late. We've already negotiated with the People's Committee.'

'Then I suggest you renegotiate.'

This is only the beginning of a full-blown confrontation. It comes upon us like a typhoon, seemingly out of nowhere. The rest of lunch, which consists of steamed pork wisely smothered in a medicinal sauce, is spent wrangling. Sau Dai, who clearly thinks a prolonged sojourn among the mangroves would do me no end of good, becomes decidedly heated. But the more he insists the more Bolshie I feel.

'Negative attitudes' toward my programme in Vietnam now start crystallizing furiously into criticisms of how the government, at all levels, manages its affairs. Apart from anything, Vietnam is the most class-ridden society I have ever been in. It's not Marxist-Leninist so much as Leninist-Confucian. At the top you have the big potato elite, then come the cadres and the intelligentsia, then come the peasants. And there is very little movement between these tiers. It is also classically male chauvinist. The elite meanwhile does everything in its power to protect its position by parading its 'socialism'.

Probably though there are other reasons for my accidie.

Prolonged exposure to the heat. The humidity. The constant travelling. The constant drinking. The constant early starts. Cao Dai and Hoa Hao. Yet it all boils down to the fact that I am ready, if the wrong occasion presents itself, to explode. And the projected mangrove swamp has all the makings of just such a wrong occasion.

(Conversely, paradoxically, I am also having the time of my life; but that is another matter.)

We drop the sturdy member off at the committee buildings and return to the guesthouse. Sau, without directly thrusting at me, makes no great effort to conceal his dudgeon. I take the line that if he is going to give himself airs, then so am I. I pointedly incarcerate myself to my room, locking the door behind me. Sure enough, within twenty minutes Truc knocks on my 'window'. We go over much of the same ground. I show him the programme for the south originally prepared for me in Hanoi. Minh Hai is there, but there is no mention of a mangrove swamp. Truc responds by suggesting it is necessary for me to 'sing for my supper'.

'But that's wholly unfair. Who taught you that phrase anyway?'

'You did.'

'Then don't throw it back at me. And in any case, what if it's a supper I don't want?'

We talk about propaganda. I tell Truc there has got to be a balance. Hanoi must sing for its supper as well. I invite him to think of my tour as a joint venture. There should be an equal input from both sides. Otherwise I am simply being exploited. And why is it that, whenever we arrive in a new town, a new place, I am never made privy to the discussions about my programmes?

'There is a limit, you know.'

'You see, there is a problem here. Some while ago the Ministry brought some Russians to Ca Mau. The Russians also wanted to leave quickly.'

'And being Russians, they did?'

'You see, we have to improve our relations with the people of Minh Hai.'

'But that's nothing to do with me. Do you understand? All that has absolutely nothing to do with me!'

I am in a rage. Truc does understand. He is silent for a while. Then he says:

'You see, Sau Dai would really like to take you there.'

And that in a way is the crux of the matter. According to the Confucian code I should respect the wishes of my age-senior. For all the other complications are only that: complications. Truc doesn't as much as say this but his meaning is quite apparent.

It is my turn to observe a minute's silence. At the end of it I tell Truc:

'I have the greatest respect for Sau. You know that everybody loves him. But I am not going to spend three days in a mangrove swamp when, in my opinion, that time could be better spent doing other things. I'm sorry, but if I'm not to have any say in my programme then I'm going back to Saigon, I'm going back to Europe.'

Truc nods. I feel sorry for him, but hold my ground. We both know that I've now been in Vietnam long enough to have gathered more than enough material for my book. The argument is not of his making, yet he is having to take the flak. His first solo outing as an interpreter is turning out a baptism of fire. Meanwhile, in Hanoi, his mother is probably dying.

He leaves, and after five minutes comes back. Nothing can be settled until four o'clock, when Mr Sau will see the sturdy member again. Meanwhile I should relax.

I walk out of the guesthouse and toward the river, ostensibly to look for cigarettes. There are several shops and coffee houses. Their chief attribute is their material emptiness. Goods from China, Thailand and Singapore are conspicuous only by the absence. A market on the river bank is a market only in name. The thought crosses my mind that Minh Hai was the southern province the French and the Americans did nothing for, and that the new regime has opted to preserve it as it was for the purposes of demonstration. The only reason people live in a place like this is there isn't any room for them anywhere else. Ca Mau is a backyard town in a backyard province.

My perceptions of course are jaundiced by the argument I have been having. But even so every instinct tells me that the thoughts I have are true.

Four o'clock comes, and with it a tap on my door. Truc tells me he and Mr Sau have had another conversation with the People's Committee. A new programme has been arranged for me. Tomorrow I will receive a history lesson in the morning, and then see the local sights in the afternoon. On Thursday we will travel by boat to a plantation. We will return to Ca Mau on Friday, and set off for Saigon on Saturday.

'This plantation,' I ask: 'is it in fact a mangrove swamp?'

Fatally Truc, too honest for his own good, prevaricates.

'But I've told you, no mangrove swamp!'

'You see, I will have to speak to Sau Dang again.'

'Do it!'

The next three hours are difficult but instructive. We take an early dinner at five. Truc outlines my objections and my feelings to Sau. Sau listens, says nothing, appears to lose his appetite and leaves the table. I, once again, vent my anger on poor Truc. Truc takes the line, which I assume is also Sau Dang's line, that the poverty of Minh Hai is insufficient reason to reject its hospitality, which is offered sincerely and from the heart. I reply that I am both aware and appreciative of the hospitality I've received not just in Minh Hai, but in every other province. But the point remains I haven't come to Vietnam to savour hospitality, I've come to find out about Vietnam now, *Viet Nam bay gio*. Truc asks, begs, me to consider his and Mr Sau's position. They have their instructions from Hanoi. They are simply not in a position to reconstruct my programme. But if that is true, I say, then why, when I was in Saigon, didn't I meet any of the people I had requested to meet when I was in Hanoi?

'But we are going back to Saigon. You still have a Saigon programme.'

'Exactly. But there won't be time for it if I spend all this time down here.'

Truc side-tracks into a long digression about the complexities of the relationships that exist inside the Company, that exist between Mr Hong, Zoom, Nguyen, Sau and himself, to name but five. Age, length of service, seniority, Party or non-Party membership and family connections are all factors. I say, that's all very interesting, but my relationship is with the Company as a whole, not with its individual ligaments.

369

'You see, it is a great pity that Mr Hong is not here.'

'But that being the case, authority should have been delegated to someone who is.'

We start to go round in circles. We have been going round in circles all along. In exasperation I tell Truc that I want a conversation with Sau Dang, one to one. As Sau does not speak English, Truc will have to interpret. But I tell him, he must only interpret. The conversation must be between myself and Sau and no one else.

Truc, I think with some relief, agrees to this. In a minute he calls me to Sau Dang's room. Sau is reading when I enter and continues reading when I sit on the bed next to his. (There are no chairs.) Through Truc, I reiterate much of what I have said before. Most strongly I express the view that I should be present whenever my programme is discussed. Again I employ the joint-venture analogy. After all, at the end of the day, however many freebies we get at the guesthouses, I shall still have to pay for the gasoline, the food and for the Company employees' time.

Sau does nothing to hide his ill humour, but at least he listens. His eyes do not move across the lines of print in his book. At length he asks me who it is I want to meet in Saigon. My list is to hand. It includes Cao Dai and Hoa Hao. Sau, without changing his expression, mutters that he will do the best he can.

The audience is over. I retire to my room before I altogether lose control of myself. Again it is not long before Truc knocks on my door. He is ready with a new tack, one that I think is entirely his own. I must, he says, understand Cochin people. To them, giving hospitality is far more important than maximizing their time and energies for business ends.

'That is why, perhaps, Vietnam is so poor. But it is our way.'

Conceivably there is a profound truth in this. A related notion has already found its way into my notes: 'The south will always nurture corruption because the south will always drink every cent it hasn't got.' But it is a truth that is also, for my purposes, a red herring.

I give Truc a much harder look than he deserves.

'Fuck it,' I tell him. 'That is not what I learned in Hanoi.'

Truc goes off to have more words with Mr Sau. There is now quite a long pause before he returns. Inevitably I mull everything

370

over. But if I conclude that I am within my rights to make a stand, I am also bitter about the wedge that it has driven into my 'team'. Arguing with Sau, whether directly or vicariously, is curiously debilitating, curiously corrosive.

Sau and Truc meanwhile have evidently concluded that the real cause of my distemper is the lack of shower-room facilities at the guesthouse. I have just decided to go to sleep without availing myself of the *mandi* at the end of the corridor when both appear at my door. Sau knows of a place I can have a steam bath. Would I like to come? My initial impulse is to say no I wouldn't, but of course I cannot be so churlish.

Sau continues sullen, but in a way this only emphasizes his magnanimity. We drive over the river to a 'tourist' hotel in the main street. By night Ca Mau is a good deal more appetizing than it is by day. The steam bath though also entails having a massage in what looks like a bedroom. No massage, no steam bath. The girl, who is nineteen and tolerably pretty, indicates a willingness to remove her clothes. For a few moments I am tempted. It would be one way to burn off the day's anger. But quickly I tell her to keep them on. If it's dollars she wants then I'll give her some dollars. The frustration fuck is not something that would go down too well at home. But also I have been eavesdropping on the conversation of three Australian Vietnamese, holidaying in the land of their birth, at the bar outside. They have come in through Bangkok. Both there, and here in Ca Mau, they have been disporting themselves. Or so they brag. It would, I suppose, be an irony of sorts, if impoverished, backward Minh Hai were to prove the first portal of AIDS in this country.

Wednesday 13th December: Ca Mau My minders are admirable. They resolutely refuse to allow our quarrel to become personal. First thing Truc brings me a shaving-bowl and a couple of Thermos flasks. Nor, when we arrive at the People's Committee, is there any sign of ill feeling. The reverse in fact. The committee is there in force to greet me. I count no fewer than seven potatoes around me when I take my place at the long table. Tran Nam Doan, the director of the Voice of Minh Hai, leads the compliments. He also delivers most of the lecture, although there is rather more discussion between members than at other long tables. I sense that because of the scandal my hosts are relatively inexperienced and need to feel their way forward collectively in a situation that is more unusual for them than it has become for me.

The obvious geographic statements are made with a flourish. Minh Hai is the 'peninsular' province, it has 307 kilometres of coastline, there are the two main towns, Ca Mau and Minh Hai (Bac Lieu), and nine districts comprising sixty villages. The land, 7,697 square kilometres of it, is relatively new. It has been created by silt from the Mekong Delta. There is not a single mountain, nor any hills to speak of. Until three hundred years ago it was largely uninhabited. 'But the Viet people came south to develop the land with a very strong will.' During the French period many farmers fled to Minh Hai in order to escape their evil landlords in more arable regions. The population today is in excess of one and a half million. Among the 'advantages' of Minh Hai are agriculture, sea products and 'the forests'. The forests comprise mainly mangrove swamps. Salt water is the abiding headache. Two-metre tides exacerbate the 'hydrological problem'. The only fresh water is rain, or 'sweet water'. But transport is not so difficult. The French saw to that, with their incredible canals, incorporating 'anti-saline dams'. Since 1975 there has been a programme to renovate the waterways. But the dams are expensive, and new canals have to be cut without them. Regularly the sea floods the land, particularly on the east coast, where, at high tide, it is only seventy centimetres above sea-level.

The committee turns to the revolutionary history of Minh Hai. The chief point they wish to make is the endemic destruction of the mangrove swamps by American herbicides. The jungle-thick swamps gave the Viet Cong perfect cover, and in its exasperation the enemy could only drench the land with chemicals from the sky. Earlier in the century there were several uprisings, directed against the puppet mandarins. The first Party cells were established in the 1930s. But because of the distance from Saigon and other revolutionary centres it was sometimes hard to co-ordinate activities in Minh Hai with what was going on in the rest of the country. Even so, at the end of 1930, fifty-nine years ago to the day, Khoai Island was successfully seized from the French, and held for nine days. Subsequently, ten revolutionaries were executed. And during the August Revolution, Minh Hai was liberated on the same day as Hué, and two days before Saigon.

In the American war the Viet Cong often lived right in the villages. 'Our heroes were the fish, the people were the sea,' says Tran Nam Doan, adopting Mao Tse Tung's saying. During the Tet Offensive the whole province rebelled, and nearly fell. The counter-offensive was launched in 1969, at the same time that Ho Chi Minh died. But Ho's death proved only a spur. 'Our sorrow renewed our determination.' Throughout the province Ho Chi Minh shrines appeared in the villages. These aroused the Saigon Army and focused the fighting. A well-placed, conspicuous shrine drew the enemy forward, sometimes into a trap. 'Thus Uncle Ho, even though he was dead, continued to help us in our struggle.'

But the Viet Cong could not spend all their time in the villages. I ask, how did they secure salt-free water? The committee takes time out for a round-table discussion. Eventually a list of six solutions is proposed: 1) the VC carried canisters of purified water; 2) they boiled salt water and used only the steam; 3) they drank rain-water in the rainy season; 4) they shook water off the trees whenever the trees were wet; 5) they got supplies from the villagers; and 6) a few of them bored wells.

I ask about the scandal. The committee confers, but seems unable to agree on a 'correct' answer. All that I am told is that it involved the vice-director of the Cimexcol wood trading company. Many big potatoes got roasted. The wrong man, a Thieu regime character, had been appointed to the wrong job at the wrong time (just after 1986 and the promulgation of *doi moi*). There was subsequently a 'violation of state property': 'In the new atmosphere we were not so careful about someone's background.' As a conse-quence a debt amounting to several million dollars – a substantial proportion of the annual Minh Hai budget – was run up 'at the bank'. Provincial finances are still recovering.

Finally we discuss my programme. I have agreed with Sau Dang beforehand that an open discussion is the only solution. I prepare my ground though. The committee has told me that Minh Hai needs all the help it can get. I tell the committee of my meeting

373

with Ben Fawcett of Oxfam, and that I'll do what I can to draw his organization's attention to Minh Hai's plight. I then tell the committee that I simply have to get back to Saigon by the weekend. I'm dying to see the mangrove swamp, but . . . well, there are forty-six provinces in Vietnam, and my time is limited. A compromise is reached. Tomorrow I will be taken to a collective swamp on a one-day trip. I can leave for Saigon on Friday. Everybody is happy.

There is no escaping southern hospitality. After lunch I am taken first to a new monument commemorating the ten heroes executed by the French for their misdemeanours in 1930, then to a state/provincial pharmaceutical company, housed in a training camp for new recruits built by the Saigon Army. It was turned over to its present beneficial use immediately after Reunification. Now it has a workforce of 120, including 12 chemists. Fifty per cent of its output is traditional, fifty per cent 'modern' (including a species of ampicillin). The traditional products include several different kinds of snake-wine. Behind the buildings is a lake where the snakes are raised. Since I am here it is suggested that I might like to sample not only some snake-wine, but also some snake-meat. In the middle of the lake is a pavilion, and although it is not yet four o'clock, in the pavilion a party convenes. An extraordinary banquet is served, appearing it seems out of nowhere. Various delicacies are thrust upon me. As well as shredded snake-flesh I am invited to try turtle's egg and turtle's brain. I am not altogether sure that along the way I do not also sample bat's ribs. And all this of course is fatal. To secure maximum efficacy the snake-wine (for which I am fast developing an inordinate taste) must be mixed with rice-alcohol. Each time I lift a hitherto unexplored foodstuff to my mouth, the toasts ring out. By five o'clock, all of us, eight or nine fellows, are roaring drunk. And once you're drunk, that's when the toasts begin in earnest. The ripples fanning out across the lake from the supports of the pavilion become small waves. Work for the day has been abandoned, if indeed it ever began. The plant's director tells me that his outfit is in difficulties. 'Today,' he tells me plaintively, 'is maintenance day' – which is why all the laboratories are empty. But then he divulges the real reason. The factory achieved its peak production targets in 1986. In 1986 it produced thirty million tablets, and a hundred and fifty million injection shots. But since 1986 there has been a steady decline. The problem has been competition from the new private sector. People would rather buy ampicillin imported from Thailand. So really, what else is there to do except sit around all afternoon in a pavilion drinking snake-wine?

Sau eats the turtle-head. Truc's point about the southern disinclination for work is made with stunning force. So much so that in a rare lucid moment it occurs to me that this is exactly what the Ministry of Information wants me to witness. It is one way to make me appreciate the necessity of Hanoi's intervention in the country at large.

Afterwards we transfer ourselves and our belongings from the guesthouse to the tourist hotel in the main street. Miraculously my room has a shower that works. Also, being on the topmost of four floors, it has a view over the rest of Ca Mau. It is not an unpleasant perch. The only problem is when I open my door. There is invariably a woman waiting behind it. Southern hospitality threatens to continue all night.

Thursday 14th December: Ca Mau–Thoi Binh We are up very very early. We have ninety kilometres of river-riding ahead of us. I go down to breakfast with a strange sentence lodged in my brain: 'Those candidates with high female relatives should sit elsewhere.' Waiting for Truc and Sau, I am accosted by a distressed Frenchman. In Saigon he trades garments. He has come down to Minh Hai for a holiday. But his minders have failed to acquire the proper papers for him, and now the police are demanding a hundred dollars. *Merde!*

The river is magic. We set off shortly after six. Excluding the boatman, who rides at the back of what is little more than a motorized canoe, there are five voyagers. Sau Dang, sitting just in front of the boatman, then Sturdy Hong, then Truc, then myself and finally, at the front of the craft, Bon. Bon is a committee member, and an ex-soldier, a thin fellow exactly my age. His features are not unlike ministry Nguyen's. His hallmark however is an Australian army hat, which he wears slung round his neck.

375

We all face forward. The boatman steers us at what, just a few inches off the water, seems a cracking pace. As we make our way through the narrow water-lanes of Ca Mau at dawn we wash a few doorsteps in our wake. The mostly wooden buildings tumble forward. Sau nurses his rifle. Truc, barely awake, reads. Bon, squatting on his haunches, keeps his eyes on the path ahead. A piece of driftwood could ruin our day.

Scarcely it is light. But once out of Cau Mau the sun stands up to warm our backs. We are travelling north-west, along the Chac Bang toward our first port of call, Thoi Binh. The river is like a road. Dwellings gravitate naturally toward it. There are shops along the way, occasionally a restaurant, a place with a table or two that sells noodles and rice. But everything is strung out. Apart from the many small craft passaging the water, evidence of humanity is scant. One is aware though of villages buried in the hinterland: the horizon trails those tell-tale snakes of smoke. There are also, at regular intervals, slim canals cut through the banks — tunnels through the earth's coarse green hair; and fronds of a magnitude and hue that would ravish an artist's eye.

By eight-thirty, when we arrive at Thoi Binh, the day is already in a swelter. There is no breeze on the river. The sun burns our faces off the water, and we have all cut banana leaves to cover our necks. The district People's Committee convenes quickly. We are invited to breakfast across the way. Thoi Binh being at a junction betwixt river and canal, there is a high iron bridge to the market on another bank. Without expecting anything I suddenly find myself looking up the canal from an elevated position. Fifty kilometres of waterway stretch in a dead straight line over the horizon north-eastwards into the next province up, Kien Giang. Taking the finest scenic photograph of my Vietnam journey, I can hardly believe that such majesty exists in so flat a country.

The committee treats us to coffee and rolls, and grants permission to travel onward — but only on condition that we call in again on our return journey. By half past nine we are back on the water. We stick to the river, which from Thoi Binh continues its north-westerly course. Accompanied by squadrons of dragonflies, the going is very slightly harder. There is more flotsam in the increasingly brackish water, and sometimes we must pause to unfoul the propeller. My

376

Swiss army knife proves somewhat more effective than Sau Dai's gun, which brings him no luck at all. The river traffic also thins out. We are on the way to Song Trem, a state-run 'wild farm'. Truc tells me I will see plenty of bees there. Discombobulated by the heat, I wonder whether there will be special hives for the Party drones.

We arrive shortly after eleven. We are not expected – there are no telephones down here, all messages must be put aboard a boat – but we are welcomed nonetheless. The farm's manager gives me a mercifully brief introduction. We are forty-three kilometres from Ca Mau. There are 10,200 hectares, and the collective supports six hundred working families. The specialities are forestry and fishing. All kinds of fruit are grown, all kinds of fish are caught. The whole is interlaced by a grid of canals created in 1984. Before 1984 there were no canals. Before 1984 Song Trem was VC country.

The manager would like to give us lunch, but we must give him time to organize his kitchen staff. In the meantime, it is suggested, we should take a look round part of the plantation. We climb back into the boat and set off up one of the minor canals. Again it is a dead-straight corridor, although at points the water is so congested with organic debris that it might be more appropriate to call it vegetable soup. After five kilometres we reach a T-junction. There is an empty leaf-roofed wooden house, a netball pitch and a fifty-metre-high iron look-out tower which Bon and Sturdy Hong invite me to climb. When I reach the top I am, I suppose, at the technical end of my journey. I will go no further from Hanoi than this. In a sense I am the luckiest of men, although for a moment this is the mind's appreciation, not yet the heart's. All around me stretches a great carpet, a well-smoothed duvet of ordered jungle. The 'farm' is scarcely profitable, but I can see that the Vietnamese are also capable of executing large-scale projects.

We return to the farm's headquarters. Lunch is rice and beer and a congees of stewed eel. Afterwards we watch a video, made by Can Tho Television. A generator is cranked up. For twenty minutes we watch a mishmash of agricultural propaganda and recreated wartime episodes, linked by two young singers who probably are in love. Then Sau decides enough is enough. In any case, there is another film in the collective's library, a film starring Sau Dang himself, in a supporting role. But Sau does not appear on the screen. Try as hard as he may he cannot find the spot. *Ma!* The video player today is no better than his rifle, and the day is not long enough to watch the film in its entirety.

On the other hand the day has been long enough for the People's Committee in Thoi Binh to prepare a banquet. The table is already laid when our boat moors shortly after four. There is chicken and duck and a lot more eel. Sau Dang, nursing triumph, because he has after all inveigled me through at least one mangrove swamp, and milking his celebrity status, makes a speech. Truc, himself a little radiant, nudges me. This, he says, is positively my last People's Committee, and Sau is telling the assembled host of my passage through Vietnam, from Hué where he met me, but also from Cao Bang in the far north. 'Nuoc Lenin' is repeated several times. All cadres beam approvingly. Then the glasses are raised.
  'Is this really the end of it?' I ask Truc.
  'Yes,' says Truc. 'This is really the end of your journey.'
  'Then,' says I, 'let's get pissed!'
  I make a speech myself. I pay homage to the tradition of national hospitality. I inaugurate my own flow of toasts, which of course incites others. More bottles of vodka are sent for from the committee's store-room. In particular I am led into a maze of *cham phan cham*s with Bon. Bon has discovered that one of the local men is also our age, forty, and so we must drink to that. Men of the same age are brothers, and three is a lucky number . . .
  Sau's face explodes with pleasure. He recognizes that at last I have decided to unrein myself. I have embraced the customs of Cochinchina. Yet even so I am not so drunk I entirely forget myself. At what I deem the appropriate moment I make the presentation. I give my water flask, which I have carried from Pac Bo and the pool outside Ho Chi Minh's cave, to the People's Committee of Thoi Binh. It is theirs to keep, a memento of the mad Englishman who brought the good *nuoc* from Cao Bang to Minh Hai. There is not a dry eye in the house.
  The light is already going when we stumble toward the water. Many hands lower me down into the boat, into Sau's arms in fact. Bon sits in front of me, and then Truc, and then Sturdy Hong. The

boatman, guiding us slowly away from the bank with the stick-engine he uses as a rudder, becomes a gondolier. The dying sun touches the faces of those who watch our departure. I might have lived in Thoi Binh ten years, such is the sadness of the send-off. But Sau tightens his grip. For him there is only cause to rejoice. For the next three hours I become his son, and he my father. For a while he absolutely refuses to let me move. I am his, I belong to Vietnam, and fellowship is Vietnam's strongest suit.

As darkness envelops the river the boat slows. At all costs we must avoid colliding with another. Some vessels display tiny oil lamps, others do not. Stars come out, but there are clouds that hide them. We move nearer the right-hand bank, to get in lane. Sometimes among the reeds we spy courting couples in smaller boats. Ripples give them away. Bon all but capsizes us when he stands up to pee. The echo of our engine, bouncing off the banks, is curious in the extreme: a high-pitched babble of children's voices, turned down. I remember My Lai and Binh Hoa and Ba Chuc. I also remember sitting on the heights above the valley on the way out of Phan Rang.

The feeling of fellowship – five men in a man's world with three sheets to the wind – intensifies: a chauvinism that is perhaps grotesque, but which is also entirely pure. I think: if this is how it was between the Viet Cong, no wonder they won! I lean forward and massage Bon's back. Sau takes the opportunity to empty his bladder into the river, then reclaims me. Truc swaps places with Bon and reclines in *my* arms. As the air chills, the heat of our bodies, which we give to each other, becomes exactly measurable. A phrase runs repeatedly through my head: *the innocence of the ordinary soldier.* I think to myself, what if this were twenty years ago, and one of us were wounded? We'd be lying here in the dark holding each other just as we hold each other now. Only we wouldn't be talking. We'd all have our ears primed for the distant patrol vessel.

With great excitement Sau draws my attention to a mulberry tree festooned with twinkling silkworms on the opposite bank. 'Christmas,' Truc translates. And then the outskirts of Ca Mau loom up on both sides, not an electric light to be seen, just the odd stray beam from an oil lamp, mingling with voices and catcalls.

And ridiculously, hanging above Ca Mau, a perfectly ponderous Dutch cheese of a moon.

And even that is not the end of it. At the tourist hotel there must be yet another banquet. Bon's brother brokers king prawn, and I must eat a bucket of the things, grilled over a charcoal fire. Also, the Chief of Police wants to meet us. Or at least, he wants to meet Sau. I think about raising the case of the distressed Frenchman, but decide this is not the moment. There are more toasts, more *chuk xu khoe*. A bottle of Russian brandy is furnished. But the odd thing now is the more I drink the more sober I become. The logic that I have been resisting for so long overtakes me at the last.

Friday 15th December: Ca Mau–Saigon   Saigon days again! We should be back in Ho Chi Minh City by nightfall, it's a 300-kilometre day, but even so our start, for some technical-bureaucratic reason, is delayed. While Truc and Sau sort it out a prostitute sits at my breakfast table. She tells me, in not altogether unconvincing English, that she has a problem. One of her clients has given her some money she 'doesn't understand'. I tell her to show it me. Discreetly she passes me a hundred franc note. So very French.

Ten kilometres outside Ca Mau the Mazda punctures. This time it's probably not a trick. There is not a repair shop in sight. Sau spends forty minutes changing the wheel. Then it's forward rather sharply. We hurtle back to the delta. Sau wants to have lunch with his friends in Soc Trang.

We have lunch with Sau Dang's friends. They are Chinese and surprisingly candid. They welcome *doi moi*, they say, yet they cannot quite believe it. Two of them have been through re-education camps. Another has a brother who has yet to be released. One of them describes himself as a former 'rice king', until 1979, when his possessions, his various properties, were all confiscated. The anti-Chinese movement left no stone unturned. Yet, although 'they' spent five years re-educating him, and although his wife is emigrating to America, he is still willing to try. 'I am Chinese, but Vietnam is my country. It is the only thing for me to do.'

The table talk reveals other aspects of recent history in the south. Before 1986, before *doi moi*, there were police road-blocks everywhere. Anyone caught carrying more than fifty kilos of rice had the surplus seized on the spot, 'as tax'. And yet at the time there was a 'big' black-market trade in rice between the south and the north. Many senior provincial officials were involved in its control. For them the road-blocks didn't exist. The trouble now is that, with the advent of an open market, the big potatoes must find other ways of making up their income. And that, it is impressed upon me, is what the 'Minh Hai scandal' was all about.

Truc translates. Sau, to my surprise, listens interestedly. Not so long ago he admonished me about 're-education types'. And yet here we are, sitting at a table with some of them, hearing them out. And I can't believe it's just that they are Chinese, and not more obvious leftovers from the Saigon regime. Rather it is a part of that enormously complicated pattern that affects all Vietnamese society, in which there is a fine, precarious balance of forces between all the conflicting loyalties that constitute the individual's life; a pattern I doubt whether any outsider can fully comprehend.

We hit the road again. Sau steams forward, squeezing the last ounce of power out of the embattled Mazda. At the ferry-stops luck is with us. We never have more than a few minutes to wait. We reach Saigon by seven. At Sau's apartment we unload a sack of rice that has been cradled in the boot. Truc offers to carry it up the stairs on his back. The sack bursts open. Sau's children come down to scoop the grain off the floor. We repair to a down-market, outdoor noodle bar. One beer is as much as any of us wants. I am left at the villa off Ky Dong Street. The owners welcome me with happy smiles. My room is waiting for me. If only because I can recognize it, it is a kind of home.

Saturday 16th December: Saigon Before I ever left Britain I promised Martha Gellhorn I would visit the 'Burn' Hospital. Gellhorn is a distinguished war correspondent. She as much as anyone perfected the modern deadpan manner of depicting man's inhumanity to man. Her writing always cuts the mustard. Of Vietnam she has written, 'It was the only war I reported on the wrong side.' Now she is the *grande dame* of her profession. But she has lost none of her fire, none of her ice. When I ring her at her home in London's Cadogan Square, a voice snaps impatiently at me. For a moment I think I've got through to Elaine Stritch. When I mention Vietnam however, and what I want to do there, the voice adjusts. Even so, Gellhorn wastes no time sorting me out. At once she compares the United States' involvement in Indochina to the behaviour of a drunken driver who has ploughed his vehicle into a row of bystanders. Simple justice demands that compensation for the injuries sustained be paid. 'But the US government just has no interest whatsoever in *people*.' Perhaps I'm not interested in people either, Gellhorn, who is also an American, suggests. But if I am then I should visit the Burn Hospital in Saigon/Ho Chi Minh City and write it up.

In the evening, after an empty day, I visit the Burn Hospital or, as it's now called, the Tu Du. Since Sau Dang knows one of the vice-directors, Madame Nguyen Thi Ngoc Phuong, I have no difficulty in gaining admittance. Dr Phuong, who is also a deputy to the National Assembly, receives me in her office. There is no need for an interpreter. She has worked at the Tu Du for twenty-one years. She is a gynaecologist and an obstetrician. She is also an abandonee. Her husband fled to Paris in 1974. In 1980 he came back to ask her to join him. She refused. So he left alone again. Madame Phuong hopes he will return again one day, but rather doubts it. From what she's heard he's found a new wife. C'est la vie. For her the important thing is her work.

Her work is geared to one great end: to demonstrate beyond reasonable doubt that the abnormally high incidence of birth defects in the delta region is related to the use of chemical weapons by American and Saigonese forces during the 1960s and early 1970s. If she can do this, then some form of compensation might one day be forthcoming.

Of 20,446 babies born in the hospital, three hundred she believes have suffered abnormalities that may be attributable to the war. The crucial statistic is comparative. In north Vietnam and the rest of SE Asia the ratio of mutants to healthy babies is 1:500; but among southern Vietnamese known to have lived in villages sprayed with Agent Orange and other herbicides, the incidence rises to 4%. 'Something,' says Dr Phuong, 'has got to be wrong somewhere.'

Equally as disconcerting are the illnesses prevalent among adult women. Among her own patients there have been 2,000 cases of chronic carcinoma during pregnancy. The majority of these have been correlated to those areas that suffered the worst bombing and spraying; and again, the percentage figure is out of all proportion to SE Asian norms. Dioxin levels in fat tissue tell the same story. In north Vietnam (where no Agent Orange was deployed) there is no significant presence of dioxin. Among those women found to have chronic carcinoma at the Tu Du, the level averages at 22.4 parts per million. This correlates closely with US servicemen hospitalized in America as a result of being in the wrong place at the wrong time. In their case the average fat-tissue dioxin level is 24 parts per million. In both cases it must be assumed that aggregate levels were higher in the past: the half-life of dioxins once they are established in the human body is not fully known.

Dr Phuong has been assisted in her research by European and North American pathologists. They too entertain no doubts about her thesis. Proper studies making use of control groups have been carried out. The real difficulty is one of attitude. The United States is unwilling to admit even limited culpability.

'It's all to do with the trade embargo,' says Dr Phuong. 'You see, after all this time, it's still a crime for an American to sell one Vietnamese one aspirin.'

Meanwhile the Tu Du, like every other hospital in Vietnam, suffers chronic shortages of funds, drugs and specialist skills. Even microscopes are lacking.

We talk about other medical problems, other illnesses. I ask whether as yet there have been any cases of AIDS in Vietnam, or SIDA as it is known, following French terminology. For a moment Dr Phuong is optimistic. No, none as yet. A team of French medics has tested 20,000 'high-risk elements' in Saigon, and 10,000 others have received mandatory testing for the Orderly Departure Program. So far nobody is HIV positive. But she knows it is only a matter of time. Tourism has its drawbacks. The incidence of venereal diseases, having dropped since 1975, is on the rise again.

'And what am I supposed to do then?' she asks. 'How will we manage? With our resources? With our equipment?'

I am not taken on a guided tour of Tu Du hospital. For that I must wait until Monday. Instead we go in search of grilled oysters. Truc is in low spirits. Hanoi has telephoned to tell him his mother's condition has deteriorated. Would I mind if he left a day or two early? Sau Dang will arrange another interpreter. I tell him to take the first plane he can get a seat on.

Sunday 17th December: Saigon   At a civilized hour Truc comes to the villa. His spirits are marginally improved. He will fly home on Monday, tomorrow. Since he has nothing else to do in Saigon he volunteers to show me around some more. We go downtown on the clapped-out Honda and hang about inside the Museum of the Saigon Revolution, formerly Diem's Presidential Palace. Ho Chi Minh in all his costumes stares out from all the walls: a manikin for all seasons. We look at the secret passage that Diem had constructed in the cellar. The man always knew how his end was likely to come. Afterwards, for an absurd price, we have coffee outside in a small, noisy park. Truc accompanies me back to the villa to use my shower. He has been staying in Soviet Nghe Tinh Street, where the amenities are on a par with those at the People's Guesthouse in Ca Mau. Much of the afternoon is spent delving into Truc's family background. Because of his mother's condition he has need to talk. He confides that his father was 'a servant of the French'. In 1954 he regrouped south. His mother however stayed behind in Hanoi, to keep one eye on the family property. Because of all this life was difficult for Truc and his siblings until 1986. Sometimes, life still is difficult.

'Are you a capitalist?' he suddenly asks, out of the blue.

'I'm not sure,' I reply. 'In some respects, yes. Capitalism is pretty good at producing wealth, though it perpetuates poverty as well.'

'But are you a capitalist?'

'What do you mean?'

'Do you ever buy things and sell them again?'

'Everybody does that once in a while.'

Truc nods, and ruminates on what I've said.

'You see,' he says at length, 'everyone in Vietnam is a capitalist.'

We have dinner at Sau Dai's palace. Sau is in the highest of spirits. Number one, he is proud to offer dinner to a foreigner.

Number two, he has just heard that his daughter is coming home from Moscow, where she has been studying. Quite apart from normal paternal anxieties, Sau Dang is clearly concerned about events in Eastern Europe which, unlike the majority of Vietnamese, he is in a position to know about and follow. He says that because there are so many overseas Vietnamese working on scholarships in eastern bloc countries, 'there must be trouble in the future'. Many of them are tomorrow's intelligentsia, and in cities like Berlin, Warsaw, Prague and even Moscow they are bound to have picked up 'too many ideas'. But his own little girl is returning, and for Papa Sau that is enough.

When at home Sau delights to play the family man. A fine duck curry has been prepared by himself. Now that I am a temporary son, he insists I eat a proper amount of bananas. His wife, though she never sits, sometimes hovers about the table. A bag of apples that I purchased as a gift across the road is treated with inordinate respect. They are first offered to Sau's ancestors, at a small altar on the sideboard. Candles and joss-sticks are lit. The apples must not be eaten, Truc explains, until the joss-sticks have burnt right down.

Later, I give Truc a list of the people I still want to interview in Hanoi, for him to pass on to Zoom or Mr Hong. There are about a dozen items, including requests for contacts with the Ministry of Justice and the Ministry of the Interior, and a reminder of the Transport College affair. Truc looks at the list and pockets it. His mind is on other things. There is the matter of his mother, and there is the matter of his job. He knows that I will be asked how he fared with me in the south, but of course he cannot ask directly. Like many who put safety first, Truc is prone to insecurity. Perhaps because of this he has taught me as much about Vietnam as anyone. I say goodbye with a hug. I cannot say it either, but when I do get back I'll root for him like hell.

Monday 18th December: Saigon With Truc gone, there is a lull in my affairs, although this does not become immediately apparent. In the morning Sau takes me back to the Tu Du for a tour of the wards. We are joined by Michael Fathers, Asia editor of *The Independent*, and his not-very-bright, gigglesome interpreter, I think another Nguyen. The interpreter however is unnecessary. At the hospital, wearing white coats, we are escorted by one of Madame Phuong's juniors, who is also called Dr Phuong and speaks good technical English. In the carcinoma ward I look at two rows of women, many of them brought in from rural districts, some of whom will shortly die. This year alone there have been twenty-seven deaths. What arouses my pity is the condition they are lying in. The room is clean, tolerably bright, and the staff does everything in its power to nurse them. But there are absolutely no frills. No television, no radio, no books, no flowers. There are simply no funds for such things. For the most part the women lie on their sides looking at each other's backs, all day every day.

Em Phuong takes us through more wards, then ushers us into the little room of horrors. Michael Fathers takes one step in and two steps out. 'I'm no good at this sort of thing,' he mutters. Around the walls are shelves and on the shelves are glass jars. Inside the jars, perhaps a gallon cubic capacity each, or a gallon and a half, are deformed foetuses and infants. But *so* deformed. They are like circus dwarfs wearing funny latex masks modelled by the makers of *Spitting Image*. In some jars all the space is taken up by imploded heads. In some it is other outsized parts of the anatomy that prevail. There are several pairs of Siamese twins, and other bundles of limbs that may represent triplets or even greater conglomerations. Infant mortality in the grotesque mode. In the worst jars though, there are little faces of great beauty, deprived of life because everything else about them turned out wrong.

Put thou my tears into thy bottle. In fact, I have been wrong-footed. I have seen footage of this display before, as I'm sure Fathers has. Like My Lai, the room is something the government likes visiting television crews to film. I should have known I would bump into what is probably the world's greatest dead freak show sooner or later. I just wasn't thinking. Where else?

I go with Sau to his office to sort out my money – then I share lunch with Fathers at a dull, modern canteen in the old Rue Catinat. When one of us shifts the salt-cellar, we find the word 'AIDS' scratched on the Formica table-top underneath.

'Well, what about that!'

'Yes,' says Fathers, 'what about that?'

We do not especially hit it off. Fathers is an old Saigon hand, I am not a Saigon hand at all. We see things from different perspectives. Fathers lived in the city in the early '70s, though he has returned a few times since. He seems deeply unimpressed by the level of material culture achieved by the Revolution. Nonetheless he offers me a window on the past. He concedes that Ho Chi Minh City is staging something of a recovery, 'but it still has a long way to go'. In the early to mid-'80s, life here was 'simply awful'. There was nothing like enough food, never mind about consumer goods. The Mekong Delta farmers were 'disgusted' with how little the government was prepared to offer for their produce, and consequently cut back on production. They grew only enough to feed themselves and their families. They even went as far as slaughtering their bullocks, rather than rearing them for the Party to steal. A lot of the problems stemmed from Hanoi's decision to send down its own managers to manage everything. 'The managers were simply incompetent. They didn't know the first thing about the delta, the first thing about farming or the first thing about management.' The crack-down on former regime employees was as unrelenting as it was hard. 'Most of the shops here were closed. It was a city full of ghosts.'

We trade a few, but not too many, notes, and wend our separate ways. There is nothing for me to do except hang about downtown for a while, mainly in Le Loi Street, and examine the stalls. The bazaar is generalized. On one corner I see a bank of Rambo T-shirts hanging above a quantity of second-hand hypodermic syringes spread out on the sidewalk on a dirty sheet. The juxtaposition is probably the image of Saigon I shall always carry with me.

At exactly the right moment my friendly cyclo driver appears out of thin air and spirits me back to the villa. I work all evening, I work all night.

Tuesday 19th December: Saigon   Ca Mau water has caught up with me at last. My oesophagus burns all the way down to the stomach. Plus I have the beginnings of an Asian flu. I spend two hours in Sau's office waiting for Le Duc Tho's secretary to return our call. Le Duc Tho is the super-big-potato interview I won't leave Saigon without. No call. Sau and I communicate almost entirely by pulling silly faces at each other. At eleven-thirty we decamp to a poorer restaurant around the corner to lunch with his friends. I recognize some of the faces from around the office compound. Beer is served out of plastic petrol cans. It's anyone's guess whether the beer tastes like petrol originally, or whether it has simply acquired that flavour. One end of the table is occupied by a gang of writers. They it is who mostly drink the stuff. Opposite me a poetess gingerly extracts a sheaf of papers from her bag and begins reciting her latest work. The man on my right nudges me, and says: 'We are all very free.' As the woman comes to the end of each poem everybody applauds and there are several *chuk xu khoe*. Two of her colleagues fall asleep. For the third or fourth time everyone introduces themselves. I discover that the poetess is in fact Dr Phuong's sister. When she discovers that I have met Dr Phuong at the Tu Du hospital she presents me with a poem. Whether she has another copy for herself I am unable to ascertain. Thoan Phuong has a hard voice. The rhythms of her lines are fiercely clipped. The effect on the ear is akin to that of Vietnamese vodka on the palate. This quality I rather admire. Other Vietnamese poetry I've heard generally strives too hard for a silken effect. The result, to one who understands it not, is often limp.

While all around us sway, Sau and I make a politic getaway. Le Duc Tho's secretary finally rings through. The good news is I will indeed meet the man. The bad news is it won't be until 9.00 a.m. on Thursday. My flight to Hanoi is booked for noon that day.

The rest of the day again is free. I consider raising Cao Dai and Hoa Hao, but it's as well perhaps I don't. I'm beginning to feel not very whole at all. I slip back to the villa and the afternoon is spent in a sort of antibiotic funk. Around five I come to and experience great lucidity in the contemplation of Vietnam's economic plight. At six I take a walk up Ky Dong Street, turn northwards at the end, arrive almost at once at a gigantic cesspool, and scuttle back. I eat at the restaurant where young men and women sing 'Saigon Saigon Saigon' all night without relishing the experience.

I am thinking about turning in when I encounter a new guest at the villa – an Australian Vietnamese who's paid $300 for his visa in Bangkok instead of waiting three months in Melbourne and paying only $10. This sheds new light on why the government is so ready to welcome Vietnam's many expatriates on short-stay visits. The expatriate I talk to though is a little different. To begin with he's a boat person who made it. Also his father was a one-star general, the commander of one of Diem's or Thieu's cavalry regiments. In 1975 the father decided not to leave, even though, according to my informant, US Ambassador Graham Martin called personally at his house. He spent the next seven years in re-education camps, until at last he died 'of natural causes'.

The son is philosophical about his father's death. That's what it was like. It wasn't much better for him either. The children of the Saigon regime couldn't go to university, couldn't go to college and couldn't usually find a job. Often the only food they could get had to be obtained on the black market. If your family didn't have any jewellery to sell, you starved. In any case it has nothing to do with why he has come back. He wants to marry his childhood sweet-heart, whom he hasn't seen for ten years. They are both Catholics.

'And what about your dad? What was his name?'

Terry looks at me.

'You really want to know his name?'

'Yes. Why not?'

'I'd have to think about that, sport.'

Terry thinks about it, and decides it wouldn't do to go giving anyone his father's name.

'Sorry, sport. But you're just a geezer, and I don't want to lose my Lilly.'

Wednesday 20th December: Saigon Sau wins again. Ever since arriving the first time in Saigon I've been threatened with a snake farm. But, as I've told Truc on countless occasions, I've seen snake farms in Thailand, Singapore, Indonesia and Hong Kong and I have no desire to see any more. In the Far East snake farms are as common as McDonald's in Texas. Nonetheless this morning Sau takes me to a snake farm. I can forget about Cao Dai and the Hoa Hao. But on balance I'm glad we go, even though we are accompanied by Fathers's inept and giggling guide, for whose services I must pay cash. Most things connected with Sau Dang do turn out better than expected.

The farm, or Yen Phung Export Factory, is on the very edge of the city. The main attractions are ten thousand pythons stored in stacked crates. The good thing about pythons is they don't smell. With so many of them in so small a space, and the temperature 105 degrees and rising, if they did smell life would be intolerable. As it is only their food smells. Their food is baby chickens. These the pythons play with in their boxes. When a python gets hungry he yawns and swallows his Easter-yellow toy-set. What surprises me is how little noise the chicklets make as they disappear almost willingly into the reptile's jaws.

There are also a few hundred water snakes, kept in shallow pens in a pond at the back of the main complex, crocodile tanks, an aviary of green parrots reared for export and a pocket-sized zoo run for the amusement of visitors and the farm's proprietor, Ho Van Than: a bear, a leopard, a porcupine and a violent creature slightly larger than a cat, wiry as a pipe-cleaner, but covered with punkster black hair, that I would have difficulty identifying outside a Maurice Sendak picture-book. Visually however the show is stolen by a frame on which hang the equal-lengthed golden python skeletons. Once these are bone dry, they will be used for the manufacture of gelatine. The flesh has already been fed to the water-snakes, while the skins are becoming belts, wallets and hand-bags.

Mr Than appears with two pet pythons squirming on his shoulders. He encourages me to hold one. It's no big deal. But when in turn I offer it to Sau, in a most un-Sau-like manner he leaps away from the thing. For a split second, before he can recover his formidable cool, his eyes actually do fill with a kind of terror. Snake-wine he can drink by the gallon, but a live snake is anathema it seems. Or perhaps it is the particular species: I wonder whether in his jungle-soldiering days Sau and the python have met before. If so, it's not something he is willing to talk about.

We are invited indoors, to the outer of two offices. I am shown a range of snakeskin goods. The belt I am wearing is taken from me, copied and returned. The new belt is presented as a gift. Sau does his bit. I ask the mandatory questions. The 'factory' has been going eighteen months, and employs seventy skilled workers. It cost $900,000 to set up. There was no overseas investor. The money came from Mr Than's own family. He typifies a southern syndrome. A lot of money remained inside the country after 1975 and was buried, literally as well as metaphorically, under floorboards. Mr Than's family has decided to take the plunge. There are many other families with as much or even more money. If they all put their trust in *doi moi* then *doi moi* would be working faster, better. If everybody dug up their gold, thinks Mr Than, then there could be no question of Vietnam returning to its former, Stalinist ways.

This year his turnover will be close on two million dollars. He has already found markets for his merchandise in Singapore and Hong Kong and he is looking at others. He is also, he emphasizes, a 'friend of nature'. He doesn't think it right to go into the jungle and kill animals or reptiles for their skins. All his skins have been reared 'artificially' at the farm. Sometimes he takes a few of his snakes back to the forests and releases them. He likes to put back more than he takes out. In addition, his company supports a 'research unit' that investigates the medical 'spin-offs' of his livestock.

Evidently my credentials as a sincere and friendly journalist are established, for I am now asked to accompany Mr Than into the inner office. All I have done in fact is nod and smile. The inner office is not unlike a People's Committee reception room. There are a long table and many chairs and ever-ready tea. The walls however are lined with charts, graphs and schedules. This is the nerve-centre of Mr Than's operation. More goods are fetched and displayed by tongueless assistants. I am now, to Sau Dang's enormous satisfaction, presented with a water-snake wallet, in addition to the belt. Perhaps I would like to buy something for my mother or my sweetheart? I choose an elaborate attaché case. Immediately I am rewarded with a second wallet, python skin this time, and large enough to hold a passport. Only if he is paying his workforce cadre wages, I reflect, can the man be making a profit.

My eye shifts to the charts and wall-planners. Mr Than has a five-year programme and a ten-year programme. By the year 2000 it is his intention to have a million water snakes, half a million pythons and God knows how many crocodiles. Diversification is the name of the game. There is, for example, an ambitious scheme to revolutionize cosmetics. But even this pales into insignificance

391

beside the hopes entertained within the final column, marked SIDA.

I quiz Mr Than quite closely about this, but his mind is already made up. When AIDS comes to Vietnam, he says, his snakes will certainly provide a treatment. Snakes, once you know about them, contain a treatment for everything. He has spent all his life with snakes and he has never once been seriously ill.

'And will your snakes furnish a cure as well as a treatment?'

'We don't know yet,' replies Mr Than. 'It is not impossible. Everything I know about snakes I have taught myself, and there is no guessing what I may learn tomorrow.'

Which is my lot for today. Contact with Mr Than's reptiles has not improved my flu. In the afternoon I buy a few things in the downtown international shop – real whisky for Sau Dang, a calculator for Mr Hong, a roll of Sellotape for Em Binh – and then I pack it in. Tomorrow I leave Saigon, but before that I shall have to be on my mettle.

Thursday 21st December: Saigon–Hanoi My interview with Le Duc Tho gets off to the best possible start. Instead of Fathers's man, Hanoi Hannah is sitting in the back of Sau Dang's Mazda when he calls to collect me from the villa. Nobody could ask for a better interpreter. Not only is her command of political English impeccable, but she also conveys the inflections of the speaker's voice, those tiny pushes and hesitations that can substantially alter the substance of what is said.

Le Duc Tho is known to the world as the man who negotiated with, and generally outsmarted, Henry Kissinger in the talks between Hanoi and Washington that began secretly in Paris in 1970. He is one of the few surviving heavyweights of the Vietnamese Revolution – the others being Pham Van Dong and General Vo Nguyen Giap. Born in the northern province of Nam Dinh in 1911, he was a founder member of Ho Chi Minh's Indochinese Communist Party (1930). Twice imprisoned by the French in the 1930s, he became a permanent member of the Central Committee in 1944. After the 1945 August Revolution he was the party's organizational anchor man. In the war against the US he directed insurgency in the South. He also took political command of the final drive for Reunification after America had quit. Famously, at a critical moment during the Ho Chi Minh Campaign, he arrived unannounced in the dead of night on a motorcycle from Hanoi at the communist army's headquarters in the South.

Since 1975 Le Duc Tho has remained a dominant figure in Vietnamese politics, to the extent that in some circles he is perceived as his country's ultimate authority. Given the persistence of a strong Confucian ethic, whereby seniority of rank gives way to seniority of age, this is not altogether improbable. Among his protégés who hold high position are the Foreign Minister, Nguyen Co Thach, and General Secretary Linh himself; while his younger brother, Mai Chi Tho, a leading conservative, is Minister of the Interior.

My meeting with Le Duc Tho takes place at his 'Saigon residence', a comfortable villa in one of the city's leafier suburbs. Numerous aides, including a medical staff, dance attendance. He is dressed, as I have been led to expect, in a simple suit of Chinese design. But he does not, as I have also been told to expect, pause every five minutes to recover his strength. Nor is he the austere, cold, grey, aloof figure of the American history books. Pink faced, soft featured and white haired, bespectacled, he smiles almost continuously, projecting an aura of immaculate courtesy. The interview is at once intimate and studied.

Appearances can deceive, however. His revolutionary fervour remains undiminished. From discussing the current situation in Vietnam, he moves to a jeremiad that offers trenchant criticisms of the entire communist world. But it is not communism that has failed, he tells me: it is individual communists. Finally I have met someone who is prepared to tell me, albeit in the most general terms, that all is not as it should be inside the Red House.

Doi moi, Le Duc Tho sets out, would never have been necessary if the Party hadn't made grievous mistakes in the past. I ask whether Saigon, seemingly born again, is not the Trojan Horse of the counter-revolution. But Le Duc Tho's defences are prepared. Gently he taps my knee. *Socialism in Vietnam, far from being under threat, has never actually happened.* A start was made in the

North after Dien Bien Phu in 1954, but much of what was built – schools, hospitals, factories – was destroyed by Nixon's B52s. Then, following 1975, there was the war in Cambodia and the Chinese invasion of 1979.

Yet none of these factors, Le Duc Tho stresses, should deflect blame from the Party. A key mistake was the post-1975 decision to go for heavy industry. In the circumstances this was 'unrealistic, an impatient and slavish emulation of socialism in the USSR'.

At the Fifth Party Congress of 1982 another 'incorrect policy' was introduced: 'socialist accountancy'. State supervision was rolled back, the provinces told to manage and balance their own books. But the provincial bosses had even less economic nous than the former warriors who staffed the Politburo. Inflation soared, the exchange rate collapsed, corruption set in. Which is why, in 1986, an accommodation with western-style capitalism had to be made.

The quest for indigenous heavy industry has been shelved. Under *doi moi* the priorities are agriculture, light industry and the development of export markets. At the same time the Party itself is to be revamped. 'First and foremost we must consolidate the Party, make it firm, politically stable and strong organizationally.' In the past, says Le Duc Tho, the Party has been too 'subjective' (uncritical? authoritarian?) in its bid to solve Vietnam's problems. Sweeping changes of personnel are needed, coupled with greater intra-Party democracy. 'But we must not hurry this' – and there is no question of allowing any alternative to the Party. 'We accept that there is only one Party. We do not accept many parties.'

It is here that Le Duc Tho gets properly into stride. It was the Party that defeated the French, and the Party that defeated the US and China, and so it is easy to see why he is wedded to the concept of the Party. He cannot concede that, historically, the Party may already have served its purpose. 'We freely admit that some cadres at some levels are corrupt. I will tell you. Now the economy consists of many elements, and naturally there is competition between those elements. So there is a tendency toward chaos, even anarchy, a tendency toward speculation and bribery. And from these other social evils have begun to flow: unemployment, embezzlement, robbery, prostitution . . .'

But what he says about Vietnam applies in even greater measure to other socialist countries. Each regime has its own pathology, but, in Le Duc Tho's estimation, the common fault has been degeneration of the leaderships. Bureaucracies have distanced the leaders from the people, therefore the leaders can no longer respond to the wishes of the people. 'You can always force the people to listen to the Party, but that doesn't mean they will always act upon what they hear.' Instead, the leaders should listen to the people, and then take 'strong' action.

Referring to Eastern Europe he uses the word 'debauchery'. The systems of privilege spawned by the Parties inevitably gave rise to bribery, and now the Parties are paying the price. Some have seen the need for auto-criticism (always a strong point of the Vietnamese Revolution in its heroic phase), but they have reacted in haste. Others have handed the job over to the press: 'So there is no limit now. I have to say that the press, where it is free, is criticizing rather wantonly.'

And Vietnam? Are the accounts I have heard about divisions within the Party true?

For a moment Le Duc Tho drops his smile. Yes, he concedes, there are differences of viewpoint within the Party; but 'there is unanimity of purpose, and that is to renovate the economy'.

Perhaps he senses the doubts of his interviewer. Perhaps Hanoi Hannah is translating my inflections as well. In any event Le Duc Tho tightens his fingers around my kneecap.

'Yes, the problems in The USSR are enormous, and it is easy to think we must one day have the same problems here. Such things do happen. I think mistakes have been made during seventy years of socialism in the Soviet Union. But at the same time we must not neglect their achievements. Seventy years ago Russia was backward, a backward capitalist country. The Revolution in Vietnam is not so old, and . . . well, there is still time yet.'

Time for me however is running out. My plane leaves soon. It is comic, but after ninety minutes I am the one who strives to wrap up the interview. Before I leave though I cannot resist asking Le Duc Tho about Kissinger. What kind of person was he?

Almost imperceptibly the smile thickens. To describe someone, he cautions, isn't simple. 'It involves too many abstracts. We judge a person by his actions, but sometimes that is artificial. For example, if you have a sweetheart, sometimes you can understand her, but sometimes you cannot, even after many years. As for Henry Kissinger, we met, we negotiated, many times. But the total time spent together was less than one month. Our longest meeting didn't last more than three or four days, and my concern was to regard him as the essence of US diplomacy. As a diplomat ... well, he was rather ordinary. He had many manoeuvres, and his manoeuvres were rather wicked. I could see through them all I think. I told him frankly that he could be regarded as one of the bellicose personalities. But in a way that was irrelevant. His real weakness lay on the battlefield. It was the battlefield that decided the negotiations, not the negotiators.'

And then, rising to shake my hand, he adds: 'I would have to say, though, that Kissinger was also a very joyful person. He made many jokes.' *

We rush to the airport, only to discover that the plane is delayed two hours. There is nothing for it but to hang about in the bar drinking coffee. Sau Dang perforce must wait with me until the gates to the departure lounge open. Otherwise there will be no one to handle my papers, no one to make sure my bags are not unnecessarily searched. It is a sadly downbeat end to our relationship, a too-long goodbye. The father must hug the son and the son must hug the father, but when the hug too is delayed some of the heart goes out of it. The gesture loses its spontaneity, an unwelcome formality takes over.

The flight is called at last. We hug, and suddenly Papa Sau is no more. On board the Russian aircraft the seats are narrow and cramped. I've known more room in a third-class train in Java. I sit opposite a Finnish hydrologist who bears an uncanny resemblance to Lee Marvin and whose shoulder-bag bulges with cans of Heineken. Every ten minutes he opens a new one, to the dismay of his half-French, half-Vietnamese girlfriend. The heat of the cabin has us all perspiring until a few minutes after take-off, when an awful chill takes over. The flight itself though is smooth enough, and there's nothing wrong with the pilot. I gaze at the central provinces

* Le Duc Tho was to die in Hanoi on 13 October 1990.

396

below. From twenty thousand feet they are simply not the same entity as they were from the window of the Mazda. Then the clouds take over. Many of the Vietnamese passengers, dressed in florid tropical garments, disappear to the toilet, only to emerge a few minutes later wearing the nondescript apparel of the cadre. Pith helmets are produced by the dozen.

The cabin temperature warms up again close to boiling, the plane comes down and lands. Outside the weather is exceedingly cold and exceedingly damp. Immediately the symptoms of my flu redouble. I make my way to the aerodrome forecourt, expecting to see Nam's minibus and either Zoom or Truc beside it. There is no one there. I hang about for twenty minutes. Cowboy taxi drivers offer to take all my dollars. Still no one from the Ministry comes. But no worry. The Finn is waiting too. In the event I ride into town in the back of a chauffeur-driven Mercedes Benz.

At least the Sofia has been advised of my return. The smallest of its three rooms is ready and waiting. The Sofia itself though, during my absence, has been transformed. The ground-floor restaurant has been ripped out. In its place is an overlit shop selling colour televisions, video recorders, radios and imported cosmetics. A little bit of old Hanoi has gone forever. The future has arrived.

I think about going to Zoom's office, but decide it can all wait until tomorrow. In any case, probably he's gone home by now. I unpack my bags and lie on the small, hard, unsouthern bed. I was looking forward to returning to Hanoi, but now I'm not so sure. To an extent I too have become corrupted by the opulence and easy attitudes of Cochinchina. Austerity and order are games like any other games. I have become part of what I have elected to call Reverse Reunification.

Afterwards I order beef brochettes and Russian mineral water. At least Hanoi can still be gentle on the liver.

Friday 22nd December: Hanoi I collect seven weeks' worth of mail from the British Embassy and make my way to Quan Su Street. Zoom greets me with ecstasy, but the ecstasy is necessarily short-lived. His office is in one of its busy periods. He apologizes profusely that there was no one to meet me at the airport. It was not because the plane was late however, but because nobody was available. He tells me Truc has given him my request list, but warns me not to be disappointed if some items get left out. He assures me though that my interviews with Vo Nguyen Giap and Foreign Minister Thach will definitely go ahead. General Secretary Linh is ill, so I may have to make do with a signed photograph and written replies. As for the Interior Minister, Mai Chi Tho, that looks doubtful. In fact Zoom thinks it unlikely the Ministry will field any kind of spokesman.

'But not to worry, Mister Justin. You've done so much. You've met so many big potatoes.'

'And what about this military parade I was supposed to be back in time for?'

Momentarily Zoom's face puzzles. 'Oh that,' he says. 'I think we've missed it. But you don't mind, do you? We'll have a party before you leave instead. You and Mr Hong and Truc and Nguyen and Mister Nam and Mister Zoom, all the gangsters!'

I take the hint, though before I leave Zoom requests that I rewrite my submitted questions for Thach and Giap. Mr Hong thinks my originals were insufficiently detailed. Back at the Sofia I find my embassy has lost no time in issuing me with an invitation to Christmas lunch. I plough through my mail. Inevitably at lunchtime I mosey toward the Thong Nhat. There I meet the two people I will spend most time with before I leave Vietnam: Peter Macdonald and his son Alexander. Peter, a historian, novelist and former British Army brigadier, has come to Hanoi to research a book he is writing about Vietnam's military. Alex is an artist who specializes in painting fat people.

I see them again in the evening, when we dine together. Afterwards I linger at the Thong Nhat bar, hoping for some lobby talk. Suddenly though I'm no longer the novice, but the old-timer. My three months have made of me a Vietnam hand. To a degree my opinions are sought after. I get very little in exchange, except one titbit concerning Ambassador Davies. Rumour has it that London has been pushing Hanoi to take back the boat people stranded in Hong Kong a mite too hard, and that Davies has been summoned at least once to the Foreign Ministry for an official drubbing.

* * *

Saturday 23rd December: Hanoi   If my Hanoi programme is to resume it doesn't resume today. I spend the morning sorting out the notes I've made in the south. The aim is to begin writing them up, but their volume overwhelms me. The best I can do is make notes on notes. After lunch I stroll around the Lake of the Restored Sword. Despite the chill damp, being back in the capital is not altogether unsatisfactory. At the Gallery I rediscover Miss Hoa and her ebullience. 'How very very nice to see you,' she shines. She invites me to a party on West Lake on Sunday night. All her friends, she says, will be there. I continue on my way. I take a look at streets that should be completely familiar, but which in fact are changing out of recognition. Everywhere I look old buildings are being either demolished or renovated. Nor is the Sofia the only establishment turned over to the sale of consumer goods. Even some of the sidewalks are stacked high with boxes marked JVC and Sony and Panasonic. If all this means *doi moi* is working, then I'm pleased. No people deserve a break more than the Vietnamese. But if it means the submergence of Hanoi beneath a tide of common commercialism, then I'm upset.

I dine again with the Macdonalds. Alexander comes to life. He has a line in taking the piss that has tap-roots in the deepest soil of English humour. There is a recklessness about him that keeps his father, himself a restless figure, perpetually amused. They provide, as the saying goes, good company; but because they are so English, they distance me somewhat from my Vietnamese surroundings, my Vietnamese friends. The withdrawal symptoms have begun.

'Bloody hell!' says Alex, when he comes back to my room to borrow a book. 'Who do you think you're playing at? Graham Greene?'

Sunday 24th December: Hanoi   All day I make more notes on notes. After dinner I regroup at the Gallery. Miss Hoa, Miss Dun and Miss N. are waiting for me. We set off on bicycles. The 'party' is an art junket being held on board a two-decked boat. Outside it is too dark to appreciate the drawings and paintings mounted on the deck railings. Inside there is dancing. I dance with Miss N. At first she is a little loath to talk to me. She thinks I have been having an affair with Mai Trang – the woman whose brother introduced me to the dissident writer Nguyen Huy Thiep. Should it upset her so much? I tell Miss N. the thing's untrue. Away from the others, I suggest we make an evening of it sometime before I leave Vietnam. Miss N. agrees.

We return to our table. There is one other foreigner, an Israeli called Rufi Kott. 'Any relation of Jan Kott?' I ask. Rufi's face lights up. Why yes Jan Kott – a scholar who, in *Shakespeare Our Contemporary*, wrote what is still perhaps the most provocative essay about *King Lear* – is his father. At once we fall deep in conversation. Rufi is a doctor. He has been working outside Hanoi on one or other of the aid programmes. He has been in the country nine months and has taken the trouble to learn the language well. But this has not altogether endeared him to his hosts. As the party threatens to continue into the small hours, we leave together and set off on the long walk back to the downtown area. Along the way there are many things that Rufi rails against. In his own field, health care, he is constantly exasperated by the way the hospitals lay on hospitality for overseas visitors, when the resources could be spent on looking after patients. That's why, he says, the health system is breaking down. When I tell him about my good impressions of the hospital in Hué, he scoffs. The reason why it was empty is because no one can afford its services. He knows of one district where so much is spent on entertainment that coconut milk has to be used as a blood-substitute in transfusions. No wonder the masses are flocking back to traditional medicine!

We pass several police road-blocks. Again, Rufi knows the reason. There has been of late a dramatic increase in the number of street gangs. Hanoi is not the tranquil city it appears by day. Now the police are hitting back. There have been 600 arrests in the last week alone. Operation Clean-Up. Youth unemployment runs at fifty per cent. And that's not just because the army is shrinking following the pull-out from Cambodia. It's because the economy can't support the population. And on the subject of Cambodia, I shouldn't pay any attention to what the government says. Vietnam pulled out because the army couldn't take it any longer. It wasn't the Khmer Rouge so much as the malaria. Also, Hanoi couldn't afford the occupation any more. Russia had withdrawn its support.

400

But that doesn't mean the army is inactive now. On the contrary, the province of Kontum is 'riddled' with divisions. On the Laotian border there's a little war going on no journalist is allowed anywhere near. A band of reactionary subversives supported by some of the hill peoples. And that's something else I shouldn't believe either, the 'one nation, one people' crap. There are biddable minorities and not-so-biddable minorities, and the latter have a thin time of it.

'There's anarchy here,' says Rufi, 'there's totalitarian lawlessness.' As evidence he cites the swell in drugs trafficking. New trade routes have been established through Laos and Cambodia out of Thailand. Saigon and Danang are the points of exit. Via Singapore, heroin finds its way to America.

'And you know why it's happening? Because the provincial bosses allow it to happen. They are the organizers. At least, some of them.'

He also tells me about the dangers of driving in the country after nightfall. Even Highway One, he says, is dangerous after ten.

'There are bandits everywhere. It's total totalitarian lawlessness.'

How much of all this should I believe? Rufi speaks with the passion of the convinced. But there is his own cultural background to be taken into account. I recall a line from his father's essay: 'The theme of *King Lear* is the decay and fall of the world.' People find what they want to find.

We part near the Russian compound, a huge fortified complex that has its own generators, its own water-purification systems. Attempting to take a short cut back to the Sofia I get lost almost immediately. For the first time in Hanoi, I experience the prick of fear. Could these groups of friendly adolescents flitting in the unlit back streets in fact be hoodlums? I begin looking for a cyclo, but it is not until I stumble on the main railway station that, among the shadows, I find one. I ask how much to Hang Bai Street. The man holds up two fingers. *Hai cham dong.* 200! He's got to be joking. I offer him a thousand, and with some uncertainty climb aboard his vehicle. He sticks to the back streets. At times squadrons of young male cyclists insist on providing an escort. It's Christmas Eve, mister. Are they simply curious about my western face, or is it my dollars they're after? I keep my hands clenched to the sides of the cyclo, ready to coil-spring away at a moment's provocation.

401

But all is well. In Hanoi it always is. When we arrive at the Sofia the cyclo driver demands two thousand *dong*, which I let him have. Then he holds out his hand and starts rubbing his stomach, at the same time grimacing. Give me more *dong* for some noodles, give me more *dong* for some beer. I tell him to be gone. His face turns ugly, but then he melts away.

Monday 25th December: Hanoi Wake up cold, chilled right through, still fluey. But, contrary to my expectations when I first get back to Hanoi, Christmas Day is a day of treats. The biggest treat is General Giap. Zoom knocks on my door early to tell me the interview is on for the afternoon: he will pick me up from the Sofia at 3.00 p.m. The General has promised me an hour of his time. It would be more, but he has to see the Thai Ambassador at 5.00 p.m. 'So be ready!' says Zoom, and zooms away.

Before then, lunch at the British Ambassador's residence. If it is true Emrys Davies has been hauled in by Thach, and hauled over the coals about the boat people, he doesn't show it. Today is a family day. One notices he doesn't wear a tie. The turkey – and it is a great fat beast of a turkey – is served in a back room, at a table that seats twenty. Large pots of cranberry jelly, which I cannot quite believe in, are placed strategically down the cloth. Emrys sits at one end, his wife at the other. Between them a motley company, half diplomatic crowd, half odds and sods like myself. The embassy chemist, or apothecary (the mission's not big enough to rate a doctor), quotes Shakespeare non-stop. On everyone's plate a gift. A staff member on my left, the lovely Pippa, explains: everybody present has been asked to bring something costing a dollar or less, to give to somebody else. She tried to get hold of me to tell me about this arrangement, but failed. But whatever happens I mustn't feel bad about it. There are enough presents to go round, so I should sit back and enjoy the wine.

I sit back and enjoy the wine too much. I'm aware that I should conserve my sobriety for Giap, but my resolve drains with each little swallow. Every gift is accompanied by a cryptic versified message, and since most of those present have nothing else to do for the remainder of the day, the gifts are queried, discussed, pondered upon before being opened, in a hyper-orderly fashion clockwise round the table. Mine turns out to be a Chinese army knife popular in Kenya. Someone else gets a striking teapot nesting in a covered bamboo basket lined with a pretty, padded cloth. Cries of 'Cheat!' go up, but it is true, it only cost 3,500 *dong*.

The ritual spins out, everyone waits their turn. The restraint shown by all and sundry is wonderfully, woefully English. I am in two minds about whether I feel at home. Also, I begin to wonder whether I shall get any lunch. Having decided to leave at two-fifteen I reschedule my departure for two-forty-five. The last present is opened, the food is served. Platters of roast potatoes appear, proper roast potatoes. I celebrate with another glass of claret. Claret, I determine, is good for flu. The conversation hots up. I begin seriously to entertain notions about standing Giap up. Would the old boy mind?

Pippa comes to my rescue. At five to three she asks whether I shouldn't be on my way. 'Good heavens! Is that really the time?' I beetle back to the Sofia, collect my camera and notepad. Then I wait, gulping coffee on the balcony overlooking Hong Gai Street. At 3.40 p.m. Nguyen shows up, on a motorcycle. 'Zoom can't come,' he laughs hoarsely. 'But don't worry, I've done Giap many times before.' We skid round to the Government Guesthouse opposite the Thong Nhat, another old jaundicey French building that used to be the Governor of Hanoi's residence. At 4.00 p.m. dead the General's battered Russian limousine noses through the front gate. I am waiting for him on the porch.

'Don't be nervous,' says Nguyen, who has never interpreted for me before.

'I'm not nervous. I'm drunk. Why should I be nervous?'

The limousine stops, two aides leap out, followed by the victor of Dien Bien Phu. In a trice he is standing in front of me. Even though the sky is overcast, the four stars twinkle on his shoulders. Otherwise it is a plain, even slightly shabby, uniform he has on. He holds my hand in both his as he rattles off compliments. I notice that his left eye twitches somewhat. I try not to look at it, with the result I stare a little too hard. It is not until after Nguyen has taken photographs and we've gone inside that I take in the rest of the man. Short of stature, he is full of beans. His face is smooth, polished, regular, slightly Chinese, his receding hair pure white.

Vo Nguyen Giap (pronounced Zap, and meaning 'metal') was born in Annam in 1911, the son of a scholar. At Hanoi University he read law. He joined Ho Chi Minh's Communist Party and for several years played a key role organizing propaganda. He was then given the task of creating and commanding the Viet Minh army. By 1975, in the space of thirty years, that army had grown from one platoon into the fourth largest standing army in the world, and it had defeated both the French and the Americans. Giap's contribution had been immense. The doyen of all Third World strategists, he has as fair a claim as any to the title 'greatest living soldier'. Dien Bien Phu, a humiliating defeat for the French, effectively ending their presence in Indochina in 1954, has become a classic, one of the undisputed 'decisive battles' of history. The French, not altogether unwisely, decided to create a super-garrison in a long valley up in the north-western mountains of Tonkin. Their aim was twofold. Firstly they sought to cut Giap's lines into Laos, where the Viet Minh were opening up a new front that threatened to outflank the French occupation of Vietnam. Secondly they hoped to draw the Viet Minh out of their hide-outs for a decisive engagement. The French had no doubt that in such a confrontation their superior arms would rout the enemy.

The Viet Minh obligingly played ball, and attacked Dien Bien Phu. The French had made at least three miscalculations. They had not believed that the Vietnamese could ever get artillery up into the surrounding hills. They had not believed that the Vietnamese in any case had the artillery to do the job. And they had underestimated the Viet Minh's ability to organize the logistical operation necessary to keep their massed divisions supplied. But a hundred thousand porters, bringing food and ammunition over distances of three hundred miles up and down narrow mountain passes, and heavy artillery donated by the Chinese, put paid to France.

The room we sit in is large and brightly lit. The General constantly has one hand on my knee, which he squeezes whenever he wants to emphasize a point. It is a curious kind of intimacy. Halfway through he jumps to his feet and demonstrates how he used to pace up and down in his headquarters during the Dien Bien Phu campaign. He really wants me to know, to appreciate how it was. 'This is how I did it, up and down, up and down, all night, just like this, thinking to myself, how can I beat them? Where are they vulnerable? And then I would look at my watch. I expected my watch to tell me it was one or two in the morning, but usually it was five or six. Sleep didn't matter at all.'

His leather shoes squeak on the wooden floor. Then Giap sits next to me again. One of his aides immediately darts forward to do up a button on his tunic that has come undone, and the interview continues.

I begin by asking, what were the principal differences in strategy in the two wars, against the French and against the Americans? 'Our military strategy came from the political outline,' Giap replies. He would hesitate to say there was any authentic strategy at all. It was all very much *ad hoc,* 'synthetic'. The Viet Minh leadership worked together closely, so that military, political and diplomatic initiatives were highly co-ordinated. In the field he had to rely on small units until the big units were ready; but thereafter the use of the two was always combined. This succeeded because military discipline was nearly always good; and military discipline was good because the political wing always got its act together. In both wars his troops fought for the same ends: independence, freedom and socialism. In both cases the enemy was an invader. Therefore it was easy to mobilize the whole people, the old as well as the young, women as well as men.

'Recently I paid a visit to Pac Bo. Seeing that place again made me think. In 1941, when Ho Chi Minh returned to Vietnam, we had no weapons at all to fight against the French. But then Ho gave us the best weapon of all. It was the idea, *independence and socialism.* This idea was absorbed into the Vietnamese mind. I met many old ladies who had been young women then. They knew that if the French caught them helping our Viet Minh forces then they would be shot. But still they helped us. Everybody, you see, was ready to sacrifice life for the nation. Leclerc thought the war would only last a few weeks. But it was not so. He was the only French general I had any respect for, because he came to see the war in its true terms. He came to recognize that it wasn't a small army he was fighting, but the whole nation.'

Giap rejects the notion that what the Viet Minh, and subsequently the Viet Cong, fought was a guerrilla war. It was a people's war, in which guerrilla tactics played only a part. 'I am not a strategist of guerrilla war,' he says, pumping my knee, 'I am a strategist of people's war.' As regards weapons, he was always at a disadvantage, even after Chinese and Soviet help began pouring in. But he always had two advantages: the human factor, and logistical support. Decisiveness, intelligence and creativity were the qualities that ensured victory.

'I was a decisive man, that was the thing,' he recalls, swelling with pride. 'There was no other option. After Dien Bien Phu, Ho Chi Minh used to make a joke. General Giap, he said, had won the war without losing a single plane or tank. That was because he didn't have any! I used to repeat this to the Russian marshals, and the marshals used to repeat it to their colonels. But the Russian colonels couldn't get it at all.'

The difference between fighting the French and fighting the Americans was one of scale. On the Viet Cong side the same political determination and willingness for self-sacrifice persisted. On the US side, the same over-reliance on superior weapons. In 1972, for example, the Americans still thought they could win because they believed North Vietnam only had simple missiles, and these would be ineffective against the B52s. Yet the B52s came down just the same.

'Of course to win a war you must be stronger than the enemy, but that shouldn't be interpreted mechanistically. It's how you fight that counts. What we did was show that the principle of reliance on weapons alone is not enough. If we had fought the way the Russian Army fights, for instance, we'd have lost, as the Russians lost in Afghanistan. Our secret was involvement of all the elements, and patience. We learned how never to attack a position until we were certain we were strong enough to take it. So for many years we took only small positions. Yet these minor victories had enormous strategic value. They boosted our morale, and undermined the enemy's.'

Perhaps the most remarkable aspect of Giap's career is that he came late to the military life. It was not until he was thirty-three that he first donned a uniform. 'That gave me an advantage though: I had a broader view of things than people trained as soldiers from an early age.'

406

Were there any theorists or commanders in history whom he admired? Sun Tzu perhaps, or Napoleon?

No, not Napoleon. Napoleon understood the importance of surprise, but he also mobilized huge armies. 'That was not our way at all. We depended in the main on smaller units. The only commanders I read about who taught me anything were the heroes of Vietnamese history, men like the Emperor Le Loi back in the Middle Ages. He had a similar problem against the Chinese Army. How to get rid of a strongly armed, well-supported invasion force from a much richer country. He had to use his ingenuity. In a thousand years, little has changed.'

Now that the topic of heroes has been broached, Giap wades in to Ho Chi Minh. It is a great pity, Giap says, that I couldn't meet Ho Chi Minh – as if Uncle Ho had left town the day I arrived, but was still around in general terms. 'The ideals of independence and emancipation he entertained for Vietnam he also entertained for all the world. We talk today of openness, but Ho Chi Minh was the most open person you could ever meet. He was a humanist, a man of the new era. I never came across anyone who, having met him, didn't like him. He saw that socialism and happiness depended on each other. His heart was as open as his eyes. But at the same time he preserved the national spirit. That was the goal he gave himself, and the goal he gave to those of us around him.'

The interview rapidly becomes a pep talk. It is our task, the General exhorts, to put Ho Chi Minh's statements into practice. There have been mistakes, naturally, but the way forward is to rely upon the people, work for the people and share the problems of the people. In particular the young people need our serious attention. Since *doi moi* the economy has gradually improved, but the same cannot be said of the social situation. 'Individual freedom is the precondition of everybody's freedom. Therefore discipline and order are needed.' Giap describes his present role as that of a 'strategist for national social and economic development'. The present enemies are poverty and backwardness. The way to victory consists of training people to love their country and to love socialism . . .

This goes on for quite a while. At the age of seventy-eight the General still bats vigorously and splendidly for his country. I am however a little relieved when one of his aides discreetly draws his attention to the time. The Thai Ambassaor has already been kept waiting twenty minutes.

We stand for a long shake of the hand, during which Giap, whose left eye has mysteriously stopped twitching, expresses his hope for better Anglo–Vietnamese relations in the future and earnestly implores me to remember Uncle Ho in my book. There is a moment's hesitation, and then he hugs me, twice.

During the second hug my lips briefly brush his clean-shaven cheek. It is my turn to twitch, though the twitch is mental, hidden, unrevealed. Partly it is a twitch of real pleasure – the honour of being hugged by such a man is after all considerable – but partly it is a Judas twitch. I know more about him than I should. I know that in 1982 he was 'retired' from the Politburo. One theory is that his colleagues feared his popularity – he had just emerged, for the nth time, top of the Army Poll – and acted collectively to remove him. The nation was already deep in trouble, and there were murmured calls for a supremo to assume near-dictatorial powers. Giap was the obvious choice. But given his intransigently doctrinaire economic ideas, which he still airs sometimes in official publications, his colleagues probably did the right thing. Another theory is that they had simply become bored of having to listen to those views.

I on the other hand have not been bored, except perhaps in the closing straight. As interviews go I hardly count it a scoop. I doubt whether he has said anything he hasn't said a dozen times before, for the benefit of a dozen other journalists – he is easily the most interviewed man in Vietnam; but that is hardly the point. One does not object to listening to an aria sung by Maria Callas simply on the grounds that others have already heard it.

Halfway out of the building I remember I have left my hat on a stand in the hallway. I dart back in to fetch it. General Giap, I observe, is on his feet, being straightened out by his aides, ready for his next performance.

Outside, the Thai Ambassador's aide scowls at me the way only a Thai male knows how. Nguyen drops me off at the Sofia. To avoid sobering up I have dinner with the Macdonalds. Both are in good form, Alexander hilarious in his disrespect for anything in a uniform. Peter, who will meet Giap for his own research, squeezes more out of me than I would have allowed on any other day of the year. To get my own back I tell him I think it's a cheap trick for a retired brigadier to bring his son along as an unpaid aide-de-camp. Peter takes this in good humour, Alexander slightly less so.

At 8.30 p.m. we remove to the Thong Nhat. Where is everyone? The hotel is deserted, the bar closed. Alexander says he won't stand for that, and leaps over the counter to liberate a bottle of Russian brandy and three glasses. We stuff *dong* into the unwilling hands of a receptionist who looks at us with near-racist contempt. I tell the Macdonalds about lunch. The brigadier explodes. The embassy, he says, has done nothing for him since he arrived. He swears he will write to the Foreign Office as soon as he returns home (to his house in Germany). Alexander giggles. I do my best to placate him. The ambassador, I say, has been preoccupied of late with the boat people, but this doesn't wash at all. Peter retorts that the ambassador wasn't too preoccupied to have me around. Then he calms down. I ask what rank in the army would be the equivalent of ambassador. Peter says, ambassador to where? I say ambassador to Hanoi for instance. Peter says around second lieutenant. We laugh. It's 9.30 p.m. and Christmas is over.

Tuesday 26th December: Hanoi   I wake up in what I now regard as my prison cell at the Sofia even colder and more chilled through to the bone. It is the dampness that is getting me down. And yet I feel guilt. Conditions are not half as bad as they are for millions of Vietnamese living out on the paddies. Also, I must only endure this for a couple more weeks at the most; and the Macdonalds have told me to come and use their bath anytime.

Zoom too seems out of sorts, when he knocks on my door. He is later than usual, arriving at about 10.30 a.m. His head feels bad, though he assures me he prefers the cold to the hot weather. Partly he feels bad because Truc's mother died yesterday. But at any rate he has good news for me. The Foreign Minister, Nguyen Co Thach, will see me later in the afternoon. One big potato follows another. So be ready!

I ask him about my other requests for interviews. He's still working on the Transport College. The good news is Ho Chi Minh's former personal secretary has agreed to talk, though no date has been fixed; also, I'll be very glad to hear, the director of the Women's Union.

For now, the Company is ready to sort out my finances. I accompany Zoom to his office. Mr Hong, in a flurry of overwork, greets me and vanishes. I collect my money from Binh's safe. Binh looks prettier than ever, but to my grave disappointment the amount contained in my sealed envelope is not a dollar more than my recollection tells me it should be. The Ministry of Information does not pay interest. Out of $3,200 I must pay all my expenses, barring the trips to Cao Bang and Thai Binh, which I settled before leaving for the south.

We sit at Zoom's desk which, like every other desk in the office except Mr Hong's, has an absolutely clean, bare top. Zoom finds some paper in one of the drawers, scribbles a few notes, looks at it and frowns. Clearly he hates figures just as much as I do.

'Is it bad?' I ask. Mentally I am rehearsing a whole string of arguments to prevent my being led away to the debtors' prison. My main defence is: why should I pay a dime for fifteen weeks' propaganda? My auxiliary defence is: hey guys, what happened to the spirit of joint venture? The prosecution case looks sounder though: look at all the man-hours you've swallowed up, look at all the petrol, think of all the big potatoes we introduced you to! And did we ever tell you you wouldn't have to pay for our propaganda? Didn't we lay it on the line from the beginning? Propaganda's wholesome, and so should be paid for. Then think of all the money Sau Dang saved you in the Mekong Delta. You've had a good time, haven't you?

The final imagined riposte is unanswerable. The last thing I want to do is have any kind of row with Zoom, or with Mr Hong, or with anyone else in the Company. They have all behaved toward me with commendable sincerity.

'Just let me check it through,' Zoom replies.

'How many kilometres have I done?'

'About six and a half thousand.'

Clonk! But when I think about it, including Zoom and Nam's

410

drive back to Hanoi from Hué, and Sau's drive up from Saigon, and all the toing and froing, the figure sounds about right.

'We'll charge you 30 cents a kilometre,' says Zoom. 'That's the best we can do. Usually it would be somewhere between 40 cents and 55 cents. Anything less and we'd be making a loss. But Mr Hong really doesn't want to overcharge you.'

'Thanks,' I say, thinking, hell! there goes two thousand dollars, and there's still the bill for services, for interpreters and drivers and organization to come. I shall be lucky if I get to Bangkok with enough to buy a cut-price boiled cicada on a street stall.

Zoom asks me how much I have. I tell him. Zoom frowns even harder and crosses everything out that he has already written.

'Can you give me $2,200?' he asks at length.

'Of course. But it must come to more than that?'

'Oh sure. But we told you when you came you'd leave with around $1,000. We don't want to go back on our word.'

'I'm very grateful.'

'You'll have to owe us, that's all. I don't know the exact amount yet. I'll have to speak to Mister Hong. We'll have to ask you to sign a note, but don't worry. There's no need to pay until you can afford it. We've done this before. We can always wait a year or two. Just bring some extra dollars the next time you visit Vietnam. Is that okay?'

'Yes,' I say, 'that's A1 okay.'

It's as if the court, having listened benignly to the accused, had told the prosecution to stuff itself.

I walk back to the Sofia mildly elated. And something else nice happens on the street. I discover deep-fried banana fritters. An old woman is cooking them in a frying pan on the pavement. I nibble one, think how wonderful, and order three. How much? I inquire. Three hundred *dong*, she replies. At today's rate, less than eight cents. And they're the best antidote I've discovered yet against the penetrating cold.

Mid-afternoon, Zoom comes to my room again. We walk to the Foreign Ministry, well over a mile away. Another impressive French building. Inside, the finest kept I've seen so far in Hanoi, and very decently lit. We must linger at the gate however. We are met by

411

two or three cadres who preserve an unusual degree of formality. The Foreign Ministry, the implication seems to be, is not the place for laughs. I am given a document three pages long. Written answers to my prepared questions. (My questions, I note, are the ones I prepared before going south, not those I prepared, at Mr Hong's request, after I returned.) Does this mean the Foreign Minister hasn't the time to see me after all? No no, it doesn't mean that at all. It simply means that Nguyen Co Thach wants me to know what he thinks before I see him.

We are ushered into the building and up a beautiful open staircase to Thach's office. It is a little like visiting an up-market doctor in Harley Street. Thach himself, waiting for me in his doorway, is bursting with friendliness and reassurance. This I find a touch unsettling. One expects a foreign minister to be a man perpetually on the ropes. It is his job, after all, to take the rap for his country's errors, and there's not a government in the world, except maybe Iceland's, which hasn't got something to hide. But just because of that, most foreign ministers are bland and reassuring. If they aren't they soon get fired.

The interview goes, if anything, too smoothly, which means I do nothing to unsettle Thach, or draw his fire. The main problem is I have been inside Vietnam too long. Deprived of access to the foreign press I'm not as up to date with what's been happening as I should like to be. As with a lot of countries, if you want to know the news, then keep your distance. Depend upon Reuters or APC. And it's not just that I'm behind on the hot news in Vietnam, I'm also behind on the hot news anywhere else. It will be a few days yet, for instance, before anyone tells me about the climactic, calamitous events in Romania.

Then again, what Thach does say, though he says it seemingly with the best will in the world, is utterly predictable. For minutes on end I feel as if I could have written the script myself.

I kick off by asking how ill Linh really is (anything to get away from the pro forma of the written questions), and about the real authority of Le Duc Tho. At once Thach smiles sweetly. A big bear of a man, in fact he approximates more closely to the stereotype of a country doctor than his overpaid city counterpart. Linh has been ill, very, but is making an excellent recovery. He will be back at his

412

desk as soon as Tet is over. As for Le Duc Tho, well, he has no role in decision-making. But his advice is highly valued. He has great experience, though not as much in foreign affairs as Pham Van Dong, and knows the Party well. I should however beware of thinking Confucianism still prevails. 'We respect older people, but we are not dependent on them for our thinking.' Vietnam is a modern socialist state, and those who wield power are those who have actual positions of power. Which, given that Thach is a known protégé of Le Duc Tho's, doesn't mean a thing.

I am unwilling however to let Confucianism slip so quickly through the net. It gives me an angle on another aspect of Vietnam that also has nothing to do with foreign relations. Women. I tell Tach that from all I've seen women have not come on as much in Vietnam as they have in some western societies. I tell him I've met dozens of People's and Party Committees, and only once was I introduced to a female member. Doesn't that show that Confucianism, the essence of antique chauvinism, has got at least one over socialism?

Again Thach smiles sweetly. Yes, what I say is a little bit true. Vietnam does have a mixed heritage, East and West. The war however brought about drastic changes. There were many women in the battlefield. A lot of them died. And they hold down good jobs in education, health and even trade. It is true that at present there are no women on the Politburo. There has never, for example, been a lady foreign minister. But (the Minister's smile seems to imply) you can't have everything. Or at least, women can't. Next one please?

We turn to foreign affairs. Thach gives an elegant, almost affectionate rerun of what I've mostly heard or know about already. His theme is America, and how America has consistently played the 'China card'. Vietnam would like to be friendly with both super-powers – and for Vietnam China definitely is a superpower – but by playing the China card America inhibits progress. By implication, it is not the case that China has also consistently played the America card. China, the insinuation is, would have become a good pal again long ago if Beijing hadn't allowed its hand to be played by Washington.

Washington's attitude toward China is deeply ambiguous. When

413

China and Russia fell out, Nixon leapt in to the breach by courting Beijing. The purpose of this was not to encourage Chinese development, but to contain Moscow. Washington in fact is equally anxious to contain China.

The United States' greatest error has been to consider Vietnam a pawn in Sino–American relations. Hence American support for France post-1949, following the victory of the Red Army, and the Chinese intervention in Korea. Washington never considered Vietnam on its own merits, and hence, in the 1960s, was unable to understand Vietnamese culture, Vietnamese psychology.

There was a wonderful chance in 1945–6 when America, the champion of liberty, could have helped Ho Chi Minh's newly established government to preserve Vietnam's newly won independence. But Washington didn't help because Washington was preoccupied with Europe. In particular Washington was scared that communism might take over in Paris. So right from the beginning America's attitude toward Vietnam was determined by its global strategy, and not by a reading of the local situation.

And global strategy still determines American attitudes. Thach plays down the 'bad loser' theory of the United States' current hostility toward Vietnam. (Washington maintains a strict trade embargo, which it encourages its allies to share, and has still failed to repeal the 'trading with the enemy act' enforced in 1970.)

All this is exemplified by the situation in Cambodia. In 1978, exploiting the differences between Beijing and Moscow, the United States persuaded China to abandon its support for the orthodox socialist regimes in Indochina in return for economic aid. Vietnam meanwhile was being harassed by the evil, non-orthodox regime of the Khmer Rouge in Phnom Penh. The only solution was to crush Pol Pot and his army. And this Vietnam would have done comprehensively, had China, with the full connivance of America, not chosen to support the Khmer Rouge once they had been pushed back to the Thai border, and also to invade Vietnam in 1979. For the invader the consequences of that action were disastrous, but China nonetheless pursued the policy preferred by her American paymasters.

No wonder, says Thach, that following 1979 Vietnam steered toward a deeper relationship with the Soviet Union. The Soviet

Union was the only superpower able to understand Vietnam's problems. But this has been 'wilfully misread' by the Americans and their Chinese allies. Whereas Vietnam has sought Soviet co-operation only to rebuild an economy devastated by almost forty years of warfare, Washington and Beijing have seen in the alliance only a threat to their own geopolitical hegemonic ambitions.

The truth of the matter however is that 'Vietnam wants only to be friends with everyone'. But all her gestures of friendship are repulsed. The Americans said they would restore diplomatic relations once Vietnam withdrew all her forces from Cambodia. That was their promise. But now Vietnam has done just that, Washington is setting preconditions. Washington now says there must first be a 'comprehensive' settlement in Cambodia. Yet the prospect of peace so long as Washington continues its support for Prince Sihanouk, and through Sihanouk its support for the Khmer Rouge, is slim.

And in case I should be in any doubt about the duplicity of United States foreign policy, Thach invites me to consider the position of Thailand, Washington's strongest ally in the region. The Cambodian resistance forces would be unable to continue were it not for the sanctuaries and supplies they find in Thailand. But the Thais, guided by America, allow these arrangements to continue. In addition, there is an agreement between Thailand and China, dating back to 1978 (when Thailand was to all intents and purposes still a monarchical military dictatorship), whereby, in return for China ceasing its support to Maoist insurgency groups inside Thailand, Thailand agreed to help anti-Vietnamese forces in Indochina. Thus at America's instigation, on the one hand you had a right-wing government aiding and abetting forces of the extreme left (the Khmer Rouge); and on the other, the socialist powerhouse of Asia actively undermining the interests and stability of a socialist sister-state.

Thach looks at me as if to say: well, I ask you!

'And what about the so-called neutralist tendencies in Laos?'

I am referring to recent reports that, very much against the wishes of Hanoi, Laos has sent a top-level delegation to Beijing, and that some sort of deal has been concluded. In a roundabout way I am trying to discover whether China still represents a threat to Vietnam's security.

But the Foreign Minister will not be fazed. He quickly 'reminds' me that Ventiane has also sent delegations to Taiwan and Japan. 'We are all Indochinese,' he comments, 'and we all need help from wherever we can get it. We certainly support any improvement in relations between Laos and China.' Then he puts in a good word for 'Madame Thatcher', on account of Britain's recent announcement that it will oppose the Khmer Rouge's continuing to have a seat at the United Nations. 'But then you see, Madame Thatcher doesn't have a China strategy, except in relation to Hong Kong.'

I decline to be drawn into a discussion on the boat people, as I know that every journalist in town thinks of nothing else. Instead I quiz Thach about the MIAs.

The Foreign Minister's face lights up with pleasure.

'We are doing everything we can to assist American agencies to recover the dead bodies of their fallen heroes. It proves that we are sincere in our overtures of friendship. As for the other thing, the idea that we are still holding some captured Americans as prisoners of war, that is a domestic problem among Americans which they must resolve among themselves. I have however myself issued a challenge. I have said that I will take anyone anywhere they like in Vietnam in search of these POWs. But they do not exist, and my challenge has never been taken up.'

Next please?

But I have no more questions. The problem is that, quite apart from his unwillingness to divulge anything new, the way Thach puts Vietnam's case it would indeed be churlish to do anything but agree. Vietnam *has* been the victim of horrendous geopolitical machinations. I only object to the untrue claim, which I have heard many times, that a primary motivation of Vietnam's 1978 invasion of Cambodia was 'humanitarian concern'. But since Thach has not made that claim today I have no gripe.

I look at my watch, see that I have had eighty minutes' worth of Thach, and prepare to leave. The Foreign Minister I know must be a very busy man, I say. But as I rise to my feet the Foreign Minister leaps to his.

'What, no more questions? Please, ask me some more questions. That is why I am here, to answer your questions!'

I am all but pushed back into my chair.

416

'Okay then,' I respond, 'what about the boat people? The forced repatriation.'

'Ah yes. As you know, following talks with your government, we are receiving some of the so-called boat people back from Hong Kong. The programme is already under way. What amuses us is how your people use the term *mandatory* repatriation. *Forcible* is the word we use.'

End of topic. We fall back on *doi moi*. I raise the question of 'black videos'. Do black videos, I ask, spell the end of communism in Vietnam? The import of high-tech consumer goods surely means, sooner or later, the import of high-tech consumer values.

Thach replies: 'Everything has two sides, a positive and a negative. If you are afraid of the negative side, then you must close your door. But we are not afraid. We want to establish a decentralized market, a macro-economy. We want to get away from an economy of shortages. But as for the end of communism, that is not our intention. A free market is not the exclusive property of capitalism.'

It's almost as if Karl Marx, whose achievement was precisely to link political forms to systems of economy, had never lived. But as I struggle to digest what to me seems a gargantuan slice of double think, Thach is telling me a joke:

'You see it's like this. Last year one duck-egg would exchange for five kilos of steel. But this year, one kilo of steel goes for five duck-eggs. We are learning all the time.'

Given that Vietnam has a great many more duck-eggs than kilos of steel, the point of this is entirely lost on me. But one thing I will say for Nguyen Co Thach. He got through a hundred minutes with me without once mentioning Ho Chi Minh. He is the man for the future.

Zoom, who has had no interpreting to do (Thach's command of English is buoyant), and I walk back through dusk and the rush-hour. Hanoi seems more alive, more purposeful than ever. During my six-week absence it has become hectic even. Millions of bicycles converge upon and pass each other with alarming velocity. Perhaps this only reflects a need to keep warm, but to the indoctrinated eye it betokens a city really on the move.

417

In the evening I again dine with the Macdonalds, who have had a first session with Giap. Alex can do little but laugh. In the bar of the Thong Nhat afterwards I have a fruitless argument with Alain Robins, a Belgian Médecins sans Frontières worker. I tell him that I was struck, during my drive south, by how very close most Vietnamese live to nature. They have a compelling, ineluctable physical relationship with their environment that few farmers in Europe would recognize. Alain, a young man recovering from hepatitis picked up in Africa, whom I like immensely, tells me I am being 'romantic'. I endeavour to turn the tables on him. 'I never said that the Vietnamese peasant's relationship with the land and water that make up his living is a good thing or a bad thing. I merely said he had it.'

'But you are still being romantic,' insists Alain. 'More brandy?'

The bar is still open, thanks to a team from the *Daily Mail* who arrived today. So long as you keep ordering drinks the bar doesn't close, and the *Daily Mail* never stops ordering drinks.

Alex is having a terrific argy-bargy with the chief of them. 'God I hate journalists,' he keeps telling him. 'You're all such slime.' His line is that because their paper has probably paid a great deal of money to send them to Hanoi (to cover the first returnees from Hong Kong), they are under an absolute obligation to come up with something sensational.

'And what do *you* do for a living?' the *Mail* man retorts with equal venom.

'Me? Me, I just laugh at you lot, that's what I do for a living,' says Alex. 'You really are a bunch of wankers. If you want the real news, just walk around the streets here. Nothing terrific is happening, and that's the truth of the matter. That's the news. Nothing's happening, baby, nothing's happening. So why don't you all pack up and go home?'

Before anyone can hit him, I leave, my loyalties too keenly divided to enter the debate.

Wednesday 27th December: Hanoi First thing Zoom comes to the Sofia to beg my forgiveness. Everybody in his department is taking the day off to attend Truc's mother's funeral. So do I mind not having any programme today?'

'How could I?'

Zoom laughs, tells me to have a good rest and do some writing.

In the event I do very little of either. As soon as Zoom has gone I walk to the airline office a couple of blocks away to reconfirm my flight out on 10th January. My seat is booked, but now my ticket is no longer valid. The girl tells me it's no good, and unbooks my seat.

'Why is it no good?'

Because it's made out from Ho Chi Minh City to Bangkok, not from Hanoi, she explains. I explain that that's no problem, that her office has already agreed on the switch-round.

'Why not you just buy new ticket?' she pleads.

'No I'm not going to buy a new ticket. I'm going to stick by the agreement I made with you in November.'

But there's nothing she can do to help. The only way out of the impasse is for me to speak to the director of Thai International in Hanoi.

'Good. Where is he?'

The girl has no clue at all where her boss is. All she knows is that he works at the Thai Embassy and may be there in the after-noon.

The rest of the morning dissipates itself. I buy a quantity of banana fritters and take them to the Gallery. Miss Hoa is madly excited, but then she is always madly excited. I look through a dozen portfolios of etchings and drawings, make my usual hollow promise that I will certainly buy something before I leave, then linger at the bookstalls in Trang Tien Street. I think about taking lunch at the Sofia, but settle for the Bac Nam, where the manageress lures me into changing dollars for something like a Saigon rate. At the Sofia the staff have largely lost interest in serving anybody. The waiters and waitresses, dressed in new clothes that approximate to uniforms, are themselves constantly seated round tables these days, embarked on a seemingly endless suc-cession of 'celebrations'.

'What is it that you are celebrating?' I ask.

'Season of Tet!'

'But Tet isn't for another four weeks.'

'Another four weeks! Is that all? Tet very very soon now!'

419

My narrow, north European, book-keeping mentality seriously wonders where the money for all this jollification comes from, but I know better than to ask. Perhaps they really are selling a lot of televisions and radio cassettes downstairs. I am invited to join them, but since joining them would mean drinking Heineken I decline. Beer and cold damp weather are not good friends.

On my way out I meet Madame Oanh.

'How are you?'

'Very good!' Then she tells me she is leaving. Her daughter and her son (a teacher and a doctor) in Saigon have asked her to join them. I ask whether she won't miss Hanoi. They earn, she says by way of reply, ten times what they could earn here. Three or four hundred thousand *dong* a month at least. Yet she looks peculiarly miserable. It may just be the weather, but a certain plainness, an over-scrubbedness, that has always vied with an ageing, comfortable prettiness for control of her features looks to have the advantage today. Her eyes are more than a little anaemic.

'Perhaps you'll find a husband?'

A wan half-smile thinks about landing on Madame Oanh's face, but clears off quickly.

'I'm too old,' she says.

I gallantly protest this comment, but her mind appears made up.

'No no no. I'm too old, too old, too old.'

In the afternoon I take a long cyclo ride to the Thai Embassy, miles out in the sticks. I shiver as the poorly rubbered wheels negotiate endless pot-holes. Because the streets I am passing are new to me, I am impressed by the sheer size of Hanoi. It is not just a pretty French *ville*, it is also a huge breeding ground for proletariats. Small factories are interspersed with single-storey concrete dwellings unglamoured by any nearby landmarks. I think to myself: if I can, I'll bring my departure date forward a day or two. The conversation with Madame Oanh has depressed me, forces me to be objective. I sensed in her a person who doesn't know what to think because what she does think is not what she's supposed to think.

So what's new?

Vietnam is winding down. There's nothing further that is useful for me to do here. For the first time since I arrived I find myself

420

actively wanting to leave. The affair is over, the romance is out of it. If I push hard enough, I can still do more interviews. But do I want to? Will I learn anything new? At what point will my good humour at being fed the line collapse into irritation and anger? I am frightened that if I stay too long there will be an erosion of the pleasures I have had. I might, for instance, begin, in a day or two, actively to dislike Hanoi. No, not dislike. Become indifferent to. But even that would give me guilt. Like fickleness toward a former sweetheart.

Nothing though is done to hasten my departure today. The Thai International manager is not at the embassy, and nobody there knows where he is. For once the Thais I talk to are unwarmed by my attempts to speak their language. I hang around for an hour or so, hoping he will come back. Just long enough for my cyclo driver, whom I have asked to wait, to vanish. The manager never shows up. It takes me a while to find another cyclo. The man, knowing he has little competition and that I am a long way from base, gets the better of the negotiation. We trundle back. In the evening I dine yet again with the Macdonalds. I learn that the father's second wife is younger than the son's current girlfriend. Alex describes himself as a necrophiliac, not on account of his girlfriend, but on account of emotions once felt in the Egyptian rooms of the British Museum.

'A necrophiliac, that's what I am. It's the only thing to be, isn't it Dad?'

'Don't look at me,' says the brigadier, 'for God's sake don't look at me.'

Thursday 28th December: Hanoi The reason why Nguyen Co Thach laid off mentioning Ho Chi Minh is made manifest when I find Zoom in his office. Today I finally get to see the man. A megadose of H.C.M. Which is why, presumably, I didn't need a shot on Tuesday.

Zoom is taking me to the Mausoleum. Since his father has prior claim to his motorcycle we walk. It is still early, before ten, and Hanoi, more monochrome than ever, is swathed in operatic mists. Slightly, it rains.

It takes half an hour to get there. The Mausoleum is modelled on the Lenin Mausoleum in Moscow, a small square Greek temple, refashioned in the social-realist fashion, raised on a soviet wedding-cake plinth. Entering it is like entering a *bijou* cinema in Tokyo. There is a bevy of ushers wearing gleaming white gloves.

These ushers are in fact soldiers. But before we deliver ourselves into their custody we must first stop off at the guardhouse opposite a road-block that, during the daytime, seals off Duong Hung Vuong. I duly surrender my camera, which is whisked off to another building over the road. For a while we hang about, then we are given the green light. As we advance toward the Mausoleum's steps I observe a long line of schoolchildren marching in single file also advancing in the same direction. Zoom quickens his step. If we don't reach the entrance first then we'll have to wait at least half an hour before being allowed in.

Barely we escape convergence. By now we are being accompanied by an usher, who hurries us along. On the steps, he hands us over to another white-gloved, po-faced and poker-backed guard. In a fairly ungentlemanly manner he checks me over. Having been warned by Peter Macdonald not on any account to have my hands in my pockets – the brigadier was reprimanded on the same point – I pass muster, although it is obvious the man disapproves of my tailor.

Now we go inside. The soldier leads the way, turning round every few seconds to make sure I am following exactly two paces behind. The corridor has several turns, and there is a sort of downward tendency. Other ushers stand at the corners, rifles to hand, and I know that were I to sneeze violently then I would probably be shot. How Alex contained his hilarity and survived is altogether beyond me.

Behind me, Zoom's face has blanked out. His expression is a void, something I have seen before, either when his head wound is giving him trouble, or at the end of the day when he is wiped out and thinks nobody is looking.

We come at last, with measured steps, to the chamber within, a gloomy place. But something here is brightly lit. Ho Chi Minh's face.

I slow down, to take a longer, better look. But at once a

dignified white glove beckons me forward. The body lies in a central pit, raised up and under glass. Visitors must keep moving around the roped-off gallery that hugs the walls. Exposure is controlled, timed. It is an experience designed to arouse awe and respect. A fleeting dream-image of the saintly Great Leader, not dead so much as asleep. Whatever you do, you musn't awaken him.

If you did awaken him of course, then the outcome might be unsalutary for Vietnam and the ruling Party. Because this is exactly what Ho Chi Minh didn't want for himself. What he did want was for his body to be cremated, and then:

> Let my ashes be divided into three parts, to be put into three ceramic boxes: one for the North, one for the Centre, and one for the South. In each part of the country, let the box of ashes be buried on a hill. Let no stone stele and bronze statue be erected on the grave. Instead there should be a simply designed, spacious, solidly built and cool house, where visitors could rest. A plan should be worked out to plant memorial trees. With the passage of time, the trees will form forests which will benefit the landscape and agriculture. Care for the trees should be entrusted to local old people.

Instead he has been embalmed, and housed in a costly mausoleum. Far from having his grave tended by local old people, he has his corpse guarded night and day by an infantry detachment which hails (as Zoom loses little time in telling me afterwards) from really rather far away.

Uncle Ho's wishes, expressed in his Testament, have only just been made public. An earlier, doctored version of the Testament, published almost immediately after his death, in 1969, omitted all mention of ashes and ceramic boxes and hills. All that was retained was: 'When I am gone, a grand funeral should be avoided in order not to waste the people's time and money.' Quite why the Party has suddenly decided to release the original document in its entirety (if that's what it is) is the subject of vigorous speculation and a bit of a mystery.

My own theory is that the Party and Hanoi People's Committee

423

have realized that the Mausoleum occupies a prime and therefore very valuable site in the middle of Hanoi. By publishing Uncle Ho's expressed wishes now, they may be hoping to raise such a storm that those wishes will have to be belatedly respected, clearing the way for the erection of the capital's first multi-storey car-park.

I also think that Ho Chi Minh, being the shrewd old dog he was, understood the innate advantages of being buried three times over in three different places. As things stand, any counter-revolution could remove him at a single stroke. To go and disinter him thrice however would surely smack of vulgarity. The counter-revolution would also incur the wrath of a lot of elderly gardeners, and it is well known what staunch resistance elderly gardeners can offer during a time of counter-revolutionary turbulence.

I crane forward as much as I dare, while continuing to work my feet. The light spreads down across his chest, but his lower parts are obscured in shadows. This very much gives him the appearance of a horizontal genie. His eyes are closed, his world-famous goatee unstiffened. The skin is waxen, no doubt hugely chemicalized. Above all, I am struck by the smallness of him. He really does resemble a Chinese mandarin modelled in ivory.

And of course it is precisely because, in the nation's unconscious, Ho Chi Minh is the mandarin *par excellence,* that they have gone to such great trouble to preserve his remains.

In a trice I find myself being ushered out of the chamber into the daylight at the back of the building. To my great annoyance I find little twitches of awe and respect fiddling with my limbs.

'So what did you think?' asks Zoom.

'Intensely ghoulish I'm afraid.'

I glance at Zoom to see whether I've struck a chord. But his face stays inside its mask a few minutes more. He gives a very slight shrug, as if to say it takes different people different ways. Possibly it's more than his job is worth to feign agreement with me. Or perhaps 'ghoulish' is foreign to him. Even with the best of interpreters it's sometimes unpredictable what words he does and does not know.

'And where are we going now?'

'To look at his house.'

Behind the Mausoleum is an unexpectedly opulent park, in the middle of which looms the biggest French building in the north. The former residence of the Governor of Indochina, it is square, classical and stately. Today it is used as a sort of super state guesthouse. But this is not where Ho Chi Minh spent the last fifteen years of his life. His place is down by a circular lake, and conforms very much to the 'simply designed, spacious, solidly built and cool house' of his will. The ground floor is open, and is mainly taken up with the long table, flanked by high-backed chairs, where he used to chair Politburo meetings *en plein air*. Upstairs, a simple square private study next to a simple square bedroom.

The sight of an antique heater on the floor is what particularly gains my attention. It's the only such thing I've seen in all Hanoi.

'Do you think I could borrow that?' I ask.

Zoom laughs, his old, usual self again.

'Maybe,' he says.

'And what did he do about his toilet? I don't see a bathroom anywhere.'

'Over there,' says Zoom, pointing to some outhouses on the other side of the lake.

'Oh come off it. You don't seriously mean to tell me that Uncle Ho, in the middle of winter, went dashing round there every time he wanted a pee? I'll bet you any money he had a potty under the bed.'

'Shhh,' replies Zoom. 'Somebody might hear you.'

'Honestly, I'd like to know. How else can I become his authorized, his trusted biographer?'

But Zoom is already making his way toward the other two things to be seen: a standing white dovecote full of underfed white doves, and an ancient pagoda which Zoom advises me not to spend any time on since it's been burnt down at least once in its recent history.

We collect my camera and head back towards the centre. A ghastly, sustained blast of iced air whips at us whenever we pause to cross a road. Zoom takes me down some narrow back streets and stops at a particularly good noodle shop to buy me noodles. I outline the difficulties I am having with Thai Inter. Zoom perks up a hundred per cent as soon as he hears this. 'Leave it to Mister Zoom, Mister Zoom knows how. Just give me ten dollars.' I give him ten dollars, we go to the airline office and in no time at all the thing is done.

'You're confirmed out on the third,' he announces, waving my ticket under my nose.

'The third?'

'Isn't that what you wanted?'

Nearly, but not quite. I do not, though, have the heart to ask Zoom about my programme: whether five days will be enough to complete it. My programme is rapidly running out. For today, it has run out completely.

'I'm sorry, but Mister Zoom must be very busy this afternoon. You know, a lot of people are coming soon. And still many many things to fix for you. Have a rest. Do some writing. Hang about. I'll see you tomorrow.'

But something more is in store for me. I pass the afternoon huddled over the tiny desk in my room at the Sofia. When I stand up I discover my torso, from my belt to my neck, is rigid, as though my chest has been filled with concrete. It hurts to move. In particular it hurts right across the chest.

Notwithstanding, I make my way, slowly, painfully, to the Dang Chu, where, for the third or fourth night running, I've agreed to have dinner with the Macdonalds. I begin to pick at the slab of undercarpet that pretends it's beef, but soon give up. The pretty, petite, seven-month-pregnant waitress serving us, whom I've always regarded as an absolute madonna, has lost so much of her charm that I start seriously to wonder whether she ever had any. Alex is prattling on brilliantly, but also very very boringly. The concrete is turning to fire, a great block of fire around which my soon-to-be-frazzled epidermis has been taped. Inside, my bones are sharding. The pain across my chest spasms frightfully every time I touch my knife.

It occurs to me that I know what this is. I'm having, or am about to have, a coronary. The fruit of all that booze, all that tobacco, in the Mekong Delta.

Should I tell Peter? Should I just lean across the table and say, excuse me old chap, but I'm having a heart attack?

What determines me against this course is the ignominy I'll

426

almost certainly have to endure afterwards, particularly at the hands of Alex, if, as I also suspect, it isn't a heart attack. Instead I push my plate forward and announce, as loudly as I can muster, that I feel very slightly queasy and would they mind terribly if I left them to it?

Peter stares at me, blinks, and then with a wave of the hand gives me permission to get down from the table. Without further ado I rise to my feet and make for the door. My thoughts suffer various revolutions. Uppermost in my mind is the notion that it is rank ill-mannered to die in front of other people, especially nice people like Peter and Alex. But I'm also thinking, if this is the onset of a cardiac arrest, then I'm doing the right thing by encouraging it with movement. The brigadier will know what to do simply by virtue of being a brigadier. And then again, there's not a minute to lose. If the facilities exist in Hanoi to resuscitate me then it's imperative to reach them fast, because in another hour or so the whole city will have gone to sleep, and my poor attacked heart will have to wait until morning.

I reach the street however without crashing to the ground, which leaves only two options: I either go down in the street, or wait till somehow I make it up the stairs to my room and go down there.

The fresh air, the wind, does me some little good. I make it to my room. I lie on my poky little bed. Or rather I attempt to lie down, for the dreadful thing is my body simply will not straighten out. Each time I endeavour to lower my back on the mattress the agonies redouble.

In the end I prop myself up in the sitting position, exactly like one's bedridden grandmother before lunch, and contemplate my next move.

The longer I remain still, the more it hurts when I do shift. Patiently, correctly, I run through the dictionary of symptoms in my head. But this is an appallingly slender pamphlet, and at the end of an hour I've still got no clue at all what's ailing me. The closest I can get is a sudden chill, but the word 'chill', sudden or otherwise, seems much too slight a thing to warrant so much discomfort. I add in bronchitis. A sudden chill complicated by sudden, acute bronchitis. Yet my breathing seems fair enough, it's certainly not the most painful feature of the present crisis. Also, I have no discernible temperature whatsoever.

427

The notion of cardiac arrest though gradually recedes. At ten o'clock I tell myself that if I haven't had a terminal seizure within thirty minutes, then it's definitely something else.

The most probable/improbable candidate suddenly presents itself: rabies. Dr Georg was wrong on both counts. (a) Rats can give you rabies, and (b) the quarantine period is a lot longer than eight weeks, whatever the almanac says.

I begin secretly to wish for the cardiac seizure, because at least there'd be a chance of survival. I imagine Peter bursting in just as it happens, because of course he suspected something serious all along and has come to see what's wrong. But the minutes tick by, and even though palpitations have me, half past comes and goes.

I relax, and for good measure rule out rabies as well. I tell myself that I may be able to help myself. Using the cord of my dressing-gown I lasso my medicine tin. I prepare a small salad of antibiotics and aspirin. Then I turn myself round 40 degrees and discover a position that is not so wholly unsatisfactory as every other position.

At some point I fall asleep. At some point soon after I wake up again. A rat is scratching away, either in the room or just outside. *Oh God, please God, not him again!* That I think would kill me.

There is no fever, no delirium. Rather there is a sort of coldness in the brain. Even so at one point I do whisper to myself in the dark: '*He* has done this to me. It's his revenge for imputing ghoulishness to his crypt.'

Friday 29th December: Hanoi The ampicillin has done some good. The early morning finds me marginally more flexible than last night. Nonetheless it is adventitious that Zoom, when he comes to the Sofia, declares this to be a free day. 'Don't worry,' he promises, 'we'll do something tomorrow.' I explain my condition to him, but emphasize that from tomorrow I want to push ahead with my programme, to get as much as possible done in the short time that's left. Zoom nods understandingly. One thing though, General Secretary Nguyen Van Linh is still not well enough to see me. His office however has promised the written answers to my questions before I leave.

Zoom goes, I climb back into bed. If I can't seen Linh, then I do the next best thing: study his works. But his works, in the shape of *Vietnam: Urgent Problems,* issued by the Foreign Languages Publishing House in 1988, are if anything more painful than my frozen shoulder and chest muscles. The man is obviously a raving anal retentive. While many of the ideas expressed are familiar to me from my interviews with Le Duc Tho and other big potatoes – the necessity for economic reform, purification of the Party, the preservation of 'correct' thinking – the language is stuffy, quite unable, or unwilling, to break with the mould of Marxist-Leninist rhetoric. But there is one passage that does stand out amongst the others in the fog:

> With regard to the small commodity production economy and private capitalist economy (small capitalists) in some branches of production and servicing domains, they are controlled according to the motto: 'Use them for transformation, and transform them for better use.'

Marxist-Leninists may understand some coded message here, but the qualms of the would-be entrepreneur would seem to have a locus too.

Saturday 30th December: Hanoi   When Zoom doesn't materialize at breakfast I walk to the office. Again, there is nothing lined up for me, either today or for tomorrow (Sunday). But he has made two appointments on my behalf, for Monday and Tuesday. One is with Nguyen Thi Dinh, the other with Vu Ky. Nguyen Thi Dinh, Zoom tells me enthusiastically, is the biggest potatoess there is: a former Viet Cong general, part creator and co-ordinator of the *toc dai*, or long-haired army, she is now president of the Women's Union, as well as a member of the Council of State (though of course not a member of the Politburo). Vu Ky is . . . Ho Chi Minh's former secretary.

'And what about the Transport College? You know I really want to get the details on that story.'

'I'm sorry. I've asked. But they've declined. You see there was an article by an Australian journalist which got things wrong. So they're rather nervous about seeing you.'

'But that's stupid,' I respond, playing the Friend of Vietnam card for all its worth. 'Surely it's better to set the record straight. I've told you so often, the Transport College affair, from what I've heard, is the best way to scotch apprehensions that Tiananmen Square could happen here in Hanoi, or in Saigon.'

'Yes, I know,' Zoom soothes, 'but . . . I'm sorry!'

Okay then, I won't put the record straight, I won't scotch apprehensions that Tiananmen Square could happen in Vietnam.

'That's a brick wall you've given me there,' I snort. 'What else?'

'Your farewell party's set for Tuesday lunchtime. Do you mind if we have it here at the office? It will cost you less, and everyone from the Company can come.'

'That's fine.'

'Binh will do the cooking. We'll have a good time.'

'What about the Macdonalds? They're leaving the following day as well.'

'Yes, we'll invite them too.'

'Good.'

Mr Hong breezes in and breezes out. I take my leave. Outside in the forecourt I see Truc. I offer him condolences and a hug. He looks drained, defeated. He tells me that among his mother's effects he has found a small bag of colonial *piastres*. Do I know how much they're worth?

In the afternoon I set off for a walk around the Hoan Kiem Lake. Immediately I run into Alain Robins, who is chatting to the girls in the Gallery. He is feeling as spare as I am. The medical supplies essential to his work have been held up, and there's nothing else for him to do. We set off together. He takes me into a large hall where citizens can sell and buy gold. I take him into the Post Office, where, remembering Graham White's purchases, we pore over sheets of yesteryear's stamps. These are kept in dusty cardboard boxes that the assistant has some difficulty locating. Most of them are gumless on the back. We both buy hundreds. There are some particularly fine monochrome specimens depicting men and women engaged in various industrial and agricultural pursuits in the mid-revolutionary period. I walk out less than three dollars the poorer.

We look for other things to buy, but fail. In the 'foreign' department stores on the north side of the lake I search in vain for anything that resembles a heater. Quite simply there aren't any. To warm up I return to the Thong Nhat with Alain and borrow the Macdonalds' bath. Peter is trying to make up his mind whether a bottle of Johnny Walker Red Label he has purchased from the bar is or isn't the real thing. Alex is going mad with an extremely sophisticated video camera they have hired from the Services Centre. (The camera was given Mr Hong's department by a German TV crew in settlement of outstanding service charges.) It records sound, has automatic focusing and offers instant playback on a miniature screen next to the viewfinder. Just about I keep him out of the bathroom.

'It's all here,' he keeps saying, 'you and Dad and the whole fucking show.'

What fucking show? I might as well have left Vietnam yesterday. The *longueurs* are beginning to tell. The Sofia, when I return there much later in the evening, is in a state of inebriation on all floors. The night porter, lounging in the doorway, inquires whether I want a madame, and can't believe me when I say I don't. Tuan, who passes, with his Italianate good looks, for the nearest thing they have to a head waiter, grabs me on the stairs and repeats my name over and over. In the upper restaurant, two of the waitresses are drinking beer and chewing the rice pancakes one of them has made. A Russian in the room next door to mine spends most of the night vomiting. Another day has passed without reward, and I can't believe tomorrow will be any different.

Sunday 31st December: Hanoi It isn't. Except in the evening, at the Thong Nhat, there's a New Year's Eve party. The usual noisy rumpus, with the best of the action at the bar and not inside the dining room, that has been cleared for the occasion. The *Daily Mail* gang turns out in force, even though it has removed to the Ministry of Energy's guesthouse – one of them didn't like my story about being bitten by a rat one little bit. The leader goes off to dance and comes back scared out of his wits because a Vietnamese boy has felt his crotch. Alex laughs long and loud. 'So much for our intrepid Fleet Street muck-raker!' he crows. I take the man to one side and tell him how he can make his fame and fortune in Vietnam. 'How's that?' the *Mail* man immediately perks up. Join the boat people on one of their outings, I reply. The *Mail* man tells me I'm the sickest thing since Uncle Adolf. A marginally more adult television crew present themselves. The Russian brandy runs out at eleven. Midnight becomes a duty. One minute into 1990 and the hotel empties.

But the Sofia is still upbeat. The tables in the gallery above the shop space are full of young people watching more or less 'black' videos. Several seventeen- and eighteen-year-old girls are dressed in gleaming white tracksuits. God knows where they're from. Their hair is done, their faces well made up, their hearts undetermined. And why should they be? Hanoi is changing changing changing. Hanoi is changing by the hour.

1990

Monday 1st January: Hanoi The show is on the road again. Zoom motorbikes me to the headquarters of the Women's Union, a house not far from the British Embassy which wouldn't look wholly out of place in north Oxford. Madame Nguyen Thi Dinh greets me at the doorway, flanked by assistants. I have already been told about her in Ben Tre. She is elderly, big, impressive, neo-mandarin and exudes the colour green. She wears a rather rich brocaded dress topped by a tasselled shawl. He manner is avuncular, her mindset orthodox. She eschews the anecdotal.

She tells me about the war, and she tells me about the condition of women in Vietnam today. She was born in 1920, in Giong Trom District, Ben Tre. She joined the Revolution in 1936, running messages between her local resistance base and its superior headquarters. At secret meetings she often played the part of watchman. In 1939 she married a fellow Party member. Three days after the birth of their son, her husband was imprisoned on Con Dao Island. When the boy was six months old, she herself was captured and sent to a detention centre close to the Cambodian border: 'a harmful place, poisonous water, miserable conditions, torture'. She was interrogated and beaten many times, but she didn't break. There was no hard evidence against her. Released in 1943 she immediately joined the Viet Minh. Her husband, she learned, had died in 1942, still in Con Dao, tortured to death.

She worked for the Viet Minh in Ben Tre Province right through to 1954, helping to shape and motivate the women's resistance movement. After Dien Bien Phu and the Geneva Accords many of her fellow leaders were regrouped north, but Nguyen Thi Dinh stayed south. For several years she restricted her activities to the political arena, pressing for the implementation of the promised

433

election. But as time went by and the prospect of an election receded, armed conflict was inevitable. In 1959 President Diem's relationship with the United States was cemented, and that 'was the beginning of the undeclared war against us'. Soon after the killings started. Men and women alike were seized and tortured by the Saigon security forces: it was, Madam Dinh recalls, 'the bloody year'.

Soon 'the people were clamouring for the Party to give them arms'. The Ben Tre Uprising, in which Madame Dinh played her part, was followed by copy-cat uprisings in other delta provinces. 'Diem and his US cronies called this the Special War, but we called it the War Without Declaration. Long before the Marines landed at Danang, the Americans had two thousand men deployed in the South. They were advisers, but they often joined combat. And then of course there was the strategic hamlet programme, another US intervention. It was this that gave my *toc dai* their opportunity.'

A long-haired female cadre was expected to work on three fronts. She had to be a political organizer, an agitator and a fighter – part of an armed 'shock force' that the enemy could never identify until it had struck. Her sex was her camouflage. Her face hidden beneath her conical sun hat, and her messages or weapons concealed in her basket, she walked the roads and jungle paths to market like countless other women.

Madame Dinh recalls with pride that six of her women in Ben Tre later received the title 'national heroine'. She herself slogged through the jungles in the role of a 'logistics mother'. But her experience and organizational ability quickly won her promotion. By the end of 1961 she was assigned to regional headquarters (the region comprising six central delta provinces). In 1965 she became a 'deputy regional commander-in-chief' of liberation troops in the whole of the South – a general, no less.

She continued to direct *toc dai* operations. 'The long-haired army never failed,' she tells me. 'We were always victorious. We were fully equal with the men, and the Americans were especially afraid of what they called the "bees". They were afraid of our bombs, our spikes, our mines. They were even afraid of our arrows. And of course, we made brilliant spies.'

Madame-General Dinh had perforce to move around continuously. For year after year she had no home. Frequently she had to sleep under other people's houses, burying her face in the earth. She only spent a short time in the relative safety of Cu Chi, three or four days at the most. And thus she continued, right up until 1975 and the fall of Saigon.

The war's immediate aftermath saw her installed as the president of the South Women's Liberation Union. But she was quickly transferred to Hanoi, where she became first vice-president and then president (1980) of the national Women's Union. She has also been a vice-minister in the Ministry of Social Affairs (since renamed the Ministry of Labour), and is one of four vice-presidents of the Council of State – a somewhat supine body that does little more than rubber-stamp the decisions of the Central Committee and Council of Ministers.

I ask about the Saigon Army. How was it that so many non-Catholic Vietnamese were recruited into it? Because this is the thing that most threatens the myth of unsullied glory that surrounds the Revolution.

Madame Dinh gives a little shrug. Many were forced to join, because of their situation. There was little other work, and the pay was relatively good. One should not underestimate the degree to which young people were under the control of the puppet government. The Saigon regime had its ways and means. And being Vietnamese, the soldiers had also to consider the suffering of their families, and how, if only in the short term, that suffering might be alleviated . . .

'But the important things to remember are that many of the men who enlisted in the Saigon Army deserted, and the low morale of that army itself. That is why the Ho Chi Minh Campaign was brought to such a swift and victorious conclusion!'

We turn to the other topic, the woman question.

'It is true, we have not yet achieved equality. Sixty per cent of the labour force is female, yet only ten per cent of the higher positions are held by women cadres. There are many reasons for this. Women are still tied down by family work. They suffer educational disadvantages. We have set ourselves a target: thirty per cent of women to receive a college education! But still we are a long way off. And yes, there is the fact of male chauvinism. Even

435

some high-ranking leaders look down on us. There are vestiges of feudalism, and in that respect the Revolution has yet to find its strength. The task of the Women's Union is to keep on raising political consciousness, to lobby the state for benefits and to realize its own educational programme. Currently we are teaching women how to defend and promote their interests, including how to choose a partner, and how too to run a home.'

The Union has a publishing wing, and circulates its own newspaper. But 'The state subsidy is very limited. Female emancipation is not a high priority.' And the Union, because it is a government-approved body (and if it wasn't it wouldn't exist), must also concern itself with other matters. 'We support *doi moi*, of course. But it is our duty to combat the negative factors. There is the question of bankruptcy among young people, both pecuniary and moral. Too many of the films they have been allowed to watch are unsalutary. Prosperity is not preferable to poverty in every case. At the moment we are conducting a nationwide campaign to draw attention to the new evils that are creeping into the land. Now that women are becoming aware of luxuries, now that those luxuries are becoming available, too many of them are turning to prostitution. Wealth and health are by no means concomitant . . .'

An assistant timorously insinuates herself into the room and after a while reminds Madame Dinh that she has state business to attend. Unhurriedly, Madame Dinh prepares to leave. But there is no need for me to go, she insists. I should stay behind and share some noodles with her staff.

Zoom and I stay behind for noodles. Among the four staff who eat with us is a young, pretty trainee interpreter. We flirt with her, in the customary manner. Zoom makes most of the running. An older woman asks me questions. Do I like Vietnam? Will I come back? Yes of course I adore Vietnam, and yes of course I want furiously to come back.

'And the women of Vietnam?'

'The women of Vietnam are wonderful. So self-controlled, intelligent, unpretentious.'

'And beautiful?'

'And very beautiful. *Dep lam*. Why not?'

The woman relaxes, smiles. When I do come back, she says, I

must remember the Union. There are many pretty girls who work at the Union, so should I ever want for female company . . .

Eat your heart out, Betty Friedan. A right gobsmack for Madame Greer. After lunch I visit the new international shop in Trang Tien Street, to buy a bottle of authentic scotch for tomorrow's office thingy. Back at the Sofia I contemplate packing. At four there is a tap on my door. Le Tien has come to say goodbye. Since my floor is now covered with the trophies of three months' journeying, we stand outside. Le Tien too is leaving Hanoi. He is going to run a publishing house in Saigon. I sense this is a sideways promotion, if indeed a promotion at all. I wish him luck. He wishes me luck. The parting compliments are long and florid. Then he hesitates. There is something on his mind. Oh yes. Ho Chi Minh. There will be a chapter about Uncle Ho in my book, won't there?

I repeat what I said on my first day in Vietnam. There will be no chapters, but how can anyone write a book about Vietnam without referring to Uncle Ho on every other page? How indeed. Le Tien, who has a sad face anyway, countenances dismay. An absolute conviction rides me: that's what I'm doing here, that's why some unrevealed higher hand has let me come and spend so long.

It also occurs to me that if I don't deliver the desired encomium, the unrevealed higher hand may tighten its fingers around those in the Ministry of Information who have done nothing but their best to render an at-times difficult English writer the assistance he required. My recalcitrance will be read as their failure.

We hug. I am saddened too, but try not to show it. There is a sudden vacuum of emotion that I'm sure we both feel. Then Le Tien leaves, to pursue a new destiny in H.C.M. City.

I reach halfway with my packing, which is to say that point when one is completely unpacked, when everything that is going to be packed is centrifuged as far is it will go. I think to myself: later, and abandon my room. At the Thong Nhat, fearing lest I become a pest to the brigadier, I take a bath in Alain's room. This has a double pay-off since Alain has just received a food parcel from his mother. He tells me to help myself to a generous box of Belgian chocolates. I do. Then I head off for my date.

My date is with Miss N. Principally I am anxious to discover what, in Hanoi, people do on a date. I meet her outside the Sofia, and we walk south-eastwards (always assuming my map of the city is compassed north) toward and into a quarter I have never set foot in before. The streets are narrow, dark, a little furtive. Every other house is a workshop of some sort, and there is a dismal clanging of metal on metal that is replicated every dozen paces. Miss N. proposes we eat noodles, but at each noodle joint we pass she hurries me on.

'That looked okay to me.'

'But I might be seen. Some of the people I know eat there sometimes.'

'You are afraid of Security?'

'No. Not at all. These days, it is no problem. But if we go to a place and my friends are there they won't leave us alone. And afterwards they won't leave me alone either.'

We plod on. At last we find a shabby little two-table restaurant that meets Miss N.'s requirements. The other diners would appear to be out-of-town mechanics who have more important things than noodles to spend their *dong* upon. A tiny, wizened waitress-cum-manageress-cum-cook plucks mightily at my sleeves, muttering 'Lien Xo, Lien Xo' in short marching syllables. After a while she places before me a bowl of thick white rubberoid strips stranded in a pale broth to which has been added half a sliced spring onion and some unidentified aspect of a pig's viscera.

'Eat!' commands Miss N., and for a minute or two I obey. When I can continue no longer she pulls a piece of paper out of her bag and hands it to me. It is a forecast of her life, prepared, in English, by an Indian astrologist. It is also the first documentary evidence I have come across in Hanoi that anyone has access to a word processor. Miss N. is promised a little health, a little wealth and much true love.

'Do you believe in this?' I ask.

Miss N. smiles non-committedly.

'Does it say you'll get what you want out of life?'

The artist lifts her spoon to her mouth and shakes her head.

'What do you want?'

'What do I want? Who? Me?' (Miss N. frequently is Japanese in

438

her manner.) 'I think what I would like, most of all, is a Rolls-Royce.'

She eats through to the last noodle. We take to the streets again. From her behaviour I gather that the way to make a date in Hanoi go with a swing is to keep walking and say nothing. Hanging about à deux. The spell is broken however when we pass a church. Behind a wooden stockade some dark ritual is being enacted. We peer through cracks and slits to observe a procession of choirboys, in full throat, following a statue of Jesus as it is taken around the building's perimeter. Miss N. is wholly mesmerized.

'Shall we go in?'

'Who? Us? You and me? No no no.'

'Why not?'

'Are we allowed?'

I take her through a stone archway into the churchyard. The last of the choirboys disappears inside the church. The service is about to begin.

My first impression within is that the church must have its own generator, or some other source of energy, for the lights are simply of a different calibre than anywhere else in Hanoi. The altar is incredibly bright. And not just the altar, but a huge, and incomparably vulgar, mock-up of the Bethlehem crib to the left. Further, there is, on wall, ceiling and pillar alike, an incredible profusion of what looks (and smells) like fresh paint. There is also an incredible profusion of people. The right aisle is full-housed with women, mainly small and old and beshawled. The left aisle, containing men of all ages, but mainly younger souls, shows a few empty spaces in the pews. Even as I lead Miss N. to one of these, I realize my mistake. The place is segregated. Hence maybe its popularity?

Miss N. realizes my mistake the moment she has sat down. Briefly she manifests a consternation laced with shame. But the congregation around us seem not to mind, and within moments Miss N. is locked into proceedings. Hymns from the choir flow uninterruptedly from the organ gallery behind. Incense rakes the indoctrinated.

My friend, who is not the spoiled person her cupidity for an English motorcar might suggest, is wondrous in her appreciation of the audio-visual spectacle. She has become abstracted in her concentration. I certainly have ceased to exist. Or have I? Having had enough of priests, hymns, incense and all other such witchcraft for one lifetime, I gaze at her face instead. And I must concede it is a very beautiful face, not just the eyes, whose sleek slim orbs trail in unbroken lines toward her distant temples, but the temples themselves, the nose, the gently pouted lips, the chin, that is delicate without being fragile . . .

With each moment that passes my reasons for this 'date' revise. There is a double danger present. Danger one is that Miss N. will want to come back to this place. Danger two, I will want to come back with her.

Is this Vietnam's last attempt to suck me in, irrecoverably, for good? The thought of my imminent departure spells both relief and misery.

I gaze at Miss N.'s face. It is simply not possible that she is unaware of my attention. The way her head inclines, thus. Her peripheral vision, her proximal sense of the other . . . And yet, must one not always make allowances for the sheer artlessness of women, which always surpasses art? For they, like us men, are nature's puppets too.

The service ends, or we leave beforehand, I forget which. I remember only the charade of the Eucharist, enacted incompletely in the peripheries of my own vision. We discover ourselves once more strolling the streets, 'hanging about' as Zoom would have it. We find a deserted video-café and sit in a back room. Miss N. has a Coke, I – for want of a Russian brandy – a Heineken. The manager, mistaking our intentions, makes the already dim lights dimmer.

On a corner of Han Bai Street we say goodbye. No kisses, no tears, but no compliments either. Shunning the Sofia, for fear of the lasses in spanking, spankable white tracksuits, I head for the Thong Nhat. Peter and Alex are in a crowd at the bar. They are just a little hurt when I tell them how I availed myself of Alain's bath in the late afternoon. Do they have nothing to match a Belgian chocolate? I promise I will use their bathroom tomorrow. When they inquire where I've been all evening, I tell them: to church. The brigadier slips his son a wink. I have just confirmed, perhaps, their absurd ruling that I am G. Greene redivivus.

Tuesday 2nd January: Hanoi   The office party, which commences at noon, is a raging, howling success. Within minutes the assembled company, which includes more or less every cadre I have shaken hands with at the Ministry since arriving, has risen to a state of extreme boisterousness. The sheer dinginess of the room itself serves only to emphasize the uppishness of the closely compacted human spirit. For a Vietnamese office, particularly a Vietnamese office in Hanoi, has none of the presentation, none of the self-congratulation, of its western counterpart. There are no pie charts, corporate-celebrity photographs, year planners, framed certificates or any of the other paraphernalia that ritually affirm the desk-slave's cosmic importance. The walls of the room in the basement of the Ministry's building in Quan Su Street are distinguished principally by their barrenness. An ancient map of the world, a hangover perhaps from the days when international Marxism-Leninism dreamed of such things, is the sole visual. A classroom blackboard provides the only opportunity for less global data. And of course, lampshades have not been invented yet.

The desks have been formed into a line down the middle of the room. Twenty or so chairs have been scrambled from adjacent departments, and twenty or so males occupy them. But again, seat occupancy is not a settled business. Rather the seats are deployed as springboards. A slow-motion Mexican wave dominates proceedings. Again and again everyone rises to his feet to toast everyone else. And having toasted everyone else, everyone must be toasted by everyone else. A lot of office amities are settled today. The bottle of Famous Grouse that I procured yesterday vanishes in a vociferous flash, as do two bottles of dreaded vodka. Our tumblers are refilled with beer poured from a five-gallon petrol can. Somebody knows somebody at Hanoi Brewmex. Or is it gasoline? For when the great moment comes, we are fuelled to the skies.

The great moment is the arrival of Peter and Alex, delayed by their final session with General Giap. They come bearing a vast box between them. The cry, the universal shout (led by Truc) goes up: Heineken! At once the already incredible energy level redoubles. Two cadres relieve the white men of their burden and in a trice the air is thick with flying green tins, lobbed like hand-grenades into outstretched hands with the timing and accuracy of a meticulously prepared assault.

441

In the thick of it all Mr Hong, blue-bereted and striving for control, flounders badly. His colleague-subordinates are merciless in their good humour, teasing him about an affair with Madame Tuk (Thuk? Thuc? Tuc?) of many years' standing. There are no grounds for this calumny, which is why (apparently) it is given full rein now. On my right Zoom explains all: 'Poor Mister Hong! But really, you should tease him a little too.'

'Maybe,' I say.

As for Madame Tuk, who has been interpreting for Peter, she alone preserves composure. She sits at the far, door end of the 'table' untroubled by any mere remark.

The only other female present is Binh. She has worked hard all morning to prepare the food. Plates of chicken, rice, salad and spring rolls abound everywhere, scarcely touched. In reality they are but obstacles, set strategically between the drinker and the source of his next drink. Binh, demure, pinch faced today, seems pleased by this. Did we munch her preparations in silence things would have gone horribly awry. But if anyone addresses her she at once dives into a tizzy of confusion. She is the hostess who wants only to be an inconspicuous ornament.

Mr Hong has already made one speech, at the beginning, to mark my presence. At the appropriate moment I make mine. I keep it short, and hope it's lively:

'What can I say? I've been here three months. I've been everywhere, seen everything. I am the luckiest of men. But more than that, I've met the people, the wonderful, warm, vital inhabitants of Vietnam. When I arrived I didn't know what to expect. To be frank I was apprehensive. And what happened? In exchange for my fears I gained three brothers, two uncles, a sister and a father. No sooner did I step off the aeroplane than I was accosted by this energetic adolescent – Dung!' (Zoom laughs, claps his hands, falls off his chair.) 'And no sooner had I met him, my first brother, than I met my first uncle, Mr Nam, waiting in the minibus.' (Nam, gangster-grinning to the last, raises his hand, sees that there is a glass in it and swallows.) 'And no sooner had I met my first uncle than I met my second. At my hotel Mr Hong gave me a truly heartfelt welcome to your country.' (Mr Hong momentarily surfaces from his anxieties and waves both hands.) 'And that was only the beginning. When I came to your office, I found a sister – except that Em Binh is too sexy for me to actually want to call her sister.' (Binh blushes cadmium and buries her head in her lap.) 'Then when I travelled south I was escorted by my second brother, the redoubtable Truc!' (Truc jumps up, cries, 'Heineken!') 'In Saigon – oh Saigon! – my third, and most dangerous, brother was ready to pounce: Tiger!' (Nguyen roars hoarsely). 'And finally, all over the south, I was driven, protected, promoted and cherished by Sau Dang.' (Cheers of 'Sau!' 'Sau Dang!' 'Mr Six!' 'Sau Dai!') 'Could anyone ask for a more fantastic family?' (Mixed, babbulous, bibulous responses.) 'A toast therefore to you all. But in particular, because he is absent, a toast to Papa Sau!'

The room stands to its feet and Sau is deeply celebrated in the collective oesophagus. Alex remains standing and makes his speech, an artist's appraisal of the charms of Hanoi. His feelings overcome his words so that those who do not understand the English tongue (nobody is translating anyone) understand him perfectly. Then it is Peter's turn. The pro.

Truth to tell, Alex and I have not been heard out in perfect silence. Our remarks were addressed to that end of the table where sit Mr Hong, Nam, Zoom, Truc, Nguyen and Binh. The other end went its own sweet way, though at a reduced raucousness. The balance was roughly that sometimes obtained by the BBC during Prime Minister's Question Time on a Wednesday afternoon in the House of Commons. The brigadier, old campaigner that in more warlike times he might have been, sorts this one out at the double. At first he displays extreme reluctance to say anything at all. This focuses attention on him wonderfully. He has virtually to be pulled out of his chair. But it is his opening gambit, repeated, that tells most convincingly, that delivers the killing shot. 'As the oldest person present ... mmmhhmmm ... As the oldest person present ...' And the rest of what he has to say (a somewhat sober, or sobering, appraisal of hospitality received, good work done and the hopefully bright future of Anglo–Vietnamese relations) is heard in a hush absolute.

A mandarin trick, designed to profit from the innate, Confucian respect a Vietnamese has, or is supposed to have, for his elders – though to be fair to ourselves Peter does have the advantage of

443

addressing Mr Hong over the heads of the recalcitrants, who therefore have good reason to hold their tongues. The point is made though: it's not what you say that matters, it's how old you are when you say it. The applause is loud and long, though exactly when it ceases to be applause and becomes simple noisy drinking again is indeterminate. That this is clearly the last of the speeches is an added cause for stoking up the coals of jubilation.

How long the proceedings continue I don't know. In a minute or two Zoom, who has changed places several times, is at my side.

'I think we must be going. We can't be late for Vu Ky.'

I have never been so thoroughly disarmed. Nam takes us – the last ride of the gangsters – in the minibus to Ho Chi Minh's house. The recurrence of the man, whom I have only seen in an embalmed state, his domicile and Government Park, combined with the mixture of whisky, rice-wine and beer coursing my arteries, serves to make this, my last afternoon in Vietnam, pronouncedly dream-like. And Vu Ky fits beautifully into that dream. He wears his years – he is well into his seventies – not lightly but hardly at all. The skin on his pink, alabaster face has not weathered in the least. Rather it emanates moral purity. Only a wisp of white hair, trailing from his chin, belies his age. For the rest, he has been painstakingly renovated.

There is only one topic of conversation. This is my final induction, the last attempt to convert me to the cult of H.C.M. My efforts to establish Vu Ky's biography meet with scant reward. It takes me half an hour to drag it out of him that he was born in Ha Son Binh. 'There is nothing important about my life,' he keeps telling me, 'except of course that I had the inestimable privilege to work alongside Uncle Ho for twenty-two years as his secretary.'

We sit on the steps that lead down into the small lake in front of the house. The three of us – Vu Ky, myself and Zoom – are squashed up together, so that our thighs and knees touch. A secretary's secretary and a semi-uniformed observer crouch within hearing distance. The latter I suspect is security. Vu Ky has been in trouble once, for publishing articles in which he indirectly criticized the lifestyles of some Politburo members by harping on about the great simplicity of H.C.M.'s own arrangements. (I also suspect that spying on the activities of big potatoes on behalf of other big potatoes forms the broad mass of Security's workload, but I would emphasize that is only speculation.)

The pond is full of large carp, presented by all the different provinces of Vietnam. Vu Ky, his voice unctuous with respect, but also self-assured (for he has imbibed the Way, and the Way makes him strong), remembers how at the end of every day he and Uncle would sit, exactly where we are sitting now, and feed these fish. And how, after Uncle died, he continued the practice, certain that the carp rose to the surface only because they expected to see the Great Leader.

'I often tried to imagine how they felt when the only person they could find here was a mere secretary! But I went on feeding them, because that was my duty.'

Vu Ky became H.C.M.'s secretary in 1945, two days after the August Revolution. Until then he had been a secret cadre, living in three different houses in Hanoi, with three different 'wives', who afforded him alibis when the French Sûreté came a-sniffing. He had been thinking of marrying one of his wives when the call to vicarious greatness came. H.C.M. never married, and Vu Ky followed suit.

'You see, he loved his country completely. If he had taken a wife, and there was an endless queue of women who wanted to become Madame Ho, then that would have caused jealousy among the others, and well . . . you know what wives can do!'

Vu Ky's thigh pushes meaningfully against mine. He knows what I want to ask, and he wants me to ask it.

'Yes of course,' he answers, 'before the Revolution, Uncle Ho had girlfriends. And why not? He was young, handsome and human. What else would you expect?'

Much of his work involved 'editing' articles about Ho Chi Minh submitted to his office. Ho Chi Minh himself had no time for such labour – the ultimate token of self-effacement perhaps. The image noised abroad therefore was partly Vu Ky's creation. But Ho did give him guidelines for this too-onerous task. When Vu Ky asked how he should know what was 'right' and what was 'wrong', H.C.M. gave him three criteria. He should always ask himself, when reading a piece: (1) Is it logical? (2) Will it improve the lives of young people? And (3) is it 'correct'?

445

'He loved the truth, he loved his country, and he loved the Revolution.'

But H.C.M. was not above telling lies about his age. Oh no. He was human like the rest of us. Vu Ky recalls the occasion of Uncle's seventy-fifth birthday in 1965, a very big birthday in Vietnamese society. So profoundly apprehensive was Ho Chi Minh of receiving *personal* attention that he threatened to leave Hanoi and not come back until everyone had forgotten his age. The Politburo engineered a compromise. On the day a dinner party would be held, but nobody, absolutely nobody, would mention the reason for the dinner.

The dinner party was held, and all went well – for a while. Everybody talked about the war against America in the South and not much else. But then a younger cadre, who had no idea why the dinner was being held, innocently asked his Leader, 'By the way, how old are you?'

'Uncle Ho replied immediately, "I am twenty!" Everybody looked at him. Then he explained. Twenty years had elapsed since the August Revolution, twenty years since the birth of the modern nation . . .'

'Is it true,' I interject, 'that he smoked forty cigarettes a day?'

Vu Ky beams. Why yes, of course! 'But he stopped after 1947. His country had first claim on his body.'

We have shifted now. We are sitting inside the house, on the ground floor. Not of course at the great table itself – that would be sacrilege – but on the low wall around the building's base.

Vu Ky signs and presents me with a little book (it measures two and a half inches by one and a half) he has written about H.C.M. Before handing it over he leafs through its pages. He hastens to reassure me that it is not the first edition. In the first edition he omitted any mention of Ton Duc Thang, the second President of Vietnam. That was a terrible thing to do! Quite accidental! So in the second edition he inserted a passage (which he shows me) where he describes how Uncle Ho and Uncle Ton often walked together through the park at dusk.

'And I would often watch them, arm in arm through the garden in the distance. And really, it was just like watching two wise old peasants take a stroll!'

The little biography is followed by a very large picture book containing a selection of the photographs of H.C.M. I have seen in countless museums, meeting halls and streets during my Vietnam journeys.

We go upstairs. Vu Ky demonstrates how he used to crouch on the floor by Ho Chi Minh's bed when Ho Chi Minh was in the bed, for their late-night chats.

'Is this where he died?'

'No. But would you like to see where he did die?'

'Oh yes please.'

We leave the house and walk to some low out-buildings (formerly the President's staff offices) at the rear. In one of them is a big room with another big table, close to which is a very small bed. Beside the bed is a tiny table, and on the tiny table is an alarm-clock. Since Ho Chi Minh's death this has never been wound up, but is stopped at the hour of his death on 3rd September 1969.

The table was for the Politburo.

We walk around the pond toward the exit. Uncharacteristically Vu Ky volunteers a piece of information about himself. It is his intention to retire, from his post as director of the Ho Chi Minh Museum, in April, the hundredth anniversary of Uncle Ho's birth. On the same day the museum will reopen in its brand-new building, which rises in the distance something like a Singapore department store.

'But please, you mustn't tell anyone. It is my little secret.'

Hugs are exchanged. We say goodbye. As I walk back with Zoom through the crowding streets of Hanoi I struggle desperately to shake loose from the suspicion that good ol' Uncle Ho actually was a saint.

Thus my programme finishes. I return to my room, finish packing, have dinner and wind up, *mutatis mutandis*, at the bar of the Thong Nhat. The bar is closed and very lively. The *Daily Mail* has turned out in force, and it's help-yourself time. A perplexed, anxious receptionist is told, in no uncertain terms, where to shove it. In my own country, if a band of orientals jumped the counter of a hotel bar, it would be a police matter. In Hanoi the police are not called. It is merely enough to wave a fistful of dollar bills to get your way. The money also covers you for any racial slur that may have found its way into your comments.

I leave. At ten o'clock on a Tuesday night the town (I will always have difficulties in thinking of Hanoi as a city) is quiet. Just a few dark cyclists gliding in the shadows of the stage-set street. A cold steam hugs the forlorn houses and hangs above the roads. Behind me, the Opera House. In front of me, the little round lake. Around the perimeter of the lake, isolated lovers embracing each other, a mixture of passion and the need to keep warm.

The Sofia too is having a rest, a night off. It is a while before the night porter opens up to my banging and shouts of 'Ciao anh!' On the other side of Hang Bai Street two drunks sit in the doorway of the department store. An old, cone-hatted woman shuffles past them along the colonnade, two panniers hanging from the ends of a pole laid across her shoulders. An empty cyclo creaks by.

Because of the cold I am rubbing my arms. I am impatient to be let in, but in a sense I want to be left where I am outside. I could drink Hanoi by night forever, but this is my final draught.

Wednesday 3rd January: Hanoi–Bangkok So it's time to go. Zoom comes early. He will not alas be able to come to the airport with me. The office is so busy today. He is very sorry about this. Madame Tuc will take myself and the Macdonalds in Nam's van. I must be ready by eleven. Therefore we must say goodbye now.

We say goodbye. It is sad. Thanking someone you have come to like for his professional services seems inadequate but still it must be done. Zoom gives me a pair of handsome Chinese gloves he bought on the border during our trip to Cao Bang. He also gives me an envelope containing Nguyen Van Linh's 'written answers', and an official letter from the Ministry clearing the export of my Cham head. I give Zoom an envelope that contains a gift for his wedding later in the year.

'For your wife-to-be,' I say. 'Mind you marry her!'

Zoom laughs. We hug. Then he is gone.

Will I ever see him again?

I look through Linh's written answers. The envelope contains the General Secretary's potted biography, as well as his photograph –

448

passport size and pasted onto a small piece of paper. As for the main course, it is hard not to scoff. The questions which Mr Hong request I revise and rewrite after my return to Hanoi appear not to have been put. Instead only two of the questions I wrote out before leaving Hanoi are addressed, and one of these has been mutilated. My 'How deep do the divisions within the Party that one hears about run?' has become 'How far advanced are the preparations for the Seventh Party Congress and what are the prospects for Vietnam in the 21st Century?'

Linh's responses – if indeed they are his – are utterly predictable, utterly starched and utterly undeserving of quotation.

At ten Truc comes bounding up to my room. Am I ready? The van is waiting outside.

'No, I'm not ready. I thought I was leaving at eleven.'

'You have to go now. Sorry.'

So at the end it's a mad undignified rush which leaves me no time to say goodbye to anyone at the Sofia and also leaves me no time to bid a proper farewell to Truc himself, who is under orders to return as quickly as possible to Quan Su Street. The presence, in the back of the van, of a television crew, adds to the downbeat. They are not leaving, only coming along for the ride, in order to reel off background footage somewhere on the way back from the aerodrome. Only Alex is in spirits of any sort. Peter smoulders. It really isn't right that a brigadier should be seen off in such a one-stone two-birds manner.

Madame Tuc though performs wonders with the emigration officials. None of us has our baggage searched. My Cham head passes through into the departure lounge under my arm without even being looked at. In a way I feel cheated. I am leaving with my original Friend-of-Vietnam status apparently untarnished. I am happy still to be a Friend of Vietnam, I hope I will always be a Friend of Vietnam, but wonder whether, investigation-wise, I've done all that I could have done.

Soon I am sitting between two windows inside the Thai Inter jet. The choice is simple. Either I crane my neck backwards blessed awkwardly to take a lingering last look at Vietnam, or I settle back to study a copy of today's *Bangkok Post* at my leisure.

I choose the latter. Any emotions I have lie scattered up and down two thousand kilometres of Highway One.

449

Friday 5th January: Bangkok   KING/ORVILLE D./348 44 9152/
A NEG/BAPTIST. I haven't forgotten. In the morning I ring the
United States Embassy and make an appointment with Lt-Col
James D. Spurgeon III for the late afternoon. I duly present myself
at the embassy gatehouse. There I am met by a hulk of undeclared
rank named Garnett E. Bell. Bell walks me across the embassy
compound (in reality a spacious mini-park) and into a central
building. As he ushers me through a multiplicity of security checks,
some human, some electronic, he chaunters on about his 'time in
'Nam'. I try not to listen. At last we come to the room of the Joint
Casualty Resolution Centre, a division of the Department of Defense. Bell sits me down in his office, gives me some corfy, hears
out my spiel about backstreeting Hué and scrutinizes my scrap of
paper. Then he looks up Orville D. King in his register of MIAs.
There are four or five Kings, but not one of them is an Orville D.
As I had rather suspected, the thing is a hoax of some kind.

'But don't worry,' grunts Bell, 'we'll check it out and let you
know.'

Having gained access to this superpower sanctum however I am
reluctant to leave so soon. I ask whether we can discuss the whole
issue of MIAs. Knowing just what I mean, Bell suggests perhaps I
should meet the colonel after all.

James D. Spurgeon III is a tall, elegant, relaxed, suave man.
Dressed in civvies, he could easily pass for a New York publisher.
As soon as I have him in my sights I put it to him: does he or
doesn't he have any hard evidence that there are any Americans still
held hostage in Vietnam?

It is not just that Spurgeon ducks and hedges which intrigues me:
it is how he ducks and hedges. No, he says, there is no watertight,
absolutely conclusive, *hard as you put it* evidence. Uh-uh. 'But we
are getting closer all the time.' His office is in receipt of reports
every week, and these are being constantly sifted, assessed and
correlated. Yes, many of the reports are thoroughly dubious. There
are plenty of Vietnamese wanting to leave Vietnam who believe
they can improve their chances of joining the Orderly Departure
Program by fabricating stories about Americans they have met in
the re-education camps; and there are plenty of sightings of Americans in the jungle who turn out to be Russians, Czechs, Swedes or

450

Australians engaged on legitimate aid projects. But every once in a while a report comes in that doesn't fit these categories. 'And at some point, when there are enough of these, they'll begin correlating.'

'And then?'

'And then, if need be, we'll go in hard.'

'What do you mean?'

'Just that. We'll go in hard.'

As for Foreign Minister Thach's challenge, Spurgeon dismisses it as 'meaningless'.

'Sure, we can tell Thach that we have reason to believe there is a POW camp in such-and-such a valley in such-and-such a mountain province, and he can take us there in his chopper. But any Americans will have been cleared well in advance.' Evidently it hasn't occurred to Spurgeon that one way to respond to Thach might be to get airborne with him first, then give him the co-ordinates. But then, as Spurgeon is all too well aware, he doesn't have anywhere specific for Thach to take him to.

Yet. What strikes me about the research programme of Spurgeon's unit, which has been going on eight years now, and which presumably enjoys the benefits of America's considerable satellite surveillance facilities, is the double take, the spurious scientificity. What the programme is trying to do is akin to proving the existence of unicorns. Unicorns may not exist, but the fact of their non-existence can never be adequately demonstrated according to the most exacting requirements of scientific logic.

On the other hand, if unicorns do exist, and you try hard enough, one day you might come across some evidence.

The same with POW MIAs. Scientifically their non-existence can never be absolutely proved. Which is why, I suspect, the Defense Department has opted for a programme that has all the glamour and authenticity of 'controls' that allow for and therefore dispose of negative indications. What is left out is the probabilities of the thing. The plain brutal truth of the matter is that if, for any reason, Vietnam did retain any American POWs after the war, it is likely they have long since been liquidated. Vietnam simply has too much to lose, and has had too much to lose for the past half-dozen years, by keeping them alive. Liquidating people is scarcely

451

pleasant, but if you go to someone else's country to fight some-one else's war then you should expect, from time to time, to be liquidated.

Two further reflections. Currently the number of US servicemen listed Missing in Action in Indochina stands at around 1,650. This compares with the 75,000 listed MIA as a result of World War II, and 8,000 as a result of Korea. Secondly, the Defense Department's continuing belief in the aliveness of some Indochina MIAs in Vietnam could actually be interpreted as a tacit acknowledgement of the more humanitarian aspects of the Vietnamese character. What Defense seems to be saying is, 'We don't actually believe the Viets would do away with any POWs they may have retained.' If the department began listening to its own unconscious reasoning, then it might cease impeding the development of US–Vietnamese relations which is so obviously in the interests of both countries.

James D. Spurgeon III gives me a pamphlet that sets out his unit's position. For reasons best known to himself he also gives me an enrolment form for the Bangkok Foreign Correspondents' Club.

On my way out I ask Bell for the return of my number one souvenir from Hué. It is retrieved from a cabinet where it has already been filed, along with four photocopies.

Tuesday 23rd January: London England. I take my Cham head to Spink's, the fine art dealer in St James's. The head of the South-East Asia department is away, but one of his young assistants is available to see me. I don't think he has ever seen a Cham piece before, but he is sufficiently impressed to have me shown round the 'stone room' in the underground vault. Most of the exhibits are Hindu, of Indian provenance. There are sculptures there which pierce the very soul. I leave cautiously optimistic. It appears my treasure really may not be a fake. I must wait a week or two, however, before they can suggest a value.

And since I am in St James's, I visit Christie's as well, next door. By pure accident I have my little hoard of Vietnamese stamps on my person.

My reception at the auctioneer's is far less satisfactory. It is even forlorn. I am made to wait on a chair in a corridor, then I am

452

interviewed by a Ugandan Indian, a tall, well-oiled fellow born in Goa. At least though he doesn't beat about the bush. There is, he says, no interest in Vietnamese stamps in the stamp world whatso-ever. He gives the contents of one of the three envelopes I place before him a cursory glance, and then explains: the market is controlled by American and Japanese money, and neither the Americans nor the Japanese will touch Vietnam. To support his argument he hands me a somewhat ancient looking catalogue. Ten cents seems to be the going price for most older Vietnamese stamps. Then he offers me his good advice: if I know of any children with a violent disposition, I should give them my haul and tell them they can destroy it.

Wednesday 7th February: Milford Haven, Wales Ghastly weather. My country has been racked by storms for days on end. Even though they are new, double glazed, PVC, all the windows of my sea-house whistle as gale-force winds home in from across the Atlantic. The water in the haven lurches from side to side, from end to end. Last night a trawlerman up at Bob Mackee's bar described how two tugs have been employed 26 hours non-stop just keeping a small tanker on her moorings. This morning a lifeboat put limpingly into port, which is strange because Milford doesn't have a lifeboat of its own.

At lunchtime I hear on the radio that Mikhail Gorbachev has won a 'watershed' vote at a plenum of the Central Committee, paving the way for multi-party democracy in the Soviet Union, and wonder how that will go down in Hanoi. I now see why neither Le Duc Tho nor Nguyen Co Thach wanted to distance himself from China, despite all the trouble China has given Viet-nam. The Politburo must have grasped a while back that it would only be a matter of time before Russia followed the lead given her by East European satellites, so ideologically China must have looked a safer bet.

I am filled with sorrow for that poor orphan of a country, always looking for a parent, and never getting anything more than one bad uncle after another. There's nothing socialist about Red China in its present incarnation, rather it's just another nasty

453

fascist military dictatorship. I am filled with sorrow, and I am also filled with nostalgia. The inclement weather drives home how far away Vietnam is now, and so I begin missing, quite intensely, the likes of Zoom and Truc and Mr Nam and Sau. It would be so nice to have a Heineken with them, to climb into the Mazda and go tootling off on another madcap ride full of fellowship and adventure.

But of course it would be full of propaganda too. I am under no illusions about the 'programme' which the Ministry of Information had more to do with the planning of than I ever did. The more I think about it, the more it strikes me that my visit must have been orchestrated, at least in the initial phase of my application, at a higher level than was ever revealed to me. *Yes, by all means, let Mr Wintle come and write a book. And let us show him what we would like the rest of the world to read about.*

I sit in my study watching the water. The sea is up to its usual, age-old trick. Minute after minute, hour after hour, day after day, year after year, century after century, it sends in its waves. Here comes another, it seems to be saying, and another and another. Am I not infinitely clever, infinitely resourceful? But it is all a con. Every wave is made up out of the same material as its predecessor. Strictly speaking there's no such thing as a brand-new wave. The sea is a permanent recycling job.

And so I think it is with the Vietnamese Revolution. Its part is played, but still it keeps on rolling in, the same old stuff, in an attempt to keep the people mesmerized.

But who is really mesmerized?

It is the politicians, the big potatoes who are mesmerized.

Even so, in my imagination I plant the flag of the Socialist Republic in the middle of the heaving haven, if only for aesthetic reasons. There is little colour in the 'scape today, everything is boiling lead, so that the bright cadmium red and inlaid golden star would look just swell.

I am thinking of course of the drive from Hanoi to Halong Bay, and the red flag flying above the deserted railway stop amid the infinitely dreary, raincast flatlands between the antiquated capital and Haiphong.

They asked me to include a chapter on Ho Chi Minh. This I put

454

down to a morbid desire to pretend that he is in some abstruse manner still alive. Yet I suspect that if he were still alive, or if he were to be resurrected, the advice he would give his people would run something like this: *Yes, I am the most remarkable Vietnamese that ever lived, but that's no reason to depend on me so much. Learn rather to depend upon yourselves, for you are good enough, and actually there's no need to go on projecting your fears and cravings upon the image of my person.*

Everywhere I went I saw the image of Ho Chi Minh. He is recycled ceaselessly. There were posters of him in every town, in every street almost, certainly in every public building that I entered; statues, sculptures, busts; painted portraits in the art shops; and, of course, the endless photographs of him in the museums. And these images were, to an astonishing degree, differentiated. Sometimes it was Uncle Ho in peasant garb, or Uncle Ho the children's friend, or Uncle Ho weeping with anguish in front of a radio microphone. Other times it was Ho Chi Minh the political supremo, or Ho Chi Minh the Party man, sleeves rolled up, even Ho Chi Minh the warrior.

No man perhaps has a better claim to have been all things to all men, no man was a better patriot. But by clinging on to him, by pinning all their aspirations on his chest, the Vietnamese thwart their own eclecticism.

Saturday 10th February: Milford Haven   Letter from Spink & Son Ltd. Bad show. 'Our director has now had the chance to look at the stone three-headed deity which you left with us. I am afraid that the prognosis is not very encouraging and we have come to the conclusion that the piece is probably not of the period it purports to be. It must be stressed that this is, of course, a matter of opinion . . .' My inquiries pinpoint the source of their doubt. The head-dress is too high. Nothing wrong with the stone, but stone is very difficult to date. Damn!

Saturday and Sunday 14th and 15th April: Milford Haven   Easter. I sleep, not unusually, with my radio switched on and tuned to the

BBC World Service. In the middle of the night I am awoken by a Vietnam report. The gist of it is that what Washington is really after is a return to Cam Ranh Bay. The Russians are pulling out and the US Navy would like a new lease on its old base.

Can that really be what it's all about? For the next few days I will search the press for confirmation, but nothing shows.

Perhaps I was dreaming, though history suggests I wasn't.

Justin Wintle
Vietnam and Milford Haven 1989–90

Postscript

October 1990   It transpires I may have been bitten by a rat in Bangkok, as well as at the Thong Nhat in Hanoi. At the end of September the *Financial Times* sent me a copy of *Kiss the Boys Goodbye* to review. The subtitle of this book, written by Monika Jensen-Stevenson and her husband William Stevenson, was *How the United States Betrayed its Own POWs in Vietnam*. Its purpose was to demonstrate that after 1973 Vietnam retained some of the Americans captured during the Vietnam War, and that these men are still alive, kept in the jungle camps and mountain caves. In addition it sought to show how other American servicemen, taken prisoner during the course of the CIA's secret operations in Laos, both before and after 1973, are similarly withheld.

My instinct was to dismiss these claims. Amnesty International, Vietnam's Foreign Minister Nguyen Co Thach and the Joint Casualty Resolution Center had painted an altogether different picture for me. But when I got down to reading *Kiss the Boys Goodbye* I was strongly persuaded to reconsider. The evidence gathered by the authors was simply too powerful to be ignored.

The Stevensons also contended that official US agencies had known about the POWs all along. Despite public demands for information and action, intelligence reports had been deliberately 'buried', they claimed, in the name of 'national security', mainly to protect illegal CIA activities which included drugs dealing out of the Golden Triangle. Indeed, every effort had been taken to silence anyone who either had or offered evidence that contradicted the declared government position.

A long list of those whom various US government agencies had endeavoured to gag included Bobby Garwood (see pp. 238–9). In the Stevensons' account, Garwood was not a deserter but a frightened

459

soldier who had evolved his own strategy for survival inside the Vietnamese prison camp system after 1973. In 1979, having gained the trust of his Vietnamese minders, he effected his escape by passing a note to a Finnish diplomat. In the same note he intimated the existence of the POWs. Washington's response was to have him reincarcerated. He was not properly debriefed until 1988, and even then steps were taken to conceal his revelations.

On the Vietnamese side, the Stevensons claimed, the purpose of retaining American prisoners was to provide Hanoi with bargaining chips for future negotiations with Washington. This the communists had done before. In 1954 not all French captives had been returned immediately to France. The Viet Minh held back some men, called 'pearls', so that they could be 'sold' later on. The motive in the 1970s seems to have been the same. In particular Hanoi wanted Washington to honour Richard Nixon's pledge of in excess of three billion dollars to 'help heal the wounds of war'.

Because of the far-reaching implications contained in *Kiss the Boys Goodbye* my review expanded to become the lead feature of the *Weekend FT* at the end of September. Since the *Financial Times* was the first major newspaper anywhere to accord the Stevensons coverage, my article inevitably attracted attention. The feedback included a lengthy communication from John LeBoutillier, Republican member of the House of Representatives for New York from 1981 to 1983, and also a member of the House Foreign Affairs Committee for the same period. His fax included this passage.

> For example, Robert McFarlane, President Reagan's national security adviser and before that a key member of Henry Kissinger's coterie during the Paris peace talks which ended American involvement in the Vietnam War, admitted that 'there are ... there have to be living Americans held over there.' Richard Nixon, on whose watch the Paris Peace Accords were signed, recently said: 'The POWs are there ... everyone admits it.' ... Six weeks ago, Senator Claiborne Pell, the Chairman of the Senate Foreign Relations Committee, confided that there are 'probably a handful of POWs over there.'

Meanwhile Nguyen Co Thach had been visiting the United States to hold talks aimed at normalizing US–Vietnamese relations. Both governments put 'resolution of the MIA issue' high on the agenda. This in itself was curious, since Washington and Hanoi have previously adopted an identical position, namely that there are no POWs alive in Vietnam. But most tellingly, on Wednesday the 17th of this month, according to the BBC World Service News Thach emerged from a meeting with General John W. Vessey (former Chairman of US Joint Chiefs of Staff) to tell reporters that, while he could 'vouch' there are no POWs still held captive by the Vietnamese, there may nonetheless be a 'few' US servicemen alive in 'remote' regions of his country.

I doubt very much whether in the fifteen years since the fall of Saigon there is a single remote region of Vietnam that hasn't been rigorously searched by a government obsessed with security. Perhaps the right question to have put to Thach was whether, to the best of his knowledge, there are significant numbers of Americans held prisoner in Laos. Perhaps too by the time *this* book is published the 'MIA issue' really will have been resolved. Yet if what Monika Jensen-Stevenson and her husband have written is accurate, American democracy has been fundamentally compromised. As has, indeed, this journalist from a friendly nation. For I would then have to conclude that what I took from James D. Spurgeon III in Bangkok was disinformation cunningly designed to steer me away from the truth.

And so it comes full circle. I went to Vietnam partly to furnish an alternative to the *Rambo* and *Missing in Action* films. Yet, despite the violence of its fantasy, that cinema may yet be vindicated.

J.W.

Some Vietnamese Dates

200 BC   The northern part of present-day Vietnam conquered by the Chinese.

AD 939   Chinese rule overthrown, although Vietnamese independence is not finally established until 1428.

The Viet people continue expanding southwards, eventually establishing themselves in the Mekong Delta.

1545   Vietnam divided north and south by warring factions.

1772   A rebellion by the Tay Son brothers begins the process of national reunification.

1802   With French help, Nguyen Anh becomes Gia Long, the first of the Nguyen dynasty of emperors.

1859–83   Indochina becomes a French colony. Vietnam divided into three: Tonkin, Annam and Cochinchina (north, centre and south).

1930   Indochinese Communist Party created by Ho Chi Minh, in exile in Hong Kong.

1940   Control of Indochina effectively passes to Japan, although French administration remains.

1945   In the vacuum created by the defeat of Japan in World
        War II, the Viet Minh (a 'broad' front of Vietnamese
        patriots and nationalists, but controlled by the
        Communist Party) seize power. Ho Chi Minh announces
        his country's independence in Hanoi, August (the August
        Revolution). The emperor, Bao Dai, abdicates.

1946   French forces attack the Viet Minh in Haiphong,
        November. Beginning of the war of resistance against
        France.

1950   Ho Chi Minh's Democratic Republic of Vietnam
        recognized by China and the USSR.

1954   France's Expeditionary Force decisively defeated at Dien
        Bien Phu, March–May. At the Geneva Conference,
        Vietnam is divided North and South at the Seventeenth
        Parallel, pending nationwide elections. Ngo Dinh Diem, a
        Catholic, heads new Saigon government with American
        support.

1955   Diem rejects Geneva Accords. Becomes President of a
        newly promulgated Republic of Vietnam.

1956   Diem begins his campaign against political dissidents.

1957   Beginning of communist insurgency in the South: many
        former Viet Minh will become Viet Cong.

1959   Weapons and men begin infiltrating South Vietnam from
        North Vietnam, down what will become known as the Ho
        Chi Minh Trail. Diem steps up persecution of dissidents.

1960   National Liberation Front established in Saigon. Increased
        American aid to Diem.

1962   The number of US military advisers in South Vietnam
        rises to 12,000. Growth of 'strategic hamlet' programme.

1963	Battle of Ap Bac, 2nd January. Viet Cong defeat South Vietnamese Army (ARVN) units. 1st November: President Diem overthrown in US-backed coup. 2nd November: Diem and his brother Nhu murdered.
1964	The *Maddox*, a US destroyer, attacked by North Vietnamese patrol boats in the Gulf of Tonkin, 2nd August. Pre-planned American bombing of North Vietnam begins almost at once.
1965	US Marines land at Danang, 8th March: officially the first American combat troops to arrive. 200,000 more arrive by December.
1966	The number of US troops committed in Vietnam rises to 400,000 . . .
1967	. . . then 500,000.
1968	The Tet Offensive begins, 31st January: a combined NVA (North Vietnam Army) and Viet Cong assault on US positions. US government begins to lose the publicity war.
1969	President Nixon begins withdrawal of US ground troops from Vietnam. At the same time he begins 'secret' bombing of Cambodia.
1970	Henry Kissinger and Le Duc Tho start talking in Paris. By December, fewer than 300,000 US troops in Vietnam.
1972	The NVA strikes across the Seventeenth Parallel. Fall of Quang Tri. Bombing missions against the North intensified. Haiphong harbour mined.
1973	Cease-fire agreement signed by Kissinger and Le Duc Tho in Paris, against the wishes of President Thieu. US troop pull-out completed by end of March.

1975   The 'Ho Chi Minh Campaign': the NVA and Viet Cong
        co-ordinate attacks on Saigon Army positions. Fall of the
        southern cities, culminating in the fall of Saigon, 30th
        April. The war finishes as Vietnam is 'reunified'.

1978   In December, Vietnam, now aligned with the USSR,
        invades Cambodia, ousting the Chinese-backed Khmer
        Rouge. Repression of Chinese minority inside Vietnam.

1979   China retaliates by attacking Vietnam. Chinese forces
        repulsed. Increasing number of 'boat people': illegal
        emigrants leaving Vietnam, hoping to begin life again
        elsewhere.

1986   At its Sixth Congress, the Communist Party, under the
        leadership of Nguyen Van Linh, promulgates *doi moi*, a
        policy of economic renovation designed to save Vietnam
        from bankruptcy. Limited liberalization as attempts are
        made to create a market economy.

1989   In September, Vietnam withdraws its army from
        Cambodia, despite continued activities of the Khmer
        Rouge. The United States however maintains its trade
        embargo against Vietnam. At the end of the year, despite
        the collapse of communism in Eastern Europe, Linh insists
        that the one-party system will remain in place in
        Vietnam.